INTERNATIONAL LAW

Fourth Edition

Linda A. Malone
Founding Director, Human Security Law Center
Marshall-Wythe Foundation Professor of Law
William & Mary Law School

The *Emanuel Law Outlines* Series

Wolters Kluwer

Published by Wolters Kluwer in New York.

Wolters Kluwer Legal & Regulatory US serves customers worldwide with CCH, Aspen Publishers, and Kluwer Law International products. (www.WKLegaledu.com)

To contact Customer Service, e-mail customer.service@wolterskluwer.com, call 1-800-234-1660, fax 1-800-901-9075, or mail correspondence to:

Wolters Kluwer
Attn: Order Department
PO Box 990
Frederick, MD 21705

Printed in the United States of America.

1 2 3 4 5 6 7 8 9 0

ISBN 978-1-5438-0587-1

Library of Congress Cataloging-in-Publication Data in process

SUSTAINABLE FORESTRY INITIATIVE Certified Sourcing www.sfiprogram.org SFI-00756

About Wolters Kluwer Legal & Regulatory U.S.

Wolters Kluwer Legal & Regulatory U.S. delivers expert content and solutions in the areas of law, corporate compliance, health compliance, reimbursement, and legal education. Its practical solutions help customers successfully navigate the demands of a changing environment to drive their daily activities, enhance decision quality and inspire confident outcomes.

Serving customers worldwide, its legal and regulatory portfolio includes products under the Aspen Publishers, CCH Incorporated, Kluwer Law International, ftwilliam.com and MediRegs names. They are regarded as exceptional and trusted resources for general legal and practice-specific knowledge, compliance and risk management, dynamic workflow solutions, and expert commentary.

Summary of Contents

Contents

CHAPTER 1
THE CONCEPT OF PUBLIC INTERNATIONAL LAW

CHAPTER 2
SOURCES OF INTERNATIONAL LAW

CHAPTER 3

INTERNATIONAL LAW AND MUNICIPAL LAW

CHAPTER 4
STATES

CHAPTER 5

STATE JURISDICTION

CHAPTER 6
INTERNATIONAL ORGANIZATIONS

CHAPTER 7
INTERNATIONAL DISPUTE SETTLEMENT

CHAPTER 8

THE RIGHTS OF INDIVIDUALS—INTERNATIONAL LAW OF HUMAN RIGHTS

Chapter 9

THE LAW OF ARMED CONFLICT

CHAPTER 10

THE LAW OF THE SEA

CHAPTER 11
AIR AND SPACE LAW

CHAPTER 12
INTERNATIONAL ENVIRONMENTAL LAW

CHAPTER 13

INTERNATIONAL CRIMINAL LAW

Preface

Thank you for purchasing this *Emanuel Law Outline*. I hope you will find it helpful in your study of international law.

International law is a constantly evolving area to teach and to learn by any standard. This Outline first and foremost seeks to make its complexities accessible and comprehensible. It is, of course, not meant as a substitute for your casebook, but does clarify the connections between issues and cases that your casebook might not explain. In particular, the Outline highlights the recent and extensive case law developments in the area, and projects what issues and resolutions might be expected from these developments in a way that should prove useful to you for either exam preparation or the preparation of research papers in advanced classes. This Outline also includes the most extensive coverage of any international law study aid of rapidly expanding areas of international environmental law, international criminal law, and international humanitarian law from the perspective of someone experienced in that area.

Here are some of the special features of the *International Law Emanuel Law Outline*:

- **Casebook Correlation Chart:** This chart, located just after the Preface, correlates each section of the Outline with the pages covering the same topic in the leading international law casebooks.
- **Capsule Summary:** This is a summary of the key concepts of international law, specifically designed for use in the last week or so before your final exam.
- **Quiz Yourself:** At the end of many chapters there are short-answer questions and answers for testing yourself on the key concepts and issues in international law.
- **Exam Tips:** Many chapters also include exam tips that alert you to issues most often appearing on exams, and factual patterns used to test those issues.

This book is useful both throughout the semester and for exam preparation. Here are a few suggestions for using it:

1. During the semester, use the book in preparing each night for the next day's class. To do this, first read your casebook. Then, consult the Casebook Correlation Chart to determine what part of the Outline to read. Reading the Outline will give you a sense of how the cases in your casebook fit into the overall structure of the subject. You may want to use a highlighter to mark key portions of the Outline.

2. Use the Outline to provide a preliminary structure and to supply black letter principles to your own course outline. The Capsule Summary is also helpful for this purpose.

3. When studying for exams, read the Capsule Summary to get an overview. This will probably take about one day.

4. Either during exam study or earlier in the semester, do the Quiz Yourself short-answer questions. When working through the questions: (1) record your short "answer" on the small blank line provided after the question and (2) write out a "mini-essay" on a separate piece of paper.

5. Three or four days before the exam, review the Exam Tips appearing at the end of each chapter. The Tips can help you spot the issues in the short-answer questions. You may want to follow up your Exam Tip review by re-reading the discussion of the topic in the Outline chapter.

6. The night before the exam: (1) do some Quiz Yourself questions to review the most likely sections to be tested and (2) re-scan the Exam Tips (spending about two to three hours).

I also suggest that a good way to prepare for an exam is simply to read a newspaper with good international coverage, and to look for the issues of international law residing in current controversies. Many professors devise their exam questions in that way, and it will have the added benefit of teaching you to evaluate and understand today's conflicts and controversies at an entirely new level.

Even if you never practice as an international lawyer, the knowledge you have acquired in this field is fundamental to today's law practice in an era of globalization. Aspects of international law now pervade almost every area of the law—including corporate law, real estate law, bankruptcy, and securities law.

Good luck in your course. If you'd like any other publications of Wolters Kluwer Law & Business, you can find them in your bookstore or at www.WKLegaledu.com.

Linda A. Malone
Founding Director, Human Security Law Center
Marshall-Wythe Foundation Professor of Law
William & Mary Law School

Acknowledgements

With grateful acknowledgment to the William & Mary faculty support center, specifically Felicia Burton, Derek Mathis, and Tonya Cosby, and for the research assistance of Ryan David Franklin, Miranda Riva, Michael Heard Snow, and Kaila Desaix.

Casebook Correlation Chart

(**Note:** General sections of the outline are omitted for this chart.
NC = not directly covered by this casebook.)

Malone: International Law Emanuel Law Outline *(by chapter and subheadings)*	**Carter, Weiner, & Hollis:** *International Law* (7th ed., 2018)	**Damrosch & Murphy:** *International Law: Cases and Materials* (7th ed., 2019)	**Dunoff, Ratner, & Wippman:** *International Law: Norms, Actors, Process* (4th ed., 2015)	**Ohlin:** *Ohlin's International Law, Evolving Doctrine and Practice* (1st ed., 2018)	**Paust, Van Dyke, & Malone:** *International Law and Litigation in the United States* (3d ed., 2009)
CHAPTER 1 THE CONCEPT OF PUBLIC INTERNATIONAL LAW					
I. Introduction	Ch. 1	Ch. 1	Ch. 1	Ch. 1	Ch. 1 (1)
Chapter 2 SOURCES OF INTERNATIONAL LAW					
I. The Statute of the International Court of Justice	Ch. 1 (A)	Ch. 2 (1)	Ch. 2	Ch. 8 (A)	Ch. 1 (1)(A)
II. International Conventions/ Treaties	Ch. 2 (A)	Ch. 4	Ch. 2 (I)	Ch. 2 (A); Ch. 3 (A)–(B)	Ch. 1 (2)(A)
III. International Custom	Ch. 2 (B); Ch. 3 (D)	Ch. 2 (2)	Ch. 2 (II)	Ch. 2 (B)	Ch. 1 (2)(B)
IV. General Principles of Law	Ch. 2 (C)	Ch. 4 (1)	Ch. 2 (II)(F)	Ch. 2 (E)(1)	Ch. 1 (1)(E)
V. Judicial Decisions and Publicists	Ch. 2 (D)	Ch. 4 (2)	Ch. 2	Ch. 2 (E)(2)	NC
VI. *Jus Cogens*—Peremptory Norms	Ch. 2 (A)(3); Ch. 7 (A)(14)	Ch. 4 (2) Ch. 2 (2)(E)	Ch. 2 (I)(D)(4); Ch. 6 (IV)(E)	Ch. 2 (D)	Ch. 1 (1)(F)(3)
VII. Equity in International Law	Ch. 9 (E)(4)	Ch. 4 (1)	NC	NC	Ch. 1 (1)(D)
Chapter 3 INTERNATIONAL LAW AND MUNICIPAL LAW					
I. Dualism and Monism	Ch. 3 (A)	Ch. 10 (1)	Ch. 5 (I)	Ch. 14 (Intro)	NC
II. Treaties in Municipal Law	Ch. 3 (B)–(C)	Ch. 10 (3)	Ch. 5	Ch. 3	Ch. 2 (2)(C)
III. Customary International Law in Municipal Law	Ch. 3 (D)	Ch. 10 (2)	Ch. 5 (IV)	Ch. 14	Ch. 2 (2)(D)
IV. Foreign Relations Law of the United States	Ch. 3 (C)(1)	Ch. 10 (4)–(5)	Ch. 4 (III); Ch. 5 (II))	Ch. 3 (E)	NC
Chapter 4 STATES					
I. Definition of a State	Ch. 5 (A)(1)	Ch. 5 (1)	Ch. 3 (I)(B)	Ch. 4 (A)–(B)	NC
II. State Territory	Ch. 5 (A)(7) & (B)	Ch. 5 (5)	Ch. 3 (I)–(II)	Ch. 4 (B)	NC
III. Recognition of States and Governments	Ch. 5 (A)(3)–(4)	Ch. 5 (1) & (4)	Ch. 3 (I)–(II)	Ch. 4 (E)	NC
IV. Recognition of States	Ch. 5 (A)(3)	Ch. 5 (1)	Ch. 3 (I)	Ch. 4 (A)	NC
V. Recognition of Governments	Ch. 5 (A)(4)–(6)	Ch. 5 (4)	Ch. 3 (II)	Ch. 4 (E)	NC
VI. Recognition of Insurgents and Belligerents	Ch. 5 (B); Ch. 11 (B)(6)	Ch. 5 (4)(C)	Ch. 3 (II)	Ch. 4 (A)	NC
VII. The Rights and Obligations of States	Ch. 5 (A)(2)	Ch. 5 (2)	Ch. 3 (I)–(II) Ch. 5 (III);	Ch. 4 (C)	NC
VIII. Heads of State, Government Officials, Diplomats, and Officials of International Organizations: Roles and Status in International Law	Ch. 7 (A) (16)–(17)	Ch. 12 (4)	Ch. 6(IV)	Ch. 16 (A)–(B)	Ch. 4 (2)–(4)

Malone: International Law Emanuel Law Outline *(by chapter and subheadings)*	**Carter, Weiner, & Hollis:** *International Law* (7th ed., 2018)	**Damrosch & Murphy:** *International Law: Cases and Materials* (7th ed., 2019)	**Dunoff, Ratner, & Wippman:** *International Law: Norms, Actors, Process* (4th ed., 2015)	**Ohlin:** *Ohlin's International Law, Evolving Doctrine and Practice* (1st ed., 2018)	**Paust, Van Dyke, & Malone:** *International Law and Litigation in the United States* (3d ed., 2009)
Chapter 5 **STATE JURISDICTION**					
I. Definition of Jurisdiction	Ch. 6 (A)–(B)	Ch. 11 (1)	Ch. 6 (I)	Ch. 15 (Intro)	Ch. 3 (1)
II. International Jurisdictional Principles	Ch. 6 (A)	Ch. 11 (2)–(3) & (6)	Ch. 6	Ch. 15 (A)	Ch. 3 (1)–(3)
III. Extradition	Ch. 12 (A)	Ch. 16 (1)(C)	Ch. 6 (III)(C)	Ch. 15 (A)(5)	Ch. 3 (4)
IV. Jurisdictional Principles in U.S. Law	Ch. 6 (C)	Ch. 11 (2)-(3)	Ch. 6	Ch. 14; Ch. 15 (A)	Ch. 2
V. Immunities from Jurisdiction	Ch. 7	Ch. 12	Ch. 6 (IV)	Ch. 16	Ch. 4 (1)
Chapter 6 **INTERNATIONAL ORGANIZATIONS**					
I. The United Nations	Ch. 5 (C)(3)(a)	Ch. 13 (2)(A) –(B)	Ch. 3 (III)	Ch. 5	Ch. 1 (1)(B)
II. Regional Organizations	Ch. 8 (B)(10)	Ch. 13 (3)	NC	Ch. 11 (A)	NC
III. Supranational Organizations	Ch. 5 (C)(3)(c)	Ch. 13 (3)(A)	NC	Ch. 8 (B)(2)	NC
IV. The World Trade Organization	Ch. 5 (C)(3)(b)	Ch. 9 (5)(E)–(F)	Ch. 12 (I)-(II)	Ch. 17 (A)	NC
Chapter 7 **INTERNATIONAL DISPUTE SETTLEMENT**					
I. Dispute Defined	Ch. 4 (A)	Ch. 9 (1)(B)	NC	Ch. 7 (Intro)	NC
II. The Role of the United Nations	NC	Ch. 9 (1)(A)	Ch. 3 (III)	Ch. 8 (A)	Ch. 1 (1)(C)
III. Other Treaty Obligations of Peaceful Settlement	NC	Ch. 9 (1)(A)(3)–(4)	Ch. 2 (I)	NC	Ch. 5 (2)(B)–(C)
IV. Non-Judicial Methods	Ch. 4 (A)	Ch. 9 (2)	Ch. 3 (III)(H)	Ch. 5 (D)	NC
V. Quasi-Judicial Methods/ Arbitration	Ch. 4 (D)	Ch. 9 (3)	Ch. 3 (III)(H)	Ch. 7 (B)(1); Ch. 17 (A)–(B)	NC
VI. The International Courts	Ch. 4 (B)–(C)	Ch. 9 (4)–(5)	Ch. 8 (III)(D); Ch. 9; Ch. 13 (III)(C); Ch. 14 (I)(C)-(D)	Ch. 7	NC
VII. The World Trade Organization	Ch. 4 (C)(2)	Ch. 9 (5)(E)–(F)	Ch. 12 (I)-(II)	Ch. 17 (A)	NC
Chapter 8 **THE RIGHTS OF INDIVIDUALS—INTERNATIONAL LAW OF HUMAN RIGHTS**					
I. Status of Individuals	Ch. 8 (B)(1)	Ch. 13 (1)(A)	Ch. 7	Ch. 11 (Intro)	NC
II. Brief History	Ch. 8 (B)(1)	Ch. 13 (1)(A)	Ch. 7 (I)	Ch. 11 (Intro)	NC
III. Human Rights and the United Nations	Ch. 8 (B)(2)–(3) & (5)	Ch. 13 (1)(A) & (2)(A)	Ch. 7	Ch. 11 (Intro)–(A)	Passim
IV. Fundamental Human Rights	Ch. 8 (B)(3)	Ch. 13 (2)(A)	Ch. 7	Ch. 11 (B)–(E)	Passim
V. Newly Emerging Rights and Fundamental Rights Recognized as Customary International Law	Ch. 8 (B)(6)	Ch. 13 (2)(E)	Ch. 7	NC	NC
VI. Enforcement of Human Rights Law in U.S. Courts	Ch. 8 (B)(9)	Ch. 13 (5)(H)	Ch. 5 (IV)(B)–(D)	Ch. 11 (A)(3)	Ch. 2 (2)(D)(2)
VII. Derogation from Protection of Rights	Ch. 8 (B)(10)	Ch. 13 (5)(B)	Ch. 7 (I)	Ch. 11 (E)	NC
VIII. Regional Human Rights Law and Institutions	Ch. 8 (B)(10)	Ch. 13 (3)	Ch. 7 (I), (III) & (IV)(B)	Ch. 11 (A)	NC
IX. International Humanitarian Law	Ch. 8 (B)(11)	Ch. 15 (8)	Ch. 8; Ch. 13 (IV); Ch. 14 (II)(E)	Ch. 12	Ch. 2 (2)(D)

Malone: International Law Emanuel Law Outline *(by chapter and subheadings)*	Carter, Weiner, & Hollis: *International Law* (7th ed., 2018)	Damrosch & Murphy: *International Law: Cases and Materials* (7th ed., 2019)	Dunoff, Ratner, & Wippman: *International Law: Norms, Actors, Process* (4th ed., 2015)	Ohlin: *Ohlin's International Law, Evolving Doctrine and Practice* (1st ed., 2018)	Paust, Van Dyke, & Malone: *International Law and Litigation in the United States* (3d ed., 2009)
Chapter 9 THE LAW OF ARMED CONFLICT					
I. Armed Conflict Generally	Ch. 11 (A)–(C)	Ch. 15	Ch. 13	Ch. 12	Ch. 7 (1)
II. The Humanitarian Law of Armed Conflict	Ch. 11 (D)	Ch. 15	Ch. 8; Ch. 13 (IV); Ch. 14 (II)(E)	Ch. 12	Ch. 2 (2)(D)
III. Civil Wars	Ch. 11 (B)–(F)	Ch. 15 (6)-(7)	Ch. 3 (II)(E); Ch. 13 (III)	Ch. 12 (Intro)–(A)	Ch. 7 (1)
Chapter 10 THE LAW OF THE SEA					
I. Generally	Ch. 9 (A)	Ch. 17 (1)	Ch. 10	Ch. 7 (B)(1); Ch. 14 (A)	Ch. 6 (1)
II. Nationality of Vessels	Ch. 9 (B)	Ch. 17 (1)–(8)	NC	NC	Ch. 6 (1)
III. Baseline Determinations for Measuring Coastal Zones	Ch. 9 (C)(1)	Ch. 17 (2)	10 (I)	NC	Ch. 6 (1)
IV. Internal Water and Ports	Ch. 9 (C)(2)	Ch. 17 (2)(C)	10 (I)	NC	Ch. 6
V. The Territorial Sea and Contiguous Zone	Ch. 9 (C)– (D)	Ch. 17 (3)–(4)	Ch. 10 (I)	Ch. 2 (A)	Ch. 6 (4)
VI. Exclusive Economic Zone	Ch. 9 (E)	Ch. 17 (5)	Ch. 10 (II)(C)	Ch. 7 (B)(1)	Ch. 6
VII. Continental Shelf	Ch. 9 (E)	Ch. 17 (6)	Ch. 10 (III)	Ch. 7 (B)(1)	Ch. 6
VIII. Exploiting the Mineral Resources of the Deep Seabed	Ch. 9 (H)	Ch. 17 (11)	Ch. 10 (III)	NC	Ch. 6 (7)
IX. Freedom of the High Seas	Ch. 9 (F)	Ch. 17 (8)	Ch. 10 (II)	Ch. 1 (B)	Ch. 6 (2)
X. Preservation of the Marine Environment	Ch. 9 (A)–(B)	Ch. 17(1)(C); Ch. 18 (3)(D)	Ch. 10 (III); Ch. 11 (I)	NC	Ch. 6 (9)
Chapter 11 AIR AND SPACE LAW					
I. Defining State Sovereignty over Airspace	NC	Ch. 11 (3)(B)	Ch. 6 (II)(C)	NC	NC
II. Liability of Air Carriers	NC	NC	NC	Ch. 15 (A)(4)	NC
III. Violations of Airspace	Ch. 11 (A)(1)	Ch. 15 (8)	NC	NC	NC
IV. Offenses Committed Aboard Aircraft	Ch. 11 (B)	Ch. 11 (3)(E)	Ch. 14 (I)(B)	NC	NC
V. Outer Space	Ch. 9 (H)	Ch. 5 (1); Ch. 11 (3)(B)	NC	NC	NC
VI. Celestial Bodies	Ch. 9 (H)	Ch. 11 (3)(B)	NC	NC	NC
Chapter 12 INTERNATIONAL ENVIRONMENTAL LAW					
I. Emergence of International Environmental Law	Ch. 10 (A)	Ch. 18 (1)	Ch. 11	Ch. 18 (Intro)	NC
II. Transboundary Pollution	Ch. 10 (A)	Ch. 18 (2)	Ch. 11 (I)(D), (II)	Ch. 18 (Intro)–(A)	NC
III. Ozone Depletion and Global Warming/Climate Change	Ch. 10 (B)(3)–(4)	Ch. 18 (3)(A)–(B)	Ch. 6 (II); Ch. 11 (II)–(III)	Ch. 18 (C)	NC
IV. Wildlife Preservation	Ch. 10 (B)(2)	Ch. 18 (3)(C)	Ch. 2 (I); Ch. 10 (II)	NC	NC
V. Hazardous Waste, Radioactive Pollution, and Environmental Emergencies	Ch. 5 (A)	Ch. 18 (3)(D)	NC	NC	NC
VI. Antarctica	Ch. 9 (J)	Ch. 18 (1)	NC	NC	NC
VII. Deforestation	Ch. 10 (B)(4)	NC	NC	NC	NC
VIII. Desertification and Land Degradation	NC	Ch. 18 (1)(B)	NC	NC	NC
IX. Marine Environment	Ch. 9 (A)–(B)	Ch. 18 (3)(D)	Ch. 10 (III); Ch. 11 (I)	NC	NC
X. International Trade and Environment	Ch. 10 (B)(5)	Ch. 18 (4)	Ch. 12 (I)	Ch. 18 (C)	NC
XI. Military Activities and the Environment	Ch. 11	Ch. 2 (2)(C)	NC	Ch. 12 (E)	NC
XII. Extraterritorial Application of United States Environmental Law	NC	NC	NC	NC	NC

Malone: International Law Emanuel Law Outline *(by chapter and subheadings)*	**Carter, Weiner, & Hollis:** *International Law* (7th ed., 2018)	**Damrosch & Murphy:** *International Law: Cases and Materials* (7th ed., 2019)	**Dunoff, Ratner, & Wippman:** *International Law: Norms, Actors, Process* (4th ed., 2015)	**Ohlin:** *Ohlin's International Law, Evolving Doctrine and Practice* (1st ed., 2018)	**Paust, Van Dyke, & Malone:** *International Law and Litigation in the United States* (3d ed., 2009)
Chapter 13 INTERNATIONAL CRIMINAL LAW					
I. The Principles of Individual Responsibility and Criminal Liability	Ch. 12 (B)	Ch. 16 (1)	Ch. 9	Ch. 13 (Intro) & (C)	NC
II. The International Criminal Tribunals	Ch. 12 (C)(2)–(3)	Ch. 16 (3)	Ch. 6 (III); Ch. 9	Ch. 13 (A)(1)	NC
III. The International Criminal Court (ICC)	Ch. 12 (C)(4)	Ch. 16 (4)	Ch. 9 (IV)	Ch. 13 (A)(2)	Ch. 1 (1); Ch. 4 (2)
IV. State Prosecution of "International Criminals"	Ch. 12 (C)	Ch. 16 (2)	Ch. 9	Ch. 13 (B)	Ch. 2 (2)
V. Barriers to Prosecution	Ch. 12 (B)(2)(a)	Ch. 12	Ch. 6 (III)–(IV); Ch. 9 (IV)	Ch. 16 (C)	Ch. 2 (2)

Capsule Summary

This Capsule Summary is useful for a quick review of the course in preparation for the exam. It is not intended as a substitute for mastering the material in the main outline.

CHAPTER 1

THE CONCEPT OF PUBLIC INTERNATIONAL LAW

I. INTRODUCTION

A. Defined: Historically, international law was defined as *"the body of rules and principles of action that are binding upon civilized states in their relations with one another."* The modern approach expands the definition to include not only relations between states but also relations between international organizations and states, relations among the international organizations themselves, and the relationship between states or international organizations and natural or juridical persons, such as the law governing human rights. [1]

B. The importance of public international law: Public international law concerns the conduct of states and international organizations, while private international law focuses on the conduct of individuals, corporations, and other private entities. Public international law is important because it (1) defines the very existence of "states"; (2) provides the framework for diplomatic relations; (3) governs international agreements; (4) sets forth rules for the operation of international commerce; (5) governs individual human rights; and (6) regulates protection of the global environment, as well as the use of the air, land, sea, and other global resources. [1-2]

C. History of public international law: International law began to develop in Europe as a moral and theological construct during the twelfth to fifteenth centuries. Early international law was derived in large part from the Roman law of *jus gentium* governing relations between Roman citizens and foreigners and the canon law of the papacy. Writers and theologians like St. Thomas Aquinas and Francisco de Vittoria developed natural law theory as a blend of Christian beliefs, economic pragmatism, the appeals of weak kingdoms for protection, and the idea of a united Christian Europe. These ideas evolved into the two main theories in the study of international law: the ***natural law approach*** of the sixteenth and seventeenth centuries and the ***positivist movement***, which was predominant in the nineteenth and twentieth centuries. [2]

1. **Natural law:** The theory of natural law is based on the notion that ***each state, just as each individual, is endowed with certain natural rights.*** These natural rights are not human constructs; they exist as a result of a mandate from God or, after the Enlightenment's secularization of thought, they exist as the "dictate of right reason." [2]

2. **Positivism:** Unlike natural law, which exists without the affirmative consent of nations, positivism teaches that international law is that body of law ***to which states have consented to be bound.*** A state's consent may be either ***express***, as in the form of a treaty, or ***implied***, as with acquiescence to customary law. Positivism developed during the Enlightenment as an

alternative to the natural rights approach to international law that was dominant in the sixteenth and seventeenth centuries. [2]

3. **Liberalism:** Liberalism draws from both natural law and positivism, holding that international law should be broadly agreed upon and formed by consensus, but its rules are universal and bind all states regardless of their consent. Liberalism is distinct from positivism in that it argues for the use of international law as a reformist tool that can further human progress. Liberalism is distinct from natural law theory in that the rules of "logical morality" that govern the international system are to be arrived at by a broad consensus of states and peoples rather than by simple "right reasoning." Liberalism holds that ***international law should be a body of law based on logical morality***. [3]

CHAPTER 2
SOURCES OF INTERNATIONAL LAW

I. THE STATUTE OF THE INTERNATIONAL COURT OF JUSTICE

C A P S U L E S U M M A R Y

A. **Article 38:** The sources of international law, set forth in article 38(1) of the Statute of the International Court of Justice (ICJ), are (1) ***international conventions***, whether general or particular; (2) ***international custom***; (3) the ***general principles of law*** recognized by civilized nations; and (4) ***judicial decisions*** and the ***teachings of the most highly qualified publicists*** of the various nations, as a subsidiary source. [5]

B. **International conventions/treaties:** In the broadest sense, an international convention or treaty is *any agreement governed by international law*. [5]

1. **The Vienna Convention:** The Vienna Convention on the Law of Treaties, which entered into force in 1980, is the ***primary source for the law of treaties***. Most provisions of the Vienna Convention were declaratory of existing law, while others went beyond the existing law to create new law at the time they were adopted. The United States has not ratified the Vienna Convention, but the State Department does recognize it as the authoritative guide to current treaty law and practice. The Vienna Convention applies only to those treaties meeting the Convention's requirements for a treaty. Some international instruments that fall outside the Convention's definition of a treaty, however, are nevertheless recognized as treaties. [5-6]

   a. **Vienna Convention definition of a treaty:** The Vienna Convention sets forth a basic definition for a treaty as "an international agreement concluded between States in written form and governed by international law, whether embodied in a single instrument or in two or more related instruments and whatever its particular designation." In short, to be a treaty within the scope of the Convention, a document must (1) ***be between states***; (2) ***be in writing***; and (3) be ***governed by international law***. [6]

2. **International law governs all treaties:** Governance by international law is required of all treaties, whether or not they are treaties within the scope of the Vienna Convention. Although the presumption is that an agreement between two or more states is a treaty, evidence that domestic law was intended to control the agreement rebuts that presumption. [6]

3. **Non–Vienna Convention treaties:** The concept of a treaty under international law is not limited to that defined in the Vienna Convention. The Vienna Convention states that its definition of a treaty

does not affect the legal force or applicability of international law to agreements that do not fall within the definition. Agreements involving international organizations as parties are also generally considered treaties. [6]

4. **U.S. distinction between treaties and executive agreements:** U.S. domestic law distinguishes between an executive agreement and a treaty in the procedures necessary for the agreements to be given legal effect and in the legal effect accorded the agreements. [6]

   a. **Treaty:** Treaties are concluded by the President with the advice and consent of the Senate. Senate ratification of a treaty requires a two-thirds majority vote. [6]

   b. **Executive agreement:** An executive agreement is concluded by the President based on authority granted by Congress or based on the inherent authority granted the President by the U.S. Constitution. [6-7]

5. **Potential conflicts between U.S. domestic law and international law:** It is possible for an agreement to be *denied legal force and effect under U.S. domestic law and yet still be binding under international law*. A state's internal law, however, cannot be invoked as justification for failure to perform a treaty. [7]

6. **Name and form of treaty:** "Treaty" is the most common title of an international agreement, but the following are also used: convention, act, general act, protocol, agreement, *modi vivendi*, concordance, charter, declaration, and compromise. [7]

   a. **Components of treaty and language:** Although there is no officially correct form, treaties generally comprise four parts: the title, the preamble, the main body, and the final part. There is no universal rule as to what language or what number of languages must be utilized for the text of the treaty. Rather, the language of the treaty is selected by the contracting parties. [7-8]

   b. **Subject matter of treaty:** The subject matter of the treaty is composed of the rights and obligations of the parties. Two important limitations apply: [8]

      i. ***Jus cogens* restrictions:** The treaty may not set forth rights and obligations that conflict with *jus cogens* (the imperative norms of international law). [8]

      ii. **U.N. Charter restrictions:** The treaty may not set forth rights and obligations that conflict with those obligations that a member state has undertaken under the U.N. Charter. [8]

   c. **Classification of international treaties:** Treaties may be classified by the following criteria: contracting parties, geographic factors, possibility of accession, subject matter, form, or method of conclusion. [8-9]

7. **Treaty-making power—capacity:** Both the party (the state or international organization) and its representative must have the proper capacity to negotiate and conclude an international agreement. [10]

   a. **Nation-states and international organizations:** It is presumed that nation-states have the necessary capacity to negotiate and conclude treaties. International organizations, however, have the necessary capacity only if the constitution of the organization either expressly or impliedly gives the organization that capacity. [10]

   b. **Component states of a federal union:** An inconsistent area is the capacity of the component states of a federal union. Generally, one constituent state of a federation may enter agreements with other constituent states, but the rules may differ with regards to entering into international agreements. Two determining factors are the constitutional guidelines of the federation and recognition of international legal personalities. [10]

c. **Self-governing territories:** Another troublesome area concerns self-governing territories, as there are conflicting views as to whether they have the capacity to enter international agreements. One view holds that a territory is not a "state" and cannot be regarded as a "distinct juridical person" capable of being "a responsible party to the treaty entirely separate from the parent State." Some conventions, however, specifically include self-governing territories amongst the parties that may sign the convention. [10]

d. **Authority of persons representing a state or international organization:** Authority is issued in a document entitled a ***"full powers"*** document, which names those individuals who may negotiate and conclude a treaty on behalf of the state. [10]

   i. **Practice of state:** A state may dispense with full powers if the practice of the state involved demonstrates its intention to consider its representative as being duly authorized. [10]

   ii. **Heads of state:** Full powers are also dispensed with for heads of state, heads of government, ministers of foreign affairs, and heads of diplomatic missions. Such officers have inherent capacity to conclude treaties. [10-11]

e. **Apparent authority of a state's representative:** A state is bound to a treaty unless it is clearly evident that a representative was acting beyond his or her authority. [11]

f. **Subsequent confirmation:** When authority is lacking, the treaty is without legal effect unless the state subsequently confirms the treaty. [11]

8. **The treaty process:** The treaty process includes *negotiation, adoption, authentication,* and *forms of conclusion.* [11]

   a. **Negotiation of treaties:** The negotiation of treaties varies according to whether the treaty is bilateral or multilateral. Bilateral treaty negotiation usually begins in the foreign ministry of one of the parties and is followed up by discussions and exchanges of notes. Restricted multilateral treaty negotiation is ordinarily conducted in the same manner as bilateral treaties. General multilateral treaty negotiation is generally conducted at diplomatic conferences where diplomatic delegations act on behalf of the states. [11]

   b. **Adoption:** Adoption is generally defined as the ***formal act signifying that the form and content of the treaty have been agreed upon***. Adoption signifies that the negotiations have been completed, disputed points have been resolved, and the wording of the final document agreed upon. [11]

   c. **Forms of conclusion:** A party is not bound to a treaty ***until it has consented to be bound***. Such consent may be expressed in various ways, including signature, the exchange of instruments, acceptance, approval, ratification, and "any other means if so agreed." [11-13]

   d. **Entry into force:** Entry into force is the ***actual implementation of the treaty's terms***. Entry into force often occurs when specific requirements laid out in the treaty have been met. The provisions setting forth the manner of entry into force apply from the moment the text of the treaty is adopted, unlike the remainder of the treaty, which is implemented upon entry into force. A provisional application may permit the treaty to be implemented before the formal requirements for entry into force have been met. [13]

9. **Reservations:** A reservation is defined as "a unilateral statement, however phrased or named, made by a State, when signing, ratifying, acceding to, accepting or approving a treaty, whereby it purports to ***exclude or to vary the legal effect of certain provisions*** in their application to that State." [13]

   a. **Permissible reservations:** Article 19 of the Vienna Convention permits reservations to general multilateral treaties, unless the treaty expressly or impliedly prohibits reservations, or the reservations sought are simply incompatible with the object and purpose of the treaty. [13]

   b. **The purpose of reservations:** Many multilateral conventions seek wide participation, and reservations encourage participation by allowing a state to be a party without agreeing to every last provision of a treaty. [13-14]

   c. **Acceptance of and objections to reservations:** A reservation expressly permitted by the treaty does not require acceptance unless the treaty so provides. "When it appears from the limited number of the negotiating States and the object and purpose of a treaty that the application of the treaty in its entirety between all the parties is an essential condition of the consent of each one to be bound by the treaty, a reservation requires acceptance by all the parties." Otherwise unanimous consent to a reservation is not necessary. If the treaty itself does not prohibit a reservation in any way or expressly permit it, each state is free to decide whether to reject or to accept the reservation. [14]

   d. **Legal effects of acceptances of and objections to reservations:** If a state accepts the reservation, the treaty will enter into force between the accepting and reserving state. The treaty's provisions apply as modified by the reservation. The modification is effective only between the reserving state and the accepting state. If a state objects to a reservation, there are two possible outcomes: (1) the state may object to the reservation, yet still be willing to enter a treaty relation with the reserving state; or (2) the objecting state not only objects, but also expresses its intention that the entire treaty be of no effect between it and the reserving state. In the latter event, the reserving state and objecting state are not parties to the treaty vis-à-vis each other. [14-15]

   e. **Limitations to reservations:** Reservations are generally narrowly construed and do not apply to other provisions of a treaty by way of implication. [15]

10. **The observance of treaties:** All parties to a treaty must perform their obligations under the treaty in ***good faith***. [15]

   a. ***Pacta sunt servanda:*** Article 26 of the Vienna Convention expresses one of the most fundamental principles of public international law, *pacta sunt servanda*: "Every treaty in force is binding upon the parties to it and must be performed by them in good faith." [15]

   b. **Good faith performance:** Good faith performance is required regardless of any conflicting domestic law. Conflicting domestic law does not excuse a state from its treaty obligations unless the state's consent to be bound by the treaty was expressed in violation of the state's domestic law. This predominance of treaty obligations over domestic law holds true only in the arena of international law and is not always the rule in domestic courts. [15]

   c. **Territorial scope of treaties:** The general rule is that a treaty applies to *all the territory of each party*. [15]

   d. **Interpretation of treaties:** There are three basic approaches to treaty interpretation: (1) the ***textual approach***, which looks only to the text of the treaty and the "plain and natural meanings of the words"; (2) the ***limited contextual approach***, which regards the text as the starting point for interpretation, ascertaining the intent of the parties from written secondary sources; and (3) the ***policy-oriented and configurative approach***, the most liberal and conceptual of the three, which gleans intent from the treaty text and all pre- and post-treaty communications, with no one source predominating over another and intent being considered in the very broad framework of "giving effect to the goals of a public order of human dignity." [15-16]

e. **Fulfillment of treaties—methods of oversight:** Remedies available for non-fulfillment include submission of the dispute to the International Court of Justice (ICJ), diplomatic negotiations, and arbitration. The treaty itself will often designate the manner in which disputes are to be resolved. [16]

f. **Amendment of treaties:** The general rule is that "a treaty may be amended by agreement between the parties." Amendments take on the character of treaties themselves and are governed accordingly by the general law on treaties. [16-17]

   i. **"Amendments"** ***alter a treaty with respect to all parties.*** Article 40 requires notification to all parties of the proposal to amend. All parties have the right to participate in the decision to amend as well as in the subsequent negotiations and conclusions of any amendments. [16]

   ii. **"Modifications" are** ***made by a limited number of parties.*** Modifications are permitted only if: (1) modifications are permitted by the original treaty; or (2) modifications are not prohibited by the treaty and the modification is one that does not affect the object and purpose of the treaty as a whole. [17]

   iii. **Amendment/modification by tacit consent:** The argument has been made that customary international law recognizes amendment or modification of a treaty by actual practice of the parties that is at variance with the treaty provisions. [17]

g. **Invalidation of treaties:** The grounds for invalidating a treaty are *error, fraudulent conduct, corruption, coercion, conflict with peremptory norms (jus cogens),* and *conflict with domestic law.* The provisions of the Vienna Convention are controversial and are not necessarily accepted as reflecting customary international law. [17-18]

   i. **Separability:** Grounds for invalidation generally affect the entire treaty, but article 44 does provide for separability of the treaty provisions if: (1) the treaty itself permits separability; or (2) the objectionable clauses are "separable from the remainder of the treaty with regard to their application," "not an essential basis of the consent," and "continued performance of the remainder of the treaty would not be unjust." [18]

   ii. **Acquiescence:** A party that continues to perform under the terms of a treaty, despite its knowledge that grounds for invalidating it exist, is precluded from later invoking those grounds for invalidation. [18]

   iii. **Termination and suspension of treaties:** Treaties may be terminated or suspended by agreement of the parties if the treaty so provides, or if the goal of the treaty is realized. Unilateral abrogation of treaties without abrogation or withdrawal clauses is, in principle, not permitted; in practice, however, it is often allowed. Additionally, treaties may be terminated for reasons analogous to contract law defenses. [18-21]

   iv. **Impossibility of performance:** Impossibility of performance is based on the permanent distinction or disappearance of something indispensable to performance. [19]

v. ***Rebus sic stantibus:*** This doctrine of a fundamental change in circumstances is rarely found applicable. Four criteria must be met: (1) the ***change*** must be ***of a fundamental character***; (2) the change in circumstances must have been ***unforeseen by the parties***; (3) the ***circumstances*** at the time of entering the agreement must have been ***an essential basis*** of the treaty; and (4) the change in circumstances must radically alter the performance of obligations yet to be performed under the treaty. [19-20]

vi. **Termination due to breach:** The effect of breach varies according to whether the treaty is bilateral or multilateral. In all cases, the breach must be material. The breach itself does not automatically terminate the treaty, but it may be invoked as a ground for termination. [20]

vii. **Later inconsistent treaty between parties:** A treaty is terminated if all parties conclude a later agreement on the same subject matter and it is implied that the later treaty is to govern; or the later treaty is so incompatible with the earlier treaty that the two treaties cannot be performed at the same time. [20]

viii. **War between contracting parties:** The outbreak of an armed conflict does not *ipso facto* terminate or suspend the operation of treaties in force between the parties to the armed conflict. The nature of the treaty dictates the effect of hostilities on its operation. [20-21]

h. **Effect of state succession on international treaties:** Succession of states is the *shift of responsibility over a territory from one state to another state*. Succession affects the legal identity of the state and its treaty obligations, and occurs with secession of states, annexation, merger and consolidation, and decolonization. [21]

i. **Transfer of territory resulting from moving boundaries (the moving treaty-frontiers rule):** The international agreements of the state to which the territory once belonged are no longer applicable. The international agreements of the state to which the territory now belongs apply. [21]

ii. **Absorption of an entire state:** The international agreements of the absorbed state cease and are replaced by the international agreements of the absorbing state. [21]

iii. **Newly formed states (former colonies or states resulting from separation of a state):** The new state does not automatically become a party to the international agreements of the predecessor state. The new state, however, is not precluded from accepting such agreements. [21]

iv. **Territorial and boundary agreements:** Such agreements are unaffected by the succession of states. [21-22]

v. **Newly independent states under the Vienna Convention:** The Vienna Convention on the Succession of States in Respect of Treaties distinguishes between newly independent states (*i.e.*, former colonies) and states created by disintegration or secession. The "clean slate" doctrine states that a newly independent state begins its existence free of the obligations of its predecessor state. The newly independent state does have the right of option to be a party to general multilateral treaties by virtue of being a successor state. [22]

vi. **States created by disintegration or secession:** A new state created by secession from a former state, or by disintegration of a former state into two or more states, generally succeeds automatically to most of the former state's treaties. [22]

vii. **Effect of governmental succession on international treaties:** A change in government has no effect on the legal identity of the state. [22]

C. **International custom:** Along with treaty law, customary international law is ***one of the two principal sources of international law***. Customary international law is important for its potentially general application to states not parties to treaties, as well as its ability to supplement areas of international concern not addressed in treaties. [22]

1. **Two approaches to customary international law:** The two approaches are the *objectivist/sociological approach* and the *participatory/voluntarist approach*. [23]

2. **Establishment of an international custom:** Customary law follows the basic principle of international law that acts are permitted unless expressly forbidden. Therefore, prohibitions as well as affirmative practices must be proved by the state relying upon them. Quantitative factors in determining an international custom include: (1) ***the amount and type of past state practice***; (2) ***duration of the state practice***; (3) ***consistency of state practice***; and (4) ***the number and makeup of states adhering to the practice***. A qualitative factor is the concept of *opinio juris sive necessitatis*, the ***sense of legal obligation compelling states to follow a certain practice***. [23-24]

3. **Use of regional custom:** Customary law may also be limited to a particular region and therefore not be the practice of such a wide variety of states. [24]

4. **Local customary rights:** Local customary rights may develop from constant and continual practice between two nations, but such customary rights differ from and are independent of general international customary law principles. [24]

5. **Resolutions and recommendations of international organizations:** General Assembly resolutions are not a form of international legislation and accordingly are ***not legally binding***. The resolutions are, however, frequently used as evidence of customary international law. The resolutions are useful as evidence because the votes of the world body may show a consensus (or lack of consensus) on a particular issue. [24-25]

6. **Application of international customary law:** The predominant view is that customary international law enjoys universal application, regardless of what nations participated in its formation. Two possible exceptions to application are: (1) a clear and consistent objection, supported by action; and (2) a historic departure from a customary rule and other states' acceptance of that deviation. [25]

7. **Relationship between treaties and customary international law:** Depending on the situation, treaties may be given equal weight with custom, prevail over custom, be proof of custom, or codify custom. [26]

D. **General principles of law:** A general principle of law "recognized by civilized nations" is one that is *so fundamental that it is a basic tenet in virtually every major legal system*. [26]

1. **Limited application of general principles:** General principles of law primarily apply to fill in gaps left by treaties and customary law. [26]

2. **Decreasing importance as a source of international law:** General principles are losing importance in modern international law because many of the norms once recognized as general principles are now incorporated into treaties or are recognized as customary international law. The Restatement (Fourth) of the Foreign Relations Law of the United States now classifies general principles as "a secondary source of international law." General principles

continue, however, to be applied in procedural matters and problems of international judicial administration. [26]

E. Judicial decisions and publicists: Article 38 includes in its sources of international law judicial decisions and the teachings of highly qualified publicists as subsidiary means. The judicial decisions may be rendered by either an international tribunal, such as the ICJ, or by a national court adjudicating issues of international law. [26]

1. **The role of judicial decisions in the development of international law:** Although not required, many courts strive to follow previous rulings (*stare decisis*) and on occasion make new international law. The statute of the ICJ says that judicial decisions have ***no binding force*** except as between the parties and in respect to that particular case. Regardless of this prohibition on the doctrine of *stare decisis*, the Court does in fact often look to prior holdings as being ***highly persuasive***. In 2013, the ICJ held that it may interpret prior decisions when the proceedings were relevant in order to show what evidence was before the court and what arguments each party had made. The ICJ has made new law when necessary, which subsequently won state acceptance. [26-27]

2. **Status of the most highly qualified publicists:** The work of scholars is more influential in the international legal system than in municipal legal systems. International groups of publicists serve the development of international law both by codifying existing rules of law and by proposing new rules. [27]

3. **Resolutions of the United Nations and other international law organizations:** The significance of resolutions of the United Nations, and other similar international law organizations, as a source of law varies tremendously according to the circumstances. The following factors are to be considered in determining the impact of a General Assembly resolution: (1) internal General Assembly Resolutions; (2) declaratory resolutions; (3) state practice as proof of impact; (4) diverse majority as proof of impact; and (5) the binding effect on dissenting states. [27-28]

II. *JUS COGENS*—PEREMPTORY NORMS

A. Generally: *Jus cogens* or peremptory norms are ***those rules of international law of such fundamental importance that derogation from them is prohibited***. There are few rules that are generally accepted as peremptory norms. Some commonly accepted rules are the basic principles of *pacta sunt servanda*, prohibitions on the use of or threat of force, genocide, slave trade, piracy, terrorism, and the taking of hostages. The controversy surrounding the very existence of *jus cogens*, as well as the difficulty of identifying rules of *jus cogens*, has resulted in sparse application. [28-29]

III. EQUITY IN INTERNATIONAL LAW

A. Generally: Equity in international law can be used if the parties agree to have a case decided *ex aequo et bono*, in which equity overrides all other legal principles in a case. Furthermore, there are substantive concepts of equity common to all modern legal systems that are, therefore, general principles of international law and may be used to decide international disputes. [29]

CHAPTER 3
INTERNATIONAL LAW AND MUNICIPAL LAW

I. DUALISM AND MONISM

A. **Two theories:** There are two theoretical approaches to the relationship between international law and municipal law: ***dualism*** and ***monism***. Under the dualist theory, international law and municipal law are ***entirely separate legal systems***. The monist theory holds that municipal and international law belong to a ***single "universal legal order."*** The diminished role of the state as a legal personality results in a dominant role for international law over municipal law. In actual practice, the dualist approach appears to predominate. [31]

II. TREATIES IN MUNICIPAL LAW

A. **Treaties in U.S. law:** The U.S. Constitution includes provisions on treaties pertaining to the creation of treaties, the judicial power, the relationship of treaties with international law, and limitations on states' power to conclude treaties. [31]

B. **Terminology for treaties:** U.S. domestic law recognizes two types of international agreements: (1) treaties under Article II of the Constitution, and (2) executive agreements. Congressional/executive agreements, also called *statutory agreements*, are made by the President pursuant to statutes passed by Congress. [31]

C. **Self-executing treaties:** Some treaties may be self-executing under U.S. domestic judge-made law. A treaty cannot be self-executing, however, if the subject matter is one that lies within the exclusive law-making power of Congress. A treaty is also non-self-executing if it instructs the legislature to implement enacting legislation. [32-33]

D. **Treaties and conflicting state law—effect of the Supremacy Clause:** Self-executing treaties and legislatively implemented treaties have the status of enforceable federal law and benefit accordingly from the Supremacy Clause. [33]

E. **Treaties and conflicting federal statutes:** Treaty law and federal statutory law are ***virtually equivalent*** in status. When both address the same issue, courts attempt to interpret the terms of each in such a manner as to avoid outright conflicts. When reconciliation is not possible, the general rule is that ***the last in time prevails***. This "last-in-time" rule applies only to Article II treaties, and only under U.S. laws—a conflict with domestic law does not excuse the United States from international legal obligations. [33]

F. **Treaties and constitutional constraints:** The substantive constraints that the Constitution places on the treaty-making power are not clear, and contrasting views have been opined by the Supreme Court. [33-34]

G. **Treaties in the laws of other countries:** The relationship between international and domestic law varies among states. Regarding self-executing treaties, two doctrines are dominant: (1) the "English" rule, which incorporates treaties into municipal law only if there is legislative enactment; and (2) the civil law treatment, which generally incorporates treaties into municipal law directly. [34]

III. CUSTOMARY INTERNATIONAL LAW IN MUNICIPAL LAW

A. **Common law countries—international law as common law:** International law derived from sources other than treaties is considered by common law countries to be a special type of common law, one to which the courts resort in the absence of a treaty, executive or legislative act, or judicial decision. The United States and other common law jurisdictions consider customary rules to be automatically incorporated into the domestic legal order and thus directly applicable in domestic courts. [34]

1. **Customary law in the United States:** Customary law, like treaty law, is considered federal law and receives the benefits of the Supremacy Clause. Equal status with federal statutory law, however, is less certain. U.S. courts group customary law together with other non-treaty sources of international law to form what is called *international common law*, comprising custom, general principles, scholarly works, and judicial opinions. [34-35]

2. **Civil law countries—relationship between customary international law and domestic law:** Civil law countries rely on express constitutional provisions to incorporate non-treaty international law into their municipal law. [35]

IV. FOREIGN RELATIONS LAW OF THE UNITED STATES

A. **Generally:** Although U.S. domestic law does not directly impose itself on the international legal order, it does play a major role by allocating power among the three branches of government. [35]

B. **Executive powers:** Article II of the U.S. Constitution expressly grants the President authority for certain international powers. The extent of the President's power to make international agreements is uncertain, although the Supreme Court has upheld various agreements made by the President without Congress's approval. The executive is also given the authority to receive ambassadors and recognize foreign governments, along with any other powers consistent with Article II. [35-36]

C. **Congressional powers:** Article I of the U.S. Constitution vests the Congress with certain international powers as well. The controversial War Powers Act is one instance of congressional authority in foreign relations. [36]

D. **Judicial powers:** Article III of the U.S. Constitution allows the Supreme Court to hear cases arising under treaties made by the United States, cases involving ambassadors and other public ministers and consuls, admiralty and maritime cases, and cases between U.S. states and citizens and foreign states and citizens. [36]

1. **Act-of-state doctrine:** The Supreme Court has declined in the past to decide cases on the basis of the act-of-state doctrine. [36]

2. **Political question doctrine:** The political question doctrine is also applied by courts to avoid addressing controversies regarding the political functions of the other two branches. [36]

CHAPTER 4
STATES

I. DEFINITION OF A STATE

A. **Defined:** Under both the Restatement (Fourth) of the Foreign Relations Law of the United States and the Montevideo Convention of 1933, a state is defined as "an entity that has a ***defined territory*** and a ***permanent population***, under the control of its ***own government***, and that ***engages in, or has the capacity to engage in, formal relations*** with other such entities." [39]

1. **Defined territory:** There is no minimum territory or size requirement. A state need not be established with clearly defined frontiers. [39]

2. **Permanent population—a "people":** There is no minimum number required. Antarctica, however, has no permanent population and, in part for that reason, is not considered a state. [39]

3. **Under the control of its own government:** A state's own government must be able to assert itself without the aid of foreign troops and to carry out its duties. Exceptions may be in the cases of: (1) a state temporarily lacking an effective government as a result of civil war, newly gained independence, or similar upheavals; (2) a simple change in regime and even conflicting claims of governmental authority; and (3) a state occupied by an enemy in times of war so long as allies are fighting on its behalf against the enemy. [39]

4. **Capacity to engage in relations with other states:** A state must have the competence, within its own constitutional system, to conduct international relations with other states, as well as the political, technical, and financial capabilities to do so. [39]

5. **Role of recognition in defining a state:** An entity must be treated as a state when it meets the four requirements set forth above. Its existence as a state is independent of any formal recognition. [39-40]

II. STATE TERRITORY

A. **State boundaries or frontiers:** State boundaries, not only across land but both upward into the airspace and downward into the earth, are ***most often determined by agreements between the parties*** rather than being dictated by principles of international law. Boundary disputes are common, and contests involving relatively small areas of land may be resolved by international litigation or arbitration, or some other settlement, such as a peace treaty. [40]

1. **Effect of succession:** A succession of states, by itself, is not grounds for affecting boundaries established by treaty, or rights and obligations established by treating and relating to the boundary regime. [40]

B. **Air and outer space:** There are separate sets of treaties and agreements concerning airspace versus outer space. [40]

1. **Airspace:** The general view is that a state has ***complete and exclusive authority*** over the airspace above its territory. [40]

2. **Outer space:** The prevailing theory in the field of outer space is that every state may explore and use outer space, free of national appropriation by another state. [40]

C. International rivers: International rivers may flow through a state's territory but not be subject to the absolute authority of the state. An international river has the following characteristics: it is ***navigable***; it ***flows directly or indirectly into the sea***; it ***flows through the territory of two or more states or forms the boundary between them***; and an ***international act*** proclaims it to be an international river. [41]

D. State coastal zones: The sea is divided into several zones: internal waters, the territorial sea, the contiguous zone, the continental shelf, the exclusive economic zone, and the high seas, with the sovereign rights of the coastal state varying with each zone. [41]

E. *Res nullius* and *res communis*: *Res nullius*, or unattributed territory, and *res communis*, or common territory, refer to territory that belongs to no state. [41]

F. Acquisition of territorial sovereignty: Acquisition of territory may occur in a variety of ways, including: (1) accretion; (2) cession; (3) conquest; (4) contiguity; (5) occupation; and (6) prescription. [41-42]

1. **Other considerations:** Other factors are considered in resolving territorial disputes: (1) affiliations of the inhabitants of the disputed territory; (2) geographical, economic, and historical considerations; and (3) cultural unity. [42]

III. RECOGNITION OF STATES AND GOVERNMENTS

A. Recognition generally: Recognition is best defined as the *willingness to deal with another state or government representing the state as a member of the international community*. Public acts of recognition may take a variety of forms. Maintaining or severing diplomatic relations is not synonymous with recognition or non-recognition, respectively. [42]

B. Express and implied recognition: Recognition of a state or government is often done expressly, but certain conduct may also imply recognition. [42-43]

C. Recognition under U.S. law: Under U.S. law, only the President has the authority to recognize or not recognize an entity as a state. [43]

D. Whether recognition is discretionary or mandatory: Generally, ***recognition is discretionary***. Two limitations on this discretion exist to prevent premature recognition and premature withdrawal of recognition. [43]

1. **The Lauterpacht doctrine:** This doctrine, not widely accepted, holds that states have a duty to recognize states or governments that meet the international law requirements for recognition. [43]

2. **Non-recognition under the U.N. Charter:** Article 41 authorizes the Security Council to order members of the United Nations to "sever diplomatic relations" with a state or government. [43]

E. *De jure* and *de facto* recognition: Under the constitutive theory, treatment of an entity as a state without extending a formal recognition was called *de facto* recognition, as opposed to *de jure* recognition. With regard to governments, *de jure* recognition implies that the government is lawfully in power even though it retains little actual power, while a *de facto* government is impliedly a government that is in control, but illegally so. [44]

F. Conditional recognition: The prevailing view is that recognition generally cannot be granted subject to conditions, except for assumed conditions such as adherence to international law. [44]

IV. RECOGNITION OF STATES

A. **Two theories:** There are two theories concerning the legal effects under international law of recognition of states: the ***constitutive theory*** and the ***declaratory theory***. The constitutive theory is that an entity does not exist as a state until it has been recognized by other states; the recognition itself "constitutes" the state. This theory is not widely accepted today. Under the declaratory theory, the facts of statehood (defined territory, permanent population, effective government, and capacity for foreign relations) rather than formal recognition define an entity as a state. [44]

B. **Evidentiary value of recognition:** Recognition, nevertheless, is useful evidence of the existence of a state if enough other states recognize that state. [45]

V. RECOGNITION OF GOVERNMENTS

A. **Recognition generally:** Recognition of a government is an ***acknowledgment that it is in effective control of the state***. The traditional approach allows recognition of a government when: (1) it is in effective control of the state without the assistance of foreign intervention; (2) it has the consent, or at least the acquiescence, of the people; and (3) it shows its willingness to comply with the state's obligations under international law. [45]

B. **Estrada doctrine:** Under the so-called Estrada doctrine, the practice of recognizing governments is eliminated altogether with the focus being on recognition of states. [45]

C. **Wilson doctrine:** Under this approach, only democratic and constitutional governments were extended recognition. The United States itself no longer adheres to this doctrine. [45]

D. **Acts of recognition:** Recognition of governments is often implied through the continuation or establishment of diplomatic relations. [45]

E. **Significance in domestic law of the recognition of states and governments:** Under domestic law, recognized governments and states enjoy important benefits. In the United States, these include: (1) access to courts in the United States; (2) entitlement to property belonging to those states located in the United States; and (3) a right to claim sovereign immunity. [45]

VI. RECOGNITION OF INSURGENTS AND BELLIGERENTS

A. **Generally:** Insurgencies and belligerencies are two types of internal state conflicts. [46]

VII. THE RIGHTS AND OBLIGATIONS OF STATES

A. **Rights:** States have the rights that are generally accorded them by the international community. Some rights are protected by the U.N. Charter and other U.N. resolutions. [46]

1. **Right of sovereignty:** The right of sovereignty is ***fundamental*** because it prohibits foreign intervention in internal affairs. A state's authority is supreme within its national territory, although restrictions on territorial jurisdiction may be made in international agreements. There is dispute over how exclusive a state's jurisdiction is within its borders, particularly with respect

to human rights. States have a similar qualified right of sovereignty over their natural resources. [46-47]

2. **Equality of states:** Under international law theory, ***all independent states are equal***. All states are to enjoy equal treatment; thus, no state is permitted to intervene in the affairs of another state. [47]

3. **The right to defense:** A state has the right to take steps necessary to protect its security. [47]

4. **The right of international intercourse:** States are free to establish and regulate their own international relations, so long as they do not violate the accepted rules and principles of international law. [47]

B. **Rights of states under U.S. law:** Under U.S. law, a state has: (1) sovereignty over its territory and general authority over its nationals; (2) status as a legal person; and (3) capacity to join with other states to make international law, as customary law or by international agreement. [47]

C. **General responsibility of states:** A state injuring the rights or property of another state in breach of its international obligations incurs international responsibility. A state may bear political responsibility or civil responsibility. [47]

1. **Acts attributable to a state:** A state incurs liability only for those individual actions or omissions ***that can be attributed to the state***. The acts of its organs or agents generally ***are imputed to the state***. A federal state generally cannot deny responsibility for the acts of its member states or provinces. [47-48]

2. **Element of fault:** A state is expected to take reasonable care to prevent injury to another state or areas outside its territorial boundaries. [48]

3. **Defenses to claims against a state:** A state's apparent violation of international law may be justified on the grounds of consent, *force majeure*, distress, necessity, self-defense, and countermeasures. [48-49]

4. **The requirement of injury:** It is generally stated that actual injury is not required to give rise to responsibility to other states for breach of an international obligation unless the obligation specifically requires injury as an element of its breach. [49]

   a. ***Erga omnes*** **obligations:** All states can be held to have a legal interest in the protection of the obligations of a state toward the international community as a whole. These are obligations *erga omnes*. [49-50]

   b. **International crimes:** An international crime is an international obligation so essential for the protection of fundamental interests of the international community that its breach is recognized as a crime by that community as a whole. [50]

5. **Remedies:** Breach of international obligations may give rise to an appropriate remedy, including collective sanctions, restitution, indemnity, and satisfaction. [50-51]

6. **Implementing obligations of reparation:** Reparation may be sought through diplomatic channels or through agreed-upon procedures of dispute settlement. Regardless of the nature of the procedure, there are several common requirements: (1) standing; (2) laches; (3) prior negotiation of the dispute; (4) exhaustion of local remedies; and (5) consent to third-party settlement. [51]

VIII. HEADS OF STATE, GOVERNMENT OFFICIALS, DIPLOMATS, AND OFFICIALS OF INTERNATIONAL ORGANIZATIONS: ROLES AND STATUS IN INTERNATIONAL LAW

A. **Heads of state:** Today, most heads of state are considered organs of the state and are limited in their powers by the states' constitutions. A head of state may be held personally responsible for certain international crimes. [52]

B. **Government:** Foreign political acts of a government and statements of a prime minister (or his or her functional equivalent) made on behalf of the state are binding on the state. [52]

C. **Secretary of state/minister of foreign affairs (or the functional equivalent):** The secretary of state (or his or her functional equivalent) is a state's key figure with respect to its foreign affairs; his or her acts and statements are ***binding upon the state***. [52]

D. **Diplomatic agents:** Diplomatic agents are persons empowered to represent a state in a foreign state or in an international organization. The two categories of diplomats (regular and extraordinary) and heads of mission (ambassadors, envoys, and *charges d'affaires*) compose the diplomatic corps. Permanent diplomatic relations with another state are established by an international agreement followed by the exchange of diplomatic representatives. Diplomatic missions with a particular purpose are terminated with the completion of that job. [52]

   1. **Diplomatic immunities and privileges:** The established privileges and immunities of diplomats apply only from the moment the diplomat enters the host country and only for the period in which he or she is, in fact, a diplomat. [53]

E. **Consuls:** Consuls are authorized to protect the interests of their state in a foreign state with respect to administrative, legal, economic, and cultural affairs. [53]

F. **Officials of international organizations:** The status of international officials is regulated by treaties, such as the U.N. Charter and the U.N. Convention on Privileges and Immunities. [53]

CHAPTER 5
STATE JURISDICTION

I. DEFINITION OF JURISDICTION

A. **Generally:** Under international law, jurisdiction is understood to be the ***allocation of power and authority among the states***. Three interdependent types of jurisdiction are recognized: (1) the right to ***prescribe or apply laws*** to persons and activities; (2) the right to ***enforce those laws*** through application of sanctions; and (3) the ***power of courts*** to exercise jurisdiction over a particular person or object. [55]

II. INTERNATIONAL JURISDICTION PRINCIPLES

A. **Five main bases:** There are five recognized bases for such jurisdiction with respect to crimes:

   1. **The territorial principle:** An essential attribute of a state's sovereignty is to have jurisdiction over all persons and objects within its territory. [55]

a. **"Pure" territoriality:** The act must be commenced in the state's territory, regardless of where it is concluded or consummated. [55]

b. **"Objective" territoriality:** The act must either be completed within the state's territory or cause serious and harmful consequences to the social and economic order within the state's territory. U.S. courts have interpreted this principle broadly in the so-called effects doctrine. [56]

2. **Active nationality principle based on nationality of the defendant:** The state of a person against whom proceedings are taking place may exercise jurisdiction based on the nationality of the defendant. This is true for corporations, vessels, and aircraft as well. [56-57]

3. **Protective principle:** A state may exercise jurisdiction over crimes that threaten its security and integrity or its vital economic interests. [57]

4. **Universality principle:** Some offenses, such as piracy on the high seas, slave trading, and war crimes, are considered to be so serious to the general interest of the international community that they are subject to the jurisdiction of all states. [57]

5. **Passive personality principle based on nationality of the victim:** The state of a person suffering injury or damage may assert that person's nationality as a basis for exercising jurisdiction. [57]

B. **Jurisdiction based on agreement:** In addition to the five basic principles of jurisdiction, states may confer jurisdiction through international agreements. [57]

III. EXTRADITION

A. **Extradition generally:** Extradition is the process by which a person accused of a serious crime in one state (the requisitioning state) and found in a second state (the asylum state) is returned to the requisitioning state for trial or punishment. In the absence of a treaty, there is ***no obligation*** to extradite. [58]

B. **Extraditable offenses:** Treaties employ one of two methods for specifying the grounds for extradition: (1) a requirement of double criminality (when the conduct is an offense in both states and punishable by a specified term of imprisonment); or (2) it may list the indictable offenses for which extradition is available. [58]

C. **Nationals of the asylum state:** State treaties sometimes provide that a state may not or cannot extradite its own nationals. [59]

D. **Process of requesting extradition:** Requests for extradition often are initiated along diplomatic channels. The request is then normally subject to a judicial determination followed by consideration in the executive branch, which has some discretion in the final determination. [59]

E. **Standard treaty limitations on extradition:** Some standard treaty provisions may (1) prohibit discrimination against the accused; (2) require probable cause; (3) provide exemptions for political offenses (except terrorism); (4) include a specialty provision (the accused may be prosecuted only for the offenses for which he or she was indicted); (5) require territorial jurisdiction; or (6) list other non-extraditable crimes. [59-61]

F. **Methods employed to avoid the safeguards of extradition treaties:** Occasionally, to avoid the terms of extradition treaties, potential asylum states may deport the accused as an undesirable alien. Requisitioning states have been known to abduct the accused from an asylum state as well. [61]

IV. JURISDICTIONAL PRINCIPLES IN U.S. LAW

A. The role of international law: The jurisdictional principles of international law and U.S. domestic law affect one another and may be limiting factors on one another. The international law principles of jurisdiction sometimes restrict the exercise of national jurisdiction. Conversely, U.S. due process considerations may place restrictions on jurisdiction that would be acceptable under international law. [62]

B. U.S. grounds for jurisdiction: Under the widely accepted "pure" territorial principle, U.S. law may be applied to any conduct taking place in the United States. The controversial effects test of U.S. law is an extension of the objective territoriality principle, in which any minimal effect on the territory of the United States is a valid ground for asserting jurisdiction. The protective principle has also been applied in a few cases. [62-63]

C. Conflict of laws under U.S. law: *Comity* is the term used to describe judicial restraint practiced in order to avoid or resolve conflicts of jurisdiction, and has been used by U.S. courts to refuse jurisdiction in deference to another state. Lack of reciprocity, on the other hand, has been used to justify a refusal to enforce a foreign court's judgment. The doctrine of *forum non conveniens*, an exercise of comity, is an often-utilized method for settling problems of concurrent jurisdiction. The sovereign compulsion defense is designed to prevent unfairness to private parties subject to the conflicting commands of several states. [63-64]

V. IMMUNITIES FROM JURISDICTION

A. Immunities generally: Both international law and municipal law grant immunities from jurisdiction. [64]

B. Sovereign immunity: There are two main theories regarding sovereign immunity. Absolute immunity is based on the notion that all sovereign states are equal and are not subject to each other's authority. The modern view holds that a state may be subject to a foreign jurisdiction when it engages in commercial activity. In addition to the "commercial exception," modern law supports the traditional denial of immunity for claims to property or other immovables acquired by gift of succession, as well as claims in non-commercial torts cases. The Foreign Sovereign Immunities Act of 1976 essentially codified the restrictive theory of immunity. [64-65]

1. **Foreign Sovereign Immunities Act (FSIA):** Jurisdiction over a foreign state in federal or state courts of the United States may be obtained only through application of the FSIA. A foreign state denied sovereign immunity is liable to the same extent as a private party, except that it will not generally be liable for punitive damages. [65]

2. **Exceptions to immunity:** A state is presumptively immune unless an exception applies. Immunity does not apply under the following statutory exceptions: waivers of immunity, commercial activities, expropriation claims, property claims, non-commercial torts, maritime liens, terrorist acts, counterclaims, and international agreements. [65-69]

C. Act-of-state doctrine: The act-of-state doctrine is not a rule of sovereign immunity and, in fact, is not even a rule of international law. It is a domestic court-made doctrine, which protects the sovereignty of states by judicial deference to the public acts of a foreign state done on that state's territory. [69]

1. **Basic doctrine in the United States:** The parameters for the act-of-state doctrine today remain poorly defined, being based on vague notions of separation of powers in foreign relations between the executive and judicial branches. The Supreme Court now requires the United States to deem as valid "the acts of foreign sovereigns taken within their own jurisdictions." There are exceptions, including the treaty exception, the commercial activity exception, and the situs of property exception. Application of the doctrine is especially controversial in antitrust cases. In human rights cases, U.S. courts have generally concluded that the doctrine does not require dismissal of alleged human rights violations by a foreign state in its own territory. [69-71]

2. **Doctrine in other states:** Although international law does not require application of the act-of-state doctrine as practiced by U.S. courts, the courts of many other states do, in fact, recognize a similar doctrine. [71]

D. **Immunity of state representatives:** Just as diplomatic and consulate premises enjoy special protection, so also do various state representatives. [71]

1. **Head of state:** The immunity of a head of state relies on both ***sovereign immunity*** and ***diplomatic immunity***. [71-72]

   a. **FSIA and *jus cogens*:** The Seventh Circuit Court of Appeals held that FSIA has no provisions, implied or otherwise, that indicated that violation of *jus cogens* norms of international law provided grounds to deny sovereign immunity. [72]

2. **Diplomatic representatives:** Diplomats (and their family members) enjoy ***broad protection*** from arrest or detention, as well as immunity from criminal laws and civil and administrative jurisdiction. The Vienna Convention, also enacted as U.S. federal statutory law, provides that diplomats are, *inter alia*: (1) not required to give evidence; (2) immune from personal service; (3) excused from paying most taxes and social security provisions; and (4) excused from customs duties and inspections. The Convention provides that diplomats do not enjoy immunity with respect to: (1) actions involving purely personal property; (2) estate administration in the host state in which the diplomat is involved in a non-official capacity; or (3) any other commercial or professional conduct in which the diplomat is functioning outside his or her official duties. [72-73]

   a. **Convention on the Prevention and Punishment of Crimes against Internationally Protected Persons:** This treaty requires states to prosecute or extradite for prosecution anyone who commits a violent crime against any head of state, diplomatic agent, or consular official. [73]

3. **Status of embassies and consulates:** Although such diplomatic premises are within the territory of the receiving state, they do enjoy ***special protection***. Diplomatic and consulate premises are "inviolable, and are immune from any exercise of jurisdiction by the receiving state that would interfere with their official use." [73-74]

4. **Consuls:** Consular immunity has been codified under the Vienna Convention on Consular Relations. Under the Convention, consulars are immune from arrest or detention except for serious crimes or as directed by court decisions, and consular archives are inviolable. [74]

5. **Special missions:** Generally, immunity for special missions is covered by the general provisions of diplomatic immunity. [74]

6. **Representatives to international organizations:** U.N. civil servants are protected under the Convention on the Privileges and Immunities of the United Nations, which generally grants immunities similar to those enjoyed by diplomats and consuls. [74]

7. **Individuals participating in foreign governments:** Individuals who participated in foreign governments are not included in the FSIA-extended immunity to foreign governments. [74]

E. **Immunity of international organizations, their agents, officials, and invitees:** Immunity of international organizations has been established by treaty rather than by customary law, and not all states have been eager to extend broad protections. The General Convention on the Privileges and Immunities of the United Nations is an example of such a treaty. It provides the following immunities to the United Nations: (1) immunity from all legal process; (2) inviolability of premises, assets, archives, and official papers; (3) exemption from direct taxes and customs duties; (4) exemption for staff from income tax on salaries; and (5) diplomatic immunity for the secretary-general and assistant secretaries-general. Other staff members have limited immunities. [75]

CHAPTER 6
INTERNATIONAL ORGANIZATIONS

I. THE UNITED NATIONS

The United Nations generally: The term *international organizations* usually refers to public or intergovernmental organizations, in contrast to private or non-governmental organizations (NGOs). International organizations are established by treaties and governed by international law. The United Nations is a public organization consisting of 193 states that was established by intergovernmental cooperation on October 24, 1945. [77]

A. **The U.N. Charter:** The U.N. Charter entered into force on October 24, 1945. The four purposes of the United Nations are described in article 1 as to: (1) "maintain ***international peace and security***"; (2) "***develop friendly relations*** among states"; (3) ***achieve international cooperation*** in solving economic, social, cultural, and humanitarian problems; and (4) ***be a center for states*** to use to attain these common goals. [77]

1. **Seven guiding principles:** Article 2 lists seven guiding principles for the United Nations: (1) sovereign equality of all member states; (2) fulfillment of states' obligations under the Charter; (3) settlement of disputes by peaceful means; (4) refrainment from the threat or use of force against the territorial integrity of political independence; (5) assistance to the United Nations in any action it takes; (6) adherence by non-member states to these principles insofar as to maintain international peace and security; and (7) non-intervention in matters that are essentially within the domestic jurisdiction of a state. [77-78]

B. **Nature and function of the United Nations:** The United Nations has organizational personality (legal capacity) and immunity in the international system. [78]

C. **Membership:** There were 51 original member states. Since its inception, membership in the United Nations has increased dramatically, doubling by 1965, and tripling by 1985. As of February 2011, there were 192 member states, with the admission of Montenegro on June 28, 2006. Membership is open to "all other peace-loving states which accept the obligations contained in the present Charter" and are able and willing to carry them out. Although never actually done, a member state may be suspended or expelled. Further, there is no provision in the Charter for voluntary withdrawal by a state. [78-79]

D. Charter supremacy: Under article 103, if a Charter obligation conflicts with any other treaty obligation, the Charter prevails. [79]

E. The U.N. organs: There are seven principal organs to the United Nations—the *General Assembly*, the *four Councils*, the *Secretariat*, and the *International Court of Justice (ICJ)*. [79]

1. **The General Assembly:** The General Assembly is composed of all member states of the United Nations. It is essentially a global forum for the exchange and debate of ideas. Its resolutions are simply recommendations and not legally binding upon members as a matter of Charter law. [79-80]

2. **The Security Council:** This organ has the primary responsibility for the maintenance of international peace and security. The Security Council consists of five permanent members and ten rotating members. The permanent members have a veto vote in substantive matters. Decisions of the Security Council are legally binding upon members. [80-81]

3. **The Economic and Social Council (ECOSOC):** The ECOSOC consists of 54 elected members of the United Nations. Its primary responsibilities are to make studies, reports, and cultural matters and to prepare draft conventions for submission to the General Assembly on matters within its competence. [81]

4. **Trusteeship Council:** This organ is responsible for administering trusteeship territories that are not yet self-governing. [81-82]

5. **International Court of Justice:** The ICJ is the principal judicial organ of the United Nations and the successor to the Permanent Court of International Justice for the League of Nations. [82]

6. **Secretariat:** The Secretariat is composed of a secretary-general and any required staff of the organization. [82]

7. **Human Rights Council:** The Human Rights Council is the newest organ of the United Nations, established in April 2006. The Council grew out of the Human Rights Commission, and was established with the purpose of "promoting universal respect for the protection of all human rights and fundamental freedoms for all." [82]

F. Legislative activities of the General Assembly and International Law Commission (ILC): The ILC is composed of leading international lawyers who research international law and draft conventions. When such conventions are adopted by the General Assembly and receive broad support, they often become a generally accepted statement of international law in the area. [82]

G. Specialized agencies: Specialized agencies are those "established by intergovernmental agreement and having wide international responsibilities, as defined in their basic instruments, in economic, social, cultural, educational, health, and related fields. . . ." Membership in specialized agencies is not limited to members of the United Nations. By making recommendations and drafting conventions, specialized agencies have developed international law in many areas. [82-83]

II. REGIONAL ORGANIZATIONS

A. Regional organizations generally: Regional organizations are concerned with problems within a specific region. Some handle only specific concerns such as economic, military, or political issues, while others deal with any matter that concerns the nations in that region. The primary function of these regional organizations is to promote cooperation between the member states. Occasionally, the term *regional organization* has been loosely applied to collective defense arrangements. [83-85]

B. Relationship to the United Nations: The United Nations encourages its members in regional organizations to attempt to settle "local disputes" in those organizations before referring them to the Security Council. The issue of regional jurisdiction and the often-overlapping authority of the Security Council is unclear. [85]

III. SUPRANATIONAL ORGANIZATIONS

A. Defined: Member states of a supranational organization submit themselves and their citizens to the law-making power of the organization through treaties with the other member states. Supranational organizations result in a division of power between the individual member states and the organization. The best example of a supranational organization is the European Union. [86]

B. The European Union

1. **Mandate:** The predecessor to the European Union, the European Community, was established to promote unity and economic integration among the member states. The Community was to promote free movement of goods and capital and freedom of movement for persons between the member states. Many of these desired goals came to fruition with the Maastricht Treaty, which has since resulted in the formation of the European Union. [86]

2. **Structure:** The treaties establishing the European Union created four institutions to utilize the power held by the European Union: (1) the Commission; (2) the Council of Ministers; (3) the European Parliament; and (4) the European Court of Justice. [86]

3. **Community and domestic law:** The treaties signed by the member states in the European Union are treated as the constitution of the Union and are binding on each of the nations and individuals in lieu of the failure to ratify a European Union constitution. The European Court of Justice has held that Union laws are superior to any conflicting domestic laws. [87]

IV. THE WORLD TRADE ORGANIZATION (WTO)

A. Generally: The WTO came into being in 1995 in order to implement and administer agreements designed to liberalize and regulate international trade. It is a direct successor to the General Agreement on Tariffs and Trade (GATT). [87]

B. Functions: The WTO, beyond overseeing and implementing WTO agreements, provides a forum for negotiating and, more importantly, settling disputes. It also reviews national trade policies to ensure transparency and global economic policy making. The Organization has also taken on the task of assisting developing nations to adjust to WTO rule. [87]

C. Structure: The World Trade Organization has four primary levels in its hierarchy, not including special committees: (1) the Ministerial Conference; (2) the General Council; (3) the Councils for Trade; and (4) the Subsidiary Body. [87-88]

CHAPTER 7

INTERNATIONAL DISPUTE SETTLEMENT

I. DISPUTES GENERALLY

A. Defined: An international dispute is a contest of some specificity, the resolution of which has some practical effect on the relations between the states involved. [91]

II. THE ROLE OF THE UNITED NATIONS

A. The Charter: The U.N. Charter includes several provisions calling for ***peaceful settlement of disputes***, particularly through "negotiation, enquiry, mediation, conciliation, arbitration, judicial settlement, resort to regional agencies or arrangements, or other peaceful means of their own choice." [91]

B. General Assembly: If a state brings a dispute to the General Assembly, the General Assembly may establish fact-finding missions and make recommendations. States are under no legal obligation to cooperate with the fact-finding missions or to follow recommendations. [91]

C. Security Council: The Security Council has discretion to deny a request for dispute settlement or accede to it by placing a dispute on its agenda. The recommendations of the Security Council exert great political influence but create no legal obligations. [91]

III. OTHER TREATY OBLIGATIONS OF PEACEFUL SETTLEMENT

A. Generally: Since the U.N. Charter, the treaties calling for peaceful dispute settlements are primarily regional treaties. In addition, many treaties on various subjects include provisions for the peaceful settlement of disputes. [91-92]

IV. NON-JUDICIAL METHODS

A. Generally: Methods of non-judicial dispute resolution are: (1) ***negotiation***, a face-to-face discussion between the disputing parties; (2) ***inquiry***, an attempt to clarify the facts in the hopes that agreement on factual matters will facilitate a final resolution; (3) ***mediation/good offices***, the use of a third party to aid in discussion; and (4) ***conciliation***, a non-binding proposal by a fact-finding third party. Each method may be used alone or in any combination with the other methods. [92-93]

V. QUASI-JUDICIAL METHODS/ARBITRATION

A. Arbitration generally: Arbitration, unlike any of the five methods discussed above, results in ***legally binding settlements***. Arbitration has several ***advantages***: (1) it is more conclusive than the other forms of non-judicial dispute settlement because the decisions of the arbitral panels are binding upon the parties; (2) the disputing parties retain greater control in the arbitration process because they appoint the arbitrators; (3) the parties may designate the procedures and the laws to be applied; (4) arbitration is less formal and less contentious than adjudication; and (5) both the arbitration proceedings and decisions can be kept confidential, a great advantage in disputes regarding sensitive matters. There are also ***disadvantages***, however: (1) if the parties do not specify procedures, arbitration may be a very cumbersome and time-consuming process; (2) arbitration panels do not have the authority of courts to conduct discovery or subpoena witnesses; and (3) the parties themselves pay for the entire cost of the arbitration. [93]

B. **Types of international arbitral clauses:** Arbitration may be mandated by a treaty clause, may be the main subject of a treaty on dispute settlement, or may be agreed upon after the dispute has risen. [93-94]

C. **Consent to arbitrate and the *compromis*:** There is no international law requirement to arbitrate. Parties may consent to arbitrate. The subsequent agreement on the details of the arbitration procedure is called the *compromis d'arbitrage*. [94]

D. **Composition of the arbitral tribunal:** Normally, a tribunal has a tripartite structure, in which each party selects one member independently and then the third member is selected by a joint decision of the parties. [94]

E. **Choice of location:** Choice of location can be important because some countries' laws provide that their courts have jurisdiction over arbitration proceedings. [94]

F. **Rules of arbitration—ad hoc versus institutional arbitration:** Parties may choose between the established sets of rules for arbitration or may develop their own ad hoc rules. [94-95]

G. **Applicable law:** The *compromis* usually sets forth the governing rules to be applied by the arbitrators, and those rules in turn stipulate the choice of law. [95]

H. **Arbitral award:** As a general rule, arbitral awards are binding on the parties and are not subject to appeal. Certain defenses to enforcement of an award do exist. Some include: (1) the arbitral tribunal exceeded its powers; (2) the enforcement of the award is contrary to the public policy of the forum country; (3) the award resulted from arbitration of matters considered incapable of settlement by arbitration under the laws of the forum country; (4) the defendant proves that it was "not given proper notice . . . or was otherwise unable to present [its] case"; and (5) the award is in "manifest disregard" of the law. Additional bases for challenging an award are: (1) corruption on the part of a member of the arbitral panel; (2) failure to state the reasons for the award; (3) serious departure from a fundamental procedural rule; (4) the agreement to arbitrate or the *compromis* are a nullity; or (5) the tribunal exceeded its powers. Other defenses may be available. [95-96]

I. **The role of the International Court of Justice (ICJ):** A *compromis* may confer jurisdiction of particular legal questions to the ICJ and indicate the rules of law to be applied by the court. [96]

VI. THE INTERNATIONAL COURTS

A. **The International Court of Justice:** The International Court of Justice (ICJ) is the ***principal judicial organ*** of the United Nations. Only states may be parties in contentious proceedings before the court. [96]

1. **Structure and composition:** The ICJ is composed of 15 judges elected by both the Security Council and the General Assembly. [96-97]

2. **Contentious and advisory jurisdiction:** The court may hear only cases governed by international law. Contentious jurisdiction is based on either the express or implied consent of the parties. Decisions in contentious cases are binding on the parties. The court also may issue non-binding, advisory opinions. [97]

3. **Compulsory jurisdiction under the optional clause of article 36(2):** A state may at any time declare that it recognizes as compulsory *ipso facto*, and without special agreement, the jurisdiction of the court in all legal disputes before the court. A state accepting the jurisdiction of the ICJ under the optional clause does so only with respect to other states that have made a similar declaration. Some declarations state no time limits, while others remain in effect for specific periods (usually five or ten years). Reservations to declarations may be conditioned on other states accepting the court's compulsory jurisdiction for a certain time, or for a wide variety of reasons. A common reservation is the so-called self-judging reservation, such as the "Connally Amendment" of the United States, which excludes from the jurisdiction of the ICJ disputes over matters that are essentially within the domestic jurisdiction of a state. Matters related to national security and defense are also often excluded. [97-98]

4. **Effect and enforcement of judgments:** Judgments of the ICJ are binding upon the parties. The Security Council makes recommendations or decides upon measures to be taken to give effect to the judgment. [98]

5. **Advisory jurisdiction:** The ICJ may give advisory opinions on any legal question at the request of a body authorized by the United Nations. Although advisory opinions are legally non-binding, they are, nevertheless, very influential in the development of international law. [98-99]

B. **Other international courts:** There are also a number of regional and specialized tribunals, particularly in Western Europe. Three regional courts sitting in Europe are the European Court of Justice, the Benelux Court of Justice, and the European Court of Human Rights. Newer additions to the list of specialized jurisdictions include the African Court of Human and Peoples' Rights, the International Tribunal for the Law of the Sea, the International Criminal Courts, and the International Criminal Tribunals for Rwanda and for the former Yugoslavia. [99-100]

VII. THE WORLD TRADE ORGANIZATION

The dispute settlement process under the WTO is considered a central pillar in resolving problems in the multilateral trading system and purports to offer stability in the global economy. [100]

A. **The Understanding on Rules and Procedures Governing the Settlement of Disputes:** Agreed upon in 1994, the Understanding on Rules and Procedures Governing the Settlement of Disputes (DSU) allows member states to engage in consultations to resolve trade disputes in regard to a "covered agreement" or, if that fails, to have a WTO panel hear the case. The operation of the dispute settlement process involves parties and third parties to a case and may involve Dispute Settlement Body panels, composed of representatives of all WTO members and responsible for administering the DSU, the Appellate Body, the WTO secretariat, arbiters, independent experts, and several specialized institutions. [100]

CHAPTER 8

THE RIGHTS OF INDIVIDUALS—INTERNATIONAL LAW OF HUMAN RIGHTS

I. STATUS OF INDIVIDUALS

A. **Modern international law:** The human rights of individuals are protected *without regard to their status as nationals or aliens.* [103]

II. BRIEF HISTORY

A. **Generally:** Historically, a state's treatment of individuals in its territory was considered a domestic affair and not a matter of international law. After World War I, a number of treaties and international organizations began to focus on individual rights. The modern concept of international human rights law is the result of the world's reaction to the Holocaust and other Nazi atrocities during World War II. The body of law concerning international human rights is still growing and evolving. [103-104]

III. HUMAN RIGHTS AND THE UNITED NATIONS

A. **The U.N. Charter:** The U.N. Charter was the first attempt to provide comprehensive protection of all individuals. In the decades since its foundation, the United Nations has continued to promote and protect human rights and has drafted treaties for global adoption dealing with many aspects of human rights. The U.N. Charter contains articles concerning human rights, which pledge the members' active support for "human rights and fundamental freedoms." These articles are the foundation of modern human rights law. [104]

B. **The Universal Declaration of Human Rights:** The rights in this General Assembly resolution fall into two general categories: (1) civil and political rights; and (2) economic, social, and cultural rights. Although a simple resolution and not legally binding, some of the rights listed have clearly evolved into customary international law. [105]

C. **The U.N. human rights covenants:** The two groups of rights set forth in the Declaration of Human Rights were the basis for subsequent treaties outlining in greater detail the protected rights of individuals: the International Covenant on Civil and Political Rights, and the International Covenant on Economic, Social, and Cultural Rights. [105-106]

D. **The role of specialized agencies of the United Nations:** A number of specialized agencies have been active in the area of developing human rights law. [106]

IV. FUNDAMENTAL HUMAN RIGHTS

A. **The right of peoples to self-determination:** Self-determination is the *right of people in a territory to decide the political and legal status of that territory*. The right of the inhabitants of an *established* state to determine their own government is well established, but there is little or no agreement on the right of groups to secede from states of which they form a part, on reunification of peoples in divided states, or the right of minorities to preserve their own separate identities within a state. [107]

B. Defining a "people": The objective element is the existence of an ethnic group linked by some common history. The subjective element is the group's own identification of itself as a "people."[107]

C. Legal status of principle of self-determination: The principle of self-determination is subject to some uncertainty as a result of its lack of concrete definition, as well as its conflict with the well-established principle of sovereignty. [107]

D. Rights of indigenous peoples: Indigenous peoples have asserted a right to self-determination to prevent their complete absorption into states dominated by non-aboriginal populations. Indigenous peoples may be seeking to secede to form their own states, or to retain control over their own communities and land. The U.N. General Assembly approved a Declaration on the Rights of Indigenous Peoples on September 13, 2007. [108]

E. Civil and political rights: These may include prohibitions on torture; discrimination on grounds of race, gender, religion, language, political opinion, nationality, ethnicity, birth, or other status; and arbitrary arrests or interferences with privacy. [108]

F. Economic, social, and cultural rights: These include the right to social security, full employment, fair work conditions, education, health care, an adequate standard of living, and participation in the community's cultural life. [108]

G. Prohibition of slavery: The prohibition against slavery is a fundamental right as a matter of customary international law and the norm is recognized as *jus cogens* from which no derogation is permitted. [108]

H. Genocide: Genocide, or acts committed with the intent to destroy a national, ethnic, racial, or religious group, is a crime for which individuals are punishable under international law. [108-109]

I. Crimes against humanity: "Crimes against humanity" are defined as "murder, extermination, enslavement, deportation, and other inhumane acts committed against any civilian population, before or during the war, or persecutions on political, racial, or religious grounds." [109-110]

J. Prohibitions of discrimination: Every individual is protected from discrimination, whether racial, gender-based, religious, or otherwise. [110-111]

K. Freedom from torture: There are no justifications for torture or exceptions to its prohibition. States must adopt measures to prevent torture in their jurisdictions, and ensure that torture, complicity, and attempts to commit torture are criminal offenses. [112-113]

L. Rights of refugees: The 1951 Geneva Convention addresses many civil rights for refugees. At present, customary international law does not appear to recognize a right to asylum, although this rule has been the subject of much criticism. [113-114]

V. NEWLY EMERGING RIGHTS AND FUNDAMENTAL RIGHTS RECOGNIZED AS CUSTOMARY INTERNATIONAL LAW

A. Generally: Many of the rights recognized in the international agreements above are also recognized as customary international law. Section 702 of the Restatement (Fourth) of the Foreign Relations Law of the United States provides a list, which is neither complete nor closed, of human rights that are generally accepted as customary law. Section 701 of the Restatement suggests that customary human rights law is established in a manner different from other customary law because historically, human rights have been a matter between a state and its own citizens. [114]

B. Methods of creation: Customary human rights law may be established through: (1) virtually universal adherence to the U.N. Charter or the Universal Declaration of Human Rights; (2) widespread participation of states in preparation and adoption of international human rights agreements and General Assembly resolutions on human rights; or (3) frequent invocation and application of international human rights principles in both domestic practice and diplomatic practice. [114-115]

VI. ENFORCEMENT OF HUMAN RIGHTS LAW IN THE U.S. COURTS

A. Current law: Because the United States has failed to ratify and implement so many human rights treaties, enforcement of human rights law in U.S. courts is largely dependent on incorporation of custom into U.S. law and specific legislative provisions, such as the Alien Tort Statute. [115-116]

VII. DEROGATION FROM PROTECTION OF HUMAN RIGHTS

A. General concept: Agreements ensuring protection of fundamental human rights often allow derogation from the rights in times of "public emergencies." The most basic human rights ***may not be derogated from***, including torture, slavery, genocide, and like crimes. Examples of the derogation principle may be taken from the International Covenant on Civil and Political Rights and the European Convention for the Protection of Human Rights and Fundamental Freedoms. [120]

1. **The International Covenant on Civil and Political Rights:** Derogation from the Covenant's obligations may be made under the following circumstances: (1) it must be a "time of public emergency which threatens the life of the nation"; (2) the existence of such dire circumstances must be "officially proclaimed"; (3) derogation is permitted "only to the extent strictly required by the exigencies of the situation"; (4) the measures may not be "inconsistent with their other obligations under international law"; and (5) the measures may not "involve discrimination solely on the ground of race, color, sex, language, religion, or social origin." [120-121]

2. **European Convention for the Protection of Human Rights and Fundamental Freedoms:** The derogation provision of the European Convention is similar to that of the Covenant on Civil and Political Rights. It permits derogation: (1) "[i]n time of war or other public emergency threatening the life of the nation"; (2) "only to the extent strictly required by the exigencies of the situation"; and (3) "provided such measures are not inconsistent with its other obligations under international law." [121]

B. Clauses of limitation: A number of the rights enumerated in the European Convention on Human Rights also have their own clauses of limitation, which allow restrictions on the rights as necessary to protect national security, safety, and health or morals. [121]

VIII. REGIONAL HUMAN RIGHTS LAW AND INSTITUTIONS

Regional human rights generally: Regional human rights regimes operate mainly in Western Europe, the Americas, and Africa. [121-122]

A. **The European system of human rights law:** European human rights law is contained primarily in the European Convention for the Protection of Human Rights and Freedoms and subsequent protocols for civil and political rights, and the European Social Charter for economic and social rights. [122]

1. **The European Convention on Human Rights:** The European Convention has established an effective human rights regime, enforcing rights through the European Commission of Human Rights, the European Court of Human Rights, and the Committee of Ministers of the Council of Europe. [122]

2. **The European Social Charter:** The European Social Charter promotes and protects economic and social rights. [122]

3. **The European Convention on Human Rights and Biomedicine:** Also known as the Oviedo Convention, this Convention bans all forms of discrimination based on genetic makeup and allows for predictive genetic testing for medicinal purposes only. [123]

4. **The European Convention on Action Against Trafficking in Human Beings:** This Convention calls on state parties to cooperate in stopping the practice of human trafficking and to bring violators to justice. [123]

B. **The original institutions of the European regime:** The European Convention of Human Rights has established an effective human rights regime, enforcing rights originally through the European Commission of Human Rights, the European Court of Human Rights, and the Committee of Ministers of the Council of Europe. [123]

1. **European Commission of Human Rights:** The Commission has both compulsory and optional jurisdiction. [123]

2. **European Court of Human Rights:** The court is composed of a number of members equal to the number of states party to the Convention. Originally, cases could be referred to the court by states, the Commission, or individuals, and the court's judgments were final and binding. The court was vested with the power to award damages. The court also had limited authority to issue advisory opinions. Decisions of the court were originally enforced by the Committee of Ministers. [123]

3. **Merger of the European Commission and the Court of Human Rights:** There has been a ***merger*** of the dual European court system (the European Commission and the Court of Human Rights), under Protocol 11 to the European Convention. Protocol 11 entered into force in 1998. [123-124]

4. **Committee of Ministers of the Council of Europe:** The committee was made up of one representative for each member state of the Council of Europe. It appointed the members of the Human Rights Commission and decided those cases that the commission failed to settle and that were not referred to the European Court within three months after the commission's report. [124]

C. **The process of implementation and enforcement:** The European Convention and the European Social Charter detail their respective adjudicative procedures. [124-125]

D. **Inter-American system—human rights law:** Outside of Europe, the most developed regime of human rights law is in the Americas. The primary sources for human rights law in the Americas are the Charter of the Organization of American States (OAS) and the 1969 American Convention on Human Rights. [125]

E. **Institutions of the Inter-American system:** The two organs responsible for supervising implementation and enforcement of human rights are the Inter-American Commission on Human Rights and the Inter-American Court of Human Rights. [125-126]

1. **Inter-American Commission on Human Rights:** In 1987, OAS established the Inter-American Convention to Prevent and Punish Torture.

2. **Inter-American Court of Human Rights:** Another convention was adopted in 1994 called the Inter-American Convention on the Prevention, Punishment, and Eradication of Violence Against Women.

   In 2016, the Court held that the American Convention on Human Rights only applies to natural persons, not legal persons. The Court also held that indigenous and tribal communities are protected by the Convention and that labor union organizations are protected by the Protocol of San Salvador.

F. **Process of implementation and enforcement:** As in the European system, claims of human rights violations are first considered by the Commission, and then referable to the court. [127]

G. **African regional system—human rights law:** The primary source of law is the African Charter of Human and People's Rights, which differs significantly from the European and American human rights regimes. It guarantees economic, social, and cultural rights as well as political and civil rights; it is concerned with the rights of "peoples" as well as individuals; and it proclaims the duties as well as rights of individuals. [127-128]

1. **African regional system—human rights law:** In July 2008, the protocol to the African Charter on Human and Peoples' Rights on the establishment of an African Court on Human and Peoples' Rights and the Court of Justice of the African Union was created. It is in the process of being ratified by the African Union countries. As of 2016, 24 countries had ratified the Protocol.

H. **League of Arab States and Human Rights:** The League of Arab States adopted an Arab Charter on Human Rights in 1994 and revised it in 2004. It tracks most of the U.N. human rights conventions, but there are some notable exceptions. [128]

I. **ASEAN:** ASEAN adopted a governing treaty in 2007 that recognized the importance of human rights. ASEAN created a commission on human rights in 2009, but it is only a consultative group with no judicial powers. In 2012, the ASEAN Human Rights Declaration was created. Though this marks a significant step forward for the human rights framework in Asia, the Declaration has been criticized for multiple shortcomings. [128]

CHAPTER 9
THE LAW OF ARMED CONFLICT

I. ARMED CONFLICT GENERALLY

The law of armed conflict is that area of international law that governs the circumstances under which a state may use military force. In addition, once armed hostilities have commenced, the law of armed conflict places limitations upon the means by which force may be exerted and the targets against which such force may be directed. This area of law can be divided into two sections—*jus ad bello*, the law leading up to war, and *jus in bello*, the law during war. [131]

A. Definition: The two terms may be used interchangeably to mean any armed conflict of a certain degree between the armed forces of states. The degree of conflict required to constitute a war will vary depending upon the circumstances, the states involved, and other similar factors. [131]

1. **Relevance of a declaration of war:** Traditionally, a state had to declare war before international law would recognize the war's existence. In recent years, however, many states have engaged in hostilities without a formal declaration of war. The Geneva Conventions apply to any armed conflict between states, even if there is not a recognized state of war between them. Art. 2. [131]

B. Legal prohibitions against international armed conflict: During the nineteenth century, every sovereign state was considered to have the right to wage war. In the twentieth century, however, many international agreements, most notably article 2(4) of the U.N. Charter, have ***renounced force as a policy*** and encouraged first resort to peaceful settlement of disputes. [131-132]

C. Threat or use of force authorized by the U.N. Charter: Even within the U.N. Charter, the prohibition on the use of force is not absolute. The Charter expressly permits member nations to exert force in ***self-defense***. The Security Council is also authorized to order force when it finds a threat to peace, a breach of peace, or an act of aggression. [134]

1. **Questions raised by article 51:** Like the prohibition against the use of force, the scope of the right of self-defense has been the subject of considerable debate. There are questions as to whether the conditions in article 51 are the only grounds for self-defense, and whether anticipatory self-defense, self-help, or humanitarian intervention are allowed, as well as questions about collective self-defense. Furthermore, it is unclear whether the right of a state to act in self-defense comes to an end as soon as the Security Council has taken action. [134-135]

2. **Requirements for a valid act of self-defense:** First, there must be a "necessity of self-defense, instant, overwhelming, leaving no choice of means, and no moment of deliberation." Second, the actions justified by the necessity of self-defense "must be limited by that necessity and kept clearly within it." These two requirements are often referred to as the ***requirements of necessity and proportionality***. First and foremost, there must be an "armed attack" against a state under article 51. Self-defense against terrorism has introduced the controversial policy of anticipatory self-defense. [135]

3. **U.N. Security Council enforcement actions under the U.N. Charter:** The Security Council may act with respect to "threats to the peace, breaches of the peace, or acts of aggression." It may call upon member states to implement measures not involving the use of armed force in order to give effect to its decisions. "Should the Security Council consider that such measures are inadequate, it may use force, including demonstrations, blockades, and other operations by air, sea, or land forces of Members of the United Nations." Action taken under Chapter VII is binding on all members of the United Nations, and such decisions are subject to the veto power. [136-138]

4. **Enforcement action by the General Assembly:** It is questionable whether the General Assembly can take enforcement action under the Uniting for Peace Resolution, in light of the *Certain Expenses* case. [139]

5. **Enforcement actions by regional organizations:** In the past, some regional organizations have tried to justify the use or threat of force under article 53, although such enforcement action is prohibited without the authorization of the Security Council. [139]

D. **Humanitarian intervention as a possible justification for the use of force:** It is generally agreed that the state using force would have to ***act from humanitarian motives*** (not against "the territorial integrity or political independence" of the target state) and ***cease military operations as soon as the humanitarian objective was achieved***, even assuming humanitarian intervention is permissible under international law. [140]

E. **Protection of nationals and property:** Protection of nationals is distinguished from humanitarian intervention based on the nationality of the victims. It is legally distinguishable because advocates of the right have asserted that attacks on a state's nationals triggers a right of self-defense under a broad reading of article 51 or a right of self-help under customary international law. [140]

F. **Reprisals:** The term "reprisal" means an otherwise illegal act committed by one state against a second state, in order to remedy a prior violation of international law by the second state, to protect its interests, or to achieve some other objective. Often, the illegal act involves the use of force. A state that engages in a reprisal in retaliation for past acts is presumably in violation of international law. [140-141]

II. THE HUMANITARIAN LAW OF ARMED CONFLICT

A. **Sources of the law of armed conflict:** The International Military Tribunal at Nuremberg found the provisions of the Hague Conventions of 1907 to have entered into customary international law as of 1939. Many international treaties have attempted to regulate the conduct of warfare. Among the more important of these treaties still in force are the Hague Conventions and Declarations of 1907, especially the Convention Respecting the Law and Customs of War on Land and the Protocol for the Prohibition of the Use in War of Asphyxiating, Poisonous or Other Gases, and of Bacteriological Methods of Warfare. The Geneva Conventions of 1949, and the Protocols of 1977 added to them, are also very important in detailing the law of war. [141-142]

B. **Protections provided by the Hague and Geneva Conventions:** Protection in times of war is afforded to certain individuals, including: (1) ***wounded, sick, or shipwrecked combatants***; (2) ***prisoners of war***; and (3) ***civilians***. As with individuals, the degree of protection extended to any particular piece of property depends largely upon its nature. As a general rule, the destruction or confiscation of enemy property is forbidden except for situations of military necessity. In no event is looting of enemy property permissible. [142-143]

1. **The civilian populace:** The 1907 Hague Conventions provided that undefended buildings, towns, and the like were not to be attacked. [143-144]

2. **Areas with special protection:** The 1949 Geneva Conventions extended special protections to medical facilities (both military and civilian) and provided for the establishment of hospital, neutralized, and safety zones in which attacks are forbidden. [144]

C. **Conflicts encompassed by the Geneva Conventions and protocols:** Which provisions of the Geneva Convention and protocols apply depends upon whether the conflict is an international conflict, a civil war, or a war of self-determination. [144-145]

D. Sanctions and enforcement: The Hague Conventions of 1907 provided that a state might be required to pay reparations if it, or any member of its armed forces, violated the Convention, although it established no procedural framework for claims. The Geneva Conventions of 1949 provide that once a violation has been established, the parties shall "put an end to it and repress it with the least possible delay." The Geneva Conventions also contain provisions allowing a state to subject any individual, regardless of nationality, to criminal prosecution for violations of the Conventions. States have an obligation to punish individuals alleged to have committed grave breaches. [145-146]

The Charter of the International Military Tribunal at Nuremberg provides for individual criminal responsibility for "crimes against peace," war crimes, or "crimes against humanity." The fact that an individual acted pursuant to the orders of his government or superior is not a defense. An official or commander who has, through reports received by him or through other means, information that troops or other persons subject to his control are about to commit or have committed war crimes, and fails to take the necessary and reasonable steps to ensure compliance with the law of war, is responsible for such crimes. [146-147]

E. Limitations on the methods of warfare: There are several limitations imposed on the conduct of warfare by the Hague Conventions of 1907 and the Geneva Conventions of 1949, among other treaties. Restrictions on conduct of warfare cover ***types of weaponry*** (*e.g.*, prohibitions on poisonous gas and chemical weapons) and ***tactics*** (*e.g.*, false surrenders). There are also prohibitions on extending warfare to neutral states or demilitarized zones. [147]

III. CIVIL WARS

A. Generally: International law ***does not prohibit civil war***. Civil wars may be fought for control of the government of the state, for the creation of a new state, or to gain independence from colonial rule. There are three categories of internal conflicts: (1) ***rebellions***; (2) ***insurgencies***; and (3) ***belligerencies***. [150]

B. Traditional rule: Under the traditional rule, states could support the governing authorities ***until a belligerency was recognized***, at which point they had to remain neutral. Now, the focus is more upon the general norms of non-intervention and self-determination under the U.N. Charter. [150]

C. Non-intervention: Non-intervention is well established as customary law. A state intervenes when it sends armed forces to either side in a civil war, supplies war materials, or allows its territory to be used as a base for forces. It is less clear when aid from a state's nationals is intervention. A state may, however, provide humanitarian aid. [150-151]

1. **Possible exception:** It has been argued that outside states may aid insurgents if the war is one of ***national liberation***. [151]

2. **Other justifications:** States have put forth several other justifications for intervention, such as: (1) ***consent of governing authorities***; (2) ***self-defense***; and (3) ***counterintervention***. With the exception of self-defense, recognition of these justifications in post-Charter international law is strongly debated. [151-153]

CAPSULE SUMMARY

CHAPTER 10
THE LAW OF THE SEA

I. NATIONALITY OF VESSELS

A. **Generally:** Three basic principles that govern the freedom of the seas are: (1) a ship of any state can navigate the oceans freely; (2) the state of the ship's nationality has exclusive jurisdiction over the ship on the high seas; and (3) no other state can exercise jurisdiction over that ship absent some affirmative rule authorizing concurrent jurisdiction. The nationality of a ship is that of the state whose flag it is authorized to fly. A ship may fly the flag of only one state. A ship without a nationality may be prevented from engaging in international trade or commerce or navigation of any sort on the high seas. [157]

B. **The right of states to confer nationality upon a ship:** Each state may set its own standards for nationality. [157-158]

1. **Limitations:** A state may not grant its nationality to a ship that is already authorized to fly the flag of another state. Furthermore, a state must have a ***genuine link*** to a ship in order to confer its nationality upon it. Proof of a genuine link between a flag state and a ship may include: (1) ownership by nationals; (2) national officers; (3) national crew; and (4) national build. [158]

C. **Documentation and registration:** A state that authorizes ships to fly its flag must: (1) ***maintain a register*** of ships containing the name and description of each ship so authorized; and (2) ***issue documents*** to the registered ships ***evidencing authorization***. [158]

D. **Duties of the flag state:** Under international law, each state has a duty to "effectively exercise its jurisdiction and control in administrative, technical, and social matters over ships flying its flag." Each flag state also has the obligation to: (1) maintain a register of ships authorized to fly its flag; (2) govern the internal affairs of each ship; (3) ensure the safety of each ship at sea with regard to seaworthiness, crews, communications, and the prevention of collisions; (4) ensure that each ship is surveyed by a qualified surveyor of ships and has on board appropriate charts, nautical publications, and navigational equipment; (5) ensure that each ship is manned by a qualified master, officers, and crew; and (6) ensure that the master, officers, and crew are fully conversant with, and are required to observe, applicable international regulations. [158-159]

II. BASELINE DETERMINATIONS FOR MEASURING COASTAL ZONES

A. **The baseline generally:** The baseline is the ***starting point from which a coastal state's various maritime jurisdictions are measured***. Waters on the landward side of the baseline are considered internal waters of the state. [159]

B. **Delineation of the baseline:** The baseline is the low-water line along the coast. [159]

1. **Rivers:** If a river flows directly into the sea, the baseline is drawn straight across the mouth of the river between the low-water points of its lands. [159]

2. **Bays:** Bays are considered to be internal waters of a state when the bay's area is as large as or larger than the area of the semicircle for which the diameter is a line drawn across the mouth of the bay, so long as that line is less than 24 nautical miles. If the line between the natural entrance points of the bay exceeds 24 miles, a straight baseline of 24 miles can be drawn so as to enclose

the maximum area of water possible with a baseline of that length. Exceptions may be made for "historical bays." [159-160]

3. **Islands:** An island is "a naturally formed area of land, surrounded by water, which is above water at high tide." Every island has the right to claim each and every coastal zone. [160]

4. **Indented coastlines and island fringes:** A straight baseline method may be used for a fringe of islands or deeply indented coastline by joining appropriate points, if: (1) the baseline does not depart from the general direction of the coast and is sufficiently linked to the main coast; (2) the low-tide elevation is not used; (3) if the straight baseline does not cut off the territorial sea of another state from the high seas or an exclusive economic zone; and (4) innocent passage is granted through any newly created internal waters. [160]

C. **Demarcation of baseline with adjacent and opposite states:** Where the coasts of two states are opposite or adjacent to each other, neither state is entitled to extend its territorial sea beyond the median line. The delimitation of the continental shelf and economic zone between states is determined by agreement. In the absence of agreement, the boundary is the median line, where opposite states are involved; and an equidistant line, where adjacent states are involved. [161]

1. **Boundary Disputes:** As demonstrated in *Ghana v. Ivory Coast* (2017), there has been a growing trend of favoring a simple, single maritime boundary for the water column, the seabed, and the extended continental shelf (ECS).

III. INTERNAL WATERS AND PORTS

A. **General definition:** Internal waters are the ***waters of lakes, rivers, and bays landward of the baseline of the territorial sea***. A port is a place for loading or unloading a ship. A coastal state has ***full sovereignty*** over its internal waters and ports. [161]

B. **Freedom of access to ports:** Freedom of access to ports by foreign merchant vessels is governed by the principal of ***reciprocity***. Landlocked nations may not be denied freedom of access to ports solely because of their inability to reciprocate. Ports may be closed to foreign vessels only when the vital interests of a state require it. A coastal state may condition a foreign ship's access to port upon compliance with the laws and regulations of the port. [161-162]

C. **Inland waters:** If a state within the United States may claim submerged lands based on the area's status as historic inland waters, it must demonstrate that the United States exercises authority over the area, has done so continuously, and has done so with the acquiescence of foreign nations. [162]

D. **Jurisdiction over foreign vessels:** A foreign merchant ship that enters any port of a state subjects itself to the administrative, civil, and criminal jurisdiction of that state, although a ship's internal matters are left to the flag state. Foreign vessels are not subject to a state's jurisdiction when the vessel is seeking refuge because of distress. The flag state also has jurisdiction, and the Law of the Sea (LOS) Convention grants the port state in certain situations enlarged jurisdiction. [162]

IV. THE TERRITORIAL SEA AND CONTIGUOUS ZONE

A. **Coastal state sovereignty over the territorial sea:** A state has the ***same sovereignty over its territorial sea, airspace, seabed, and subsoil thereof as it has with respect to its land***. [163]

B. **Breadth of the territorial sea:** According to the LOS Convention, every state has the right to establish the breadth of its territorial sea up to 12 nautical miles as measured from the baseline. The United States adheres to a 3-mile territorial sea for domestic law purposes. For international relations, however, the United States has extended its territorial sea to 12 miles. Many states have extended their claims of a territorial sea from 3 miles up to as much as 200 miles. [163]

C. **The right of innocent passage:** Ships of all states have a ***right of innocent passage*** through the territorial sea of any coastal state. [163]

1. **General definition:** *Passage* means navigation through the territorial sea for the purpose of either traversing that sea without entering internal waters or proceeding to or from internal waters. [163]

2. **Prohibited activities for innocent passage:** Many activities not having a direct bearing on passage violate "innocent passage," including: (1) threat or use of force; (2) exercise or practice with weapons; (3) collecting information that prejudices the defense or security of the coastal state; (4) propaganda affecting the defense or security of the coastal state; (5) aircraft activity; (6) any activity involving a military device; (7) loading or unloading any commodity; (8) pollution in contravention of international law; (9) fishing; (10) research or surveying; or (11) interfering with communications of the coastal state. [163]

3. **Coastal state's rights:** Within the territorial sea, the coastal state retains several rights for monitoring activity in the area, including: (1) the unilateral right to verify the innocent character of passage; (2) the ability to suspend the right of innocent passage if essential for protection of the state's security; (3) the adoption of regulations relating to innocent passage; (4) the exercise of fairly broad criminal jurisdiction over foreign ships; and (5) the exercise of more limited civil jurisdiction over foreign ships. [163-164]

4. **Warships:** No prior notification is required for warships in innocent passage under the LOS Convention. [164]

D. **Transit passage:** The right of transit passage exists "through straits which are used for international navigation between one part of the high seas and another part of the high seas or the territorial sea of a foreign state." The right does not exist where a strait is broad enough to allow navigation through a high seas route in its middle. Unlike innocent passage, transit passage extends to aircraft and submarines, and the ***coastal state must place fewer limitations on it***. [165]

E. **Contiguous zone:** The coastal state may exercise the control necessary to prevent infringement of its customs and fiscal, immigration, or sanitary laws and regulations in a zone contiguous to its territorial sea. The contiguous zone may not extend beyond 24 nautical miles from the baseline from which the breadth of the territorial sea is measured. The United States has claimed such a contiguous zone. [165]

V. EXCLUSIVE ECONOMIC ZONE

A. **High seas to fishery zones to exclusive economic zones:** The exclusive economic zone (EEZ) was created to give coastal states exclusive economic water rights beyond the contiguous zone. The 200-mile zone was adopted at the Third U.N. Conference on the Law of the Sea under the 1982 LOS Convention. The EEZ is generally treated as part of the high seas, although states may exercise exclusive exploitation of its resources. The United States has adopted a 200-mile EEZ. [165-166]

B. Management and conservation of the living resources within the EEZ: The coastal state has several responsibilities in the management of the resources within the EEZ, including the duty to prevent overexploitation and to promote optimum utilization of living resources. In granting access to its EEZ, a coastal state must give special consideration to the rights and needs of geographically disadvantaged and landlocked states in the region. [166]

C. Right of geographically disadvantaged states and landlocked states in the EEZ: Geographically disadvantaged states are coastal states that can claim no EEZ of their own or whose geographic locations make them dependent upon exploitation of the EEZ of other coastal states in the region. These states and landlocked states have the right to participate, on an equitable basis, in the exploitation of any fishery surplus in the EEZs of coastal states in the region. [166-167]

D. Species subject to special rules: Several species have been singled out for special treatment within EEZs, such as ***migratory animals***, ***marine mammals***, and ***sedentary species***. [167]

E. Enforcement of conservation and management measures: Enforcement of conservation and management measures depends upon whether the violation occurred within the EEZ or beyond it. A coastal state has enforcement rights within the EEZ, but has limited enforcement powers beyond the EEZ. [167-168]

F. Other uses of the EEZ: A coastal state may exploit non-living resources in its EEZ. [168]

G. Marine scientific research: Coastal states may regulate, authorize, and conduct marine scientific research within their EEZs. If the proposed scientific research is for peaceful purposes for the scientific benefit of all humankind, the coastal state must consent to another state's request to do research. [168]

H. Artificial islands and installations: The coastal state has the ***exclusive*** right to construct and regulate construction, operation, and use of any artificial islands, and of installations and structures built for economic purposes in its EEZ if they do not obstruct recognized sea navigation lanes. [168]

VI. CONTINENTAL SHELF

A. Definition and delimitation: The continental shelf is that submarine area that ***begins at the shore and ends where the continental slope to the deep seabed begins***. The 1958 Continental Shelf Convention and the LOS Convention establish more detailed measurements. [169]

B. Rights and duties of the coastal state over the continental shelf: The coastal state has limited obligations in managing the continental shelf and has extensive rights over the natural resources of the shelf. [169]

C. Sedentary fisheries: The coastal state has sovereign rights over all sedentary fisheries on its continental shelf. [169]

D. Marine scientific research on the continental shelf: The same rules apply to continental shelf research and to the EEZ. [169-170]

E. U.S. practice and legislation relating to the continental shelf: In the United States, control over the continental shelf area is divided between the federal government and coastal states of the United States. States have full jurisdiction and rights over the inner continental shelf area. However, the federal government has reserved its powers to regulate commerce, navigation, defense, and international affairs within the inner shelf. [170]

VII. EXPLOITING THE MINERAL RESOURCES OF THE DEEP SEABED

A. **Current status of the legal regime of the deep seabed:** Three views have developed regarding the legal status of the deep seabed: (1) the ***common heritage of mankind*** view, adopted in the LOS Convention, under which the mineral resources of the deep seabed may be exploited only through an international authority acting on behalf of all countries and which is advocated by the LOS Convention and the developing states; (2) the ***freedom of the high seas*** view, under which the right to explore and exploit the mineral resources of the deep seabed is a freedom of the high seas; and (3) the ***res nullius*** view, under which the seabed belongs to no one and the mineral resources there may be explored and exploited to the exclusion of all others by the first state that claims them. [170-171]

B. **Seabed mining under the LOS Convention:** No state may claim, exercise sovereign rights over, or appropriate any part of the deep seabed or its resources because the mineral resources of the seabed are the common heritage of mankind. The seabed is governed by the Deep Seabed Authority established by the Convention to oversee exploitation and distribute the benefits of exploitation throughout the international community. [171-172]

C. **U.S. legislation:** The United States has promulgated its own regulations on the seabed in the 1980 Deep Seabed Hard Mineral Resources Act. The United States has rejected the deep-seabed regime under the LOS Convention because of the way in which it provides for sharing of technology and profits. [172]

VIII. FREEDOM OF THE HIGH SEAS

A. **General principles:** Freedoms of the high seas include but are not limited to: (1) ***freedom of navigation;*** (2) ***freedom of overflight;*** (3) ***freedom of fishing;*** (4) ***freedom to lay submarine cables and pipelines;*** (5) ***freedom to construct artificial islands, installations, and structures;*** and (6) ***freedom of scientific research.*** These freedoms must be exercised with due regard for the interests of other states. States may exercise high-seas freedoms in the EEZs of other states if there is due regard for the rights and duties of the coastal state, and there is compliance with internationally legal regulations of the coastal state. [172]

B. **Reservation of the high seas for peaceful purposes:** The high seas must be used for ***peaceful purposes***. Naval forces may use the high seas, but use or threat of force violates the law of the sea and article 2(4) of the U.N. Charter, absent other justification of international law (*e.g.*, self-defense). [172]

C. **Freedom of navigation:** Every state has the right to sail ships on the high seas bearing its national flag. Warships and state-owned ships on the high seas have complete immunity from the jurisdiction of any state other than the flag state. The flag state of merchant ships has exclusive jurisdiction in terms of arrest or other physical interference, subject to the following exceptions: (1) treaty provisions allowing interference; (2) collision cases; (3) right of visit; (4) hot pursuit; (5) necessity; (6) self-defense; and (7) action authorized by the United Nations. [172-174]

D. **Freedom of overflight:** All aircraft have the right to fly over the high seas. [174]

E. **Freedom of fishing and conservation measures:** All states have the right to fish the high seas. This is limited by treaties (e.g., the Central Arctic Ocean Agreement) and regards for the rights and duties of other states. [174] The U.N. is currently hosting negotiations for a formally binding instrument to conserve biodiversity on the high-seas, scheduled through 2020. [174]

F. Freedom to lay submarine cables and pipelines: Cable and pipeline laying is subject to coastal state regulation on the continental shelf. [174]

G. Freedom to construct artificial islands: Construction and operation of artificial islands, installations, and structures is subject to coastal regulation of such activities on the continental shelf or in the EEZ. [174]

H. Freedom of scientific research: All states and competent international organizations have the right to conduct scientific marine research outside of EEZs. [175]

IX. PRESERVATION OF THE MARINE ENVIRONMENT

A. The 1958 High Seas Convention: The only provisions of the 1958 High Seas Convention specifically addressed to the preservation of the marine environment are articles 24 and 25. Article 24 requires states to regulate to prevent pollution of the seas by oil discharge from ships, pipelines, or deep-seabed activities. Article 25 calls on states to take measures to prevent pollution of the seas from radioactive materials. [175]

B. Generally: In exercising their sovereign rights to exploit their resources, states must ensure "that activities within their jurisdiction or control do not cause damage to the environment of other states or of areas beyond the limit of national jurisdiction." [175]

C. Third U.N. Conference on the Law of the Sea: States are required to take all measures necessary to prevent pollution of the marine environment from any source. [175]

D. Vessel-source pollution: States are required to establish international guidelines governing vessel-source pollution through international organizations. Flag states are required to adopt laws and regulations for the prevention of pollution of the marine environment from ships flying their flags or of their registries. Coastal states may adopt laws and regulations for the prevention, reduction, and control of marine pollution from foreign vessels within their territorial seas but may not hamper innocent passage. States may regulate vessel-source pollution in their EEZs through an international organization or diplomatic conference. A state may also make a request to the appropriate international organization for additional coastal state regulation of vessel-source pollution in the EEZ if international rules provide inadequate protection. The North American Emission Control Area requires states to reduce allowable emissions of sulfur, nitrogen oxides, and particulate matter from ships in the coastal Atlantic and Pacific waters. [176]

E. Pollution from land-based sources: All states must adopt laws or regulations to prevent pollution of the marine environment from land-based sources. [176]

F. Ocean dumping: States are required to adopt laws and regulations to prevent pollution of the marine environment by the dumping of sewage, sludge, and other waste materials into the ocean. These laws must be comparable to global standards. Dumping in the coastal zones of states requires consent and also is regulated under the Dumping Convention. [176]

G. Pollution from seabed activities subject to national jurisdiction: States are required to adopt all laws and regulations necessary to prevent pollution of the marine environment arising from, or in connection with, their exploration and exploitation of the seabed and subsoil. [177]

H. **Pollution from deep-seabed mining:** The LOS Convention authorizes the Authority to adopt appropriate rules and regulations to prevent pollution of the marine environment from deep-seabed activities. [177]

I. **Pollution from or through the atmosphere:** All states are required to adopt laws and regulations to prevent pollution of the marine environment from or through the atmosphere. [177]

J. **Protection of fragile ecosystems:** States are obligated to take measures necessary to protect and preserve rare or fragile ecosystems, as well as the habitat of depleted, threatened, or endangered species and other forms of marine life. [177]

K. **Fisheries:** In 1999, despite jurisdictional challenges offered by Japan, the International Tribunal for the Law of the Sea (ITLOS) ordered Japan to refrain from conducting an experimental fishing program. Parties to the Convention on the Conservation of Migratory Species of Wild Animals have agreed to share information, cooperate with regional fisheries management organizations, and regulate the capture of sharks in order to help conserve sharks. [177]

L. **Liability:** A state that fails to fulfill its obligations to protect and preserve the marine environment is liable in accordance with international law. [177-178]

M. **Enforcement:** Flag states, coastal states, and port states may all enforce rules and regulations relating to the marine environments depending on the source of pollution, the location of the violation, and the degree of harm to the environment. A state is obligated to compensate the flag state for any injury or loss attributable to unlawful or excessive measures taken against a foreign ship. [178-179]

N. **Notification and cooperative action:** As soon as a state is aware that injury to the marine environment has occurred or is imminent, it must notify immediately the appropriate global or regional international organizations and all states likely to be affected. [179]

O. **Government non-commercial ships:** Ships that are used by governments for non-commercial purposes are not subject to the international rules, standards, and enforcement procedures discussed above. [179]

P. **The International Tribunal for the Law of the Sea (ITLOS):** The ITLOS was constituted in 1996 upon the election of 21 judges with the court seat in Hamburg, Germany. The Tribunal has exclusive jurisdiction over certain specified matters under the treaty, including release and detention of vessels, and deep-seabed mining (which is exercised by the 11-judge Deep Seabed Chamber of the Tribunal). [179]

CHAPTER 11
AIR AND SPACE LAW

I. DEFINING STATE SOVEREIGNTY OVER AIRSPACE

A. **Generally:** Common law doctrine held that a state's control over airspace ***extended to the end of the universe***. Early attempts to define states' sovereignty over airspace balanced the inherent nature of airspace as free from sovereign control against the need of the sovereign to provide for self-preservation and the defense of its citizens. [181]

B. Exclusive control: In 1919, the Paris Convention established each state's ***exclusive control over the airspace over its territory and its territorial waters***. No state has control over the airspace over the high seas. [181]

C. Developing law after World War II: With the dramatic rise in international air traffic, a need arose to establish some general principles to govern international air travel. [181]

1. **The "five freedoms":** At this time, free airspace had been broken down into five components. These so-called ***five freedoms*** became the basis of the international agreements of the World War II era. The five freedoms are: (1) ***overflight***; (2) ***non-traffic landing***; (3) ***putting down traffic***; (4) ***picking up traffic***; and (5) ***international traffic***. [181]

2. **The Chicago Convention:** The most important of the World War II–era agreements was the Chicago Convention on International Civil Aviation, which created the International Civil Aviation Organization (ICAO) and the International Air Services Transit Agreement. It also outlined a number of other general principles. [181-182]

3. **International Air Services Transit Agreement extends limited freedoms to scheduled air service:** Only the first two freedoms, *i.e.*, overflights and non-traffic landings, are generally available under the International Air Services Transit Agreement for scheduled air service. The remaining three freedoms are not generally agreed upon. [182]

4. **Definition of "scheduled international air service":** Because the rules governing scheduled and non-scheduled international air service differ, the International Civil Aviation Organization promulgated the following definition. A "scheduled international air service" is a series of flights that: (1) ***overflies more than one state***; (2) is ***open to the public***; and (3) ***has regular service***. [182-183]

5. **Prescriptive jurisdiction for international air travel:** When an aircraft engages in international air travel, it will at all times be traveling either in airspace governed by a state's domestic regulations or in airspace above the high seas. Regulations regarding air travel differ by jurisdiction. When the aircraft is in airspace above a state or its territorial waters, the regulations of that state apply. When the aircraft is in airspace above the high seas, rules promulgated by the ICAO under article 12 of the Chicago Convention apply. Additional rules may apply for specially designated zones, such as flight information regions (FIRs) or air defense identification zones (ADIZs). [183]

6. **Aircraft has nationality of state of registration:** Article 17 of the Chicago Convention defines the nationality of any aircraft as the state in which it is registered. [183]

II. LIABILITY OF AIR CARRIERS

A. Limitations on liability needed to foster airline industry: The original purpose for placing limits on the recovery from airlines for damages was to assist the growth of the fledgling airline industry, help airlines attract capital, and make obtaining insurance financially feasible. Many U.S. courts construe the limitation of liability provisions very ***strictly*** against air carriers on the theory that the original purpose behind the provisions is no longer valid. [183-184]

B. Standard of liability: In exchange for the limitation on liability, the Warsaw Convention for the Unification of Certain Rules Relating to International Carriage by Air provided a stricter standard of liability for the airlines. Under the Convention, a carrier is liable for death or personal injury unless it can prove that it or its agents have taken all necessary measures to avoid the damage or that it was impossible for the carrier to take such measures. [184-185]

C. **Jurisdiction:** The Warsaw Convention of 1929 specifies when a state has jurisdiction for actions brought under its terms. Under article 28, there is jurisdiction in the state of: (1) the carrier's domicile; (2) the carrier's principal place of business; (3) the location at which the ticket was purchased; and (4) the passenger's place of destination. [185]

III. VIOLATIONS OF AIRSPACE

A. **Violation of airspace:** Under the various international conventions and bilateral agreements governing international aviation, an aircraft normally needs authorization to enter a state's airspace and is required to follow certain procedures while operating in that airspace. [185]

B. **Use of force to terminate a trespass:** By analogy to the law of the sea, states may use only "necessary and reasonable force" in response to intruding aircraft. [185-186]

IV. OFFENSES COMMITTED ABOARD AIRCRAFT

A. **Jurisdiction generally:** Because an aircraft takes on the nationality of the flag state, that state may assert jurisdiction over offenses committed on board the aircraft. In addition, the subjacent state over which the aircraft flies may assert concurrent jurisdiction based on territoriality. Other states may also assert jurisdiction for offenses committed based on other aircraft principles, such as the nationality of the defendant, universality, or the nationality of the victim. [186]

B. **Hijacking and sabotage:** Hijacking involves the ***use or threat of force to exercise control over an aircraft***. Sabotage generally addresses efforts to place the safety of the aircraft in jeopardy. The international community has established conventions to govern both of these offenses. The Convention for the Suppression of Unlawful Seizure of Aircraft (the Hague Convention) governs hijacking, and the Convention for the Suppression of Unlawful Acts Against the Safety of Civil Aviation (the Montreal Convention) deals with sabotage. Many of the articles of the two conventions are identical. Both conventions recognize ***hijacking and sabotage as universal crimes*** and require that a state either prosecute or extradite the alleged offenders. [186]

V. OUTER SPACE

A. **Definition of outer space:** A controversy exists as to whether a definition of outer space is even necessary and, if it is, whether it should be scientifically based or politically based. At least seven possible definitions have been supported over the years: (1) the ***limit of the atmosphere***; (2) the ***limit of air flight***; (3) the ***point at which the atmosphere will no longer sustain human life***; (4) the ***lowest point at which a satellite can orbit***; (5) the ***point at which centrifugal force replaces aerodynamic forces***; (6) the ***limit of a state's effective control over its airspace***; and (7) the ***current orbital minimum***. [186-187]

B. Control of outer space: The widely adopted Treaty of Principles Governing the Activities of States in the Exploration and Use of Outer Space, Including the Moon and Celestial Bodies (Outer Space Treaty) generally provides for free access to outer space and celestial bodies by all nations. [187]

C. Liability for damage caused by space objects: Under the Outer Space Treaty and the more detailed Convention on International Liability for Damage Caused by Space Objects (the Liability Convention), a state that launches or authorizes the launching of an object, or from whose territory an object is launched, can be held liable for damages caused by the object. The standard of liability varies depending upon where and how the damage occurs. Damages are determined under the Liability Convention by the amount needed to return the injured party—whether that party is a person, state, or international organization—"to the condition which would have existed if the damage had not occurred." [187-188]

1. **Obligation to consider rendering assistance:** In cases in which the damage caused "presents a large scale danger to human life or seriously interferes with the living conditions of the population or the functioning of vital center," the responsible state shall examine the possibility of rendering assistance to the damaged state. [188]

2. **Responsibility for activities in outer space:** States bear international responsibility for national activities in outer space regardless of whether the activity is carried out by governmental or non-governmental entities. [188]

3. **States retain jurisdiction over objects it launches into space:** States retain jurisdiction over objects launched into space that are registered to it. [188]

D. Military applications in outer space: The Outer Space Treaty bans military use of outer space and celestial bodies but permits some military use of orbiting spacecraft. The Treaty does not, however, prohibit the use of military personnel in the conduct of research or for other peaceful purposes. [188-189]

E. Geostationary orbits: A satellite in a geostationary orbit remains over the same position on Earth. Such orbits occur only over the equator. Although some states along the equator claim special rights to geostationary orbits, the prevalent view is that such orbits are properly considered "outer space" and therefore are under no state's control. [189]

1. **Regulated use of geostationary orbits:** Because geostationary orbits are so valuable and are limited in number, the international community has sought agreement on their use. [189]

VI. CELESTIAL BODIES

A. Territory not subject to state control: Under the Outer Space Treaty, *no state may exercise any claim of right to the moon or any other celestial body*. The moon and other celestial bodies may be used only for peaceful purposes. [189]

B. Control of resources on the Moon and other celestial bodies: Only a few states have signed the Agreement Governing the Activities of States on the Moon and other Celestial Bodies, which addresses exploitation of the Moon's resources. The Agreement provides, *inter alia*, for the development of a governing regime for the exploitation of the Moon's resources. The treaty also provides that the Moon and its resources are the common heritage of mankind. [189-190]

CAPSULE SUMMARY

CHAPTER 12
INTERNATIONAL ENVIRONMENTAL LAW

I. EMERGENCE OF INTERNATIONAL ENVIRONMENTAL LAW

The principles of modern international environmental law began to emerge in 1972 during the Stockholm Conference and culminated in the 1992 "Earth Summit" in Rio de Janeiro and the 2002 Johannesburg World Summit on Sustainable Development. Many international organizations, including the United Nations, have played a fundamental role in its development. [191]

A. **Stockholm Conference:** The Stockholm Conference, sponsored by the United Nations, was the first global environmental conference. It was attended by 113 parties, who adopted two major documents: the Stockholm Declaration on the Human Environment and the Action Plan for the Human Environment. [191]

1. **Stockholm Declaration:** The Stockholm Declaration established a global approach to environmental problems. Its most important provisions state the principles that humans have a "fundamental right to . . . an environment of a quality that permits a life of dignity and well-being (Principle 1)"; states have the right to exploit their own resources but must ensure that activities within their jurisdictions do not cause damage to areas outside their jurisdictions (Principle 21); and that states should develop international law regarding liability and compensation for pollution victims (Principle 22). [191]

2. **Action Plan:** In the Action Plan, the parties adopted 109 resolutions aimed to assist states in assessing environmental problems and providing solutions. [191]

B. **U.N. Environment Program (UNEP):** UNEP was established in 1973 partly as a result of the Stockholm Conference. It is a subsidiary organ of the United Nations and coordinates its environmental activities. UNEP has a Governing Council, a Secretariat in Kenya, and an Environment Fund. Functions of UNEP include gathering information on environmental problems, recommending possible solutions, and funding programs. It has played a lead role in the formulation of international environmental law and has sponsored major global agreements. [191-192]

C. **World Charter for Nature:** The World Charter for Nature was drafted in 1982 by the World Conservation Union (IUCN). Its preamble and 24 articles set forth global environmental principles that focus upon the value of nature and the importance of integrating nature with economic planning and suggest ways that states can implement these goals. [192]

D. **Articles on State Responsibility:** The International Law Commission (ILC) has drafted various articles that focus upon state liability with regard to transboundary pollution and other environmental damage. Article 1 states that "every international wrongful act of a state entails the international responsibility of that state." Article 19(3)(d) lists among international crimes "a serious breach of an international obligation . . . for the safeguarding and preservation of the human environment. . . ." Articles 29 to 31 describe situations that preclude the liability of a state for an otherwise wrongful act: "1. an act made with consent by the affected state, 2. an act legally made in response to a wrongful act by the affected state, and 3. an act due to extraordinary events that made it materially impossible for the state to act in conformity with its obligations." [192-193]

E. **Restatement (Fourth) on the Foreign Relations Law of the United States:** The American Law Institute has drafted a Restatement on foreign relations that provides, in section 601, that a state is obligated to take measures to ensure that activities under its control conform to general international principles regarding transboundary pollution and are not conducted so as to cause significant injury to another state. It also states that a state is legally responsible for such an injury. [193]

F. **The 1992 Rio Earth Summit:** The U.N. Conference on Environment and Development (UNCED), or "Earth Summit," was held in Rio de Janeiro, Brazil, and was the largest global conference on the environment. The Earth Summit produced five major documents: the Convention on Biological Diversity, the Climate Change Convention, the Declaration of Principles on Forest Conservation, the Rio Declaration, and Agenda 21. [193]

1. **The Rio Declaration on Environment and Development:** The Rio Declaration, the modern equivalent of the Stockholm Declaration, contains 27 non-binding principles, endorsed by the Conference and U.N. General Assembly. It reflects a compromise between developed and developing nations and specifically includes the "right to development." Principle 2 provides that states have a right to exploit their resources pursuant to environmental and developmental policies, a revision of Principle 21 of the Stockholm Declaration. Other key provisions relate to notification of environmental disasters, environmental impact assessments, and liability for transboundary pollution and compensation to its victims. [193-194]

2. **Agenda 21:** This 800-page document contains a plan of action for sustainable development and environmental preservation. It includes a set of priority actions and means to accomplish them. A Commission for Sustainable Development is established to monitor and review implementation of Agenda 21. [194]

3. **The 2002 World Summit on Sustainable Development:** Held in Johannesburg, South Africa, the 2002 World Summit on Sustainable Development was the most important world conference on sustainable development since the 1992 Earth Summit in Rio de Janeiro. The summit emphasized the growing gap between rich and poor; participating nations attempted to address the problem by setting global targets in poverty reduction, clean water and sanitation, and infant mortality. [194]

   a. **Johannesburg Declaration on Sustainable Development:** The summit concluded with the adoption of the Johannesburg Declaration on Sustainable Development, which reaffirmed participants' commitment to Agenda 21, the plan created ten years earlier in Rio de Janeiro. [194]

II. TRANSBOUNDARY POLLUTION

A. **General rule:** *No state may use or permit the use of its territory in a manner that is injurious to another state or its persons or property.* [195]

1. ***Pulp Mills* case:** The *Pulp Mills* Case was brought in the International Court of Justice (ICJ) by Argentina against Uruguay reinforces the notion that states are obligated to inform adjacent states regarding their proposed plans that will significantly affect the environment of the region and held that Uruguay breached its duty regarding adequate notification even if it did not breach substantive environmental protection obligations. [195]

2. ***Trail Smelter* case:** This landmark case, brought by the United States against Canada, established two fundamental principles of liability under international law for transboundary pollution: (1) a state must show damage and causation; and (2) a state has a duty to prevent, and may be responsible for, pollution by private parties within its jurisdiction. The Tribunal held

that Canada was legally responsible for harm caused to U.S. forests in Washington State by a smelter near Trail, British Columbia, Canada. [195]

3. ***Corfu Channel* case:** The *Corfu Channel* Case was brought in the International Court of Justice (ICJ) by the United Kingdom against Albania for damages to British warships by mines in the Straits of Corfu. The court held against Albania and established the principles that every state has an obligation not to knowingly allow its territory to be used contrary to the rights of other states, and a duty to notify other states of imminent danger. [195-196]

4. ***Lake Lanoux Arbitration:*** This case was brought by France against Spain, and it established the principle that a downstream state does not have the right to veto an upstream state's use of water, but the upstream state must consider counterproposals of the downstream state. [196]

5. ***Nuclear Test* cases:** These cases, brought in the ICJ by Australia and New Zealand against France, left the legality of nuclear testing unresolved on the merits. However, the ICJ did preliminarily enjoin France from testing while it heard the dispute. [196]

6. ***Gabcikovo-Nagymaros Project:*** In this 1993 case, which was the first time the ICJ ruled on an environmental dispute, both Hungary and Slovakia claimed the other had breached a treaty for constructing a system of dams on the Danube River. The ICJ found that both states had breached their obligations, but it found specifically that Hungary's breach was not justified by its claim of "ecological necessity." [196]

7. ***Question of Compensation* case:** The *Question of Compensation* Case was brought in the International Court of Justice (ICJ) by Costa Rica against Nicaragua. In the ICJ's first environmental compensation case, the ICJ held that damage to the environment is compensable under international law, separate from compensation for expenses incurred by environmental damage. "Overall valuation" is used to determine the amount of compensation awarded.

B. **Theories of liability for transboundary pollution under international law:** Such theories include: (1) strict liability for ultrahazardous activities; (2) liability for negligent or intentional acts (abuse of rights); and (3) liability for pollution that exceeds an amount a state's neighbors can reasonably endure (good neighborliness). [196]

1. **Specific treaties focusing on transboundary pollution:** Treaties in this area take a variety of approaches, including agreeing to try to reach agreement (framework conventions), establishing substantive standards, "freezing" pollution at current levels, providing for notification and consultation, and authorizing an international organization to establish rules. [196]

2. **Example—the acid rain treaties:** Various agreements have been drafted that address the problem of acid rain. The Convention on Long-Range Transboundary Air Pollution of 1979 went into effect in 1983 and has 51 parties, including the United States, as of February 2011. Its purpose is to "limit, and as far as possible, gradually reduce and prevent air pollution including long-range transboundary air pollution." The Convention provides for research, exchange of information, and an Interim Executive body to monitor pollution in Europe. The Convention does not contain specific ceilings and timetables. Additional protocols to the Convention have been adopted by some of the parties, establishing standards for reduction of sulfur, nitrogen oxides, and other pollutants. [196-197]

III. OZONE DEPLETION AND CLIMATE CHANGE/GLOBAL WARMING

A. Protection of the ozone layer: The ozone layer protects the earth by filtering out harmful ultraviolet radiation from the sun. It is ***currently being depleted*** primarily by chlorofluorocarbons (CFCs) from air conditioning, aerosols, styrofoam, and refrigerators. ***Two major treaties*** address this problem. [197]

1. **The Vienna Convention for the Protection of the Ozone Layer:** The 1985 Vienna Convention is a framework convention that focuses upon information exchange and cooperation among states for research with a goal to protect human health and the environment from the adverse effects of a diminished ozone layer. [198]

2. **Montreal Protocol on Substances that Deplete the Ozone Layer:** This protocol to the Vienna Convention was adopted in 1987, significantly amended in 1990, and several times since. The original protocol sets forth timetables for a 50 percent reduction in use of CFCs by 1999. The 1990 amendments establish an escalated timetable for reduction in use of CFCs, placing a total ban on them by the year 2000. The amendments also establish a fund to assist developing countries in the transition to technology free of CFCs. Amendments have added other substances and timetables and have accelerated previously established timetables. [198]

B. Protection of the climate: Another serious global environmental problem is climate change due to the greenhouse effect, which results when certain gases in the air trap infrared radiation near the Earth's surface, thus elevating global temperatures. [198-199]

1. **U.N. resolutions on climate change:** In 1989, the United Nations passed two resolutions that formally recognized climate change as a global concern to be given high priority. They emphasize the need for governmental efforts to prevent climate change, and reviewed possible elements for an international climate change convention. [199]
2. **U.N. Framework Convention on Climate Change:** This Convention was signed at the 1992 Earth Summit and emphasizes the global concern about climate change caused by greenhouse gases. Its objective is to stabilize gas concentrations in the atmosphere, and it had an implicit goal of returning to 1990 levels of emissions by 2000. The parties do not agree to specific goals or deadlines. However, they do commit to periodic national inventories of emissions; mitigation programs; development of technology to control emissions; consider climate change in decision-making processes; and cooperate in the exchange of information, education, and public awareness. Developed countries also agree to use the best available scientific technology, and assist developing countries with financing their obligations under the agreement. The 1997 Kyoto Protocol to the Convention, which entered into force in February 2005, commits developed countries to an additional reduction in greenhouse gas emissions of at least 5 percent from 1990 levels during the period from 2008-2012. [199]
3. **Asia-Pacific Partnership on Clean Development and Climate:** In 2005, the United States partnered with Australia, China, India, Japan, and the Republic of Korea to attend to climate change issues and invest in new technologies to address these concerns. These countries represent approximately half of the world's economy and population, as well as half of the world's greenhouse gas emissions. [199-200]
4. **Climate change before the U.S. Supreme Court—international applicability of U.S. statutes:** In a 5-4 decision, the U.S. Supreme Court held that the EPA not only could but was

required to regulate greenhouse gases from mobile sources such as cars under the Clean Air Act if these gases were found by the EPA to endanger the public health and welfare. [200-202]

5. **Future regulation of greenhouse gases:** In 2015, the Parties to the U.N. Framework Convention on Climate Change adopted the Paris Agreement to further limit and adapt to global climate change. The objectives of the Agreement were to limit average global temperature to 2 °C above pre-industrial levels and to increase adaptability and responsiveness to the negative effects of climate change. Each Party to the Agreement would determine its own national contribution, to progressively increase every five years, but there would be no enforcement mechanism beyond a public registry of contributions. The Agreement requires ratification by at least 55 countries representing 55 percent of global greenhouse gas emissions to enter into force. In the United States, some critics argue the Agreement restricts American industry too harshly compared to developing, high-emission countries such as India or China, while other critics argue it will not reach far enough without enforcement. U.S. legislation to impose a cap-and-trade system of regulation became unlikely after the election of Barack Obama in 2008. [202]

IV. WILDLIFE PRESERVATION

A. Provisions Under the Stockholm Declaration and the World Charter of Nature:

1. **Stockholm Declaration:** Principle 4 of the Declaration states that ***plants and animals are a world heritage***, and that humans have a responsibility to safeguard nature and also consider conservation when planning economic development. [203]

2. **World Charter for Nature:** Principle 2 of the Charter stresses the need to safeguard habitats to protect global genetic viability, and maintain animal populations to ensure their survival. In Principle 3, the Charter states that all areas of the earth are subject to conservation. [203]

B. International Convention for the Regulation of Whaling: This Convention, adopted in 1946, established the International Whaling Commission and was intended to regulate the fishing industry. It is increasingly being directed to the conservation of whales. Under the Convention, an annual schedule of whaling regulations is published, which the Commission may modify. In 1990, the Commission set a ten-year moratorium on whaling. Any member may opt out of its obligations under the Convention by objecting. [203]

C. Convention on International Trade in Endangered Species of Wild Fauna and Flora (CITES): This Convention has over 100 parties, and it sets up a system of import and export permits and regulations to protect endangered species from overexploitation. The Convention establishes a Secretariat at UNEP to prepare scientific studies and coordinate national record keeping required by the Convention. The parties are required to meet every two years to modify the Convention if necessary. The permits required under the Convention are nationally administered and keyed to categories of endangered species as described in Appendices I-III of the Convention. No permit may be issued for a species, or a recognizable part or derivative thereof, that is threatened with extinction. [203-204]

D. U.N. Convention on Biological Diversity: This Convention was signed at the 1992 Earth Summit. Its objectives include conserving biological diversity and the sustainable use of biological resources, and equitable sharing of the benefits of genetic resources. The parties to the Convention are committed to developing and implementing national strategies to protect biological diversity.

The Convention establishes a Conference of the Parties to review implementation and adopt protocols or amendments, a Secretariat to arrange meetings and prepare reports, and a technical body to provide scientific advice to the Conference. [204]

E. **Cartagena Protocol on Biosafety:** This protocol seeks to regulate and control the risks that the transboundary movements of living modified organisms (LMOs) pose to human health and biodiversity. The parties of the Protocol will provide information when exporting LMOs to other party countries so that they might make an informed decision prior to importation. [204]

V. HAZARDOUS WASTE, RADIOACTIVE POLLUTION, AND ENVIRONMENTAL EMERGENCIES

A. **Early conventions on civil liability for nuclear damage:** These conventions include the Paris Convention of Third Party Liability in the Field of Nuclear Energy of 1960, the Brussels Convention Supplementary to the Paris Convention, the Vienna Convention on Civil Liability for Nuclear Damage of 1963, and the Joint Protocol Relating to the Application of the Vienna Convention and the Paris Convention of 1988. [205]

B. **The Chernobyl accident and resulting conventions:** In 1986, an explosion occurred at the Chernobyl nuclear power plant in the Soviet Union. The accident raised questions about the adequacy of international law to address this type of emergency. Two conventions were negotiated as a result of the accident: the Convention on Early Notification of a Nuclear Accident, and the Convention on Assistance in the Case of a Nuclear Accident or Radiological Emergency, both signed in 1986. The Convention on Early Notification provides for notification "forthwith" and information regarding a nuclear accident that may have a transboundary affect. The Convention on Assistance provides for cooperation between states in the event of a transboundary radiological release. It focuses upon efforts prior to and after nuclear accidents. The International Atomic Energy Agency (IAEA) has a central role under this Convention to coordinate emergency response. [205-206]

C. **Basel Convention on the Control of Transboundary Movements of Hazardous Wastes and Their Disposal and Bamako Convention:** The Basel Convention regulates international trade in hazardous wastes, with an objective to limit such trade. Under the agreement, a party may not export hazardous waste to another party without the consent of that party and proof that it has adequate facilities to dispose of the waste. The Convention contains labeling standards and prohibits trade with non-parties. The 1991 Bamako Convention prohibits African countries that are parties from importing specified chemicals at all. The 2011 "Ban Amendment" prohibits the export of hazardous waste for final disposal to developing countries. [206]

D. **Rotterdam Convention on the Prior Informed Consent Procedure for Certain Hazardous Chemicals and Pesticides in International Trade:** This Convention, which entered into force on February 24, 2004, seeks to protect human health and the environment by promoting shared responsibility among nations that import and export specified hazardous chemicals. [206]

E. **Stockholm Convention on Persistent Organic Pollutants (POPs):** Adopted in 2001 and entered into force on May 17, 2004, the Stockholm Convention seeks to eliminate or restrict the use or release of 12 persistent organic pollutants (POPs), toxic chemicals that travel great distances and infiltrate the food chain. [206]

VI. ANTARCTICA

Antarctica composes about 10 percent of the Earth's land and water mass and is the ***only continent that has not been exploited for commercial purposes***. There are five principal mechanisms that protect the Antarctic environment. [207]

A. Antarctica Treaty of 1959: This treaty was the first to protect the Antarctic environment. It assured continued scientific research and suspended states the right to claim "sectors" of the continent. The Antarctic Treaty Consultative Parties (ATCPs) include 38 states, 12 original signatories, and 26 other states that have signed the treaty and conducted substantial scientific activity in Antarctica. Key environmental provisions prohibit nuclear explosions and disposal of radioactive waste and require the ATCPs to meet annually to consult and formulate, if necessary, measures to preserve or conserve living resources in Antarctica. [207]

B. Convention for the Conservation of Antarctic Seals: This 1972 convention establishes a regulatory system for the hunting of seals, which had almost disappeared due to excessive hunting. Some species are completely protected. [207]

C. Convention on the Conservation of Antarctic Marine Living Resources: This Convention, signed in 1980, establishes a system for conservation of marine resources within the entire Antarctic marine ecosystem extending to the boundaries of the Antarctic Ocean, called the Antarctic Convergence. The Convention permits a "rational use" of resources within the context of its conservation goals. [207]

D. Agreed Measures for the Conservation of Antarctic Fauna and Flora: These measures, adopted by the ATCPs in 1964, declare the Antarctic Treaty Area a "special conservation area" and establish a ***regulatory permit system*** for activities that harm wildlife in the area. They also require that states take steps to minimize habitat interference and water pollution. Areas of scientific interest are designated "specially protected areas" and are subject to special regulatory protections. [207]

E. The 1991 Madrid Protocol: The Madrid Protocol provides the most comprehensive protection of the Antarctic environment. Article 3 establishes the basic environmental principle that protection of the Antarctic environment "shall be the fundamental consideration in the planning and conduct of all activities in the Antarctic Treaty Area." The Protocol provides standards by which to assess the environmental impact of all human activities in the Treaty area, requires that adverse impacts on the environment be limited, and provides for "regular and effective monitoring" to assess environmental impacts. Its annexes provide procedures for environmental impact assessment and waste disposal and also address conservation of wild flora and fauna, prevention of marine pollution, and area protection and management. Most significantly, article 7 of the Protocol effectively bans mining on Antarctica for at least 50 years, when the agreement first becomes open for review by the Conference of the Parties. [207-208]

VII. DEFORESTATION

Deforestation involves the ***unsustainable use of forests and their genetic resources***. Of primary concern today is the destruction of tropical rainforests. [208]

A. Consequences: A fundamental cause of deforestation is thought to be poverty. Local impacts include floods, droughts, siltation of rivers, destruction of breeding areas, and the threat to the survival of millions of forest dwellers worldwide. Globally, deforestation is considered the primary loss of biodiversity and a major contributor to global warming through the greenhouse effect. [208]

B. The 1984 International Tropical Timber Agreement: This Agreement accounts for 90 percent of the international timber trade and is the only global agreement regulating tropical timber. It is administered by the International Tropical Timber Organization and includes 60 party states. The Agreement is based upon free trade principles and is unlikely to be modified for environmental reasons alone. [208-209]

C. The Rio Forest Principles: The Non-Legally Binding Authoritative Statement of Principles for a Global Consensus on the Management, Conservation, and Sustainable Development of All Types of Forests, or Rio Forest Principles, were proposed by the United States at the 1992 Earth Summit after meeting resistance from developing countries to a more binding forestry agreement. In the Rio Principles, the parties agree to promote international cooperation on forestry but do not commit to any specific actions. [209]

D. Debt-for-nature swaps: First introduced in 1987 by NGOs, debt-for-nature swaps involve the purchase of foreign debt in exchange for domestic forest reserves or other environmental projects. Countries such as Bolivia and Ecuador have participated in swaps, and many others are currently considering them. [209]

1. Public versus private debt-for-nature swaps: The first swaps were "private," meaning at least one of the parties was private. A second generation of swaps has emerged, called "public swaps." These occur between sovereign states and account for a greater amount of debt reduction than private swaps. There are three types of public swaps: (1) government debt purchases; (2) government grants to environmental groups; and (3) debt forgiveness. [209]

VIII. DESERTIFICATION AND LAND DEGRADATION

Desertification is identified in Agenda 21 as a key global environmental problem that is critically linked to the goal of achieving sustainable development in all countries. It affects about one-sixth of the population and one-quarter of the total land area of the world. Land that is severely degraded may be permanently lost. [210]

A. Definition: The United Nations has defined desertification as land degradation in arid, semi-arid, and dry subhumid areas (including irrigated cropland) resulting mainly from adverse human impact. [210]

B. The Lome IV Convention: This Convention was signed in 1989 between the European Economic Community and the African, Caribbean, and Pacific states, and it specifically calls for national, regional, and international action to preserve resources and protect ecosystems against desertification and drought. [210]

C. Past U.N. efforts to combat desertification: The U.N. Conference on Desertification (UNCOD), held at UNEP in Nairobi in 1977, was the first world conference to set out a plan for initiating and sustaining a cooperative effort to combat desertification. It focused on technical and economic reforms and attempted to integrate national, regional, and international efforts within and outside the United Nations, but it has made little progress. [210]

D. **Current U.N. efforts:** Chapter 12 of Agenda 21 includes six program areas addressing desertification upon which states agree to focus, including developing information and monitoring systems and integrating comprehensive anti-desertification programs into national development plans. [210]

E. **Treaty envisioned:** The U.N. General Assembly formulated the 1994 Desertification Convention to establish a committee to oversee the creation of an international convention addressing land degradation and drought. [210]

IX. MARINE ENVIRONMENT

A. **Generally:** The protection and preservation of the marine environment is discussed in Chapter 10, §IX of the Capsule Summary.

X. INTERNATIONAL TRADE AND ENVIRONMENT

There is a growing recognition that ***trade and the environment are inextricably linked***. Thus, the effects of environmental policy on trade and environmental implications of trade are emerging as issues of international concern. [211]

A. **The GATT:** The General Agreement on Tariffs and Trade (GATT) codifies most of the rules governing international trade. It was established in 1948 and is periodically reviewed by the parties. GATT rules are based primarily on concepts promoting free trade, and environmental regulations are frequently viewed as a type of non-tariff barrier to be forbidden under GATT. There is no mention in GATT of environmental protection as a justification for limiting trade. However, states may legitimately restrain trade under article XX if "necessary to protect human, animal, or plant life or health" and impose measures "relating to the conservation of natural resources." The Uruguay Round of GATT talks, begun in 1985 and concluded in 1994, was the first round to link international trade and the environment, with the participants signing a pledge that they agreed to undertake a dialogue on the "interlinkages between environmental and trade policies." In 1971, GATT established a Group on Environment Measures and Trade, which first became active in 1991 following a GATT debate on environment and trade. The group initially examined trade provisions in existing multilateral environmental agreements, national regulations likely to have an international effect, and trade effects of packaging and labeling requirements aimed at protecting the environment. [211-212]

B. **The WTO.** *See* Chapter 7, §VII of the Capsule Summary.

C. **Conflicting views of traditional free trade theorists and environmentally oriented economists:** GATT negotiators have difficulty coming to agreement about the role of the environment in international trade because economists' views in this area conflict. Environmentally oriented economists argue that goods in the international market that do not reflect the environmental costs of production distort the trade process, giving an unfair advantage to those who degrade the environment, termed "ecological dumping." However, under GATT, this kind of advantage is not recognized as unfair, and the practice is not forbidden. [212]

D. **The Tuna/Dolphin Decision:** This 1991 decision by a GATT panel was the result of a formal complaint by Mexico against the United States claiming that a U.S. embargo on Mexican yellowfin tuna was protectionist and a violation of GATT. The United States had imposed the trade sanction to compel Mexico to bring down its kill rate of dolphins in the harvesting of yellowfin tuna to U.S. standards. The United States argued that it was treating the Mexican product no less favorably than products of national origin, and it also invoked the exemption for the protection of natural resources and animals. The panel found that the import ban by the United States violated the GATT, stating that a product may be regulated only according to its properties, and the natural resources exemption can only be used to protect living or natural resources in the jurisdiction of the party invoking the exemption. [212]

E. **The Shrimp/Turtle Case:** In 1998, the WTO appellate body ruled that a U.S. law that protected endangered sea turtles violated the GATT. The law restricted imports of shrimp and shrimp products caught without using "turtle excluder devices" (TEDs). The WTO found that the implementation of this law amounted to arbitrary and unjustifiable discrimination. The United States subsequently modified this law, and the WTO upheld it as GATT compliant. [212-213]

F. **The Global Environment Facility (GEF):** The GEF was established by the World Bank, UNEP, and UNDP in 1991 as a pilot program to provide financial assistance to developing countries to help them implement programs addressing global environmental problems including ozone layer protection, limiting greenhouse gas emissions, protection of biodiversity, and protection of international waters. The 1992 Biodiversity Treaty and the Montreal Protocol both contain the GEF as a funding mechanism. Contributions to the fund are currently voluntary. It is administered by the World Bank, UNEP, and UNDP. [213]

G. **North American Free Trade Agreement (NAFTA):** NAFTA is a unique trade agreement because of its incorporation of environmental protections. The preamble states that trade must be consistent with environmental protection and conservation. The agreement calls for "harmonization of the parties' domestic standards" with international environmental standards, while preserving in certain circumstances each country's ability to maintain domestic environmental standards that exceed prevailing international standards. Disputes over environmental standards may be resolved by an arbitral panel, with the burden under NAFTA on the party challenging the environmental measure. Although NAFTA, by its terms, is generally to be given priority over conflicting international agreements, exceptions are made for several major international environmental treaties. A separately negotiated environmental agreement focuses on cleanup of the Mexico/United States border area and establishment of a Commission on Environmental Cooperation to ensure enforcement of environmental standards by the parties. [213]

H. **Dominican Republic—Central American Free Trade Agreement (DR-CAFTA):** Like NAFTA, DR-CAFTA contains provisions that set forth environmental priorities and guidelines for responding to violations of members' environmental laws. The Agreement establishes "incentives and other flexible and voluntary mechanisms" for addressing environmental concerns, focused primarily on establishing a framework for regional cooperation to mitigate environmental effects of development and trade. [213]

I. **Equator Principles:** Adopted in June 2003 and last revised in July 2006, the Equator Principles are voluntary guidelines for managing environmental and social issues in project finance lending. They were created in response to the Collevecchio Declaration, which was signed by over 100 environmental advocacy groups at the 2003 Annual Meeting of the World Economic Forum, calling on financial institutions to make environmentally responsible lending decisions and policy. [213-214]

XI. MILITARY ACTIVITIES AND THE ENVIRONMENT

The international community is increasingly willing to condemn an aggressor and impose liability for environmental crimes committed during military activities. Liability may arise under a number of international agreements or customary law. [214]

A. **Protocol I to the 1949 Geneva Conventions Relating to the Protection of Victims of International Armed Conflicts:** This protocol prohibits warfare methods that "are intended, or may be expected, to cause widespread, long-term, and severe damage to the natural environment." It also states that "care shall be taken in warfare to protect the natural environment against . . . damage," and that "[a]ttacks against the natural environment by way of reprisals are prohibited." The Protocol's status as customary law is controversial. [214]

B. **Environmental Modification Convention of 1977 (ENMOD):** ENMOD was drafted during the Vietnam War in response to concern about the military's use of chemicals in Vietnam that changed the "dynamics, composition, or structure" of the environment. ENMOD prohibits member states from using environmental modification techniques that have "widespread, long-lasting, or severe" effects as a means to harm another state. [214]

C. **General customary laws of war:** Customary laws of war require proportionality and necessity of all methods of warfare. It has been argued that the body of law that restricts the use of certain weapons prohibits any method of war that causes unnecessary suffering. It is not clear whether general norms of international environmental law are suspended during armed conflict. [214]

D. **Application of U.S. domestic law:** In 2005, the National Historic Preservation Act (NHPA), which requires the United States to avoid harming cultural properties on its own or other nations' registries, was invoked to protect the dugong, an animal that would have been endangered by the construction of a planned U.S. military base in Okinawa. [214]

XII. EXTRATERRITORIAL APPLICATION OF U.S. ENVIRONMENTAL LAW

A. **Generally:** While some U.S. laws are intended for extraterritorial application, environmental legislation typically is not considered one of the areas. U.S. courts have been reluctant to apply domestic environmental law to foreign countries because these laws were designed to address domestic environmental issues. [215]

CHAPTER 13
INTERNATIONAL CRIMINAL LAW

I. THE PRINCIPLES OF INDIVIDUAL RESPONSIBILITY AND CRIMINAL LIABILITY

A. **Understanding international criminal law:** International criminal law is the body of public international law that deals with the relationships between states and international criminal tribunals, between those criminal tribunals and individuals, and between states and individuals with respect to criminal trials and punishment. [217]

B. **State responsibility:** The purposes of international criminal law are bringing closure to victims, restoring people's belief in the operation of justice, expressing the condemnation of the international community, and deterring future crimes by holding individuals personally responsible for their actions. The International Court of Justice (ICJ) is available to hold states accountable for their breaches of international humanitarian law. [217]

C. **International humanitarian law:** In order for a crime to be an "international crime" that carries individual liability and is subject to prosecution and punishment by the international community, it must be a violation of international humanitarian law, as defined by the Geneva Conventions and all of the conventional and customary law prohibiting genocide and crimes against humanity. [217]

D. **The doctrine of command responsibility:** At Nuremberg and other international criminal trials, a common defense proffered by those accused of crimes against humanity was that they were simply following the orders given to them by superiors. For international humanitarian law to have any practical application, ***someone in the chain of command must be personally accountable to the international community for his or her actions***. Criminal prosecutions have established the invalidity of the "following orders defense," but they have focused only on individuals in positions of power or command responsibility. [217-218]

E. **Broadening criminal liability:** Over the past 20 years, international criminal prosecutions have become more prevalent and the international community has become more comfortable identifying new crimes, such as aiding and abetting and incitement. [218-219]

II. THE INTERNATIONAL CRIMINAL TRIBUNALS

A. **Problems of legitimacy:** Throughout the 1990s, the creation of ad hoc criminal tribunals after wars or humanitarian disasters was widely viewed as a good way to bring closure to victims, restore people's belief in the operation of justice, express the condemnation of the international community, and deter future crimes by holding individuals personally responsible for their actions. The tribunals face several major criticisms: local communities rather than the international community should try criminals and pass judgments; the international state system cannot allow a supranational judicial body to have personal jurisdiction over individuals; the international community is not well suited to pass judgment on individuals because it can never properly understand the conflicts that lead to massive human rights disasters; and the U.N. Charter does not permit the creation of criminal courts. [219]

B. **Overcoming problems of legitimacy:** The legitimacy of the tribunals has depended mostly on the cooperation of state governments in officially recognizing the tribunals, making arrests, and extraditing the accused to the tribunals. Legitimacy is also established with the consent and agreement of the governments of the states where the human rights violations occurred. [220]

C. **Examples of international criminal tribunals:**

1. **The International Criminal Tribunal for the Former Yugoslavia (ICTY):** The ICTY is an ad hoc U.N. organ established in The Hague, Netherlands, to try those responsible for serious "violations of international humanitarian law" that occurred on the territory of the former Yugoslavia beginning in 1991. The ICTY was directed by the Security Council to complete all cases by the end of 2014. [221]

2. **The International Criminal Tribunal for Rwanda (ICTR):** The ICTR is a U.N. organization that was established in Arusha, Tanzania, to try those responsible for human rights violations during the genocide in Rwanda in 1994. The Tribunal has jurisdiction to hear criminal charges against *anyone* accused of committing crimes against humanity within Rwanda during the period of January 1, 1994, to December 31, 1994. The ICTR was also directed to complete all cases by the end of 2014. [221-222]

3. **The International Residual Mechanism:** The International Residual Mechanism was established by the Security Council to resolve lingering issues which would have been resolved by the ICTY or ICTR. The Mechanism resolves issues such as trials for current fugitives from justice, retrials, enforcement or reassessment of sentences, archiving documents from both Tribunals, and other residual issues caused by the ending of the Tribunals. The Mechanism will be assessed every two years, starting in 2016, until the Security Council decides to end it. [222-223]

4. **Hybrid or mixed trials:** Unlike the ICTY, ICTY, or ICC, many tribunals developed in the past few decades to resolve international incidents have not been exclusively international or exclusively domestic. Instead, these mixed or hybrid tribunals incorporate elements of both international prosecution and domestic prosecution to varying degrees. These hybrid trials have been used in the Lockerbie Bombing, East Timor, Cambodia, Iraq, Lebanon, Kosovo, Bosnia and Herzegovina, Senegal, Bangladesh, and Rwanda. [223-225]

5. **The Special Court for Sierra Leone:** The Special Court is an independent judicial body established in Freetown to try those who bear the greatest responsibility for serious violations of international humanitarian law and Sierra Leonean law committed in the territory of Sierra Leone after November 30, 1996. The independence of the court and its direct financing by the governments of other states make it a unique judicial entity. [225-226]

IV. THE INTERNATIONAL CRIMINAL COURT (ICC)

A. **A permanent criminal court:** The ICC is a U.N. organ and the first permanent criminal tribunal. It was established in The Hague, Netherlands, to hear prosecutions for genocide, crimes against humanity, war crimes, and crimes of aggression that occurred after July 1, 2002. [226]

1. **Creation and the Rome Statute:** The ICC was established when the Rome Statute of the International Criminal Court came into force on July 1, 2002. [226]

a. **Structure and jurisdiction:** The court has four organs: the Presidency, the Registry, the Prosecutor, and the Judicial Divisions. There are three judicial bodies that hear the cases. The Pre-Trial Division has seven judges, the Trial Division has six judges, and the Appeals Division has five judges. The court can hear cases against persons who are citizens of states parties to the Rome Statute, against persons whose alleged crimes occurred on the territory of a state party, or against persons whose crimes occurred in connection with a situation referred to the court by the U.N. Security Council. The court ***does not have universal jurisdiction***. [226-227]

B. **Criticisms:** In 1998, seven states (including the United States) voted against the adoption of the Rome Statute and, in 2002, both Israel and the United States "unsigned" the treaty by expressing their intention never to become parties. [227]

1. **Politically motivated prosecution:** Some states fear that their political leaders or military personnel will be subject to investigations and prosecutions by the ICC that are without merit and are driven by the desire to realize certain international political outcomes. [227]

2. **National sovereignty:** Commentators have argued that the ICC infringes on the sovereignty of states in the international system by supplanting national judicial systems and interfering with state policymaking. [227]

C. **Early work:** The early work of the ICC following the Rome Statute entering into force was mainly focused on various situations in Africa. In Uganda, the ICC focused on the prosecution of commanders of the Lord's Resistance Army. In the Democratic Republic of the Congo, the Court has prosecuted several commanders of Congolese rebels for various war crimes, including the conscription of child soldiers. The ICC has also been active in Darfur, Sudan, where it has brought charges against sitting Sudanese President Omar al Bashir. [227-228]

D. **Crimes the ICC can adjudicate:** The ICC only has jurisdiction over the "most serious crimes of concern to the international community as a whole." Article 5 of the Rome Statute specifies the four crimes in particular that meet this criteria: genocide, war crimes, crimes against humanity, and aggression. The ICC also only has jurisdiction over crimes committed after the Rome Statute entered into force in 2002. [228]

V. STATE PROSECUTION OF "INTERNATIONAL CRIMINALS"

A. **Early development:** The first prosecutions of individuals for crimes against humanity and war crimes by the domestic courts of a state occurred after World War II. Nazi hunters found many Germans accused of crimes and brought them for trial in Europe and Israel. After the close of Nuremberg, there were no international courts available to try war criminals, so state governments had to pass laws criminalizing the actions of foreign individuals committed on foreign territory and laws conferring extraterritorial jurisdiction on their courts. [229]

B. **Statutory schemes and universal jurisdiction:** Some states have conferred universal jurisdiction on their courts to hear criminal prosecutions for violations of international humanitarian law regardless of where the violations occurred, who allegedly committed them, or who the victims were. The universality principle is based on the idea that certain *jus cogens* norms of international humanitarian law carry *erga omnes* obligations. A violation of that law by an individual is a breach of the individual's obligation to the government and people of every state in the world, so every state has the right to prosecute. [229-230]

C. **Civil liability and tort claims as alternatives to criminal law:** In many countries, and especially in the United States, national courts are available to foreign plaintiffs for civil actions against foreign defendants for extraterritorial violations of international humanitarian law. The development of civil liability for human rights violators is far ahead of the development of criminal liability. The United States is a leader in passing legislation that allows for civil suits by victims of human rights abuses. The Alien Tort Claims Act (ATCA), Alien Tort Statute (ATS), Torture Victim Protection Act (TVPA), Hostage Taking Act, and the Racketeer Influenced and Corrupt Organizations Act (RICO) can all be used to bring lawsuits for acts that occurred outside of the United States. [230]

VI. BARRIERS TO PROSECUTION

A. **Sovereign immunity and the state action doctrine:** A major barrier to the development of international criminal law is the principle of sovereign immunity. It is customary that members of the government of a state are immune from criminal prosecution by the courts of another state. It would be very difficult to hold government leaders accountable for violations of international humanitarian law if they could always hide behind their immunity, so courts have begun to chip away at the traditional rules of immunity. [230-231]

B. **Extradition and problems with capture:** Criminal prosecutions are obviously not very successful unless the accused is arrested and present before the court. Many international criminal defendants contest their prosecutions from the outset by challenging the circumstances of their arrest or extradition. [231]

CHAPTER 1

THE CONCEPT OF PUBLIC INTERNATIONAL LAW

I. INTRODUCTION

To understand international law as a body of law, one must take a broad view of the term *law* and consider it in a context surpassing the set of well-defined rules that are applied to settle disputes brought before a tribunal. International law is applied not only for dispute resolution in a courtroom, but also for the policy-making and diplomatic relations of nations. The enforcement of international law also differs from the enforcement of most domestic law. Enforcement is less dependent upon judicially imposed civil or criminal sanctions than expectations of reciprocal behavior among nations.

A. **Definition of international law:** The definition of international law has changed over time.

1. **Historical approach:** Historically, international law was defined as ***"the body of rules and principles of action which are binding upon civilized states in their relations with one another***." J. Brierly, ***The Law of Nations*** (1963). ***See also The Case of the S.S. "Lotus" (Fr. v. Turk.)*** 1927 P.C.I.J. (ser. A) No. 10, at 21 ("International law governs relations between independent States.").

2. **Modern approach:** The modern approach expands the definition to include not only relations between states ***but also relations between international organizations and states and among the international organizations themselves, as well as the relationship between states or international organizations and natural or juridical persons***, such as the law governing human rights. This view is reflected both in the Restatement (Fourth) of the Foreign Relations Law of the United States §102 and in the Vienna Convention on the Law of Treaties Between States and International Organizations or Between International Organizations. *See also LaGrand Case (Ger. v. U.S.)*, 2001 I.C.J. 466; *Advisory Opinion on Reparation for Injuries Suffered in the Service of the United Nations*, 1949 I.C.J. 174.

3. **Public international law distinguished from private international law:** One must carefully distinguish "public international law" from "private international law." The latter focuses on the conduct of individuals, corporations, and other private entities, rather than that of states or international organizations.

   Note: The distinction between public and private international law is increasingly difficult to define because many treaties entered into by states actually affect the activities of private corporations and individuals, particularly in the area of overseas trade and investment practices. One such example is the U.N. Convention on the Sale of Goods.

B. **Importance of public international law:** International law is pervasive and directly or indirectly impacts upon many fundamental aspects of human existence. International law:

- ***Defines the very existence of "states"***;
- ***Provides the framework for diplomatic relations***;
- ***Governs international agreements***;

- ***Sets forth rules for the operation of international commerce***;
- ***Governs individual human rights***; ***and***
- ***Regulates protection of the global environment***, as well as the use of the air, land, sea, and other global resources.

C. **History of public international law:** First known as "the law of nations," international law began to develop in Europe as a moral and theological construct during the twelfth to fifteenth centuries. Early international law was derived in large part from the Roman law of *jus gentium* governing relations between Roman citizens and foreigners and the canon law of the papacy. These beginnings of international law were rooted in the idea of a "natural law" that was somewhat universal and transcended the divine right of kings to act as they pleased. Writers and theologians like St. Thomas Aquinas and Francisco de Vittoria developed natural law theory as a blend of Christian beliefs, economic pragmatism, the appeals of weak kingdoms for protection, and the idea of a united Christian Europe. International law matured and fully emerged as a distinct body of law in the sixteenth and seventeenth centuries as scholars all over Europe refined natural law theory. The natural law approach to international law was criticized by advocates of "positivism," another European jurisprudential movement that developed in the seventeenth and eighteenth centuries and became the fundamental basis for modern international law.

1. **Natural law:** Natural law is based on the notion that ***each state, just as each individual, is endowed with certain natural rights.*** These natural rights are not human constructs; they exist as a result of a mandate from God or, after the Enlightenment secularization of thought, they exist as the "dictate of right reason." The natural rights of states are basic principles of justice with a universal validity.

   a. **Influence of Hugo Grotius:** Hugo Grotius (1583-1645) transformed the law of nature from one based on divine authority to a law based on universal reason. Grotius is considered the "father of international law" and is best known for *De Jure Bellis Ac Pacis* (The Law of War and Peace). Three important principles of modern international law can be attributed to Grotius:

   - The requirement of restitution for harm done by one party to another;
   - *Pacta sunt servanda*—the obligation of a state to honor its promises; and
   - The principle of freedom of the seas.

   b. **Influence of Samuel Pufendorf:** Samuel Pufendorf (1632-1694) was a German scholar who furthered the natural law approach by stating that natural law was the true source of international law.

2. **Positivism:** The foundation of positivist theory is the idea of consent. Natural law theory holds that every state has natural rights that exist whether or not other states consent to respect those rights. By contrast, positivism teaches that ***international law is that body of law to which states have consented to be bound***. Consent to be bound by international law may be ***express***, as in a formal treaty, or ***implied***, as by acquiescence to customary practice. Positivist theorists seek an international law that works much like contractual business law. Positivism developed during the Enlightenment Era as an alternative to the natural rights approach to international law that was dominant in the sixteenth and seventeenth centuries.

a. **Influence of Emerich de Vattel:** Emerich de Vattel (1714-1767) was a Swiss philosopher and diplomat who advocated looking at international law as a science. Vattel understood international law to have "order" rather than "justice" as its primary end. In his 1758 book *The Law of Nations*, Vattel ushered in the new international law paradigm of binding contracts as the basis of global order. Vattel's application of contract theory to the international system was novel because it called for treaties to be more than just agreements between monarchs and held that contractual obligations should remain between states even when internal regimes change.

b. **Influence of John Austin:** John Austin (1790-1859) argued for the clear separation of morality and positive law. He defined law as the commands of the sovereign supported by sanctions. Austin believed that the sovereign of each state in the international system was supreme and "uncommanded," and therefore only restricted by his or her own promises to other sovereigns. The idea that sovereignty is only qualified by treaty obligations persists today, though the modern trend is toward recognition of other restraints on the power of a state's government (for example, the recognition of universal human rights that all sovereigns must respect).

3. **Liberalism:** Liberalism holds that ***international law should be a body of law based on logical morality***. Liberal theorists usually tend to be much more prescriptive than descriptive in their writings about international law. Liberalism is distinct from positivism in that it argues for the use of international law as a reformist tool that can increase human progress. Liberalism is distinct from natural law theory in that the rules of "logical morality" that govern the international system are to be arrived at by a broad consensus of states and peoples rather than by simple "right reasoning." Liberalism holds that international law should be broadly agreed upon and formed by consensus, but its rules are universal and bind all states regardless of their consent.

   a. **Influence of Immanuel Kant:** Immanuel Kant (1724-1804) was a German philosopher who introduced the "categorical imperative" to international law. Kant's categorical imperative is the idea that all people should act in accordance with rules that they would be comfortable having as universal laws. The creation of universal rules by state consensus is a powerful concept in modern international law, and since the Universal Declaration of Human Rights in 1948, it has driven the evolution of international law.

4. **In summary:** Positivism became the predominant theory of the nineteenth and twentieth centuries, although there was a resurgence of the natural law approach following World War I. The positivist approach, with its emphasis on sovereign commands and traditional sanctions as fundamental to the distinction between law and morality, was and continues to be the foundation for much of the controversy over whether international law is really "law."

CHAPTER 2

SOURCES OF INTERNATIONAL LAW

I. THE STATUTE OF THE INTERNATIONAL COURT OF JUSTICE

The sources of international law, set forth in article 38(1) of the Statute of the International Court of Justice (ICJ), are:

- "***international conventions***, whether general or particular, establishing rules expressly recognized by the contesting states"; Stat. of the ICJ, art. 38, ¶1(a).
- "***international custom***, as evidence of a general practice accepted as law"; art. 38, ¶1(b).
- "***the general principles of law*** recognized by civilized nations"; art. 38, ¶1(c).
- "***judicial decisions and the teachings of the most highly qualified publicists*** of the various nations, as subsidiary means for the determination of rules of law"; art. 38, ¶1(d).

II. INTERNATIONAL CONVENTIONS/TREATIES

In the broadest sense, an international convention or treaty is ***any agreement governed by international law***. Although treaties have been in use for centuries, many have been concluded since World War II. More than 158,000 treaties have been registered with the United Nations since 1945, and the majority of those treaties are bilateral treaties or treaties between a small number of states.

A. Introduction: The ***Vienna Convention on the Law of Treaties***, which entered into force in 1980, is the ***primary source*** for the law of treaties. Most provisions of the Vienna Convention were declaratory of existing law, while others went beyond the existing law to create new law at the time they were adopted. The argument has been made, and disputed, that the "progressive development" provisions of the Convention have been so widely accepted that they have been transformed into customary law.

Note: The United States has not ratified the Vienna Convention, but the State Department does recognize it as the authoritative guide to current treaty law and practice.

1. History of the Vienna Convention: Work commenced on the Convention in 1949 by the International Law Commission. The Convention was regarded from the beginning as primarily a codification of existing treaty law. From the outset it was assumed that the provisions would form a multilateral treaty rather than an "expository code." Drafts and commentaries were prepared by a group of four preeminent legal scholars called *special rapporteurs*. The four scholars, who are still often quoted, are James Brierly, Sir Hersch Lauterpacht, Sir Gerald Fitzmaurice, and Sir Humphrey Waldock. The *travaux preparatoires* are made up of the reports and records of the International Law Commission and the special rapporteurs and are critical for understanding and interpreting the Vienna Convention.

2. Alternate forms of treaties: Although the Vienna Convention is the primary source of treaty law, it is not the sole source. The Vienna Convention ***applies only to those treaties meeting the***

Convention's requirements for a treaty. Some international instruments that fall outside the Convention's definition of a treaty, however, are nevertheless recognized as treaties.

B. The Vienna Convention definition of a treaty—requirements: The Vienna Convention sets forth a basic definition for a treaty as *"**an international agreement concluded between States in written form and governed by international law, whether embodied in a single instrument or in two or more related instruments and whatever its particular designation.**"* Vienna Convention on the Law of Treaties, *opened for signature* May 23, 1969, U.N. Doc. A/Conf. 39/27, art. 2, ¶1(a), 8 I.L.M. 679, 681 [hereinafter *Vienna Convention*]. In short, the Convention requires that an international agreement meet the following criteria in order to be a treaty within its scope:

1. It must be ***between states***. The Convention excludes treaties between states and an international organization or between international organizations.
2. The agreement must be ***in writing***.
3. The agreement must be **governed by international law**.

C. International law governs all treaties: Governance by international law is required of all treaties, whether or not they are treaties within the scope of the Vienna Convention. Although the presumption is that an agreement between two or more states is a treaty, evidence that domestic law was intended to control the agreement rebuts that presumption. The following are examples of agreements that are not treaties because they are not governed by international law:

Example: A standard contract between two governments for the sale of beef, the contract being one normally used in the meat trade among private parties.

Example: The purchase of land or buildings in a transaction that is made subject to domestic rather than international law.

Note: The transfer of land from one state to another, however, could be governed by international law under different circumstances. For example, the cession of a small parcel of land by France to Switzerland to enlarge the Geneva airport was done by means of a treaty because the sovereignty of that parcel was transferred and sovereignty is governed by international law.

D. Non–Vienna Convention treaties: The concept of a treaty under international law is not limited to that defined in the Vienna Convention. The Vienna Convention states that its definition of a treaty does not affect the legal force or applicability of international law to agreements that do not fall within the definition. Vienna Convention, art. 3. A more recent treaty (Vienna Convention on the Law of Treaties between States and International Organizations or between International Organizations) expands the definition to include agreements not only between states but also those involving international organizations as parties.

E. U.S. distinction between a treaty and an executive agreement: While international law recognizes as treaties all agreements meeting the requirements for a treaty outlined above, U.S. domestic law distinguishes ***between an executive agreement and a treaty*** in the procedures necessary for the agreements to be given legal effect and in the legal effect accorded the agreements.

1. **Treaty:** Treaties are ***concluded by the President with the advice and consent of the Senate***. Senate ratification of a treaty requires a two-thirds majority vote. U.S. Const. art. II, §2.

2. **Executive agreement:** An executive agreement is ***concluded by the President based on authority granted by Congress or based on the inherent authority granted the President by***

the U.S. Constitution. It is unclear under U.S. constitutional law as to what matters must be concluded by treaties with Senate ratification and what may be done by executive agreement as part of the inherent authority of the President.

a. **Limitations upon presidential power and congressional domain:** The President may not conclude executive agreements regulating areas clearly within the congressional domain. The regulation of foreign trade, for instance, is vested in Congress. *See United States v. Guy W. Capps, Inc.*, 204 F.2d 655 (1953), *aff'd*, 348 U.S. 296 (1955).

b. **Presidential power in foreign affairs:** The President may, however, conclude executive agreements extinguishing U.S. nationals' claims against foreign countries. *See Dames & Moore v. Regan*, 453 U.S. 654 (1981). *But see Medellin v. Texas*, 552 U.S. 491 (2008) (President's memo stating that the United States would discharge its international obligation under an ICJ decision by having state courts give effect to the decision has been historically limited to a practice of settling civil claims between U.S. nationals and foreign governments or foreign nationals.).

3. **Potential conflicts between U.S. domestic law and international law:** It is possible for an agreement to be ***denied legal force and effect under U.S. domestic law and yet still be binding under international law***. In *Zickerman v. Korean Air Lines Co., Ltd.*, 516 U.S. 217 (1996), the Supreme Court recognized that because a treaty is not only the law of this land but also an agreement between states, negotiating and drafting history, as well as the post-ratification understanding of the parties, have all been used to interpret the treaties. This confirmed that the compensable injury is to be determined by domestic law.

Example: The President could sign an executive agreement with another state that goes beyond the constitutional authority of the President to enter into such agreements. Without Senate ratification, the agreement has no legal force and effect as a matter of constitutional law. Nevertheless, the Vienna Convention says that a state's consent to be bound can be expressed in almost any manner (Vienna Convention, art. 11), and that a state's internal law cannot be invoked as justification for failure to perform a treaty. Vienna Convention, art. 27.

Note: The Vienna Convention does provide, however, that failure to comply with an internal law concerning competence to conclude treaties may invalidate a state's consent if that violation was "manifest and concerned a rule of its internal law of fundamental importance." art. 46, ¶1. A violation is manifest if it would be "objectively evident to any State conducting itself in the matter in accordance with normal practice and in good faith." art. 46, ¶2.

F. **Name and form of treaty:** As indicated in the Vienna Convention's definition of a treaty, ***a treaty may be designated by a wide array of names***. "Treaty" is the most common title, but the following are also used: convention, act, general act, protocol, agreement, *modi vivendi*, concordance, charter, declaration, and compromise.

1. **Components of treaty and language:** Although there is no officially correct form, treaties generally comprise four parts: the title, the preamble, the main body, and the final part.

a. **Title:** A description of the type of treaty and the subject matter, the title often also includes the names of the contracting parties. Treaties concluded in simplified form do not usually have titles.

b. **Preamble:** Following the title and serving as an introduction, the preamble states the reasons for the treaty, the names of the negotiating representatives, and the authority with which the representative is cloaked.

c. **Main body:** This part sets forth the rights and obligations of the parties.

d. **Final part:** The final part comprises the provisions setting forth the guidelines for entry into force, termination of the treaty, revisions, accessions, reservation, publication, and languages in which the text will be written. The treaty finally concludes with the date and place of conclusion and the signatures and seals of the contracting parties.

e. **Language:** There is no universal rule as to what language or what number of languages must be utilized for the text of the treaty. Rather, the language of the treaty is selected by the contracting parties. When a treaty is published in more than one language, the treaty itself should clarify which text is to be the authentic and authoritative one.

2. **Subject matter of treaty:** The subject matter of the treaty is composed of the rights and obligations of the parties. Two important limitations apply:

   a. ***Jus cogens* restrictions:** ***The treaty may not set forth rights and obligations that conflict with jus cogens*** (the imperative norms of international law). (*See* §VI of this chapter, *infra*, for discussion of the concept of *jus cogens*.)

   b. **U.N. Charter restrictions:** ***The treaty may not set forth rights and obligations that conflict with those obligations a member-state has undertaken under the U.N. Charter***. U.N. Charter, art. 103.

   Example: Treaties condoning wars of aggression, slavery, or genocide are prohibited.

3. **Classification of international treaties:** Treaties may be classified by the following criteria: ***contracting parties, geographic factors, possibility of accession, subject matter, form***, or ***method of conclusion***.

   a. **According to number of contracting parties:** Treaties may be bilateral, multilateral, restricted multilateral, and general multilateral, according to the number of contracting parties.

      i. **Bilateral treaties:** Agreements ***between two parties*** are termed bilateral. They are by far the most common type of treaty and are similar to contracts in that they express a mutual exchange of rights and obligations. Bilateral treaties come in a wide variety of forms, ranging from detailed agreements effective for a fixed period of time to agreements simply stating general norms or intentions to form alliances. Some general treaties state principles that are so widely accepted as to be considered customary law.

      ii. **Multilateral treaties:** Multilateral treaties are divided into two categories: ***restricted multilateral treaties*** and ***general multilateral treaties***.

         1. **Restricted multilateral treaties:** Restricted multilateral treaties are agreements ***involving close cooperation among a limited number of states for specific purposes;*** *e.g.*, construction of a hydroelectric dam and other similar projects, or facilitating economic integration, such as establishing the European Communities. Because restricted multilateral treaties set forth interdependent rights and obligations, the consent of all states is often necessary to adopt the text of the treaty.

2. **General multilateral treaties:** General multilateral treaties, on the other hand, are ***open to all states, or to at least all states within a large geographic region*** (*i.e.*, Europe). Unlike bilateral treaties, which are often akin to contracts between parties, general multilateral treaties are more legislative in character. In contrast to restricted multilateral treaties, general multilateral treaties ordinarily do not require unanimity for adoption or entry into force.

b. **According to geographic factors:** General multilateral treaties are open to all states, no matter where they are located. Regional treaties, on the other hand, are restricted to a defined area of the world. Problems arise when a region is not well defined. For example, considerable debate took place in the European Union as to whether Turkey was a "European" country for purposes of becoming a party to many treaties of the European Community.

c. **According to possibility of accession:** A closed treaty contains no provisions allowing for subsequent accession or the joining of the treaty by a new contracting party. An open treaty does provide a right of accession to parties not involved in the original drafting and conclusion of the treaty. A hybrid is the semi-open treaty, which allows accession but only after consultation with the original contracting states. The U.N. Commission adheres to the traditional notion that ***accession is possible only if the treaty expressly provides for accession or if the original parties subsequently decide to permit accession***.

d. **According to subject matter:** Treaties are loosely categorized as political, commercial, technical, administrative, or procedural. The categories are merely a matter of convenience and have little bearing on the treaties themselves or their legal effects.

e. **According to form—written and verbal:** Although the Vienna Convention states that treaties must be written, the **Restatement (Fourth) of the Foreign Relations Law of the United States** and custom demonstrate that ***oral agreements are also enforceable as treaties***. *See* Vienna Convention, art. 3; *Legal Status of Eastern Greenland (Den. v. Nor.)* 1933 P.C.I.J. (ser. A/B) No. 53. Even a unilateral promise by a state may be binding under international law if so intended by the state.

Example: In the midst of controversy over France's testing of nuclear devices in the South Pacific, France's president declares in various public statements that France intends to stop testing. France is then bound by its declaration. *Nuclear Tests* (*Aus. v. Fr.*) 1973 I.C.J. 99 and (*N.Z. v. Fr.*) 1973 I.C.J. 135.

f. **According to method of conclusion:** Treaties may be concluded by solemn or simplified form.

i. **Treaties concluded in solemn form:** Treaties concluded in solemn form are concluded by a "special procedure" and "subject to ratification by the highest competent authority."

ii. **Treaties concluded in simplified form:** Treaties concluded in simplified form are concluded on the basis of an exchange of notes or letters. One party sends a note or letter including the draft of an agreement, and the other party returns a note or letter expressing its intentions to adopt the text as an international agreement. Ratification is rarely required for treaties concluded in simplified form. Treaties concluded in simplified form usually extend, amend, or amplify preexisting agreements.

G. **Treaty-making power—capacity:** ***Both the party*** (the state or international organization) ***and its representative*** must have the proper capacity to negotiate and conclude an international agreement.

1. **Nation-states and international organizations:** It is presumed that nation-states have the necessary capacity to negotiate and conclude treaties. International organizations, however, have the necessary capacity only if the constitution of the organization either expressly or impliedly gives the organization that capacity.

2. **Component states of a federal union:** An inconsistent area is the capacity of the component states of a federal union. Generally, one constituent state (*e.g.*, Connecticut) of a federation may enter agreements with other constituent states (*e.g.*, Michigan), but the rules may differ with regard to agreements that extend beyond the members of the federation. Two determining factors are the constitutional guidelines of the federation and recognition of international legal personality.

   Example: States of the United States must receive approval from Congress before entering "any Agreement or Compact" with foreign states. By contrast, the states of Germany and Switzerland do have the right, without the interference of their respective central governments, to enter certain treaties with states outside their federal union.

3. **Self-governing territories:** Self-governing territories also present troublesome issues, as there are conflicting views as to whether they have the capacity to enter international agreements.

   a. **No capacity view:** One view holds that a territory is not a "state" and cannot be regarded as a "distinct juridical person" capable of being "a responsible party to the treaty entirely separate from the parent State." *First Report on the Law of Treaties*, [1962] 2 Y.B. Int'l L. Comm'n 27, 37.

   b. **Capacity view:** Some conventions, however, specifically include self-governing territories among those parties that may sign the convention.

4. **Authority of persons representing a state or international organization:** Authority is issued in a document entitled a ***"full powers" document***, which names those individuals who are authorized to negotiate and conclude a treaty on behalf of the state.

   a. **Practice of state:** An exception to the requirement of "full powers" is in article 7 of the Vienna Convention. In addition to authorization through full powers, it also allows states to dispense with full powers if the practice of the state involved demonstrates its intention to consider its representative as duly designated and authorized.

   b. **Heads of state—exception to the requirement of "full powers":** Full powers are also unnecessary for heads of state, heads of government, ministers of foreign affairs, and heads of diplomatic missions. Such officers have inherent capacity to conclude treaties. *See Legal Status of Eastern Greenland* (*Den. v. Nor.*) 1933 P.C.I.J. (ser. A/B) No. 53 (concluding that the oral statements of Norway's foreign minister were binding upon Norway because he acted within his capacity under international law). Also having capacity are representatives accredited by states to international conferences or organizations. The latter's authority applies only for the purposes of the treaty concluded by the particular conference or organization.

Example: A U.S. representative to a conference on human rights may have capacity to negotiate and sign a treaty on human rights but lack capacity to negotiate and sign an unrelated treaty on the sale of goods.

5. **Apparent authority of a state's representative:** A state is bound to a treaty unless it is clearly evident that its representative was acting beyond his or her authority.

6. **Subsequent confirmation:** When authority is lacking, the treaty is without legal effect unless the state subsequently confirms the treaty. Vienna Convention, art. 8. It is not clear whether such confirmation must be expressly made or whether it is sufficient if implied by subsequent conduct.

H. **The treaty process:** The treaty process includes ***negotiation, adoption, authentication***, and ***forms of conclusion.***

1. **Negotiation of treaties:** The negotiation of treaties varies according to whether the treaty is bilateral or multilateral.

   a. **Bilateral treaty negotiation:** Bilateral treaty negotiation usually begins in the foreign ministry of one of the parties and is followed up by discussions and exchanges of notes, usually through diplomatic channels. Draft texts are prepared by legal advisors and become the basis of further negotiations. The goal, of course, is to create a draft that is acceptable to both parties.

   b. **Restricted multilateral treaty negotiation:** Restricted multilateral treaty negotiation is ordinarily conducted in the same manner as are bilateral treaties.

   c. **General multilateral treaty negotiation:** Negotiation of general multilateral treaties is usually conducted at diplomatic conferences where diplomatic delegations, including legal advisors, act on behalf of the states. The conference typically begins with draft proposals and other working papers that the participating states or organizations had prepared in advance. The proposals and working papers are the subject of the subsequent negotiations and form the basis for the final text of the treaty. The conference itself functions much like a legislature, with the designation of drafting committees, presentation of amendments, and recording of the working sessions. As with a legislature, the records become an important part of the final product, the treaty. The formal, final result of the conference is entitled the Final Act, which often serves to authenticate the treaty. Note, however, that the Final Act is not usually intended to bring the treaty into force. Vienna Convention, art. 10.

2. **Adoption:** Although the Vienna Convention itself does not provide a definition, "adoption" is generally defined as the ***formal act signifying that the form and content of the treaty have been agreed upon***. Adoption signifies that the negotiations have been completed, disputed points have been resolved, and the wording of the final document agreed upon.

3. **Forms of conclusion:** Adoption of the text of the treaty does not conclude the treaty but is rather just one step in a series of steps necessary to eventually bring a treaty into force. A party is ***not bound to a treaty until it has consented to be bound***. Such consent may be expressed in many ways as suggested by articles 7-11 of the Vienna Convention: through signature, the exchange of instruments, acceptance, approval, ratification, and "any other means if so agreed." Parties most commonly express their consent to be bound by the terms of a treaty by means of either ratification or accession.

a. **Signature:** The signing of the treaty may, by itself, signify the state's definitive consent to be bound when: the treaty states that the signature is a signal of the state's definitive consent; it is otherwise established by the contracting parties; or intent that the signature establishes definitive consent is indicated from the "full powers" document or otherwise expressed during the negotiations. Vienna Convention, art. 12.

   Note: Ratification is superfluous when the signature itself binds the party to the treaty. On the other hand, a treaty that requires the additional step of ratification before the party is bound to its terms regards the signature primarily as a method of authenticating the treaty's text and does not signify a promise to ratify later.

b. **Signature followed by ratification:** Historically, ratification was the process of verifying the authority given the representatives who had negotiated and signed a treaty, but the modern understanding in many states is that ratification is a check on the treaty-making powers of the executive branch by passing the treaty through the parliamentary/legislative branch of government. Ratification provides an additional opportunity to carefully consider the rights and obligations of a treaty before consenting to be bound by its terms. The law of treaties, as reflected in the Vienna Convention, ***does not require ratification*** for a state to be bound by a treaty, and many informal international agreements bind parties on the basis of a signature alone.

   i. **U.S. constitutional requirement of ratification:** Under U.S. law, the President must obtain the advice and consent of the Senate to ratify a treaty. The Senate must approve of the treaty by a two-thirds vote. U.S. Const. art. II, §2; *see* §II(E)(1) of this chapter, *supra*.

c. **Obligations of a party that has signed but not yet ratified:** Although a party has not yet ratified a treaty, it may still have an ***obligation not to defeat the object and purpose of the treaty*** under the following circumstances. Vienna Convention, art. 18.

   i. **Clear intent to no longer be a party:** When a party has signed a treaty or otherwise exchanged instruments indicating that the treaty is subject to ratification, acceptance, or approval, that party is obliged not to defeat the object of the treaty until it clearly expresses its intentions to no longer be a party.

   ii. **Reasonable waiting period for entry into force treaties:** A party is obliged not to defeat the object of the treaty when its consent to be bound to the treaty has been expressly made subject to the entry into force of the treaty, so long as the entry into force is not unduly delayed.

d. **Accession:** Accession is the ***process by which a state that was not a signatory of the treaty may nevertheless become a party to the treaty and be bound by its terms***. Parties to a treaty are not given different treatment according to the manner in which they became parties.

   Example: A treaty may provide that "this treaty may be ratified by all states signatories thereto. Any other state wishing to become a party to it may do so by depositing an instrument of accession."

e. **Acceptance:** Article 14 of the Vienna Convention refers to "acceptance" as "***an expression of consent to be bound either without a signature or after a non-binding prior signature***." Acceptance is not so much an actual method of consent as it is a term seen in treaty provisions, the meaning of which varies according to the context.

Example: A signature "subject to acceptance" is the equivalent of a signature subject to ratification, but a treaty that is "open to acceptance" is one that is open to accession.

f. Approval: The term *approval* was introduced into international law to correspond to the internal procedures of states that call for the "approval" of treaties.

g. Entry into force: Entry into force is the ***actual implementation of the treaty's terms*** and in the Vienna Convention is governed by article 24. Entry into force often occurs when specific requirements laid out in the treaty have been met.

i. Bilateral treaties: The contracting states indicate their intention to be bound to the treaty from a specified date, and the treaty takes effect as of that date.

ii. Multilateral treaties: General multilateral treaties usually include a provision stating that a specified number of states must ratify or accept the treaty before it is in force between those states. Alternatively, the treaty may specify that it goes into force only when it is ratified or accepted by all the parties. Note that the provisions setting forth the manner of entry into force apply from the moment the text of the treaty is adopted, unlike the remainder of the treaty, which is implemented upon entry into force.

iii. Consent of all negotiating states: If the treaty has not laid out specific requirements for entry into force, the treaty is implemented when all negotiating states have consented to be bound.

iv. Provisional application: Provisional application, recognized by article 25 of the Convention, permits the treaty to be implemented before the formal requirements for entry into force have been met. Either the entire treaty or segments of it may be subject to provisional application. Provisional application may be terminated when the terminating party informs the other states of its intent not to become a party bound to the terms of the treaty. Provisional application is increasingly important in the search for quick solutions. Entry into force of a treaty can take years, and the delays are frequently unrelated to its actual substance. Hurdles to overcome before actual entry into force often relate to translations, administrative matters, and objections by parliaments to marginal provisions.

I. Reservations: A "reservation" is defined as "***a unilateral statement, however phrased or named, made by a State, when signing, ratifying, accepting, approving, or acceding to a treaty, whereby it purports to exclude or to modify the legal effects of certain provisions in their application to that State.***" Vienna Convention, art. 2, ¶d.

1. Declarations of understanding: A reservation must be distinguished from a statement that serves as a clarification of the state's position. Unlike reservations, these declarations of understanding have ***no legal effect*** in varying the terms of a treaty under international law. Their legal effect within a state, as a matter of domestic law, will vary from state to state.

2. Permissible reservations: Article 19 of the Vienna Convention permits reservations to general multilateral treaties unless the treaty expressly or impliedly prohibits reservations, or the reservations sought are simply incompatible with the object and purpose of the treaty. *See* Reservations to the Convention on Genocide 1951 I.C.J. 15 (May 28). The treaty may prohibit reservations as a general matter, or it may prohibit specific types of reservations.

3. **The purpose of reservations:** Many multilateral conventions seek wide participation, and reservations encourage participation by allowing a state to be a party without agreeing to every provision. Some conventions, however, such as the 1982 Law of the Sea Convention, include a general prohibition on reservations because reciprocity may be vital to treaties functioning as a "package deal."

4. **Acceptance of and objections to reservations:** Reservations are ***not applicable to bilateral treaties*** because the terms of the treaty are tailored specifically to the interests of the two contracting parties. Either the parties accept one another's terms or they do not. Reservations may apply in multilateral treaties and often complicate the multilateral treaty, transforming it into a series of related bilateral treaties.

   a. **Reservation expressly permitted:** A reservation expressly permitted by the treaty ***does not require acceptance*** unless the treaty so provides. Vienna Convention, art. 20, ¶2. The other parties essentially have already indicated their acceptance by drafting it into the treaty itself.

   b. **Object and purpose require consent:** "When it appears from the ***limited number of the negotiating States and the object and purpose of a treaty that the application of the treaty in its entirety between all the parties is an essential condition of the consent of each one to be bound by the treaty***, a reservation requires ***acceptance by all the parties***." Vienna Convention, art. 20, ¶2. Otherwise, unanimous consent to a reservation is not necessary. ***See*** Reservations to the Convention on Genocide 1951 I.C.J. 15 (May 28).

   c. **Reservation neither permitted nor prohibited:** If the treaty itself does not prohibit a reservation in any way, or expressly permit it, each state is free to decide whether to reject or to accept the reservation.

5. **Legal effects of acceptances of and objections to reservations:** ***States may either accept or object to reservations***.

   a. **Acceptance of a reservation:** If a state accepts the reservation, the treaty will ***enter into force between the accepting and reserving state.*** The treaty's provisions apply as modified by the reservation. *See* Reservations to Convention on Genocide 1951 I.C.J. 15 (May 28); Vienna Convention, art. 21, ¶1. The modification is effective only between the reserving state and the accepting state, and it is of no consequence to other parties to the treaty. art. 21, ¶2.

   b. **Objection to a reservation:** If a state objects to a reservation, there are two possible outcomes:

      i. **Objecting state still a party:** The state may object to the reservation yet still be willing to enter into a treaty relationship with the reserving state. In that case, the treaty is ***in force between the objecting and accepting State, but "the provisions to which the reservation relates do not apply as between the two States to the extent of the reservation."*** Vienna Convention, art. 21, ¶3. The willingness to preserve the treaty relationship is presumed in the absence of an express objection to the contrary.

      ii. **Objecting state refuses to be a party:** If the objecting state not only objects but also expresses its intention that the entire treaty be of no effect between it and the reserving state, ***the reserving state and objecting state are not parties to the treaty vis-à-vis each other.***

Example: States *A*, *B*, *C*, and *D* are parties to a general multilateral treaty, but State *A* ratifies the treaty with a reservation to art. 10. State *B* accepts the reservation; State *C* objects but still wishes to maintain the treaty relationship; and State *D* objects both to the reservation and to entry into force of the treaty between itself and State *A*, the reserving party. The possible outcomes are as follows:

1. The treaty is in force between State *A* and State *B*, but art. 10 is modified by the reservation.
2. The treaty is in force between State *A* and State *C*, but art. 10 does not apply between the two states to the extent of the reservation.
3. The treaty is not in force between State *A* and State *D*.
4. The treaty is in force and unmodified between States *B*, *C*, and *D*.

J. Limitations to reservations: Reservations are generally narrowly construed and do not apply to other provisions of a treaty by way of implication. *See* 1984 *Advisory Opinion on Restriction of the Death Penalty*, American Convention on Human Rights, Inter-American Court on Human Rights, Advisory Opinion No. OC3 [1983] (ser. A) No. 3, 23 I.L.M. 321 (1984).

K. The observance of treaties: ***All parties to a treaty must perform their obligations under the treaty in good faith*.**

1. ***Pacta sunt servanda*:** Article 26 of the Vienna Convention expresses one of the most fundamental principles of public international law, *pacta sunt servanda*: "Every treaty in force is binding upon the parties to it and must be performed by them in good faith." This obligation of parties to observe the provisions of a treaty to which they have consented to be bound is closely related to a second fundamental principle underlying international law: good faith performance.

2. **Good faith performance:** Good faith performance is required regardless of any conflicting domestic law. Conflicting domestic law does not excuse a state from its treaty obligations unless the state's consent to be bound by the treaty was expressed in violation of the state's domestic law and the violation was manifest and concerned an internal law of fundamental importance. Vienna Convention, art. 46.

   Note: The predominance of treaty obligations over domestic law holds true only in the arena of international law and is not always the rule in domestic courts. For example, the general rule under U.S. law is that a later federal statute supersedes an earlier treaty. U.S. courts, however, first attempt to avoid conflicts between the treaties and superseding statutes by interpreting the domestic law in a manner consistent with the treaty. *See* §II(E)(3) of this chapter, *supra.*

3. **Territorial scope of treaties:** The general rule is that a treaty applies to ***all the territory of each party***. "All the territory" is defined as all land, neighboring territorial waters, and airspace.

   a. **Exceptions:** Territorial scope may be limited by the treaty itself or by means of a reservation. Note that a reservation limiting territorial scope may be invalid if the limitation is incompatible with the object and purpose of the treaty.

4. **Interpretation of treaties:** There are three basic approaches to treaty interpretation:

   a. **Textual approach:** The textual approach, advocated by the Institute of International Law, looks ***only to the text of the treaty and the "plain and natural meanings of the words."*** Adherents of the textual approach do not attempt to ascertain the intent of the parties except to the extent that the intent is clearly expressed in the words of the text. The presumption is that the four corners of the document contain all that the parties wished to express.

b. **Limited contextual approach:** The limited contextual approach, followed by the International Law Commission and incorporated into articles 31 and 32 of the Vienna Convention, regards the text as the starting point for interpretation. Interpretation, however, is ***not necessarily limited to the four corners of the document***. Intent of the parties may be ascertained from the *travaux preparatoires*, subsequent agreements regarding interpretation of the treaty, subsequent actions or practices of the parties that reflect the parties' understanding, and other relevant rules of international law.

c. **Policy-oriented and configurative approach:** The policy-oriented and configurative approach [from M. McDougal, H. Lasswell, & J. Miller, *The Interpretation of Agreements and World Public Order* (1967)] is the most liberal and conceptual of the three. ***Intent is defined as the "genuine shared expectations"*** of the parties and may be gleaned from the ***treaty text and all pre- and post-treaty communications***. No one source predominates over another, and intent is considered in the very broad framework of "giving effect to the goals of a public order of human dignity."

5. **Fulfillment of treaties—methods of oversight:** Many of the traditional methods of securing compliance with a treaty have no application today.

a. **Available remedies:** Remedies available for non-fulfillment include submission of the dispute to the ICJ, diplomatic negotiations, and arbitration. The treaty itself will often designate the manner in which disputes are to be resolved. (For further discussion, *see* Chapter 7, "International Dispute Settlement.")

Note: Although the Vienna Convention in articles 65-66 sets out the procedures to be followed for peaceful settlement of treaty disputes, the Convention does not address what happens if peaceful methods of settlement should fail.

6. **Amendment of treaties:** The general rule, as set forth in the Vienna Convention, is that "***a treaty may be amended by agreement between the parties***." Vienna Convention, art. 39. The method of amendment is often specified in the original treaty. Amendments take on the character of treaties themselves and are governed accordingly by the general law on treaties. The Vienna Convention distinguishes between an "amendment" and a "modification."

a. **Amendments (article 40):** Amendments ***alter a treaty with respect to all parties***. Article 40 requires notification to all parties of the proposal to amend. All parties have the right to participate in the decision to amend, as well as in the subsequent negotiations and conclusions of any amendments. Unless a contrary intention is expressed, a party that does consent to be bound by the amendment nevertheless continues its obligations under the original treaty with respect to those parties not joining the amended version. If not all the original contracting parties become party to the amendment, there results a split in the application of the treaty. The only version that applies between any two states is the one to which both states are parties.

Example: State *A* and State *B* are parties to an amended agreement. State *C* is a party to the original agreement only, having not joined the amended agreement. The rights and obligations of the amended agreement apply only to the relationship between States *A* and

B. Between States *A* and *C* and between States *B* and *C*, the rights and obligations of the original agreement apply.

b. Modifications (article 41): In contrast to amendments, which are open to all parties, modifications are ***made by a limited number of parties***. Modifications are permitted only if:

1. Modifications are permitted by the original treaty; or
2. Modifications are not prohibited by the treaty and the modification is one that "does not affect the enjoyment by the other parties of their rights under the treaty or the performance of their obligations; [and] does not relate to a provision, derogation from which is incompatible with the effective execution of the object and purpose of the treaty as a whole." Vienna Convention, art. 41, ¶b(i-ii).

c. Amendment/modification by tacit consent: Although the Vienna Convention has not included such a provision, the argument has been made that customary international law recognizes amendment or modification of a treaty by actual practice of the parties that is at variance with the treaty provisions.

7. Invalidation of treaties: The grounds for invalidating a treaty are ***error, fraudulent conduct, corruption, coercion, conflict with peremptory norms*** (jus cogens), and ***conflict with domestic law***. The provisions of the Vienna Convention are controversial and are not necessarily accepted as reflecting customary international law.

a. Error (article 48): In actual practice, error is rarely invoked as grounds for invalidation because the lengthy process of negotiations decreases the possibility of error.

i. Right to invalidate the treaty: ***Error does not automatically void the treaty***, but it provides the right to invalidate consent to the treaty. Consent may be invalidated only if the error pertained to an essential basis of the consent.

ii. Invalidation not allowed: If the party in question either contributed to the error or was on notice of the error, the error is not grounds for invalidating its consent.

iii. Textual errors: Errors limited to the wording of the text do not affect its validity.

b. Fraud (article 49): Fraud is not defined by the Vienna Convention, but it is distinguished from innocent misrepresentation and error because fraud not only affects the consent of a party but the entire basis of mutual confidence between the parties. ***Fraud, like error, does not void the treaty***, but it is a ground for invalidating a party's consent to be bound by the treaty.

c. Corruption (article 50): Corruption is the exercise of a substantial and inappropriate influence on the representative concluding a treaty on behalf of the state. The improper influence must come from one of the other negotiating states, not from within the representative's own state.

d. Coercion of a representative (article 51): Coercion goes beyond influence and consists of acts or threats used against a representative in order to procure a state's consent to be bound by a treaty. Consent so procured is ***without any legal effect***.

e. Coercion of a state (article 52): ***A treaty concluded with the threat of or use of force in violation of the principles of the U.N. Charter is void.*** Force or threat of force is not well defined and potentially could include everything from economic or political pressure to actual military force.

f. **Conflict with a peremptory norm (*jus cogens*) (articles 53 and 64):** The generally accepted rule is that ***a treaty is void if it conflicts with a rule of* jus cogens**. The application of this rule, however, is complicated by the fact that there is much controversy concerning the rules of *jus cogens*. It is difficult to identify which general rules of international law qualify to be rules of *jus cogens*, and the difficulty is amplified by the evolving nature of *jus cogens*. Nevertheless, there are some generally accepted principles.

Example: Treaties contemplating genocide, slavery, or the use of armed or physical force against the territorial integrity or political independence of any state are unenforceable as conflicting with *jus cogens*.

g. **Conflict with domestic law (article 46):** *See* §II(E)(3) of this chapter (discussing potential conflicts between U.S. domestic law and international law).

8. **Separability of treaty provisions (article 44):** Grounds for invalidation generally affect the entire treaty, but in certain circumstances, only parts may be invalidated. In instances of fraud or corruption, only the "victim" state may decide whether the whole treaty or parts of the treaty are to be invalidated. In instances of coercion or conflict with *jus cogens*, the entire treaty is void and there is no separability. Article 44 does provide for separability of the treaty provisions if:

a. **Separability specified in treaty:** The treaty itself permits separability.

b. **Treaty provisions are not essential:** The objectionable clauses are "separable from the remainder of the treaty with regard to their application," "not an essential basis of the consent," and "continued performance of the remainder of the treaty would not be unjust."

9. **Acquiescence (article 45):** A party that continues to perform under the terms of a treaty, despite its knowledge that grounds for invalidating it exist, is precluded from later invoking those grounds for invalidation. This provision is included to prevent abuses, and it does not apply to treaties that have been procured by coercion or are in conflict with *jus cogens*.

10. **Termination and suspension of treaties:** Treaties may be terminated or suspended for one or more of the following reasons:

a. **Termination of or withdrawal from a treaty by agreement of the contracting parties:** Treaties may fix their own duration, state a date of termination or an event or condition to trigger termination, or set forth the right of the parties to denounce or withdraw from the treaty. Article 54 of the Vienna Convention provides that a treaty may be terminated in accordance with the terms of the treaty or by consent of all of its parties. In the United States, a treaty's termination provision does not require the Senate's consent to a notice of termination. The President may terminate the treaty on his or her own authority. *Goldwater v. Carter*, 444 U.S. 996 (1979).

b. **Provisional suspension of multilateral treaties as between some of the contracting parties:** Temporary suspension of a multilateral treaty between some of the parties is permitted:

1. If provided for in the treaty.
2. If the treaty ***does not prohibit*** the suspension and the suspension is ***neither prejudicial*** to the rights of the other parties ***nor incompatible*** with the object and purpose of the treaty. Vienna Convention, art. 58.

c. **Unilateral abrogation of treaties:** Unilateral abrogation by a party, particularly when a treaty neglects to address the subject, is an area in which many treaty disputes occur.

i. **Intent of parties and nature of treaty:** ***Unilateral abrogation of treaties without abrogation or withdrawal clauses is, in principle, not permitted.*** In practice, however, the intent of the parties or the nature of the treaty determines whether unilateral abrogation or withdrawal will be allowed. For example, a treaty establishing a territorial boundary by its nature prohibits unilateral abrogation, while a commercial treaty may imply a right of unilateral abrogation. Article 56 of the Vienna Convention has adopted a middle-of-the-road approach by embracing both the principle and the practice for treaties without provisions regarding termination, denunciation, or withdrawal. It requires the abrogating party to give 12 months' notice of its intent to withdraw from the treaty. However, a treaty is not subject to denunciation or withdrawal unless the parties so intended or such a right can be implied by the nature of the treaty. Vienna Convention, art. 56, ¶1(b).

ii. **Unilateral abrogation provisions:** Unilateral abrogation of treaties containing abrogation clauses can be revoked in accordance with their own provisions. Treaties may either permit unilateral abrogation under fixed conditions or may stipulate that unilateral abrogation is valid only with the consent of all other contracting parties.

d. **Termination by reason of duration or realization of purpose:** Termination by reason of duration or realization of purpose is fairly straightforward. If the parties have agreed that the treaty is to last for only a specified period of time, the treaty ceases to be valid at the expiration date. The parties may, however, agree to extend the duration and set a new term for the treaty's validity.

e. **Grounds for termination or withdrawal:** Treaties may be terminated for reasons analogous to contract law defenses.

i. **Impossibility of performance:** Although the Vienna Convention, article 61, recognizes impossibility of performance (based on the permanent destruction or disappearance of something indispensable to performance) as a grounds for terminating or suspending application of a treaty, the closely related grounds of *rebus sic stantibus* (fundamental change in circumstances) is of more practical importance as grounds for termination or withdrawal.

ii. **Fundamental change of circumstances (*rebus sic stantibus*) (article 62):** This doctrine is invoked to terminate obligations under long-term treaties, but international courts and arbitrators rarely find the doctrine applicable. The doctrine may not be invoked when the treaty establishes a boundary or the change is the result of a breach by the invoking party of either an obligation under the treaty or of any other international obligation owed by it to any other party to the treaty. *Rebus sic stantibus*, under the Vienna Convention, applies only when all of the following requirements have been met:

1. **Fundamental change:** The change must be of a fundamental character.
2. **Unforeseen:** The change in circumstances must have been unforeseen by the parties.
3. **Essential basis:** The circumstances at the time of entering the agreement must have been an essential basis of the treaty. *But see Bremen v. Prussia*, Germany,

Staatsgerichtshof 1925-1926 Ann. Dig. 352, No. 266, stating that restrictive clauses forming an essential basis for the treaty may not be abolished without the party's consent.

4. **Radical alteration:** The change in circumstances must radically alter the performance of obligations yet to be performed under the treaty. *See Fisheries Jurisdiction* (*U.K. v. Ice.*), 1974 I.C.J. 3 (July 25).

iii. **Termination due to breach (article 60):** The effect of breach varies according to whether the treaty is bilateral or multilateral. ***In all cases, the breach must be material.*** A material breach consists of a repudiation of the treaty not sanctioned by the Vienna Convention or a violation of a provision essential to the object and purpose of the treaty. The breach itself does not automatically terminate the treaty, but it may be invoked as a ground for termination. *See Advisory Opinion on the Continued Presence of South Africa in Namibia*, 1971 I.C.J. Rep. 16.

(a) **Bilateral treaties:** A material breach by one party entitles the other party to terminate or suspend operation of the treaty in whole or in part. *Charlton v. Kelly*, 229 U.S. 447 (1913).

(b) **Multilateral treaties:** The following parties to a multilateral treaty may terminate due to breach:

1. **Parties not in breach:** By unanimous agreement, the parties not in breach may suspend the treaty in whole or in part or terminate it, either between the aggrieved parties and the breaching party or among all parties.
2. **Party specially affected:** A party specially affected by a material breach may act alone to unilaterally suspend the treaty in whole or in part between itself and the breaching party.
3. **Radical change in position:** Any party may unilaterally revoke the treaty, if the breach is such as to radically and materially change the position of every party to the treaty.

iv. **Later inconsistent treaty between parties (article 59):** A treaty is terminated if all parties conclude a later agreement on the same subject matter and it is implied that the later treaty is to govern or the later treaty is so incompatible with the earlier treaty that the two treaties cannot be performed at the same time. The earlier treaty may be merely suspended if there is an implication drawn either from the treaty or otherwise that suspension was intended.

v. **War between contracting parties:** The Vienna Convention addresses the effect of war between the contracting parties only to state that its provisions "shall not prejudge any question that may arise . . . from the outbreak of hostilities between states." Vienna Convention, art. 73. The Institute of International Law has addressed the topic, concluding that "***[t]he outbreak of an armed conflict does not ipso facto terminate or suspend the operation of treaties in force between the parties to the armed conflict.***" The Effects of Armed Conflict on Treaties: Resolution of the Institut de Droit International, article 2 (1985 Helsinki Session). The nature of the treaty dictates the effect of hostilities on its operation. ***Factors to consider are these:***

1. **Express termination:** Has the treaty been expressly terminated?
2. **Incompatibility with war:** Is the treaty's execution simply incompatible with the state of war? *See Techt v. Hughs*, 229 N.Y. 222, 128 N.E. 185, *cert. denied*, 254 U.S. 643 (1920) (stating that treaties not incompatible with the state of war remain in effect unless expressly terminated). Peace treaties or treaties of alliance, for example, are dissolved during a state of war.
3. **Intent to govern hostilities:** Is the treaty in fact intended to govern the hostilities, such as treaties on the rules of war (Hague Convention), or to prevent hostilities, such as treaties governing boundaries?
4. **Suspension during war:** Is the treaty of a type that may be suspended during the conflict? Law-making treaties and certain other general multilateral treaties may be simply suspended by war. Such treaties may remain in force because they serve the interests of the entire international community.

11. **Effect of state succession on international treaties:** Succession of states is the ***shift of responsibility over a territory from one state to another state***. This is to be distinguished from a change in government or regime within an established state, as takes place, for example, with a social revolution or an election. Succession affects the legal identity of the state and its treaty obligations. Succession occurs with secession of states, annexation, merger and consolidation, and decolonization. Succession has legal consequences concerning the transfer of rights and obligations from the predecessor state to the newly emerged state.

a. **The Restatement (Fourth) of the Foreign Relations Law of the United States §201:** The Restatement generally follows the Vienna Convention but does vary in several respects. The Restatement, unlike the Vienna Convention, does not distinguish between newly independent states (*i.e.*, former colonies) and new states resulting from disintegration of a former state or secession from a former state.

b. **The Vienna Convention on the Succession of States in Respect of Treaties:** As of 1996, this Convention had not entered into force. As with the Vienna Convention on the Law of Treaties, this Convention is intended primarily as a codification of preexisting customary law. Not all provisions, however, are considered declaratory of existing law. Most of the principles that follow are reflected in the Vienna Convention.

i. **Transfer of territory resulting from moving boundaries (Moving Treaty—Frontiers Rule):** The international agreements of the state to which the territory once belonged are no longer applicable. The international agreements of the state to which the territory now belongs apply.

ii. **Absorption of an entire state:** The international agreements of the absorbed state cease and are replaced by the international agreements of the absorbing state.

iii. **Newly formed states (former colonies or states resulting from separation of a state):** The new state does not automatically become a party to the international agreements of the predecessor state. The new state, however, is not precluded from accepting such agreements, either expressly or impliedly, and may become a party upon the agreement or acquiescence of the other parties.

iv. **Territorial and boundary agreements:** Such agreements are unaffected by the succession of states. What qualifies as a territorial treaty is controversial. It is generally defined as a treaty that either grants another state a right to use of its territory or places restrictions on the use of its territory. Examples are treaties on the rights of transit on international waterways, rights to pass through a state's airspace, use of international rivers, and demilitarization or neutralization treaties.

c. **Newly independent states under the Vienna Convention:** As stated earlier, the Vienna Convention distinguishes between newly independent states (*i.e.*, former colonies) and states created by disintegration or secession.

i. **The "clean slate" doctrine:** The basic concept is that ***a newly independent state begins its existence free of the obligations of its predecessor state***. Vienna Convention, art. 17; art. 24. There is an exception for territorial treaties, the obligations of which newly independent states do maintain.

ii. **The right of option:** Although generally free of obligations, a newly independent state does have the right of option to be a party to general multilateral treaties by virtue of being a successor state. In such cases, the newly independent state may choose to become a party to a treaty independent of the consent of other parties to the treaty. This absolute right of option does not extend to restricted multilateral treaties or bilateral treaties. In practice, most new states continue to act pursuant to treaties that applied to their territory before their independence.

d. **States created by disintegration or secession:** A new state created by secession from a former state, or by disintegration of a former state into two or more states, succeeds automatically to most of the former state's treaties. Vienna Convention, art. 34. It has been questioned whether this rule for states created by secession reflects customary international law because such new states have been viewed as entitled to invoke the "clean slate" doctrine.

Example: In 2008, the ICJ determined that Serbia would be bound by the Genocide Convention as a successor state to the former republic of Yugoslavia, which was a signatory to the Convention. In rejecting Serbia's claims that it was not bound by the Convention because it became a state after Yugoslavia's dissolution, the ICJ determined it could hear the case on the merits, in which Croatia claimed that Yugoslav officials participated in ethnic cleansing of certain regions of Croatia between 1991 and 1995. *Application of the Genocide Convention* (*Croatia v. Serbia*) (Preliminary Objections) (I.C.J. 2008).

12. **Effect of governmental succession on international treaties:** A change in government has no effect on the legal identity of the state and therefore no effect on the legal obligations arising from treaties.

III. INTERNATIONAL CUSTOM

Along with treaty law, customary international law is one of the two principal sources of international law. Despite numerous treaties, there are many topics and many parties that are not covered by treaty law. Customary international law is important for its potentially general application to states not parties to treaties, as well as its ability to supplement areas of international concern not addressed in treaties. Despite its acknowledged importance, customary law is subject to much controversy, for it eludes any definite formulation. First, the lack of sufficient consistency in state practices may make it difficult to establish a practice as customary. Second, customary law is ascertained by subjective analysis of whether states engaged in a certain practice are acting out of a sense of legal obligation (the *opinio juris* requirement) or for other reasons.

A. Two approaches to customary international law: The two approaches are the objectivist/sociological approach and the participatory/voluntarist approach.

1. Objectivist/sociological approach: The objectivist/sociological approach is that customary law is ***universal and therefore binding on every state*** of the world community.

2. Participatory/voluntarist approach: The participatory/voluntarist approach is that customary law applies ***only to those states that have participated in the custom***, and newly independent states have the right not to be bound by a previously established practice as customary international law. *See S.S. "Lotus"* (*Fr. v. Turk.*), [1927] P.C.I.J. (ser. A) No. 10, at 21 ("The rules of law binding upon States . . . emanate from their own free will as expressed in conventions or by usages generally accepted as expressing principles of law. . . .").

a. Objections by developing nations: The former Soviet Union and many developing countries object to the universal application of customary law on the principle that countries outside the developed nations of the Western Hemisphere had little to do with the establishment of many customary laws and therefore ought not be bound by them.

b. Restatement (Fourth) of the Foreign Relations Law of the United States §201: The comments to Restatement §201 reject this position and view all states as bound by whatever customs are established at the time the state comes into existence.

B. Establishment of an international custom: There are quantitative and qualitative elements to customary international law. Customary law follows the basic principle of international law that ***acts are permitted unless expressly forbidden.*** Therefore, prohibitions as well as affirmative practices must be proved by the state relying upon them. *See S.S. "Lotus"* (*Fr. v. Turk.*), [1927] P.C.I.J. (ser. A) No. 10.

1. Quantitative factors: Quantitative factors include past state practice and duration of the state practice.

a. State practice generally: States in the ***practice of their international relations*** implicitly consent to the creation and application of legal rules. State practice may be ascertained from a wide variety of sources: treaties, executive agreements, legislation, regulations, court decisions, speeches, and testimony before national and international bodies.

b. Duration of state practice: The practice must have been followed for an ***appreciable period of time***. The notion is that what began as a limited practice may, over time, ripen and widen in its adoption to become customary law. There is, however, no set standard to determine when practice is transformed into law.

i. Long-term: Long-term practice was an important consideration of the Supreme Court in the case of *The Paquete Habana*, 175 U.S. 677 (1900). The Court looked at the practices of England, France, Germany, and the Netherlands from 1403 to 1898 to conclude that fishing vessels are recognized as exempt from capture as prizes of war.

ii. Short-term: The ICJ held in the *North Sea Continental Shelf Cases*, 1969 I.C.J. 4 (Feb. 20), that a "passage of only a short period of time is not necessarily, or of itself, a bar to the formation of a new rule of customary international law," if the practice is "both extensive and virtually uniform."

c. **Consistency of state practice:** More important than the duration of state practice is the ***consistency with which it is applied***. Minor and infrequent inconsistencies do not necessarily negate a custom.

d. **Number and makeup of states adhering to the practice:** To establish custom definitively, a practice must be followed by ***a significant number of states representing diverse geographic, economic, and social characteristics***. It has, however, been suggested that the consistent practice of only a handful of states may be sufficient to establish custom, particularly when those states are the only ones capable of engaging in the practice (*e.g.*, nuclear testing on the high seas in the 1950s). The question then becomes whether custom can be established and imposed over the objection of other states. The answer depends on which approach to customary international law is followed, discussed *supra*, at §IIIA of this chapter.

2. **Use of regional custom:** Customary law ***may also be limited to a particular region*** and therefore may not be the practice of such a wide variety of states. A state may rely on regional custom but must show its existence by proving both quantitative and qualitative factors. *Asylum (Colombia v. Peru)*, 1950 I.C.J. 266 (Nov. 20).

3. **Local customary rights:** Local customary rights may develop from ***constant and continual practice between two nations***, but such customary rights differ from and are independent of general international customary law principles. *Right of Passage Over Indian Territory (Port. v. India)*, 1960 I.C.J. 6 (Apr. 12).

4. **Qualitative factor—*opinio juris*:** In addition to the quantitative factors, international lawyers often refer to the subjective element of ***opinio juris sive necessitatis*** (called *opinio juris*). *Opinio juris* is the sense of ***legal obligation compelling states to follow a certain practice***. The difficulty in ascertaining *opinio juris* is that states rarely acknowledge that they are acting under a sense of legal obligation rather than as a matter of choice, comity, or convenience.

Example: A ship was flying a French flag and collided with a Turkish ship. Criminal proceedings were brought in Turkey against the French captain of the French ship. The Permanent Court of International Justice held that there was no rule of international law at the time limiting criminal proceedings in a collision on the high seas to the exclusive jurisdiction of the state whose flag is flown on the offending ship. While the court found that states in Turkey's position had often abstained from asserting criminal jurisdiction, there was no evidence that the abstentions were based on a sense of legal obligation. *S.S. "Lotus"* (*Fr. v. Turk.*), [1927] P.C.I.J. (ser. A, No. 10).

Example: In the *North Sea Continental Shelf Cases*, 1969 I.C.J. 4 (Feb. 20), the ICJ stated that "[t]he States concerned must therefore feel they are conforming to what amounts to a legal obligation. The frequency, or even habitual character of the acts, is not in itself enough. There are many international acts . . . which are motivated only by considerations of courtesy, convenience, or tradition, and not by any sense of legal duty."

C. **Resolutions and recommendations of international organizations:** The role of international organizations' resolutions and recommendations in establishing custom, in particular the General Assembly of the United Nations, is controversial. General Assembly resolutions are not a form of international legislation and accordingly are not legally binding. Indeed, the U.N. Charter itself refers to the "recommendations" of the General Assembly, in contrast to decisions of the Security

Council, which are binding on members of the United Nations. U.N. Charter, art. 25. The resolutions are, however, frequently used as evidence of customary international law. The resolutions are useful as evidence because the votes of the world body may show a consensus (or lack of consensus) on a particular issue. A majority vote is more compelling evidence of custom when the majority represents a wide array of developed and developing countries. On the other hand, states vote in the General Assembly without expecting that they must act or have acted in accordance with their vote.

Example: The U.N. Declaration of Human Rights now has been recognized as expressing customary international law because it "create[d] an expectation of adherence" and that expectation was "gradually justified by State practice." *Filartiga v. Pena-Irala*, 630 F.2d 876, 883 (2d Cir. 1980).

D. Application of international customary law: The predominant view is that customary international law enjoys universal application, regardless of what nations participated in its formation. The issue then arises as to whether there is any way for a state to be exempt from application of a law. Two possible exceptions to application follow:

1. **Clear and consistent objection:** Dissent from a custom in the form of clear and consistent objections supported by action may prevent application of the custom to the objecting state.

2. **Historic departure:** Historic departure from a customary rule and other states' acceptance of that deviation also provides an exception to the application of a custom. Note that wholesale departure from a custom by a large number of states may eventually result in the creation of a new custom.

E. Relationship between treaties and customary international law: Depending on the situation, treaties may be given equal weight with custom, prevail over custom, be proof of custom, or codify custom.

1. **Equal weight standard:** Although article 38 of the Statute of the International Court of Justice places treaties first on the list of sources of international law, the order does not necessarily establish a hierarchy of sources. In fact, treaties and custom are generally given ***equal weight in international law*** (although a treaty that is more specific than a custom will prevail) and some peremptory norms of customs (*jus cogens*) preempt conflicting treaty law. *See* §II(K)(7)(f) of this chapter, *supra*, and §VI of this chapter, *infra*.

2. **Treaty as evidence of custom:** Treaty provisions may become so widely adopted that they are accepted as custom. Treaties can also serve to codify customary international law.

   a. **Multilateral convention provisions as custom:** Provisions of a multilateral convention that becomes widely adopted may be applicable as customary law, and therefore binding on non-party states, if the practice is uniform and widely recognized as a legal obligation. *See North Sea Continental Shelf Cases*, 1969 I.C.J. 4 (Feb. 20).

   b. **Treaties as codification of custom:** In recent years, treaties have been used to codify customary international law, as, for example, with the law of the sea treaties in 1958 and again in 1982, and with the Vienna Convention on the Law of Treaties. When utilizing such treaty provisions as evidence of custom, however, it is important to differentiate provisions that merely reiterate custom from provisions that expand upon custom or represent progressive development (*i.e.*, new) law.

IV. GENERAL PRINCIPLES OF LAW

A general principle of law "recognized by civilized nations" is one that is ***so fundamental that it is a basic tenet in virtually every major legal system***. Unlike treaties or international customary laws, general principles are derived from domestic law and are not principles originating from international relations or obligations.

Example: General principles of law are rules concerning liability for damages, unjust enrichment, right of passage over territory, the doctrine of *res judicata*, some basic humanitarian rights, the prohibition against being a judge in one's own cause, and application of the principle of good faith.

A. **Limited application of general principles:** General principles of law primarily apply to fill in gaps left by treaties and customary law. As international law expands to encompass new subject areas, general principles of law from domestic legal systems may be utilized until custom is established or treaties are developed.

B. **Decreasing importance as a source of international law:** General principles are losing importance in modern international law because many of the norms once recognized as general principles are now incorporated in treaties or are recognized as customary international law. The Restatement (Fourth) of the Foreign Relations Law of the United States now classifies general principles as "a secondary source of international law."

C. **Application of general principles for procedural matters:** Although generally decreasing in importance, general principles continue to be applied in procedural matters and problems of international judicial administration. General principles often relied on are the doctrines of *res judicata* and laches, as well as the rule that judges are to act with impartiality and independence. *Corfu Channel (U.K. v. Alb.)*, 1949 I.C.J. 4 (Apr. 9).

V. JUDICIAL DECISIONS AND PUBLICISTS

Article 38 of the Statute of the International Court of Justice includes, in its sources of international law, judicial decisions and the teachings of highly qualified publicists as subsidiary means. These sources must be used with some caution. No amount of strong language in a judicial decision or scholarly writing stressing that a given rule is the norm will make it a rule of international law if it is not recognized by states as a binding norm. On the other hand, a decision or scholarly article may be very influential in first recognizing a state practice as custom or in highlighting an emerging norm of customary international law.

A. **Status of judicial decisions:** Judicial decisions are a "subsidiary means for the determination of rules of law," and the decisions may be rendered by either an international tribunal, such as the ICJ, or by a national court adjudicating issues of international law. Many of the cases cited in international law disputes come from national courts. However, great care must be taken to be sure that the domestic court is applying international law and not its own domestic law.

B. **The role of judicial decisions in the development of international law:** Although the scope and effect of international law judicial decisions are supposed to be limited to the parties and the particular case, most courts strive to follow previous rulings (*stare decisis*) and on occasion make new international law.

   1. **International Court of Justice view:** Article 38 of the Statute of the International Court of Justice says that judicial decisions are a subsidiary source of international law, "subject to article 59." Article 59 of the Statute of the International Court of Justice states that "[t]he decision of the Court has ***no binding force except between the parties and in respect to that particular case***" (emphasis added).

2. ***Stare decisis* effect:** Although article 59 prohibits the ICJ from following the common law doctrine of binding precedent (*stare decisis*), the court does in fact often look to prior holdings as being ***highly persuasive***. Judges of the ICJ, as well as judges in national courts hearing international law issues, strive to follow previous rulings, thereby lending some certainty and predictability to the development of international law.
3. **Interpretation:** In 2013, the ICJ held that it has jurisdiction to interpret prior judgments when the proceedings were relevant because it showed "what evidence was, or was not before the Court and how the issues before it were formulated by each Party." *Request for Interpretation of the Judgment of 15 June 1962 in the Case concerning the Temple of Preah Vihear (Cambodia v. Thailand)*, 2013 I.C.J. 281 (Nov. 11). Therefore, Cambodia asked the ICJ to interpret a 1962 decision where the court found that the Temple of Preah Vihear was in a territory under the sovereignty of Cambodia. The ICJ in 2013 determined that the entire territory around the Temple of Preah Vihear fell within the sovereign territory of Cambodia, and not just the Temple building itself.
4. **Law making:** When necessary, the ICJ has made new law, which subsequently won state acceptance, as in the *Fisheries Case (U.K. v. Nor.)*, 1951 I.C.J. 116 (Dec. 18). However, the role of judges in the development of international law is somewhat contested, especially by civil lawyers who view law making as belonging only in legislative bodies.

C. **Status of the most highly qualified publicists:** The work of scholars is more influential in the international legal system than in municipal legal systems. International law scholars play an important role in the development of international law, as evidenced not only by the impact of early scholars such as Grotius and Pufendorf, but also by the inclusion of scholarly works as a source of international law in article 38.

1. **Role in systematization and codification:** International bodies of publicists, such as the International Law Commission (an organ of the U.N. General Assembly), the Institut de Droit International, the International Law Association, the Hague Academy of International Law, and the American Law Institute (publisher of the Restatement of the Foreign Relations Law of the United States), have two functions. They have served the development of international law both by codifying existing rules of law and by proposing new rules.
2. **Role of scholarly works in the courtroom:** Reference to scholarly works varies from court to court. British courts, for example, are reluctant to refer to writers, while French courts are highly influenced by the works of jurists. The ICJ often takes into account the opinions of highly qualified legal scholars, but is reluctant to actually identify them in issuing their judgments.

D. **Resolutions of the United Nations and other international law organizations:** The significance of U.N. resolutions and other similar international law organizations as a source of law varies tremendously according to the circumstances. The role of resolutions is a subject of much controversy because bodies such as the U.N. General Assembly are not intended to be legislative.

E. **Factors influencing the impact of General Assembly resolutions:** The following factors are to be considered in determining the impact of a General Assembly resolution:

1. **Internal General Assembly resolutions:** General Assembly resolutions addressed to a subsidiary organ of the United Nations or to the Secretariat are legally binding as a matter of law under the U.N. Charter.
2. **Declaratory resolutions:** A General Assembly resolution (particularly in the form of a declaration) approved of unanimously and supported by state practice is generally regarded as

evidence of customary law. Declaratory resolutions are important evidence of *opinio juris* and, if ratified unanimously or by a larger majority, are significant evidence of customary law.

3. **State practice as proof of impact:** Widespread adoption of a resolution, however, does not necessarily make it "instant custom." A General Assembly resolution, even if approved unanimously or by a majority, is not evidence of customary law if not supported by state practice unless the states intended for the resolution to express a rule of law or the states support the resolution by subsequent practice in accordance with the resolution.

4. **Diverse majority approval as proof of impact:** General Assembly resolutions may be evidence of custom if accepted by a majority of member states (rather than unanimously), the composition of which represents a variety of political, geographic, and economic interests. *Texaco Overseas Petroleum et al. v. Libyan Arab Republic*, 53 Int'l L. Rep. 389 (1979).

5. **Effect on dissenting states:** Whether dissenting states are bound by a resolution expressing custom depends upon the general rules as to when custom is binding upon a dissenting state or newly independent state. *See* §II(K)(11)(c) of this chapter, *supra* (discussing newly independent states under the Vienna Convention).

   Example: In the *Advisory Opinion on the Western Sahara*, 1975 I.C.J. 12 (Oct. 16), the ICJ stated that the General Assembly's declarations in regard to decolonization and self-determination were interpretations by the member states of customary international law established by the U.N. Charter. The ICJ therefore concluded that the right of self-determination for non-self-governing territories had become a norm of customary international law.

VI. *JUS COGENS*—PEREMPTORY NORMS

Jus cogens, or peremptory norms, are those rules of international law that are of ***such fundamental importance that derogation from them is prohibited***. *Jus cogens* may be modified only by the emergence of new peremptory norms.

A. **Subject to much controversy:** The controversy surrounding the very concept of *jus cogens* centers on the division between the natural law approach and the positivist approach to international law. Adherents of the natural law approach maintain that there are fundamental rules that exist independently of a state's actions. On the other hand, positivists question the existence of any law to which states have not expressly consented. The Vienna Convention on the Law of Treaties refers to *jus cogens*/peremptory norms, but avoids including specific examples of rules of *jus cogens*. *See* §II(K)(7)(f) of this chapter, *supra* (discussing the difficulty in identifying which general rules of international law qualify to be rules of *jus cogens*).

B. **Identifying rules of *jus cogens*:** There are few rules that are generally accepted as peremptory norms. Those generating the least amount of controversy are the basic principles of *pacta sunt servanda* ("agreements of parties must be observed") and prohibitions on the use of or threat of force. Other commonly accepted rules of *jus cogens* include prohibitions on genocide, slave trading, piracy, terrorism, and the taking of hostages.

C. **Actual application of *jus cogens*:** The controversy surrounding the very existence of *jus cogens*, as well as the difficulty of identifying rules of *jus cogens*, has resulted in sparse application.

VII. EQUITY IN INTERNATIONAL LAW

Equity in international law is best understood by distinguishing the reference to decisions *ex aequo et bono* ("by what is fair and good") from application of equity through general principles of law.

A. ***Ex aequo et bono*:** Article 38 states that it "shall not prejudice the power of the Court to decide a case *ex aequo et bono*, if the parties agree thereto." Statute of the ICJ art. 38. This provision has been interpreted to authorize a decision in which equity is not merely applied but is ***allowed to override all other legal principles***. Thus far, parties have never agreed to have a case heard *ex aequo et bono* by the ICJ.

B. General principles of law: Article 38 does, however, list general principles of law as a source of international law. Therefore, there are substantive concepts of equity common to all modern legal systems that are general principles of international law. Examples are concepts of estoppel, unjust enrichment, and abuse of rights. Furthermore, many legal scholars argue that the less tangible notion of equity as "reasonableness," "fairness," or "natural justice" is also incorporated in all modern legal systems.

C. Effect of other principles of equity—*intra legem, contra legem,* and *praetor legem*: Another method used by international lawyers to distinguish authorized from unauthorized use of equity in international tribunals is to classify the principles of equity as *intra legem* (within the law), *contra legem* (against the law), and *praetor legem* (outside the law). Decisions *contra legem* are unauthorized unless the parties agreed to confer on the court the power to hear cases *ex aequo et bono.*

Example: The maritime delimitation cases, such as the *North Sea Continental Shelf Cases*, 1969 I.C.J. 4 (Feb. 20), are examples in which the ICJ has applied equity without the parties conferring on the court the power of *ex aequo et bono*. Equity was applied as a rule of construction to prevent similarly situated states from unjustifiable differences in treatment. Using equity as an instrument of interpretation is *intra legem* (part of the law) as opposed to *ex aequo et bono* (notwithstanding the law).

Exam Tips on *SOURCES OF INTERNATIONAL LAW*

- The most important tip to keep in mind from this chapter is how often the substantive questions of international law are determined by whether a particular concept of international law is or is not a binding source of international law.

- With treaties, the initial question is whether a state is a party to the treaty. Domestically, a treaty can be approved by a state in a number of different ways. From the perspective of international law and the provisions of the Vienna Convention on the Law of Treaties, a treaty may be binding under international law even if it was defectively approved under that state's domestic law (*see* article 27).

- With reservations to treaties, a commonly raised issue is whether a reservation is valid under international law because it is not a permissible reservation that can be made under the treaty. This problem has arisen recently and controversially with the reservations by the United States and others to human rights treaty provisions.

- Exam questions often explore whether a state may be bound to a treaty under international law before it has accepted the treaty under its own internal processes because article 18 of the Vienna Convention says that a state that has indicated its preliminary acceptance of a treaty in certain ways cannot do anything to "defeat the object and purpose of the treaty" until it has clearly indicated its refusal to become a party to it.

- Finally, with treaties, it is important to understand the procedures and varying consequences of a state's acceptance or rejection of another state's proposed reservation to its acceptance of a treaty, now that international law no longer requires unanimous acceptance of every reservation by the other state-parties to a treaty (see the analysis of article 21 in §II(I) of this chapter).

- Even if a state does not become a party to a treaty, it may still be bound by a rule contained in a treaty if that provision has become so widely accepted by states as to meet the requirements for becoming a norm of customary international law or a general principle of international law. In that case, a state's best chance of not being subject to the rule is to argue that it has been a persistent objector to the rule and, therefore, is not bound by it, but many states do not recognize this exception to the formation of customary international law.

- With custom, note that both a consistent state practice and the element of *opinio juris* (states engaging in the practice because they think international law requires it) must be demonstrated for a norm to be considered binding as custom.

- General principles of international law are the most difficult to define and determine, but they often originate in basic rules of jurisprudence common to most domestic legal systems—for example, that everyone is entitled to a fair trial—and then evolve into custom and often widely accepted treaty provisions.

- Remember, too, the "supernorms" of international law, or *jus cogens*, which are norms (usually customs) that are so widely accepted that states cannot deviate from the norm even by agreement in a treaty (for example, no treaty to engage in slavery would be valid under international law).

CHAPTER 3

INTERNATIONAL LAW AND MUNICIPAL LAW

I. DUALISM AND MONISM

There are two theoretical approaches to the relationship between international law and municipal law: ***dualism*** and ***monism***.

A. Dualism defined: Under the dualist theory, international law and municipal law are ***entirely separate legal systems.*** In actual practice, the dualist approach appears to predominate.

1. Incorporation of international law in the domestic legal order: A state's constitution and domestic legal doctrines determine the effect of international laws within the domestic legal order. The constitution also imposes on international laws the same limitations imposed on municipal laws.

2. Incorporation of municipal law in the international legal order: Ordinarily, a state may not impose its municipal laws on the international legal system. Conflict with a municipal law *does not excuse a state from its international legal obligations*. Thus, a state may be legally bound to an obligation under international law that would have no legal force under its own domestic legal system. Although municipal law cannot generally impose itself on the international legal order, there are instances when an international tribunal encounters and must interpret a municipal law at issue between disputing states. In such cases, the international tribunal attempts to interpret the municipal law in conformity with the interpretations of the municipal courts.

B. Monism defined: The monist theory holds that municipal and international law ***belong to a single "universal legal order."*** The diminished role of the state as a legal personality results in a dominant role for international law over municipal law.

II. TREATIES IN MUNICIPAL LAW

Treaty law is the form of international law most commonly applied in domestic legal practice.

A. Treaties in U.S. law: The U.S. Constitution includes several provisions on treaties:

1. Article II treaties: The President of the United States has the authority to make treaties with the "Advice and Consent of the Senate." Two-thirds of the senators present at the vote must concur. U.S. CONST. art. II, §2.

2. Judicial power over treaties: The judicial power of the United States extends to cases arising under treaties. U.S. Const. art. III, §2.

3. Supremacy of treaties: Treaties, along with the Constitution and federal laws, are "the supreme Law of the Land" and prevail over conflicting state laws. U.S. Const. art. VI, §2.

4. Limitations on state powers: The individual states of the United States may not enter into treaties, alliances, or confederations with foreign nations. U.S. Const. art. I, §10.

B. **Terminology for treaties:** Although "treaties" are often referred to in a generic sense, U.S. domestic law recognizes two types of international agreements—treaties and executive agreements.

1. **Article II treaties:** Article II treaties are those international agreements made by the President with the two-thirds majority consent of the Senate.

2. **Congressional/executive agreements:** Also called *statutory agreements*, these may be made by the President pursuant to statutes passed by a majority of both the House and the Senate. The President's ability to act without any congressional participation in binding the United States to international obligations is controversial. *See* §IV(A)(1) of this chapter, *infra*. *See also Made in the USA Found. v. United States*, 242 F.3d 1300 (11th Cir. 2001) (recognizing congressional-executive agreements as a complete and constitutional alternative to the treaty power granted by the Constitution, thus permitting U.S. participation in North American Free Trade Agreement [NAFTA] and the World Trade Organization [WTO]).

C. **Self-executing treaties:** The doctrine of self-executing treaties is not explicit in the U.S. Constitution; it is a judge-made doctrine. Self-executing treaties may be applied directly in U.S. courts without the need for implementing legislation by Congress. Whether or not a treaty is self-executing depends on the intent of the government and is an issue for the courts to decide when the treaty is invoked as law. *Foster & Elam v. Neilson*, 27 U.S. (2 Pet.) 253 (1829).

1. **Origin of self-executing treaty doctrine:** The doctrine emerged in the 1829 case of *Foster & Elam v. Neilson*, 27 U.S. (2 Pet.) 253 (1829), when the Supreme Court made a distinction between treaties ***directly applicable by the courts as U.S. law*** (*i.e.*, self-executing) and treaties aimed at the legislature and requiring implementation before taking effect under the municipal legal order.

2. **Constitutional restraints on the self-executing character of treaties:** A treaty cannot be self-executing if the subject matter lies within the exclusive law-making power of Congress. For example, treaties pertaining to international crimes (*e.g.*, genocide, hijacking) or the raising of revenue require congressional action before taking effect as domestic law.

   In *Standt v. City of New York*, 153 F. Supp. 2d 417 (S.D.N.Y. 2001), the court held that private individuals have standing to sue for violations of the rights guaranteed by the Vienna Convention on Consular Relations. The court allowed a German citizen to sue the City of New York because the police arrested him without informing him of his right to communicate with the German consulate. ***Usually, treaties of the United States are not self-executing*** and do not give rights to private causes of action for alleged violations. *See also United States v. Lombera-Camorlinga*, 206 F.3d 882 (9th Cir. 2000); *Cheung v. United States*, 213 F.3d 82, 95 (2d Cir. 2000).

   The only modern guidance on distinguishing between self-executing and non-self-executing treaties came in a sharply divided opinion in *Medellin v. Texas*, 552 U.S. 491 (2008). In that decision, Chief Justice Roberts and Justices Alito, Thomas, Scalia, and Kennedy concluded that neither the ICJ Statute, the U.N. Charter, the Optional Protocol to the Vienna Convention on Consular Relations, nor the ICJ decision in *Avena* were directly enforceable as federal law in state courts. In so concluding, these Justices, according to Justice Stevens's separate and brief concurring opinion, incorrectly applied a presumption against self-execution. Justice Stevens also found "a great deal of wisdom" in the dissent, and found the case to involve a very close question as to whether the phrase "undertakes to comply" in article 94(1) of the U.N. Charter for ICJ decisions made the obligation non-self-executing. Dissenting Justices Breyer, Ginsburg, and Souter found the relevant provisions of both the U.N. Charter and the Optional Protocol, and thus *Avena* as well, to be binding.

3. **Non-self-executing treaties:** A treaty is also non-self-executing ***if it instructs the legislature to implement enacting legislation***. Strictly speaking, it is then the implementing legislation that is given effect as U.S. law, not the treaty itself. *See Hamdan v. Rumsfeld*, 548 U.S. 557 (2006) (holding that Geneva Convention norms dictate the executive's ability to create military commissions because Congress had previously passed legislation that called for application of the Geneva Convention norms). Difficulties arise if a treaty does not clearly mandate enactment through implementing legislation and the government takes no actions to implement the treaty. The question then becomes whether the treaty is self-executing and enforceable in domestic courts or non-self-executing and unenforceable without congressional implementation.

D. Treaties and conflicting state law—effect of the Supremacy Clause: Self-executing treaties and legislatively implemented treaties have the status of enforceable federal law and benefit accordingly from the Supremacy Clause. ***Thus, such treaty provisions prevail over conflicting state law***. *See Ware v. Hylton*, 3 U.S. 199 (1796) (ruling a Virginia statute was unconstitutional because it was in conflict with the Treaty of Paris of 1783); *Asakura v. Seattle*, 265 U.S. 332 (1924). "Treaties" benefiting from the Supremacy Clause include "congressional/executive" agreements and "executive" agreements.

Note: A treaty lacking required legislative implementation does not prevail over conflicting state laws. For example, a California state law barring certain aliens from owning land was upheld against conflicting provisions of the U.N. Charter. The court held that the cited provisions of the U.N. Charter were not "intended to become rules of law for the courts of this country upon ratification of the charter." *See Sei Fujii v. California*, 242 P.2d 617, 621 (Cal. 1952).

E. Treaties and conflicting federal statutes: Self-executing and legislatively executed treaties ***prevail over state law but do not necessarily prevail over federal statutory law***. Treaty law and federal statutory law are virtually equivalent in status. When both address the same issue, courts attempt to interpret the terms of each in such a manner as to avoid outright conflicts. *See United States v. Palestine Liberation Organization*, 695 F. Supp. 1456 (S.D.N.Y. 1988). When reconciliation is not possible, the general rule is that ***the last in time prevails***. *Whitney v. Robertson*, 124 U.S. 190 (1888). A later treaty may supersede an earlier federal law. Likewise, legislative action may supersede an earlier treaty. *See also Breard v. Greene*, 523 U.S. 371 (1998).

1. **The "last-in-time" rule:** This rule applies only to Article II treaties, that is, those made with the advice and consent of the Senate. An executive agreement does not prevail over previously enacted federal statutes.

2. **Effect on international law obligations:** ***The "last-in-time" rule applies only under U.S. law.*** Under international law, a conflict between treaty obligations and domestic law does not excuse the United States from its international legal obligations. *See* Chapter 2, §II(E)(3) (discussing potential conflicts between U.S. domestic law and international law).

F. Treaties and other constitutional constraints: It is far from clear what substantive constraints the Constitution places on the treaty-making power.

1. **Treaty better suited to task:** In *Missouri v. Holland*, 252 U.S. 416, 433 (1920), the Supreme Court stated: "We do not mean to imply that there are no qualifications to the treaty-making power; but they must be ascertained in a different way. It is obvious that there may be matters of

the sharpest exigency for the national well-being that an act of Congress could not deal with but that a treaty followed by such an act could…."

2. **Constitutional supremacy:** In contrast, in *Reid v. Covert*, 354 U.S. 1 (1957), the Court struck down an executive agreement authorizing military trials (without the full protections of the Bill of Rights) of dependents of armed forces personnel. "The Court has regularly and uniformly recognized the supremacy of the Constitution over a treaty." *Reid*, 354 U.S. at 17.

G. **Treaties and the laws of other countries:** The relationship between international and domestic law varies among states, but broad generalizations are possible with regard to the doctrine of self-executing treaties.

1. **"English" rule:** Most common law countries other than the United States do not permit treaties to be incorporated as municipal law without legislative enactment. In the United Kingdom, for example, a treaty may be ratified by the Crown alone but is incorporated into British law only by an act of Parliament. Thus, the United Kingdom may be bound by treaty obligations to other contracting parties, but parliamentary refusal to perform the treaty puts the United Kingdom in default.

2. **Civil law treatment:** Most civil law countries accept the concept of self-executing treaties, and explicit constitutional provisions allow for direct incorporation of treaty law into municipal law. The French constitution, for example, states that "treaties or international agreements regularly ratified or approved have, from the date of their publication, an authority superior to municipal law on the basis of reciprocity by the other state."

III. CUSTOMARY INTERNATIONAL LAW IN MUNICIPAL LAW

A. **Common law countries—international law as common law:** International law derived from sources other than treaties is considered by common law countries to be a special type of common law. As early as 1784 (*Respublica v. De Longchamps*, 1 U.S. 111), ***the law of nations was considered to be part of the law of the United States.*** This principle was stated in *The Paquete Habana*: "International law is part of our law, and must be ascertained and administered by the courts of justice of appropriate jurisdiction, as often as questions of right depending upon it are duly presented for determination. For this purpose, where there is no treaty, and no controlling executive or legislative act or judicial decision, resort must be had to the customs and usages of civilized nations…." 175 U.S. 677, 700 (1900).

1. **Incorporation of customary law into domestic law:** The United States joins other common law jurisdictions in considering *customary rules to be automatically incorporated into the domestic legal order* and thus directly applicable in domestic courts. *See Sosa v. Alvarez-Machain*, 542 U.S. 692, 729 (2004) (stating that "the domestic law of the United States recognizes the law of nations"). *But see* Harold G. Maier, *The Authoritative Sources of Customary International Law in the United States*, 10 MICH. J. INT'L L. 450 (1989) (stating courts are free to apply or not apply custom as with other principles under the common law approach). The United States, Great Britain, Canada, and India all treat customary rules of international law as part of domestic law.

2. **Supremacy Clause and customary international law:** Customary law, like treaty law, is considered federal law and ***receives the benefits of the Supremacy Clause.*** *Banco Nacional*

de Cuba v. Sabbatino, 376 U.S. 398 (1964). Customary law, thus, has supremacy over state laws. Its status with respect to federal statutory law, however, is less certain. The drafters of the Restatement (Fourth) of the Foreign Relations Law of the United States rejected their position in an earlier draft that international common law, like treaties, could supersede preexisting federal law. Note again, however, that U.S. courts will attempt to interpret a federal law to avoid conflict with international law, whether the international law is in the form of a treaty or custom. *See The Charming Betsy*, 6 U.S. (2 Cranch) 64 (1804); *see also Garcia-Mir v. Meese*, 788 F.2d 1446 (11th Cir. 1986), *cert. denied*, 479 U.S. 889 (1986) (holding that acts of the attorney general are controlling executive acts that prevail over international law).

3. **U.S. treatment of customary international law:** U.S. courts group customary law together with other non-treaty sources of international law to form what is called *international common law*. Custom, general principles, scholarly works, and judicial opinions are all consulted in order to establish a rule of international law. This practice contrasts with that of international tribunals, which consider each a discrete source of law.

B. **Civil law countries—relationship between customary international law and domestic law:** Civil law countries rely on express constitutional provisions to incorporate non-treaty international law into their municipal law. The provisions are varied. The French constitution expresses a readiness to adhere to rules of public international law. The Philippine constitution more directly expresses that it incorporates general international law principles into municipal law and assigns the legislature the task of harmonizing any conflicts. The German constitution goes so far as to give "general rules" of international law priority over domestic law.

IV. FOREIGN RELATIONS LAW OF THE UNITED STATES

Although U.S. domestic law does not directly impose itself on the international legal order, it does play a major role by allocating power among the three branches of government. The tripartite structure created by the U.S. Constitution influences U.S. conduct of foreign relations.

A. **Executive powers:** Article II of the U.S. Constitution expressly grants the President authority to be "Commander in Chief of the Army and Navy"; to make treaties; to appoint ambassadors, public ministers, and consuls; and to receive ambassadors and public ministers.

1. **International agreements:** One of the most controversial issues regarding the executive powers is the President's ability to ***make binding international agreements without congressional participation*** (so-called non–Article II treaties). In *United States v. Curtiss-Wright*, 299 U.S. 304 (1936), the Supreme Court took a very broad view of the inherent powers of the President to enter into international agreements. In 1979, the Court upheld executive orders to effectuate the settlement agreement between the United States and Iran concerning the U.S. hostages seized from the U.S. embassy in Tehran. In upholding the President's authority, the Court emphasized that Congress had acquiesced in the President's action and that there had been a long-standing practice of settling claims of U.S. nationals against foreign countries by executive agreement without the advice and consent of the Senate. *Dames & Moore v. Regan*, 453 U.S. 654 (1981).

2. **Recognition of governments:** Implicit in the express constitutional authorization to receive ambassadors is the exclusive power to ***recognize foreign governments***. The executive branch has used the recognition of governments as a political tool, but the current practice is to recognize any government in effective control of a state.

3. **Other presidential authority:** Any other presidential authority in international affairs must be premised on the ***inherent authority generally conferred by Article II***. *See Dames & Moore v. Regan, supra.*

B. Congressional powers: Article I of the U.S. Constitution authorizes the Congress to establish and collect taxes and duties; to pay debts and provide for the common defense and general welfare; to regulate trade with foreign countries; to define and punish piracy and other "offences against the Law of Nations"; to raise and support the armed forces; and to declare war. In 1973, Congress passed the War Powers Act to ensure that the President could not commit U.S. troops to combat without consulting Congress. 50 U.S.C. §1541 *et seq.* The validity of this attempt to restrict presidential powers in international relations has been questioned following *INS v. Chadha*, 462 U.S. 919 (1983), which declared legislative vetoes unconstitutional.

C. Judicial powers: Article III of the U.S. Constitution vests the Supreme Court with the judicial power of the United States, which includes cases arising under treaties made by the United States, cases involving ambassadors and other public ministers and consuls, admiralty and maritime cases, and cases between U.S. states and citizens and foreign states and citizens.

1. **"Act-of-state" doctrine:** The "act-of-state" doctrine exemplifies the tensions that exist among the three branches with respect to international relations. The Supreme Court stated that the act-of-state doctrine emerged from "the proper distribution of functions between the judicial and political branches of the Government on matters bearing upon foreign affairs." *Banco Nacional de Cuba v. Sabbatino*, 376 U.S. 398 (1964). Applying the act-of-state doctrine, the Court declined to rule in favor of the expropriated U.S. property owners and left the matter to the executive branch. Congress reacted quickly with passage of the Foreign Assistance Act of 1961 to prevent courts from declining to address similar issues in the future. For further discussion, *see* Chapter 5, §V(B).

2. **"Political question" doctrine:** The "political question" doctrine is also applied by courts to ***avoid addressing controversies regarding the political functions of the other two branches***. *See Baker v. Carr*, 369 U.S. 186 (1962) (formulating a six-point test for determining when a political question precludes jurisdiction). Recently, the Ninth Circuit Court looked at the effect of the political question doctrine on foreign relations cases. *Alperin v. Vatican Bank*, 410 F.3d 532 (9th Cir. 2005). The court noted that often the political question doctrine "lurks in the shadows of cases involving foreign relations" and that the inquiry into justiciability as required by *Baker v. Carr* is limited to "political questions, not...political cases" and should be looked at on a "case-by-case basis." *Id. at* 537-538 (citations omitted).

Exam Tips on INTERNATIONAL LAW AND MUNICIPAL LAW

- The most important point of international law in this chapter is that municipal (domestic) law systems of states differ as to whether international law and the state's own domestic law are equal or unequal (with either international law or domestic law taking precedence in the event of a conflict) sources of law.

- The United States takes a mixed approach, depending upon the source of international law. Self-executing treaties are on an equal footing with federal legislation, with the last in time prevailing if there is a conflict. If this results in the United States failing to follow a treaty to comply with federal law, then from an international law perspective, the United States is in violation of the treaty and thus international law. It is virtually impossible to articulate a helpful test for whether a treaty is or is not self-executing, despite the importance of the question. In the significant 2008 Supreme Court opinion in *Medellin v. Texas*, however, five of the Justices appeared to apply a general presumption against self-execution and to be demanding of the language necessary to make a treaty self-executing.
- Although other international law obligations (for example, non-self-executing treaties or custom) under U.S. law may not take precedence over federal law, generally they will prevail if there is a conflict with state or local law.
- Another surprisingly unresolved constitutional law issue is the extent to which constitutional provisions limit the treaty-making power. At best, it could be said that the United States could not constitutionally approve a treaty that would violate the Bill of Rights protections.
- Lastly, although a number of U.S. Supreme Court cases have said that customary international law is a part of U.S. law, and thus directly enforceable in federal court, scholars have had some success in influencing judicial opinion and political representatives to the contrary. Specifically, they argue customary international law is not part of U.S. law, and custom is not binding law in federal court unless Congress has incorporated it into our law by legislation.

CHAPTER 4
STATES

States, particularly under the dualist view of international law, are the primary subjects of international law. States have the capacity to make agreements and treaties and to make claims for breaches of international law. States have rights and obligations under international law. In short, states are the ***principal entities having legal personality in the international legal order***.

I. DEFINITION OF A STATE

Under both the Restatement and the Montevideo Convention of 1933, a state is defined as "an entity that has a ***defined territory*** and a ***permanent population***, under the control of its ***own government***, and that ***engages in, or has the capacity to engage in, formal relations*** with other such entities."

A. Defined territory: There is no minimum size for a state. Monaco, for example, takes up only 1.5 square kilometers, yet it is a state. A state need not be established with clearly defined frontiers. The United States, for example, was a state despite indeterminate claims westward into unexplored territories. In addition, many states are in existence despite long-standing border disputes with neighboring states.

B. Permanent population—a "people": ***A permanent population or a "people" is similarly not defined by size***. The Vatican, with a population of only about 300, is considered a state. Antarctica, however, has no permanent population and is, in part for that reason, not considered a state.

C. Under the control of its own government: A state cannot exist without the control of an effective government. The government must be able to assert itself without the aid of foreign troops and to carry out its duties. Exceptions are granted as follows:

- A state may temporarily lack an effective government as a result of civil war, newly gained independence, or similar upheavals.
- A simple change in regime and even conflicting claims of governmental authority alone will not disqualify an entity from statehood.
- A state occupied by an enemy in times of war continues to be a state so long as allies are fighting on its behalf against the enemy.

D. Capacity to engage in relations with other states: Under the Restatement (Fourth) of the Foreign Relations Law of the United States §201, "[a]n entity is not a state unless it has the competence, within its own constitutional system, to conduct international relations with other states, as well as the political, technical and financial capabilities to do so."

Note: ***Only capacity is required, not actual practice.*** Voluntary relinquishment of partial or complete control over foreign relations does not disqualify an entity from statehood. Liechtenstein, for example, has relinquished control of its foreign relations to Switzerland, yet is still considered a state.

E. Role of recognition in defining a state: Under the declaratory theory of recognition and under the Restatement, an entity must be treated as a state when it meets the four requirements set forth above. Its existence as a state is independent of any formal recognition. *See* §IV of this chapter, *infra*, on "recognition" of states.

II. STATE TERRITORY

The very existence of a state relies in large part on the concept of territory—that area of land, air, or water circumscribed by the state's frontiers. An entity can be a state only if it can be defined by its territory. Sovereignty is a state's ***right to exercise its authority within that territory***. In addition to the right of sovereignty, a state has certain obligations with respect to its territory. Most of the Earth's habitable area is indisputably claimed by the many states. Questions with respect to territory arise with respect to boundary disputes, claims to islands, polar regions, and forceful occupations of land.

A. **State boundaries or frontiers:** State boundaries are the barriers distinguishing one state's territory from another state's territory. These barriers extend not only across land but both upwards and downwards into the airspace and subsurface space. Boundaries are most often determined by agreements between the parties rather than being dictated by principles of international law.

   1. **Boundary dispute resolution:** Boundary disputes are common, and contests involving relatively small areas of land may be resolved by litigation before the International Court of Justice (ICJ), by arbitration, or in conjunction with the resolution of some other settlement, such as a peace treaty.

      Example: In 2010, Costa Rica instituted an ICJ proceeding against Nicaragua claiming "[i]ncursion into, occupation of and use by Nicaragua's Army of Costa Rican territory...." *Costa Rica v. Nicaragua*, 2011 I.C.J. 6 (Mar. 8).

   2. **Effect of succession:** A succession of states, by itself, is not grounds for affecting boundaries established by treaty or rights and obligations established by treating and relating to the boundary regime. The International Law Commission does recognize other grounds for challenging a boundary, such as the invalidity of a treaty or self-determination. For discussion of the effects of succession on treaties, *see* Chapter 2, §II(K)(11-12).

B. **Airspace and outer space: Relatively recent developments in the field of aeronautics have** raised many issues of territoriality. There are two important considerations. On the one hand, there is respect for the notion that a state has ***the right to use and control its airspace***, particularly for reasons of national security. On the other hand, there exists the notion that outer space, like the high seas, cannot be completely within the jurisdiction of any one state. Accordingly, there are separate sets of treaties and agreements concerning airspace versus outer space. For a detailed discussion on air and space law, *see* Chapter 11.

   1. **Airspace:** The Chicago Convention, along with a number of supplemental accords and protocols, establishes the rights of states over their territorial airspace, stating that "[t]he contracting States recognize that every State has ***complete and exclusive authority over the airspace above its territory***" (emphasis added).

   2. **Outer space:** The legal order of outer space first became an issue with the launching of the Sputnik satellite in 1957 and is an area of great uncertainty. Some guidance is available in the Outer Space Treaty (entered into force in 1967), which provides that the "exploration and use of outer space, including the moon and other celestial bodies...shall be the province of all mankind" and that "[o]uter space, including the moon and other celestial bodies, is not subject to national appropriation."

C. International rivers: International rivers may flow through a state's territory but not be subject to the absolute authority of the state.

1. Characteristics: An international river has the following characteristics:

- It is ***navigable***;
- It flows directly or indirectly ***into the sea***;
- It flows through the territory of ***two or more states*** or forms the boundary between them; and
- An ***international act*** proclaims it to be an international river.

Examples: The Danube, the Rhine, the Amazon, the Congo, and the Niger rivers.

2. The Vienna Conference of 1815: The Vienna Conference of 1815 established the general principle of freedom of navigation on international rivers. It also established the rights of states along the length of international rivers and imposed on riparian states the obligations of maintaining barge-towing paths and removing obstacles to navigation.

D. State coastal zones: The sea is divided into several zones: *internal waters, the territorial sea, the contiguous zone, the continental shelf, the exclusive economic zone*, and *the high seas*. The sovereign rights of the coastal state vary with each zone. Generally speaking, the internal waters of a state are part of its territory, and the state may apply and enforce its laws there. The band of sea extending outward from a state's coast, the territorial sea, is also the state's territory and is subject to the state's exercise of sovereignty. That sovereignty, however, is limited by foreign states' right of innocent passage. Beyond the territorial sea, the rights of the coastal state are much more limited and pertain primarily to economic interests. *See* Chapter 10, §§V-VI (discussing state sovereignty over the territorial sea, rights of passage, and economic zones).

E. *Res nullius* and *res communis*: *Res nullius* and *res communis* are terms referring to territory that belongs to no state. *Res nullius*, meaning ***unattributed territory***, gave rise to the colonial empires in the fifteenth to nineteenth centuries. *Res communis* refers to ***common or international territory***, such as the high seas, Antarctica, the Moon, and outer space.

F. Acquisition of territorial sovereignty: Acquisition of territory may occur in a variety of ways, including the following:

1. Accretion: Natural processes, such as shifting rivers and growing deltas, may expand a state's territory.

2. Cession: Sovereignty over an area may be transferred by means of an agreement between states. Although some hold that territory may be ceded to another state without the consent of the population living there, the actual practice in recent years has been to condition cession on such consent.

3. Conquest: Traditionally, territory could be annexed through complete and final subjugation followed by the conquering state's declaration of its intent to annex the territory. Title by conquest in this manner was rare because territory more frequently passes as a result of a treaty of cession. More importantly, the U.N. General Assembly's Declaration on Principles of International Law Concerning Friendly Relations and Cooperation Among States suggests that territory may not be acquired by another state from the threat or use of force in an international war.

4. **Contiguity:** There is no rule in international law permitting a state to make claims of acquisition over neighboring islands that are not part of another independent state. Mere geographic proximity is insufficient to claims of acquisition.

5. **Occupation:** Physical presence coupled with continuous and peaceful display of territorial sovereignty over territory belonging to no state (*terra nullius*).

6. **Prescription:** Acquisition of land belonging to another state through prescription under international law is analogous to the concept of adverse possession under municipal law. Lasting possession of an area, as shown by the exercise or display of a state's authority, may confirm title in that state. Prescription is distinguished from occupation; the former involves acquisition of territory previously claimed by another state, and the latter involves the acquisition of territory belonging to no state (*terra nullius*).

7. **Other considerations:** Although the ICJ puts great weight on acquiescence and recognition of territorial claims in determining which state is the sovereign power (*see Temple of Preah Vihear (Thail. v. Cambodia)*, 1962 I.C.J. 6 (June 15)), tribunals do consider other factors in resolving territorial disputes. These include affiliations of the inhabitants of the disputed territory; geographic, economic, and historical considerations; and cultural unity. These considerations are controversial and are sometimes described as political rather than legal. *See India v. Pakistan*, [1968] 50 I.L.R. 2 (1976). *See also Sovereignty over Pulau Ligitan and Pulau Sipadan (Indon. v. Malay.)*, 2002 I.C.J. 625 (Dec. 17) (In a dispute between Indonesia and Malaysia over which state was sovereign over the islands of Ligitan and Sipadan, the ICJ ruled that Malaysia's regulation of the commercial collection of turtle eggs and establishment of a bird sanctuary on the islands were sufficiently administrative to demonstrate effective control, and the ICJ recognized Malaysia's sovereignty over the islands.); *Nicaragua v. Colombia*, 2012 I.C.J. 624 (Nov. 19) (in a dispute over title in island territory, the Court found Colombia had established title to the islands by consistently acting *à titre de souverain*).

III. RECOGNITION OF STATES AND GOVERNMENTS

Recognition is a confusing mixture of international law, domestic law, and politics. It is important to distinguish political considerations from legal considerations, and to separate the legal issues that arise under international law from those arising under the domestic law of the recognizing state. Recognition is best defined as the ***willingness to deal with another state or government representing the state as a member of the international community***. Public acts of recognition include formal notes, letters, and telegrams sent through diplomatic envoys; formal oral public announcements; and the conclusion of bilateral agreements. Maintaining or severing diplomatic relations is not synonymous with recognition or non-recognition, respectively.

A. **Express and implied recognition:** Recognition of a state or government is often done expressly, but certain conduct may also imply recognition:

- ***Entry into diplomatic relations implies recognition***, but an exchange of trade missions does not imply recognition. Conversely, the lack of diplomatic relations does not imply a lack of recognition.
- ***Signing a bilateral treaty subject to ratification implies recognition.***
- ***Common membership in international organizations does not imply recognition of one another.*** For example, several Arab states that do not recognize the state of Israel are members of the United Nations along with Israel.

B. Recognition under U.S. law: Under U.S. law, ***only the President has the authority to recognize or not recognize*** an entity as a state. This exclusive authority is implied from the powers granted under Article II of the U.S. Constitution to appoint and to receive ambassadors. The President may also recognize a state by concluding an international agreement. The United States often uses recognition as a sign of approval. The current practice of the executive branch is to recognize any government in effective control of a state. *See* Chapter 3, §IV(A)(2).

C. Whether recognition is discretionary or mandatory: Generally, recognition is discretionary, although one influential scholar has taken the view that it should not be. There are two limitations on this discretion to prevent premature recognition and premature withdrawal of recognition.

1. **Recognition is optional:** Recognition is an optional and political act, and there is no legal duty to recognize. If an entity, however, meets the requirements for recognition, other states put themselves at risk legally and politically if they refuse recognition.

   a. **Recognition is optional:** The Restatement (Fourth) adds that an entity need not be treated as a state if it has attained the qualifications for statehood by violating international law, for example, by use of or threat of force. As early as the 1930s, former U.S. Secretary of State Henry L. Stimson articulated the Stimson doctrine by proclaiming a refusal to recognize any situation, treaty, or agreement that may be brought about contrary to the covenants and obligations of the Pact of Paris [Treaty of Paris].

   b. **Recognition is optional:** Note that the obligation to treat an entity as a state when it has met the requirements of statehood considerably diminishes the significance of the constitutive theory of recognition.

2. **The Lauterpacht Doctrine:** A prominent scholar, Sir Hersch Lauterpacht, contended that states had a duty to recognize states or governments that met the international law requirements for recognition. In practice, states have been reluctant to relinquish their control of recognition to this extent.

3. **Premature recognition:** If a state, or more commonly a purported government, is recognized *before it has effective control over the territory at issue, such premature recognition is illegal.*

4. **Premature withdrawal of recognition:** On the other hand, *if recognition is withdrawn before loss of control, such premature withdrawal of recognition is also illegal.* Again, note that severance of diplomatic relations is not the same as withdrawal of recognition. Because premature recognition and withdrawal of recognition are so rare, it is not clear what the remedies are or to whom they are owed.

5. **Non-recognition under the U.N. Charter:** Article 41 authorizes the Security Council to order members of the United Nations to "sever diplomatic relations" with a state or government, as was done in 1970 with the Smith regime in Southern Rhodesia.

D. *De jure* and *de facto* recognition: The terms *de facto* and *de jure* result in much confusion because they are used with varying and uncertain meanings. The Restatement avoids the terms altogether. In any case, the terms do not qualify the legal effects of recognition under international law.

1. **States:** Under the constitutive theory, treatment of an entity as a state without extending a formal recognition was called *de facto* recognition, as opposed to *de jure* recognition. Under the more modern declaratory theory, there is little use for the distinction between *de facto* and *de jure* recognition, except that *de jure* recognition may be regarded as having greater evidentiary value than does *de facto* recognition. The terms are more often used with recognition of governments.

2. **Governments:** *De jure* recognition implies that ***the government is lawfully in power even though it retains little actual power.*** A government-in-exile, for example, may be accorded *de jure* recognition. Conversely, a *de facto* government is impliedly a government that is in control but illegally so. The term *de facto* recognition is most commonly utilized when there exist unstable circumstances and a political reluctance to fully recognize the government. Notice that international law does not specify how a government must be established, nor does it prohibit a group from seizing power in a civil war. Any government with effective control is subject to unqualified recognition. Therefore, the terms *de jure* and *de facto* are more often an expression of the recognizing state's political approval or disapproval of a government, or of how the government came to power in its own domestic system, rather than a reflection of legitimacy under international law. One exception is that a government that seized control through gross violations of human rights, a violation of international law, might be referred to as the *de facto* government.

E. **Conditional recognition:** The prevailing view is that recognition generally cannot be granted subject to conditions. Conditional recognition is prohibited for fear that more powerful nations would utilize it as a form of blackmail. Reasonable conditions, however, are assumed under the international legal principles. For example, a state or government must abide by the general principles of international law.

IV. RECOGNITION OF STATES

A. **Two theories of recognition:** There are two theories concerning the legal effects under international law of recognition of states: the constitutive theory and the declaratory theory.

1. **Constitutive theory:** The constitutive theory is that ***an entity does not exist as a state until it has been recognized by other states***; the recognition itself "constitutes" the state. Acts of recognition determine statehood. This theory is not widely accepted today, as it is borne out by actual practice. The People's Republic of China, for example, was considered a state long before it was recognized by many states. Furthermore, fewer states today go through the process of formally recognizing another state.

2. **Declaratory theory:** Under the declaratory theory, the facts of statehood (defined territory, permanent population, effective government, and capacity for foreign relations) rather than formal recognition define an entity as a state. Any formal recognition is simply declaratory of the political and legal reality of statehood.

B. **Evidentiary value of recognition:** Recognition, nevertheless, is useful evidence of the existence of a state if enough other states recognize a state and recognition (or non-recognition) is based on principles of international law rather than political considerations. The limitation of the evidentiary value of recognition is that states may grant or withhold recognition for many reasons unrelated to principles of international law.

Example: In an arbitration decision between Great Britain and Costa Rica (the *Tinoco Case*), [1923] 1 R. Int'l Arb. Awards 369 (1948), Chief Justice Taft as arbitrator found that the Tinoco regime was the government of Costa Rica because it had been in effective control of the state, despite the fact that it had not been recognized by a number of states, including Great Britain. He concluded that the Tinoco regime was clearly the government in control. If control had been less clear, recognition or non-recognition based on the legal requirement of control would have had evidentiary weight in determining whether the Tinoco regime was the government, and thus authorized to act on behalf of Costa Rica.

V. RECOGNITION OF GOVERNMENTS

Recognition of a government is an acknowledgment that it is ***in effective control of the state***. Recognition under international law is not dependent upon the constitutionality of a government or its legitimacy under its own domestic laws, but solely on its effectiveness.

A. Traditional approach to recognition: The traditional approach allows recognition of a government when:

1. It is in effective control of the state ***without the assistance of foreign intervention***. Revolutionary governments are not recognized until they have clearly established control over most of the state, having reduced the prior government to control of only negligible areas;
2. It has ***the consent, or at least the acquiescence, of the people***; and
3. It shows its ***willingness to comply with the state's obligations under international law***.

B. Estrada Doctrine: Under the so-called Estrada Doctrine, the practice of recognizing governments is eliminated altogether with the focus being on recognition of states. A number of states claim to apply the Estrada Doctrine, but states often depart from it to use recognition or non-recognition as a political tool.

C. Wilson Doctrine: In the early 1900s, the Tobar Doctrine was adopted by the United States and renamed the Wilson Doctrine. Under this approach, only democratic and constitutional governments were extended recognition. The United States itself no longer adheres to this doctrine.

D. Acts of recognition: Unlike recognition of states, which is more likely to be express, recognition of governments is often implied through the continuation or establishment of diplomatic relations.

E. Significance in domestic law of the recognition of states and governments: Under domestic law, recognized governments and states enjoy important benefits, as exemplified in the Restatement (Fourth) of the Foreign Relations Law of the United States §205:

- ***Access to courts*** in the United States.
- ***Entitlement to property*** belonging to states located in the United States.
- ***A right to claim sovereign immunity***.

1. **Afghanistan:** The United States refused to recognize the Taliban as Afghanistan's official government. However, the United States did recognize the Afghan Interim Authority (AIA) in 2002, which held a *loya jirga* (a traditional communal meeting). In 2004 the first democratically elected official took office.
2. **Iraq:** In 2003, the United States invaded Iraq and ousted the government of Saddam Hussein. In 2004, the United States announced that full sovereignty was transferred to an Iraqi sovereign government, which signaled official recognition of an Iraqi government by the United States.
3. **Macedonia:** In 2004, the United States announced that Macedonia would be referred to as the Republic of Macedonia, and this reflected its recognition that Macedonia has a separate government from Greece.

VI. RECOGNITION OF INSURGENTS AND BELLIGERENTS

A. Generally: Insurgencies and belligerencies are two types of internal state conflicts, and are discussed at Chapter 9, §III(A).

VII. THE RIGHTS AND OBLIGATIONS OF STATES

Although states have been the most prominent actors in international relations, the precise content of their rights and obligations continues to be surprisingly ill-defined and uncertain.

A. Rights: There is much controversy regarding the basic rights of states, and as yet, there exists no finalized written statement of the rights and duties of states. The U.N. Charter as a whole does impose obligations on its members to respect certain rights of states. Such rights and obligations, however, are binding on the international community as a whole only if accepted as customary law with universal application. The rights generally protected by the U.N. Charter and other U.N. resolutions are as follows:

1. **Right of sovereignty:** The right of sovereignty is fundamental because it ***prohibits foreign intervention in internal affairs.*** The state is the supreme authority within its national territory. It is said to have territorial sovereignty or territorial jurisdiction. Customary international law also recognizes immunity for warships and limited immunity for merchant ships.

   a. **Restrictions on territorial jurisdiction:** Restrictions on territorial jurisdiction may be made in international agreements, such as the preamble to the Statute of the International Labour Organization, which gives the organization the right to influence labor conditions within the member-states' territories.

   b. **Exclusive, domestic jurisdiction:** The notion of exclusive, domestic jurisdiction is subject to much controversy, particularly with respect to matters affecting individual rights. The issue is whether protection of the individual is a matter of domestic jurisdiction or a matter falling under international law governing human rights.

   c. **Sovereignty over use of natural resources:** Under a number of U.N. resolutions, including the Charter of Economic Rights and Duties of States and the Stockholm Declaration on the Human Environment, states are declared to have absolute sovereignty over use of natural resources within their territories. This right has been qualified in recent years by growing recognition that a state has an obligation to ensure activities occurring within its jurisdiction or control do not cause harm in areas beyond its territory, and the International Law Commission has been studying articles of state responsibility to extend state liability to injuries caused by acts lawful *per se*.

2. **Equality of states:** Under international law theory, ***all independent states are equal.*** Neither the size of territories or populations nor the level of development has any bearing on the equality of states. The concept of legal equality is set forth in the Statute to the International Court of Justice. "[N]o circumstances may place parties to a dispute in an unequal position before the court." Likewise, states receive equal treatment when disputes arise in international organizations. The concept of sovereignty and equality are closely joined. All states are to enjoy equal treatment. Thus, no state is permitted to intervene in the affairs of another state. The U.N. Declaration on Principles of International Law Concerning Friendly Relations and Cooperation Among States provides that "armed intervention, and all other forms of interference or attempted

threats against the personality of the State or against its political, economic and cultural elements are in violation of international law."

3. **The right to defense:** A state has the ***right to take steps necessary to protect its own security.*** Before the U.N. Charter was adopted, the right to defense included the right to initiate hostilities in anticipation of an attack. A state may no longer engage in anticipatory self-defense without running the risk of being held responsible for an act of aggression in violation of international law. *See* Chapter 9, §I(C)(1) (discussing the right of self-defense under the U.N. Charter and problematic examples).

4. **The right of international intercourse:** States are ***free to establish and regulate their own international relations*** so long as they do not violate the accepted rules and principles of international law. The U.N. Declaration on Principles of International Law Concerning Friendly Relations and Cooperation Among States in fact imposes a duty on states to cooperate with one another in maintaining international peace and stability and promoting the general welfare of nations.

B. Rights of states under U.S. law: The Restatement (Fourth) §206 incorporates some of these rights. A state has:

a. ***sovereignty*** over its territory and general authority over its nationals;

b. ***status as a legal person***, with capacity to own, acquire, and transfer property, to make contracts and enter international agreements, to become a member of international organizations, and to pursue and be subject to legal remedies; and

c. ***capacity*** to join with other states to make international law, as customary law or by international agreement.

C. General responsibility of states: ***A state injuring the rights or property of another state in breach of its international obligations incurs international responsibility.*** *Chorzow Factory*, 1927 P.C.I.J., 21 (ser. A) No. 9. A state may bear political responsibility (resulting, for example, in disarmament of an aggressor state) or civil responsibility (resulting, for example, in payment of reparations for damages caused by war). State responsibility for "international crimes" is a developing area of liability.

1. **Acts attributable to a state:** A state can act only through the actions and omissions of human beings, and the state incurs liability only for ***those individual actions or omissions that can be attributed to the state***. Questions then arise as to who or what can act on behalf of the state and what type of conduct is imputed to the state. Articles of state responsibility adopted by the International Law Commission and draft articles currently being considered have been very influential in formulating this area of the law.

   a. **Acts of state organs:** The basic principle is that the ***acts of state organs or agents are imputed to the state***. An organ may be part of the formal structure of the state government, or it may be an entity empowered to exercise elements of governmental authority. The position of the organ in the organization of the state is irrelevant. It does not matter whether its function is legislative, executive, or judicial, or whether it has any responsibility for foreign affairs.

   b. **Acts of state agents:** Agents may be official authorities in government or other persons actually and justifiably exercising elements of governmental authority. Conversely, the conduct of persons not acting on behalf of the state is not considered an act of state.

c. **Acts of officials:** The state maintains responsibility for the conduct of its officials and organs with little regard to whether or not the official or organ acted within the limits of his, her, or its competency. A state may not be held responsible for insurrectional movements that do not succeed in becoming the new government of a state.

d. **Acts of member states or provinces:** A federal state cannot generally deny responsibility for the acts of its member states or provinces, for a federal state is expected to uphold its international obligations regardless of internal divisions in government.

2. **Element of fault:** The issue of whether a state can incur liability without fault arises most commonly in connection with transboundary pollution. On the one hand, a state is obliged not to use its territory in a manner injurious to other states. *See, e.g., Trail Smelter Arbitration (U.S. v. Can.)*, [1941] 3 R. Int'l Arb. Awards 1911 (1949). On the other hand, many lawful uses of a state may have an adverse effect on neighboring states. *See generally* Günther Handl, *Territorial Sovereignty and the Problem of Transnational Pollution*, 69 AM. J. INT'L L. 50 (1975). Section 601 of the Restatement (Fourth) provides:

> A state is obligated to take such measures as may be necessary, to the extent practicable under the circumstances to ensure that activities within its jurisdiction or control,
>
> (a) conform to generally accepted international rules and standards for the prevention, reduction, and control of injury to the environment of another state or of areas beyond the limits of national jurisdiction; and
>
> (b) are conducted so as not to cause significant injury to the environment of another state or of areas beyond the limits of national jurisdiction.

3. **Defenses to claims against a state:** A state's apparent violation of international law may be justified on the grounds of consent, *force majeure*, distress, necessity, and self-defense.

a. **Consent:** The International Law Commission has stated that "[t]he consent validly given by a State to the commission by another State of a specified act not in conformity with an obligation of the latter State towards the former State precludes the wrongfulness of the act...to the extent that the act remains within the limits of that consent." In no case, however, may there be any derogation from a peremptory norm.

Example: The entry of foreign troops into the territory of another is normally unlawful, but it is legitimate if done with the consent of that state.

b. **Force majeure:** An act normally in violation of international law obligations may be excused if the act was:

- "due to an irresistible force or to an unseen external event"
- "beyond its control"
- "[such that] made it materially impossible for the State to act in conformity with that obligation or to know that its conduct was not in conformity with that obligation." (I.L.C. Article 23 of the Draft Articles on Responsibility of States for Intentionally Wrongful Acts (2001).)

This defense is not available to states contributing to the occurrence of the event. Claims of *force majeure* most often arise in connection with vessels or aircraft that have entered the territory of another state without that state's consent. Claims of *force majeure* are generally not successfully invoked in seeking excuse from payment of a debt.

c. Distress: Wrongful conduct of a state may be excused if the state is acting to save the lives of persons entrusted to its care. This defense is closely related with *force majeure*, except that conformity to its obligations is actually possible for the state although it would result in a loss of lives. Incursions into foreign territory in order to save lives may be excused by the defense of distress.

d. Necessity: A state may act in violation of its international obligations in order to protect an essential state interest threatened by grave and imminent peril, but it may not do so if its conduct imperils the comparable or superior state interests of the other state. The defense of necessity does not apply if:

i. the state acting in violation of its international obligations caused the situation of "necessity";

ii. the international obligation of which the state is in breach is a peremptory norm of international law (in particular, prohibitions on acts of aggression); or

iii. the defense of necessity is precluded by the terms of an applicable instrument. (Human rights treaties, for example, often preclude necessity as a defense.)

The International Law Commission suggests that the pertinent essential state interests are the existence of the state, maintenance of essential services, keeping the domestic peace, the survival of part of its population, and ecological preservation of its territory.

e. Self-defense: To assert this defense, the state must be acting in self-defense in accordance with the U.N. Charter. *See* Chapter 9, §I(C)(1) (discussing the right of self-defense under the U.N. Charter).

4. The requirement of injury: It is generally stated that ***actual injury is not required*** to give rise to responsibility to other states for breach of an international obligation unless the obligation specifically requires injury as an element of its breach. The relative unimportance of the injury raises difficulties in determining which states are entitled to seek reparations from the offending state.

a. *Erga omnes* obligations: In *Barcelona Traction, Light and Power Company (Belg. v. Spain)*, 1970 I.C.J. 3 (Feb. 5), the court said:

> [A]n essential distinction should be drawn between the obligations of a State towards the international community as a whole, and those arising vis-à-vis another State in the field of diplomatic protection. By their very nature, the former are the concern of all States. In view of the importance of the rights involved, all States can be held to have a legal interest in their protection; they are obligations *erga omnes*.

Examples: Some examples given by the court of *erga omnes* obligations owed by every state to every other state are the prohibitions on acts of aggression, genocide, slavery, and race discrimination. The Restatement (Fourth) also includes §902, defining customary law obligations with respect to human rights and protection of the environment.

b. International crimes: Related to the concept of obligations, *erga omnes* is the concept of state responsibility for international crimes. Article 19 of the Draft Articles on State Responsibility defines an international crime as an international obligation "so essential for the protection of fundamental interests of the international community that its breach is recognized as a crime by that community as a whole...." Examples given generally correspond to the Restatement's examples of obligations *erga omnes*. The Draft Articles differentiate international crime from other illegal acts ("delects") as entailing all the legal consequences of an illegal act plus "such rights and obligations as are determined by the applicable rules accepted by the international community as a whole." Other states must not aid the offending state in maintaining the crime. It continues to be controversial whether customary international law recognizes the distinction between international crimes and delects for state responsibility.

5. **Remedies:** Breach of international obligations may give rise to the following remedies:

   a. **Collective sanctions:** Acts of aggression or gross violations of human rights are often countered by means of collective sanctions. Collective sanctions are imposed by the international community in reaction to its collective interests or common concerns, and they include severance of diplomatic relations, trade boycotts, and cessation of air or sea traffic. The U.N. Security Council may adopt collective sanctions as a non-military enforcement measure under article 41 of the U.N. Charter. For example, collective sanctions were imposed against Southern Rhodesia (Zimbabwe) in 1970. Sanctions were leveled against Iran several times between 2006 and 2010 for Iran's failure to comply with demands to halt the progression of its nuclear technology systems. During this period, similar sanctions were enacted against North Korea for that country's refusal to cease expansion of its nuclear energy development programs. In February 2011, the Security Council issued sanctions against Libya and its leader Colonel Qadhafi, as reports emerged from cities throughout the country that the dictator used extreme violence to put down peaceful protests against his rule.

   b. **Restitution:** Restitution is a form of reparation for an injury and is designed to put the injured party back in the same state in which it would have been had the wrongful conduct or omission not taken place. Restitution may be accomplished through performance of the failed obligation, revocation of an unlawful act, or abstention from further wrongful conduct.

   c. **Indemnity:** Under international law, *indemnity* is the term for monetary compensation, and it is the most common form of reparation. Indemnity should compensate all damages resulting from a wrongful act or omission, including ascertainable lost profits. Highly speculative lost profits are not awarded. Punitive damages were awarded in one arbitration decision (*The I'm Alone*, 3 Int'l Arb. Awards 1618 (1923)), but international tribunals have generally rejected claims for punitive damages.

   d. **Satisfaction:** This form of reparation is appropriate for situations in which there has been no material injury. Forms of satisfaction include official regrets and apologies, formal or judicial declaration of the illegality of an act, and punishment of guilty minor officials.

      Example: In 2011, the ICJ delivered a judgment that Greece breached Article 11 of the Interim Accord by objecting to the former Yugoslav Republic of Macedonia's membership application to NATO. The court ordered no further remedy, concluding the finding of breach was adequate satisfaction. *Former Yugoslav Republic of Macedonia v. Greece*, 2011 I.C.J. 644 (Dec. 5).

   e. **Self-help, retorsions, and reprisals:** *See* Chapter 9, §I(D).

6. **Implementing obligations of reparation:** Reparation may be sought through diplomatic channels or through agreed-upon procedures of dispute settlement. *See* Chapter 7 (discussing the International Dispute Settlement). Regardless of the nature of the procedure, there are several common requirements:

a. **Standing:** Parties may present a claim only if possessing a "legal interest." (Consider here the discussion of *erga omnes* obligations on §VII(C)(4)(a) of this chapter, *supra.*) Some international conventions permit any party to the convention to bring a claim if both parties to the dispute have agreed to a provision to that effect.

b. **Laches:** International tribunals have discretion to decide whether there has been undue delay in bringing a claim. Some tribunals deny remedies on the basis of undue delay, and others find that the principle of laches is inapplicable in international law.

c. **Negotiations as a prerequisite:** Many international agreements and tribunals require the parties to enter into negotiations, consultations, or "diplomacy" before submitting their claims to adjudication. The ICJ in the *North Sea Continental Shelf Cases*, 1969 I.C.J. 3, *supra*, stated that the negotiations must be meaningful and entered into with the purpose of reaching an agreement.

d. **Exhaustion of local remedies:** A state submitting a claim on behalf of its nationals for denial of rights in another state must first exhaust available remedies in the violating state. Exceptions have been made in cases in which the injured individual had minor and transitory connections with the violating state (such as being a passenger in its national airlines) or was injured by a space object or missile of the foreign state.

e. **Consent to third-party settlement:** Both parties to a claim must consent, expressly or impliedly, to its submission to a tribunal. Consent may be implied by the submission of arguments on the merits free of reservations on the issue of jurisdiction.

VIII. HEADS OF STATE, GOVERNMENT OFFICIALS, DIPLOMATS, AND OFFICIALS OF INTERNATIONAL ORGANIZATIONS: ROLES AND STATUS IN INTERNATIONAL LAW

A. **Heads of state:** Until the nineteenth century, the heads of state had the power to fully represent their states in foreign affairs, but today, most are considered organs of the state and are limited in their powers by the states' constitutions. Many heads of state now are competent to proclaim war, declare peace, receive diplomatic representatives, and possibly ratify international agreements. Under modern international law, a head of state may be ***held personally responsible for certain international crimes*** such as genocide, crimes against peace, crimes against humanity, and war crimes. The Charter of the International Military Tribunal at Nuremberg, after World War II, established this principle, and is discussed at Chapter 9, §II(E)(4).

B. **Government:** Foreign political acts of a government and statements of a prime minister (or its functional equivalent) made on behalf of the state are binding on the state. A person in the position of a prime minister (or its equivalent) is considered competent by other states to represent his or her state, without inquiry into his or her actual authority.

C. **Secretary of state/minister of foreign affairs (or the functional equivalent):** The secretary of state (or its functional equivalent) is a state's key figure with respect to its foreign affairs. He or she is in charge of the foreign service, holds talks and negotiations, supervises the drafting of foreign policy acts and execution of international agreements, and generally safeguards the interests of the state and its nationals abroad. His or her acts and statements ***are binding upon the state***, and other countries need not inquire into his or her actual authority.

D. Diplomatic agents: Diplomatic agents are persons empowered to represent a state in a foreign state or in an international organization. Every sovereign state has the right to send and receive diplomats. In the case of a federal state, that right is reserved for the central government.

1. **Types of diplomats:** Regular diplomats are permanent representatives in foreign states. Extraordinary diplomats serve temporarily to carry out a special mission, usually in connection with international congresses, international conferences, and sessions of international organizations.

2. **Heads of mission:** Heads of mission are technically divided into three classes (ambassadors or *nuncios*; envoys, ministers, or internuncios; and *charges d'affaires*), but the only distinctions that can be drawn on the basis of class relate to precedence and etiquette.

3. **Diplomatic corps:** Traditionally, the diplomatic corps in a state consisted only of all the heads of missions, but the modern trend is to include all diplomats.

4. **Appointment of a diplomatic mission:** Permanent diplomatic relations are established by an international agreement followed by the exchange of diplomatic representatives. *Agreement* is the term signifying ***a state's consent to the foreign state's appointment of a head of mission***, as well as the appointment of military, naval, and air attaches. Following receipt of the agreement, there is a formal ceremony in which the new head of mission presents a document called the letters of credence. The letters of credence includes the nature of his or her appointment, his or her name, the subject matter of the particular mission, and an expression of the desire to foster good relations.

5. **Diplomatic immunities and privileges:** From ancient times to the present, diplomats have had an ***independent and specially protected status***. The privileges and immunities of diplomats have been established both as a matter of customary law and treaty law. The immunities and privileges apply only from the moment the diplomat enters the host country and only for the period in which he or she is, in fact, a diplomat. For discussion of diplomatic immunity, *see* Chapter 5, §V(C)(2).

6. **Termination of a diplomatic mission:** Diplomatic missions with a particular purpose are terminated with the completion of that job. Diplomatic agents in more permanently established missions generally serve for a specific term, but their tour of duty may be cut short by death, recall, or request by the host country.

E. Consuls: Consuls are authorized to protect the interests of their state in a foreign state with respect to administrative, legal, economic, and cultural affairs. Consuls generally have no political function and are therefore distinguished from diplomats, who do have a political function. However, a consul may take on a political role if serving in a foreign state in which his or her state has no diplomatic mission. A common and important function of consuls is to oversee the growth of trade and economic, scientific, and cultural relations between the two states. The consul is also charged with administrative duties such as the issuance of passports, visas, and other travel documents.

Consulars ***enjoy immunities and privileges***, but to a lesser extent than do diplomats. For a comparison of the immunities and privileges of consuls and diplomats, *see* Chapter 5, §V(C)(4).

F. Officials of international organizations: The proliferation of international organizations following World War II has given rise to increasing numbers of international officials. The status of these officials is regulated by treaties, such as the U.N. Charter and the U.N. Convention on Privileges and Immunities, setting forth applicable privileges and immunities. *See* Chapter 5, §V(D) (discussing the immunities granted to international organizations).

Exam Tips on *STATES*

- The four generally accepted requirements of the Montevideo Convention for what constitutes a state are easily stated but not easily applied. For example, is Kosovo a state? It may have a defined territory (which Serbia disputes) and a permanent population (although shifting due to the political situation). Does it have its own controlling government? The Albanian representatives of Kosovo would certainly argue that it does, but Serbia contends that, despite the conflict there, Kosovo is and has been under the control of the Serbian government and is a part of its territory. Does Kosovo have the capacity to enter into international relations with other states? The fact that a number of states, including the United States, recognized it as a state upon its declaration of independence helps in that regard but is not determinative. The insurgency in Libya during the early months of 2011 presents an equally delicate problem if antigovernment forces effectuate a successful secession in some regions of the country but leave the current dictator in charge over the remainder.
- Note also that the U.N. Security Council, in its enforcement powers under chapter VII of its charter, may require other states to recognize or not recognize a particular state or government.
- For recognition of both states and governments, keep in mind that most states view recognition as discretionary. Even if the legal requirements are clearly met, a state may choose not to recognize in order to express its disapproval of the state or government on some level.
- Finally, consider how effective collective sanctions have been in recent years for breaches of international obligations: Can such sanctions ever replace the use of armed force if the issue is of paramount importance (*e.g.*, development of nuclear weapons)?

CHAPTER 5

STATE JURISDICTION

I. DEFINITION OF JURISDICTION

Jurisdiction can be defined as ***the authority to affect legal interests***. More specifically under international law, jurisdiction is understood to be the allocation of power and authority among the states.

A. Types of jurisdiction: Three interdependent types of jurisdiction are recognized:

- the right to prescribe or apply laws to persons and activities;
- the right to enforce those laws through application of sanctions; and
- the power of courts to exercise jurisdiction over a particular person or object.

B. Civil and criminal jurisdiction: International law in this context is most important for the restrictions it imposes on state jurisdiction over criminal matters. International law appears to impose few, if any, restraints on a state's exercise of civil jurisdiction other than sovereign and diplomatic immunity. As stated in *S.S. "Lotus" (Fr. v. Turk.)* [1927] P.C.I.J. (ser. A) No. 10 at 21:

> Far from laying down a general prohibition to the effect that States may not extend the application of their laws and the jurisdiction of their courts to persons, property, and acts outside their territory, it leaves them in this respect a wide measure of discretion which is only limited in certain cases by prohibitive rules; as regards other cases, every State remains free to adopt the principles which it regards as best and most suitable.

The comments to the Restatement (Fourth) of the Foreign Relations Law of the United States, however, say that its limitations on jurisdiction apply to civil as well as criminal jurisdiction.

C. Extraterritorial jurisdiction: A topic of much controversy in international law is the exercise of extraterritorial legislative jurisdiction. The extraterritorial claim of jurisdiction by the United States in antitrust and drug enforcement, for example, is very contentious.

II. INTERNATIONAL JURISDICTIONAL PRINCIPLES

International jurisdictional principles are concerned primarily with a state's right to prescribe or enforce its laws. Five bases for such jurisdiction with respect to crimes are recognized. It is a widely accepted principle of international law that ***the exercise of jurisdiction on any basis must be reasonable***.

A. The territorial principle: The territorial principle is a fundamental and universally accepted basis for jurisdiction, the principle being that *an essential attribute of a state's sovereignty is to have jurisdiction over all persons and objects within its territory.*

1. **"Pure" territoriality:** The pure territoriality principle is applied when acts or offenses ***are commenced within the state's territory***, regardless of whether they were also concluded or consummated there. This principle of jurisdiction is particularly applicable to conspiracies to commit crimes in foreign states.

2. **"Objective" territoriality:** The objective territoriality principle is applied to offenses or acts commenced outside the state's territory but completed within the state's territory; or causing serious and harmful consequences to the social and economic order within the state's territory.

Example: The *Lotus* case is often cited for recognition in international law of the principle of objective territoriality. Negligence occurring on board a French ship, the *Lotus*, had the effect of causing injury on the Turkish ship (a "piece" of Turkish territory). *See also United States v. Aluminum Co. of America*, 148 F.2d 416 (2d Cir. 1945).

3. **The "effects" doctrine in U.S. law:** American federal courts and the Restatement (Fourth) have adopted a broad interpretation of the objective territoriality principle based upon effects within a state's territory. Jurisdiction is sometimes exercised ***on the basis of reprehensible effects or consequences alone, no matter how minimal or attenuated***. Such broad claims to jurisdiction have been criticized by many states and may be contrary to international law in allowing a state's territorial jurisdiction to be virtually limitless.

   Example: The Central District of Illinois held that the Major Fraud Act applies extraterritorially because the United States was the ultimate payer of the subcontract underlying the alleged fraud, and therefore the actions of the defendants amounted to theft from the U.S. Treasury. The court determined it was reasonable for the United States to have jurisdiction because the United States has a right to protect itself against crimes committed against it, and the exercise of jurisdiction did not infringe upon the sovereignty of the locations where the fraud occurred. *United States v. Hijazi*, 845 F. Supp. 2d 874 (C.D. Ill. 2011).

B. **Active nationality principle based on nationality of the defendant:** The state of a person against whom proceedings are taking place may exercise jurisdiction based *on the nationality of the defendant*.

1. **Nationality of individuals:** The right of states ***to regulate the conduct of their nationals everywhere and thus assert nationality as a basis for jurisdiction is widely accepted***. International law requires that a state must have a ***genuine link with the person*** to assert jurisdiction based on nationality. *Nottebohm (Liech. v. Guat.)*, 1955 I.C.J. 4 (Apr. 6). Nationality is otherwise a question of each state's domestic law, and jurisdictional conflicts often arise when a person is a national of more than one state.

   a. **U.S. law:** U.S. law, for example, confers citizenship on every legitimate child born abroad, even when only one parent is a U.S. citizen, but requires illegitimate children born abroad to an American father and alien mother to prove a biological and personal relationship with the father. 8 U.S.C. §1409(a). This determination of nationality was unsuccessfully challenged on equal protection grounds. *Miller v. Christopher*, 96 F.3d 1467 (D.C. Cir 1996), *cert. granted and aff'd sub nom. Miller v. Albright*, 523 U.S. 420 (1998).

2. **Nationality of corporations:** Jurisdiction based on the nationality of corporations is controversial because the "nationality" of a corporation is also determined in different ways by different states. Nationality may be determined by state of incorporation, by the location of the principal place of business, or by the nationality of those owning or controlling the corporation.

3. **Nationality of vessels:** The nationality of a vessel is determined by the flag it flies, but international law requires a "genuine link" between the vessel and the state. Article 5 of the 1958 Convention on the High Seas and article 91 of the 1982 Law of the Sea Convention.

4. **Nationality of aircraft and spacecraft:** The nationality of an aircraft is determined by its place of registration under the 1944 Chicago Convention on International Civil Aviation. The state of registration may be changed, but registration may not exist in more than one state at a time. A spacecraft likewise is under the jurisdiction of the state in which it is registered under article 8 of the Outer Space Treaty.

5. **Extent of the territory to which jurisdiction applies:** The applicable territory to be used as a basis for exercising jurisdiction includes the land within the state's boundaries, the coastal zones as specified in the law of the sea, and the airspace above the lands and territorial waters.

C. **Protective principle:** A state may exercise jurisdiction over crimes ***that threaten its security and integrity or its vital economic interests***. The reasoning behind the protective principle is that an offense may have extremely grave consequences in one state, but it may otherwise go unpunished if the state where the offense was actually committed does not itself consider the conduct to be unlawful. The objection to this basis for jurisdiction is that it is subject to abuse, with each state free to determine what crimes threaten its security. The Restatement (Fourth) limits protective jurisdiction to conduct generally recognized as criminal by states in the international community. Crimes generally recognized as being detrimental to a state's interests and within protective jurisdiction include espionage, counterfeiting a state seal or currency, and violations of immigration or customs laws.

D. **Universality principle:** The international community considers some offenses ***to be so serious that they are subject to the jurisdiction of all states***. Crimes clearly subject to universal jurisdiction are piracy on the high seas, slave trading, and war crimes. *See United States v. Dire*, 680 F.3d 446 (4th Cir. 2012). U.S. law and multilateral conventions also treat torture, genocide, aircraft piracy, some criminal acts against diplomats, and other crimes as subject to universal jurisdiction. It is unclear, however, whether customary international law recognizes these and other crimes as universal crimes. *See generally Demjanjuk v. Petrovsky*, 776 F.2d 571 (6th Cir. 1985), *cert. denied*, 475 U.S. 1016 (1986) (war crimes and crimes against humanity); *Filartiga v. Pena-Irala*, 630 F.2d 876 (2d Cir. 1980) (torture is a universal crime).

Example: The D.C. Circuit and Fourth Circuit both found criminal jurisdiction over drug traffickers who aided and abetted piracies on the high seas even though the traffickers' actions occurred solely on land and in territorial waters. *See United States v. Carvajal*, 924 F. Supp. 2d 219 (D.C. Cir. 2013).

E. **Passive personality principle based on nationality of the victim:** An injured person's state may assert *the victim's nationality as a basis for exercising jurisdiction*. This principle is not widely accepted for ordinary crimes, so that the principle often overlaps with jurisdiction predicated on universal crimes.

F. **Jurisdiction based on agreement:** In addition to the five basic principles of jurisdiction, there exists the possibility that ***states can confer jurisdiction through international agreements***. The Restatement (Fourth) provides that a state has jurisdiction to prescribe and enforce a rule of law in the territory of another state to the extent provided by international agreement with the other state.

1. **Example of agreement-based jurisdiction:** An example of such an agreement exists between Cuba and the United States with respect to Guantanamo. The United States recognizes Cuba's continuing "ultimate sovereignty" over the leased area, but Cuba conferred upon the United States "complete jurisdiction and control over and within" the leased areas.

2. **Armed forces:** Jurisdiction over the armed forces taking part in the North Atlantic Treaty Organization (NATO) is also determined by a series of multilateral and bilateral treaties.

G. **Conflicts of state jurisdiction:** The various bases of jurisdiction frequently result in overlapping state jurisdiction. Although the problem is somewhat mitigated by the requirement of reasonableness in asserting jurisdiction, the possibility of conflicts remains. *See* §IV(A)(2) of this chapter, *infra*; *F. Hoffman–La Roche Ltd. v. Empagran S.A.*, 542 U.S. 155 (2004) (citing with approval the reasonableness test of the Restatement (Fourth) of Foreign Relations Law of the U.S. §403).

III. EXTRADITION

Extradition is the ***process by which an individual charged or convicted of a serious crime in one state (the requisitioning state) and found in a second state (the asylum state) is returned to the requisitioning state for trial or punishment***. Extradition arises from bilateral and multilateral treaties and many issues of extradition are matters of treaty interpretation.

A. Obligation to extradite: In the absence of a treaty, there is ***no obligation to extradite***. A state may volunteer to extradite an individual without the existence of a treaty but is obliged to extradite only by the terms of a treaty. The practice of the United States and the general modern trend are to disallow extradition in the absence of an applicable treaty.

B. Extraditable offenses: Treaties employ one of two methods for specifying the grounds for extradition. The treaty may rely solely on the requirement of double criminality, or it may list the indictable offenses for which extradition is available. In either case, treaties often prohibit extradition if prosecution of the offender would be barred in either state by the statute of limitations.

1. **Double criminality:** Treaties often provide that extradition is available for any conduct that is an offense in both the requisitioning state and the asylum state punishable by a specified minimum term of imprisonment.

   Example: In December 2010, Julian Assange, founder of the WikiLeaks Web site, surrendered to British authorities in response to a Swedish extradition request for sexual offenses. Mr. Assange fought extradition on the grounds that the extradition was politically discriminatory, based on insufficient evidence, and effectuated to allow the United States to extradite and indict him on charges related to the release of sensitive and classified national security information by WikiLeaks. The substantive weight of his arguments was less than the media interest. The U.K. court found that there was sufficient preliminary evidence based on several victims' testimony that there had been a violation of Swedish law, which satisfied the requirements of "dual criminality" under the treaty between Sweden and the United Kingdom, that Sweden's prosecution of these criminal charges was not politically discriminatory but based on evidence provided by multiple witnesses that established a preliminary case of such violations under Swedish law, and that extradition from Sweden to the United States would be determined by a separate extradition treaty if and when the United States should seek extradition.

2. **List of extraditable offenses:** A second method of listing extraditable offenses has fallen into disfavor because it is considered clumsy and results in treaties being outdated as new crimes emerge.

C. Nationals of the asylum state: State treaties sometimes provide that a state may not or cannot extradite its own nationals. A consequence of the latter type of treaty is that criminals may escape punishment altogether if their own state fails to prosecute them. Some treaties with such an exception obligate the asylum state to prosecute its own nationals for the crime if it refuses to extradite.

D. Process of requesting extradition: Although the process of requesting extradition varies, there are common characteristics. Requests for extradition are often initiated along diplomatic channels. The request is then subject to a judicial determination followed by consideration in the executive branch, which has some discretion in the final determination.

1. **Role of U.S. secretary of state:** A 1996 case reaffirmed the final power of extradition of an individual from the United States to be in the ***sole discretion of the secretary of state***. *Lobue v. Christopher*, 82 F.3d 1081 (D.C. Cir. 1996). However, the court found that the statute, which purported to give executive branch officials the power to review legal decisions of Article 3 judges, was unconstitutional.
2. **Necessity of proof that an individual has been "charged" with a crime:** In 2009, the Second Circuit held that the arrest warrant issued by a Bosnian court did not satisfy the requirement for proof that a U.S. citizen had been "charged" with a crime because the issuing court was no longer able to enforce its arrest warrant. The extradition treaty between Bosnia and the United States expressly required a "warrant of arrest" as proof that one of the country's citizens had been charged with an extraditable crime. Because the court that issued the warrant, at the time of the extradition request, lacked jurisdiction (due to constitutional reorganization within the former states of Yugoslavia) to investigate the alleged crimes and could not enforce the arrest warrant, the treaty's requirements were not fulfilled. Without being "charged" within the meaning of the treaty, the petitioner received habeas corpus relief from the court. *Sacirbey v. Guccione*, 589 F.3d 52 (2d Cir. 2009).

E. Standard treaty limitations on extradition: Extradition treaties may include exceptions under which extradition by the asylum state is not required.

1. **Discrimination:** Extradition will not be granted if it would subject the fugitive to prosecution based on race, nationality, political opinion, or other similar grounds that would prejudice the process.
2. **Lack of probable cause:** The request for extradition must include sufficient *prima facie* evidence of guilt attributable to the fugitive whose extradition is sought. This limitation is commonly found in treaties of English-speaking states. More generally, extradition does not apply to persons merely suspected of having committed an offense. Nor may extradition be utilized to obtain a person's presence as a witness or for the purpose of enforcing a civil judgment.
3. **Political offenses:** Most treaties today exempt from extradition political offenses in either mandatory or discretionary terms. The exemption for political offenses is widely accepted by non-socialist states but the term itself is subject to several interpretations. While there is no generally agreed-upon definition of political offenses, there are a few offenses that are generally recognized as not being political offenses, such as assassination of heads of state, war crimes, and genocide.
   a. **Purely political offenses:** Purely political offenses are acts directed against the state that lack the essential characteristics of a common crime. Examples are treason, sedition, rebellion, and espionage. Such acts are done with the purpose of damaging a political regime.
   b. **Related political offenses:** Related political offenses are common crimes motivated by political goals. There are three approaches to related political offenses, requiring varying degrees of connection between the crime and the political act.
      i. **The "political incidence" approach (the Anglo-American approach):** This approach requires the criminal offense to be committed in the course of a dispute between a governing party and another party with political aims. The motive and purpose of the crime must be to further the aims of the party. Application of the test in U.S. courts has been inconsistent. *Compare Eain v. Wilkes*, 641 F.2d 504 (7th Cir.), *cert. denied*, 454 U.S. 894 (1981) (granting extradition of PLO member for marketplace bombing) with *Matter of Mackin*, 668 F.2d 122 (2d Cir. 1981) (denying extradition

of IRA member for attempted murder of British soldier), and *Quinn v. Robinson*, 783 F.2d 776 (9th Cir.), *cert. denied*, 479 U.S. 882 (1986) (granting extradition of IRA member for murder of London police constable because relevant political uprising was in Northern Ireland, not Great Britain).

ii. **The "political objective" approach (the Franco-Belgian approach):** Under this approach, the means used to achieve the political objective may not be unlimited; the means used must relate to the political objective; and a degree of proportionality must exist between the political objective and the crime for which extradition is sought.

iii. **The "predominant motive" approach (the Swiss approach):** This approach demands a close and direct link between the crime and the political act, thus making it more likely for a fugitive to be extradited. A crime is a political offense if it was committed in the course of preparing to perpetrate a purely political offense; there must be a direct link between the act and the political goal; and the common law criminal element must be proportional to the political goal.

iv. **Treaty exceptions for acts of terrorism:** The trend in extradition treaties is to exempt acts of terrorism as defined by the treaty from treatment as political offenses, and thus require extradition for such acts. Such exceptions have been recognized in bilateral treaties (*e.g.*, the 1985 Supplementary Extradition Treaty between the United States and the United Kingdom) and in regional treaties (*e.g.*, the European Convention on Suppression of Terrorism). Use of this exception in extradition treaties has been criticized, particularly when done on a state-by-state basis (thus singling out certain political movements for less favorable extradition treatment) and when the extraditable offenses are broadly defined to include crimes against military and other non-civilian targets.

4. **Doctrine of specialty:** The requisitioning nation cannot prosecute the extradited person for offenses other than those stated as the grounds for extradition. American extradition treaties expressly include such a provision, and the Supreme Court has also ruled that the doctrine of specialty may be implied from the "manifest scope and object of the treaty."

   a. **Re-extradition to a third state:** The doctrine of specialty may also prevent a state from extraditing the accused to a third state without first offering him or her the "right to return."

   b. **Exceptions:** The requisitioning state may prosecute the extradited person for offenses committed after extradition. Other offenses committed before extradition may also be prosecuted if the accused first has a reasonable opportunity to depart the country.

5. **Territorial jurisdiction:** Extradition treaties often rely on the principle of territorial jurisdiction so that the crime for which extradition is being requested must have been committed within the territorial jurisdiction of the requisitioning state. Difficulties often arise when a state is requesting extradition based on non-territorial jurisdictional grounds.

6. **Other non-extraditable crimes:** A mandatory or discretionary exception for crimes of a religious, fiscal, or military nature is often included.

F. **Methods employed to avoid the safeguards of extradition treaties:** Two principal methods are used to avoid the safeguards of extradition treaties: ***deportation*** and ***abduction***. In addition, the practice of ***extraordinary rendition*** has provoked considerable controversy in recent years in the context of the U.S. global war on terror.

1. **Deportation (also referred to as "disguised extradition"):** A potential asylum state may avoid the terms of an extradition treaty by either denying the fugitive permission to enter the state initially or by deportation as an undesirable alien.

2. **Abduction:** States occasionally recover fugitives by abduction from the asylum state. Although abduction is generally considered an affront to the sovereignty of the asylum state and widely considered a violation of individual human rights, U.S. courts nevertheless accept jurisdiction of defendants brought before them by such illegal means. *See, e.g., Ker v. Illinois*, 119 U.S. 436 (1886) (kidnapping by non-governmental party); *United States v. Alvarez-Machain*, 504 U.S. 655 (1992) (kidnapping by government agents). Illegal recovery of a fugitive, however, will not be ignored by U.S. courts if the abduction, in addition to being illegal, was performed in a violent, brutal, and inhumane manner. *See United States v. Toscanino*, 500 F.2d 267 (2d Cir. 1974).

3. **Extraordinary rendition:** While *rendition* is a general term for "handing over" individuals to a foreign nation, *extraordinary rendition* refers to the extrajudicial capture and transport of terrorism suspects abroad for interrogation. Several cases have arisen in which terrorism suspects claim they were detained by the CIA and transported, in violation of the Convention Against Torture, to countries that are known to practice torture. A highly publicized example involved a Syrian-born Canadian citizen who was mistakenly identified as a terrorist at JFK Airport and deported by the United States to Syria. There, he was imprisoned for nearly a year and tortured during interrogations before being cleared of wrongdoing and returned to Canada. Canada has apologized for the provision of faulty information that led to the man's deportation. *See* Commission of Inquiry into the Actions of Canadian Officials in Relation to Maher Arar, *Report of the Events Relating to Maher Arar* (2006), accessed April 10, 2016 at www.sirc-csars.gc.ca/pdfs/cm_arar__bgv-eng.pdf. In 2009, the Court of Appeals for the Second Circuit ruled that Arar could not sue officials involved in his rendition for civil damages because such suits have not been congressionally authorized.

IV. JURISDICTIONAL PRINCIPLES IN U.S. LAW

A. **The role of international law:** The jurisdictional principles of international law and U.S. domestic law affect one another and may be limiting factors on one another. The international law principles of jurisdiction, *see* §II of this chapter, *supra*, sometimes restrict the exercise of national jurisdiction. Conversely, U.S. due process considerations of fairness expressed by tests such as "minimum contacts" and "purposeful availment" may place restrictions on jurisdiction that would be acceptable under international law.

1. **Federal legislation:** Courts may also be confronted with conflicts between customary international law principles of jurisdiction and federal legislation. Article VI of the U.S. Constitution makes federal legislation binding upon the courts. U.S. courts have upheld federal legislation even when it causes the courts to violate international law jurisdictional principles. *United States v. Aluminum Co. of America*, 148 F.2d 416 (2d Cir. 1945); *The Over the Top*, 5 F.2d 838 (D. Conn. 1925). U.S. courts do try, however, to interpret federal legislation consistently with the international principles of jurisdiction. *Murray v. Schooner Charming Betsy*, 6 U.S. (2 Cranch) 64 (1804). More recently, the Supreme Court has shown a willingness to interpret provisions of international agreements in accordance with its determinations of the interests and expectations of treaty partners of the United States. *See, e.g., Abbott v. Abbott*, 560 U.S. 1 (2010).

2. **Conflicts of laws:** Conflicts between domestic courts may arise over which state should exercise jurisdiction over a dispute, which state's law should apply, and whether to enforce a judgment of a foreign court. Conflict of laws, sometimes referred to as *private international law*, is not really part of public international law at all. Each state has developed its own legal rules as a matter of comity to resolve such conflicts, and therefore this section addresses only U.S. law governing conflicts.

B. **U.S. grounds for jurisdiction:** U.S. courts rely on several bases to assert jurisdiction.

1. **The "conduct" and "effects" tests in U.S. law for claiming jurisdiction:** Under the widely accepted "pure" territorial principle, §II(A)(1) of this chapter, *supra*, U.S. law is applied to ***conduct taking place on U.S. territory***, regardless of where the effects are felt. In looking to the place of conduct, the Fifth Circuit has held there to be no subject matter jurisdiction under the Federal Tort Claims Act for the tort of conversion of watercolor paintings by the U.S. Army when that conversion took place in Germany. *Price v. United States*, 69 F.3d 46 (5th Cir. 1995), *cert. denied*, 117 S. Ct. 295 (1996).

   The controversial effects test of U.S. law, *see* §II(A)(3) of this chapter, *supra*, is an extension of the objective territoriality principle. The effects test has been applied in antitrust, securities trading, export controls, and environmental protection, with U.S. courts finding that conduct between foreign companies on foreign soil could nevertheless subject them to U.S. jurisdiction if there are effects in the United States (*Timberlane Lumber Co. v. Bank of America Nat'l Trust & Saving Ass'n*, 549 F.2d 597 (9th Cir. 1976)), and perhaps even if only an intent to affect U.S. trade is shown. *United States v. Aluminum Co. of America*, 148 F.2d 416 (2d Cir. 1945).

2. **The protective principle in U.S. law:** U.S. courts rely mostly on the territorial basis for jurisdiction but have applied the protective principle of international law for jurisdiction in a few cases. The protective principle is recognized in the Restatement (Fourth) §402, which states that:

   > Subject to §403, a state has jurisdiction to prescribe law with respect to...certain conduct outside of its territory by persons not its nationals that is directed against the security of the state or against a limited class of other state interests.

   The Comments give as examples "espionage, counterfeiting of the state's seal or currency, falsification of official documents, as well as perjury before consular officials, and conspiracy to violate the immigration or customs laws."

C. **Conflict of laws under U.S. law:** Several states may have grounds for jurisdiction of a single case. *Comity* is the term used to describe ***judicial restraint practiced in order to avoid or resolve such conflicts*** of jurisdiction. It is not a hard-and-fast rule of law but rather stems from the notion that a state should treat others as it would wish to be treated. Comity has been used by U.S. courts to refuse jurisdiction in deference to another state. For purposes of comity, however, no conflict exists where a person subject to regulation by both the United States and a foreign state can comply with the rules of both. *Hartford Fire Insurance Co. v. California*, 509 U.S. 764 (1993).

In addition, the United States should not interfere with the laws of another sovereign regarding conduct occurring within its territory. *Denty v. SmithKline Beecham Corp.*, 907 F. Supp. 879, 882 (E.D. Pa. 1995). Lack of reciprocity, on the other hand, has been used to justify a refusal to enforce a foreign court's judgment. In determining whether jurisdiction should be exercised, the Restatement (Fourth) lists as factors to be balanced: the ***vital national interests*** of each state; ***nationality*** of the persons subject to concurrent jurisdiction; ability to ***enforce*** the judgment; the extent to which the required conduct is to take place ***in another state***; ***hardship*** to the parties from possibly conflicting national decisions; the existence of ***justified expectations***; and ***consistency*** with international traditions. The Restatement (Fourth) also concludes that customary international law requires jurisdiction to be exercised only in a reasonable manner with deference to another state if its interests are clearly greater, although it has been widely questioned whether customary international law does impose such a limitation.

1. ***Forum non conveniens*:** The doctrine of *forum non conveniens*, an exercise of comity, is an often-utilized method for settling problems of concurrent jurisdiction. It is defined by the Restatement (Second) of Conflict of Laws §84: "A state will not exercise jurisdiction if it is a seriously inconvenient forum for the trial of the action provided that a more appropriate forum is available to the plaintiff." The Supreme Court has stated that *forum non conveniens* determinations should be at "the sound discretion of the trial court," balancing "all relevant public and private interest factors." *Piper Aircraft Co. v. Reyno*, 454 U.S. 235 (1981); *see also In re Union Carbide Corporation Gas Plant Disaster at Bhopal*, 809 F.2d 195 (2d Cir. 1987), *cert. denied sub nom. Executive Committee Members v. Unions of India*, 484 U.S. 871 (1987) (upholding district court judgment as revised that Union Carbide must submit itself to the jurisdiction of Indian courts because all relevant events had taken place in India and the public interests of India were much greater than the public interests of the United States). *But see Simon v. Republic of Hungary*, 911 F.3d 1172, 1190 (D.C. Cir. 2018) ("While we accord respectful deference to district courts' *forum non conveniens* determinations, we do not rubber stamp them.").
2. **Reciprocity distinguished:** U.S. courts have refused to enforce proper foreign judgments on the grounds that the foreign states have failed to give effect to U.S. judgments. *See, e.g., Hilton v. Guyot*, 159 U.S. 113 (1895). This reciprocity requirement for enforcement of a foreign judgment, generally disfavored today, is more a political tool than a legal principle.
3. **Sovereign compulsion:** The sovereign compulsion defense is designed to prevent unfairness to private parties subject to the conflicting commands of several states. The defense most often has been applied in situations when production of foreign-based documents in a court proceeding would violate the law of the foreign state in which they are located. The Restatement (Fourth) of Foreign Relations §441, entitled "Foreign State Compulsion," gives further guidelines for resolving conflicting demands on parties, stating that:
   a. A person generally may not be required by a state
      i. to do an act in another state that is prohibited by the law of that state or by the law of the state of which he is a national; or
      ii. to refrain from doing an act in another state that is required by the law of that state or by the law of the state of which he is a national.
   b. A person of foreign nationality may generally be required by a state
      i. to do an act in that state even if it is prohibited by the law of the state of which he is a national; or
      ii. to refrain from doing an act in that state even if it is required by the law of the state of which he is a national.

V. IMMUNITIES FROM JURISDICTION

Both international law and municipal law grant immunities from jurisdiction. Municipal laws can create additional immunities not existing under international law, but municipal law restrictions on the immunities granted by international law may result in violations by the state of its international obligations. Of the three types of jurisdiction (legislative, judicial, and enforcement), the subject of immunities is most concerned with judicial and enforcement jurisdiction. However, the view is widely accepted that denial of immunity from judicial jurisdiction also implies denial of immunity from legislative jurisdiction.

A. **Sovereign immunity:** States are generally not subject to the jurisdiction of other states.

1. **Absolute theory:** Until about 1900, a state's immunities were very broad. Absolute immunity is based on the notion that all sovereign states are equal and are not subject to each other's authority. *The Schooner Exchange v. M'Faddon*, 11 U.S. 116 (1812). Even absolute immunity did not extend to litigation involving a state's interest in property or other immovables abroad, or its interests in the administration of an estate in a foreign state's territory.

2. **Restrictive theory:** The modern view holds that a state may be subject to a foreign jurisdiction when it engages in commercial activity. A distinction is made between "commercial" activity or property (*acta gestionis*) and "public" activity or property (*acta imperii*). The United States first adopted the restrictive theory in 1952 in the so-called Tate letter from the State Department to the Justice Department.

   a. **Approach of third-world states:** The approach of the former Soviet Union and various third-world states was to adhere to the absolute theory. Although the absolute theory was espoused, in actual practice the communist states concluded international agreements allowing their trade missions to be subject to foreign jurisdiction.

   b. **"Nature" test and "purpose" test:** One of two tests is employed to determine whether a state's activity is a commercial activity. Some states look to the nature of the activity, while others consider the purpose of the activity. For example, under the "nature" test, a state-owned bank extending credits to encourage investment in its country is engaged in a commercial activity. Under the "purpose" test, however, the activity may be regarded as governmental because the bank's activities are serving a public policy interest.

   c. **Exceptions:** In addition to the "commercial exception," modern law supports the traditional denial of immunity for claims to property or other immovables acquired by gift of succession, as well as claims in non-commercial torts cases.

   d. **Convention on Jurisdictional Immunities:** The U.N. General Assembly adopted in 2004 the U.N. Convention on Jurisdictional Immunities of States and Their Property. Only a few states have signed the convention, so state immunity continues to be governed primarily by the national law of every state.

3. **Foreign Sovereign Immunities Act (FSIA):** The Foreign Sovereign Immunities Act (FSIA) of 1976 essentially codified the restrictive theory of immunity.

4. **Exceptions to immunity:** A state is presumptively immune unless an exception applies. Immunity does not apply under the following statutory exceptions: waivers of immunity, commercial activities, expropriation claims, property claims, non-commercial torts, maritime liens, counterclaims, and international agreements. The party claiming immunity bears the burden of demonstrating that no exception applies. *Arango v. Guzman Travel Advisors Corp.*, 621 F.2d

1371 (5th Cir. 1980); *Diaz Aguasviva v. Iberia Lineas Aereas de Espana*, 902 F. Supp. 314 (D.P.R. 1995).

a. Jurisdiction through application of FSIA: Jurisdiction over a foreign state in federal or state courts of the United States may be obtained only through application of FSIA. *Argentine Republic v. Amerada Hess Shipping Corp.*, 488 U.S. 428 (1989). "Foreign state" is defined under FSIA to include its political subdivisions (including local governments), agencies, and instrumentalities. Agency or instrumentality is in turn defined as a separate legal entity that is either an organ of or owned by a foreign state and that is neither a citizen of one of the United States or of any third nation. F.S.I.A. §1603(b). In 2010, the Supreme Court held that an individual foreign government official is not entitled to immunity from suit as a "foreign state" within the statutory meaning of FSIA for conduct undertaken in his or her official individual capacity. *Samantar v. Yousuf*, 560 U.S. 305 (2010).

i. "Agency or instrumentality": The phrase "agency or instrumentality" of the FSIA has not been given overly broad interpretation by U.S. courts. F.S.I.A. §1605(b). The Supreme Court has held that a corporate entity can claim instrumentality status only if owned directly by a foreign state and not by an intermediate subsidiary. *Dole Food Company v. Patrickson*, 538 U.S. 468 (2003). However, property owned through an instrumentality or a subsidiary of an instrumentality is attachable to a judgment. *Heiser v. Islamic Republic of Iran*, 885 F. Supp. 2d 429 (2012). In addition, the Second Circuit has denied instrumentality status to entities that are subsidiaries of, but are not themselves, state organs. *Filler v. Hanvit Bank*, 378 F.3d 213 (2d Cir. 2004).

Example: In a state action by its employees over injuries from chemical exposure, Dole Food Company impleaded the Dead Sea Companies, which sought removal to federal court, claiming to be an instrumentality of the state of Israel under the FSIA. The U.S. Supreme Court held that the Dead Sea Companies were not an instrumentality because they were at all times owned not directly by Israel, but by one or more intermediate subsidiaries; only directly owned corporate entities could claim instrumentality status under the FSIA. *Dole Food Company v. Patrickson*, 538 U.S. 468 (2003).

Example: Chohung Bank and Hanvit Bank, both commercial banks headquartered in Seoul, were allegedly involved in a multibillion dollar fraud perpetrated by a Belgian software company. Investors who had suffered significant losses as a result of their investment in the Belgian company sued both banks. Chohung was a subsidiary and Hanvit was a second-tier subsidiary of the Korean Deposit Insurance Corporation, a governmental institution, and as such, they claimed sovereign immunity as state instrumentalities under the FSIA. The Second Circuit ruled that the two banks were not entitled to sovereign immunity because they were subsidiaries of, but not themselves, state organs. *Filler v. Hanvit Bank*, 378 F.3d 213 (2d Cir. 2004).

b. Waivers of immunity: Waivers of immunity may be explicit or implicit and may not be withdrawn except in a manner consistent with the original terms of the waiver. F.S.I.A. §1605(a)(1). Explicit waivers occur as a result of treaties or contacts with private parties, and waiver may be implied from a state's conduct. Common examples of conduct implying a waiver are the filing of a general appearance, signing of arbitration clauses, forum-selection clauses, choice-of-law clauses, and assertion of counterclaims.

Example: A U.S. court ruled that a foreign state's immunity under pre-1996 FSIA is not impliedly waived by its alleged participation in actions that violated fundamental norms of international law or by its alleged guaranty of any damages judgment against its alleged agents. *Smith v. Socialist People's Libyan Arab Jamahiriya*, 101 F.3d 239 (2d Cir. 1996), *cert. denied*, 520 U.S. 1204 (1997). In addition, the suit did not fall within FSIA exception for occurrences on U.S. "territory" when the alleged tortious conduct was the sabotage of a U.S. aircraft abroad.

c. **Commercial activities:** The FSIA codifies the commercial exception to immunity, denying immunity in any case "in which the action is based upon a commercial activity. . . ." The commercial activity must either be carried on in the United States or have a direct effect in the United States. F.S.I.A. §1605(a)(2). The act defines "commercial activity" as a "regular course of commercial conduct or a particular commercial transaction or act," with the nature of the activity, rather than its purpose, determining characterization as either a commercial or public/governmental activity. F.S.I.A. §1603(d). *Dominican Energy Ltd. v. Dominican Republic*, 903 F. Supp. 1507 (M.D. Fla. 1995) (stating that a "direct effect" must be more than mere financial loss suffered in the United States).

- Examples of commercial activity are purchasing supplies and equipment for its armed forces, issuing letters of credit, and contracting for repairs on embassy buildings.
- Activities considered non-commercial are those arising from a state's mere participation in foreign assistance programs of organizations such as the Agency for International Development (A.I.D.).
- "Commercial activity carried on in the United States" is in turn defined as commercial activity "carried on by such state and having substantial contact with the United States." F.S.I.A. §1603(e). In *Saudi Arabia v. Nelson*, 507 U.S. 349 (1993), a U.S. citizen sued Saudi Arabia, alleging that he was tortiously detained and tortured for a critical report he had written as an employee of a government-controlled hospital. The Court concluded that his suit was not "based upon" his employment but upon the tortious conduct and that the tortious conduct itself was not "commercial activity."
- When a foreign government acts as a private player within a market and not simply a regulator, the actions of the foreign government are "commercial" under the FSIA. In *Argentina v. Weltover, Inc.*, 504 U.S. 607 (1992), the government of Argentina issued government bonds payable in U.S. dollars in New York to creditors in order to refinance debts that it owed. Argentina lacked the money to repay the bondholders and unilaterally extended time of payment and offered substitute instruments for rescheduling. Two foreign banks and a corporation insisted on payment and sued in U.S. courts for breach of contract. The Court held that the issuance of bonds is a commercial activity and not a sovereign act. The reason for the issuance of bonds did not matter because that did not change the commercial nature of the act. Compare this holding with *MCI TeleCommunications Corp. v. Alhadhood*, 82 F.3d 658 (5th Cir. 1996), which held that alleged promises and negotiations made through diplomatic channels by an ambassador to pay a telephone provider for services stolen by his nationals is not "commercial activity" because the "non-commercial activity of stealing telephone services did not create a 'market' to which [the] alleged promises could relate." 82 F.3d at 663. In addition, MCI sought to carry on negotiations to cover losses and not to form a contract. The court held that these negotiations were not commercial in nature.

- For purposes of the FSIA, a court can assert jurisdiction over paintings present in the United States while on loan to a museum, so that a claimant can attempt to recover them. The paintings, which were confiscated during the Holocaust, satisfy the "commercial activity" requirement, even if on loan to a nonprofit museum, because paintings can be loaned by private parties. *Malewicz v. Amsterdam*, 362 F. Supp. 2d 298 (D.D.C. 2005). The court did not make a determination as to the substantiality of U.S. contacts for jurisdiction purposes.

- Subsequent commercial transactions involving expropriated property do not qualify as "commercial activity" for purposes of obtaining jurisdiction over claims that arise from the original expropriation. *Rong v. Liaoning Province Government*, 452 F.3d 883 (D.C. Cir. 2006); *Garb v. Republic of Poland*, 440 F.3d 579 (2d Cir. 2006); *Beg v. Islamic Republic of Pakistan*, 353 F.3d 1323 (11th Cir. 2003).

d. **Expropriation claims:** Sovereign immunity does not apply when "rights in property taken in violation of international law are in issue." F.S.I.A. §1605(a)(3). The phrase "taken in violation of international law" refers to the nationalization or expropriation of property without proper compensation and arbitrary or discriminatory takings. In a suit to recover six paintings that had been confiscated by Austria during Nazi rule, the U.S. Supreme Court held that FSIA applies retroactively to expropriations that took place prior to its enactment and even prior to the adoption by the United States in 1952 of the restrictive theory of sovereign immunity. *Austria v. Altmann*, 541 U.S. 677 (2004). A woman brought suit in U.S. federal district court against Austria and its instrumentality, the Austrian Gallery, seeking to recover six paintings that had been confiscated from her aunt during Nazi rule. The suit invoked FSIA's "expropriation exception" to sovereign immunity, which allows suit against foreign states in cases involving property taken in violation of international law. Petitioners claimed that because the alleged wrongdoing took place prior to the 1976 enactment of the FSIA, the exception did not apply. In May 2005, following remand, the parties submitted the dispute to binding arbitration in Austria. *Austria v. Altmann*, 541 U.S. 677 (2004).

e. **Property rights:** Sovereign immunity does not apply in any case "in which rights in property in the United States acquired by succession or gift or rights in immovable property situated in the United States are in issue." F.S.I.A. §1605(a)(4). Rights in property include leaseholds, easements, servitudes, and security interests in land. The denial of immunity extends to all property, including property used for diplomatic or consular purposes. *See, e.g., Mission of India to the U.N. v. City of New York*, 551 U.S. 193 (2007).

f. **Non-commercial torts:** Sovereign immunity does not apply when a foreign state or one of its agents is subject to a tort claim for money damages. Possible tort actions include personal injuries, death, and property damage. This tort exception to immunity does not apply if the conduct at issue was the discharge of a discretionary function or the claims are for "malicious prosecution, abuse of process, libel, slander, misrepresentation, deceit, or interference with contract rights." F.S.I.A. §1605(a)(5)(B).

- Discretionary acts are acts requiring the exercise of judgment rather than the mere carrying out of orders.

- This provision is generally inapplicable to torts or injuries occurring outside the United States.

g. **Maritime liens:** Sovereign immunity does not apply to suits brought in admiralty to enforce a maritime lien against a foreign state–owned vessel or cargo when the lien suit is based on commercial activity by the state. F.S.I.A. §1605(b)-(c).

h. **Counterclaims:** A foreign state that is subject to a counterclaim is denied immunity if it would also have been denied immunity had the claim been brought as a direct claim against the state, or the counterclaim arises from the same transaction or occurrence giving rise to the foreign state's claim. F.S.I.A. §1607.

i. **Attachment, arrest, and execution:** The FSIA also provides immunity for the property of foreign states from attachment, arrest, and execution. F.S.I.A. §1609. The exceptions to this immunity are generally the same as the exceptions to immunity from jurisdiction. *See* F.S.I.A. §1610(a). Some forms of state property are immune without exception. F.S.I.A. §1611.

j. **International agreements:** The FSIA states that "[s]ubject to existing international agreements...a foreign state shall be immune...except as provided in sections 1605 to 1607." It is unclear whether "international agreements" refers only to treaties or whether it is broad enough to encompass non-immunity as established by custom.

   - In *Smith v. Socialist People's Libyan Arab Jamahiriya*, 101 F.3d 239 (2d Cir. 1996), *cert. denied*, 520 U.S. 1204 (1997), the U.S. court held that FSIA §1604, which provides that a foreign state's immunity is "[s]ubject to existing international agreements to which the United States is a party at the time of enactment of [FSIA]" did not contemplate a dynamic expansion whereby FSIA immunity can be removed by action of the United Nations taken after the FSIA was enacted. The U.N. action was the U.N. Security Council Resolution 748, adopted March 31, 1992, that committed Libya to pay compensation to the victims of Pan Am Flight 103 on which Libyan nationals allegedly planted a bomb.

k. **Terrorist exemption:** This exception allows civil suits for damages against foreign states designated as terrorist states by the U.S. State Department for personal injury or death "by an act of torture, extrajudicial killing, aircraft sabotage, hostage taking, or the provision of material support or resources" for such an act. Some states so designated are Cuba, Iran, Syria, and Sudan. Agents of these states are also non-immune. *See, e.g., Flatow v. Iran*, 999 F. Supp. 1 (D.D.C. 1998).

l. **Extent of liability under FSIA:** A foreign state denied sovereign immunity is liable to the same extent as a private party, except that it will not generally be liable for punitive damages. An exception to the exception is made when a state's laws award only punitive damages in wrongful death actions, in which case the foreign state is liable for them, but only to the extent that the award reflects actual or compensatory damages. F.S.I.A. §1606.

B. **Act-of-state doctrine:** The act-of-state doctrine is not a rule of sovereign immunity and, in fact, it is not even a rule of international law. It is a ***domestic court-made doctrine***, but because it is related to the concept of sovereign immunity, it is often discussed in that context. It is a doctrine that protects the sovereignty of states by judicial deference to the public acts of a foreign state done on that state's territory. Courts accord such deference to avoid the adjudication of delicate international political issues. While the doctrine of sovereign immunity looks to the limits of a court's jurisdiction, the act-of-state doctrine functions more like a choice-of-law rule by which courts defer to a foreign state's prescriptive authority within its own territory. Furthermore, while sovereign immunity may be employed only by "foreign states," the act-of-state doctrine is available to private litigants. In the United States, recent cases have focused on the doctrine as an outgrowth of separation of powers in foreign relations between the executive and judicial branches.

1. **Basic doctrine in the United States:** The United States has applied the act-of-state doctrine since the late 1800s. The development of the doctrine has given rise to several exceptions that have decreased its scope.

   a. **Early cases:** The early version of the act-of-state doctrine was developed by the courts in several cases ranging between the late 1800s and early 1900s.

   Example: In *Underhill v. Hernandez*, 168 U.S. 250 (1897), an American citizen seeking damages resulting from detention by the armed forces of Venezuela was denied relief on the grounds that "the courts of one country will not sit in judgment on the acts of the government of another, done within its own territory." *See also Oetjen v. Central Leather Co.*, 246 U.S. 297 (1918) (holding that a Mexican citizen from whom hides had been seized and sold to a Texas leather company as a military levy could seek remedy only in the courts of Mexico or through diplomatic channels).

   Example: In *Bernstein v. Van Heyghen Freres Societe Anonyme*, 163 F.2d 246 (2d Cir. 1947), *cert. denied*, 332 U.S. 772 (1947), the court applied the act-of-state doctrine and refused to return to a Jewish plaintiff property that had been seized by Nazi officials. Later, the same case (*Bernstein v. N.V. Nederlandsche-Amerikaansche, Stoomvaart-Maatschappij*, 210 F.2d 375 (2d Cir. 1954)) gave rise to the so-called Bernstein exception. This rule of exception provided that the act-of-state doctrine was inapplicable in the face of explicit statements from the State Department that such judicial restraint was not required.

   b. **Recent Supreme Court decisions:** Supreme Court decisions from 1964 to the present combined with congressional action have resulted in poorly defined parameters for the act-of-state doctrine based on vague notions of separation of powers in foreign relations between the executive and judicial branches.

      i. **The height of the act-of-state doctrine:** In ***Banco Nacional de Cuba v. Sabbatino***, 376 U.S. 398 (1964), the Cuban government had expropriated a Cuban sugar company (C.A.V.) owned by U.S. nationals. The dispute before the courts regarded the distribution of the proceeds, and Sabbatino, essentially acting on behalf of the expropriated U.S. owners, argued that the proceeds belonged to him rather than the Cuban government. According to Cuban law, however, the proceeds were the property of the Cuban government. The U.S. Supreme Court, applying the act-of-state doctrine, refused jurisdiction and stated that the courts "will not examine the validity of a taking of property within its own territory by a foreign sovereign government…in the absence of a treaty or other unambiguous agreement regarding controlling legal principles, even if the complaint alleges that the taking violates customary international law." *Banco Nacional*, 376 U.S. at 428. The Court asserted that the act-of-state doctrine was premised upon the "distribution of functions between the judicial and political branches of the Government on matters bearing upon foreign affairs." *Banco Nacional*, 376 U.S. at 427. Congress reacted by passing the Sabbatino Amendment to the Foreign Assistance Act of 1961 (also called the Second Hickenlooper Amendment), which stated that courts were required to adjudicate claims to property taken in violation of international law. The lower courts have narrowly construed the amendment to apply to cases in which the property is physically present in the United States.

ii. **Decline of the doctrine:** *First National City Bank v. Banco Nacional de Cuba*, 406 U.S. 759 (1972), like the *Sabbatino* case, involved the expropriation of property by Cuba. The State Department notified the Supreme Court that it need not apply the act-of-state doctrine. The Court did not in fact apply the doctrine, but only three of the five Justices in the minority regarded this outcome as an application of the Bernstein exception. In the course of *Alfred Dunhill of London, Inc. v. Republic of Cuba*, 425 U.S. 682 (1976), the State Department wrote a "Bernstein" letter suggesting an end to the application of the act-of-state doctrine under any circumstances. The Court nevertheless rejected the State Department's suggestion, even while refusing to apply the act-of-state doctrine to the repudiation of debts owed by Cuban-nationality cigar companies. The results of this case, as well as the *First National City Bank* case, leave the current status of the Bernstein exception unclear. In *W.S. Kirkpatrick & Co. v. Environmental Tectonics Corp.*, 493 U.S. 400 (1990), the Supreme Court ruled on the act-of-state doctrine for the first time since 1976. The Court concluded by stating that the doctrine requires U.S. courts to deem as valid "the acts of foreign sovereigns taken within their own jurisdictions." *Kirkpatrick*, 493 U.S. at 401. The act-of-state doctrine was found to be inapplicable because "no foreign sovereign act [was] at issue" in a suit against a Nigerian citizen by an unsuccessful bidder for disbursing bribes to obtain a government contract for another bidder.

2. **Exceptions to the act-of-state doctrine:** The development of the act-of-state doctrine has given rise to the ***treaty*** exception, the ***commercial activity*** exception, and the ***situs-of-property*** exception. Furthermore, the act-of state doctrine cannot be pleaded to defend against charges of war crimes, crimes against peace, or crimes against humanity.

   a. **Treaty law exception:** This exception was referred to in the *Sabbatino* case and applied in *Kalamazoo Spice Extraction Co. v. Provisional Military Government of Socialist Ethiopia*, 729 F.2d 422 (6th Cir. 1984). Many treaties call for the "prompt payment of just and effective compensation" when property is expropriated by one of the nations party to the treaty. The State Department suggested in *Kalamazoo Spice* that the judiciary need not abstain from adjudication because the applicable treaty had provided the "controlling legal standard for compensation." It remains unclear, however, whether this "treaty exception" applies in every case involving a similar treaty or only in those cases in which the court receives a special letter from the executive branch permitting adjudication.

   b. **Commercial activity exception:** This exception is analogous to the commercial activity exception to sovereign immunity. The act-of-state doctrine is inapplicable to "the repudiation of a purely commercial obligation owed by a foreign sovereign or by one of its commercial instrumentalities." *Alfred Dunhill of London, Inc. v. Republic of Cuba*, 425 U.S. 682 (1976).

   c. **The situs of the property:** The "situs" of the property at issue is important because the act-of-state doctrine applies only to acts of a foreign state done on its own territory and not to seizure of property located in the United States. The situs of the property presents a difficult issue with respect to intangible property, and it remains unclear whether the situs is to be determined by federal law or by the applicable state (of the United States) law. *See Callejo v. Bancomer*, 764 F.2d 1101 (5th Cir. 1985) (applying federal law to determine that the situs of certificate of deposits was Mexico because the CDs were issued in Mexico and called for payment in Mexico).

d. Cases of mixed causes of actions: The Ninth Circuit Court of Appeals permitted plaintiffs to pursue 18 causes of action against the government of Argentina for torture and expropriation of property. It held that FSIA did not bar the lawsuit because the case fell within the exceptions to sovereign immunity for cases concerning commercial activities and cases concerning property taken in violation of international law. *Siderman De Blake v. Argentina*, 965 F.2d 699 (9th Cir. 1992).

3. **Act-of-state doctrine in antitrust cases:** Application of the doctrine is especially controversial in antitrust cases, in which the defendant may be liable for treble damages. Defendants raise the act-of-state doctrine to shift blame for damages incurred by the plaintiff to the conduct of a foreign state. This defense has met with varying success. *See Hunt v. Mobil Oil Corp.*, 550 F.2d 68 (2d Cir. 1977), *cert. denied*, 434 U.S. 984 (1977).

4. **Doctrine in other states:** Although international law does not require application of the act-of-state doctrine as practiced by U.S. courts, the courts of many other states do, in fact, recognize a similar doctrine. *See, e.g., Habib v. Commonwealth*, 2010 FCAFC 12 (Fed. Ct. 2010) (Austl.).

C. **Immunity of state representatives:** Just as diplomatic and consulate premises enjoy special protection, so also do various state representatives.

1. **Head of state:** The immunity of heads of state relies on both sovereign immunity and diplomatic immunity. A suit against the head of state is often treated like a suit against the state itself for purposes of immunity. Heads of state traveling abroad also enjoy the privileges and immunities accorded to diplomats. This immunity applies to heads of state so long as the U.S. government recognizes a person as the head of state. *Lafontant v. Aristide*, 844 F. Supp. 128 (E.D.N.Y. 1994). Not as well developed are issues pertaining to former heads of state and other government officials, particularly with respect to prosecution for human rights violations. In 2002, the International Court of Justice (ICJ) held that under customary international law, an incumbent minister of foreign affairs has full immunity while abroad, even in cases of war crimes or crimes against humanity. *Arrest Warrant of 11 April 2000 (Congo v. Belg.)*, 2002 I.C.J. 121 (Feb. 14).

The court ruled that a Belgian arrest warrant issued for an incumbent Congolese minister of foreign affairs for crimes against humanity violated the official's "full immunity from criminal jurisdiction and inviolability." The court held that, because of the nature of the post, no distinction can be made between his private and official actions. Under customary international law and in state practice, there is no exception to the immunity of an incumbent minister of foreign affairs while abroad, even in cases of war crimes or crimes against humanity. The ruling contradicted a Belgian law creating universal jurisdiction over such crimes and was a setback to those seeking avenues for prosecution of the most grievous offenses committed by persons acting in their "official" capacity.

a. FSIA and *jus cogens*: The Seventh Circuit Court of Appeals held that the FSIA had no provisions, implied or otherwise, that indicated that violation of *jus cogens* norms of international law provided grounds to deny sovereign immunity. The decision reinforced the rule that resolving human rights crises in foreign countries is a matter for the foreign policy of the executive branch and not for the courts of the United States. *Wei Ye v. Jiang Zemin*, 383 F.3d 620 (7th Cir. 2004).

2. **Diplomatic representatives:** Diplomats have enjoyed personal immunity (personal inviolability) from the times of ancient Greece to modern-day codification of custom in the widely

adopted Vienna Convention on Diplomatic Relations. Diplomatic privileges and immunities are regarded as indispensable to the diplomat's performance of duties. Diplomats (and their family members) enjoy broad protection from arrest or detention, as well as immunity from criminal laws and civil and administrative jurisdiction. art. 31, ¶1.

a. **Specific protections and limitations under the Vienna Convention:** The Vienna Convention, also enacted as U.S. federal statutory law in 22 U.S.C. §254(a-e) (1982), provides that diplomats are:

- ***not required to give evidence.*** art. 31, ¶2.
- ***immune from personal service.*** art. 35.
- ***excused from paying most taxes*** and Social Security provisions. arts. 33-34. *See Tabion v. Mufti*, 73 F.3d 535 (4th Cir. 1996) (holding that the contractual relationship with a domestic servant was not commercial activity because commercial activity does not include such contracts for goods and services that are incidental to daily life).
- ***excused from customs duties and inspections.*** art. 36.

The Convention provides that diplomats do *not* enjoy immunity with respect to:

- actions involving ***purely personal property***;
- estate administration in the host state in which the diplomat is involved in a ***non-official capacity***; or
- any other commercial or professional conduct in which the diplomat is functioning ***outside his or her official duties***. art. 31, ¶¶a-c.

The U.S. legislation extends its protection even to diplomats of states that are not parties to the Vienna Convention. 22 U.S.C. §254(b).

b. **The Iranian hostages case:** The protections granted diplomats both by customary international law and its subsequent codification in the Vienna Convention on Diplomatic Relations were strongly reaffirmed by the ICJ in *United States Diplomatic and Consular Staff in Tehran* (*U.S. v. Iran*), 1980 I.C.J. 3 (May 24). The court found that Iran had breached its fundamental international law obligations and that these rules of diplomatic immunity could not be violated even in the alleged extraordinary circumstances.

c. **Convention on the Prevention and Punishment of Crimes Against Internationally Protected Persons:** This treaty requires states to prosecute or extradite for prosecution anyone who commits, attempts to commit, or threatens to commit a violent crime against any head of state, diplomatic agent, or consular official. The United States has implemented the Convention in 18 U.S.C. §112 (1982).

d. **Administrative, technical, and service staff of a diplomatic mission:** Such staff has complete immunity from criminal jurisdiction, but immunity from civil and administrative jurisdiction only with respect to their official acts.

3. **Status of embassies and consulates:** Diplomatic mission and consular post properties are not considered an extension of the foreign state's territory. Although such diplomatic premises are within the territory of the receiving state, they do enjoy special protection related to the issue of sovereign immunity. Diplomatic and consulate premises are "inviolable, and are immune from any exercise of jurisdiction by the receiving state that would interfere with their official use." Restatement (Fourth) of Foreign Relations §466; *see also 767 Third Avenue Associates*

v. Permanent Mission for Republic of Zaire to United Nations, 988 F.2d 295 (2d Cir. 1993), *cert. denied*, 510 U.S. 819 (1993) (holding Zaire mission to United Nations immune from eviction for its failure to pay rent).

- The host state is to refrain from search, seizure, attachment, or any other form of enforcement jurisdiction that interferes with the official use of the premises. Vienna Convention on Diplomatic Relations, art. 22.
- Furthermore, the host state is obliged to protect the diplomatic premises from interference by private parties, art. 22. The United States, for example, has enacted statutes prohibiting congregation within 500 feet of diplomatic premises.
- Authorities of the territorial state are not permitted to enter the building and other premises of a diplomatic mission unless they have gained the permission of the head of the mission. In fact, the territorial state is further obliged to prevent any unlawful entry by others. art. 22.
- Diplomatic missions are generally exempt from all taxes of the host country. arts. 23, 28.
- Correspondence, records, and documents of the mission are inviolable. art. 24. Diplomatic mail may not be opened or detained by the host country. art. 27.
- The host country is obliged to make all necessary facilities available for the proper functioning of a diplomatic mission. art. 25.
- Diplomatic agents enjoy freedom of travel within their host country, but they may be barred from designated zones related to national security interests. art. 26.
- Diplomatic missions have the right to use all suitable means of communications, with the exception of radio transmitters, for which they must seek special permission. art. 27.
- Diplomatic agents may not be arrested or subjected to coercive measures. Diplomats' dwellings, correspondence, and other property are likewise inviolable. art. 30.

4. **Consuls:** Historically, consuls were granted only very limited immunity because they were often merchants in addition to consuls. More recently, a consulate position is often a career in itself, and states have negotiated specific immunities for their consulates. Consular immunity has been codified under the Vienna Convention on Consular Relations. Under the Convention, consulars are immune from arrest or detention except for serious crimes or as directed by court decisions, and consular archives are inviolable. The primary difference between diplomatic and consular immunity is that consuls enjoy immunity only with respect to their official acts. Diplomats enjoy a much broader "personal" immunity.

5. **Special missions:** In recognition of "itinerant envoys, diplomatic conferences, and special missions sent to a State for limited purposes," the General Assembly has approved a Convention on Special Missions. The Convention went into effect on June 21, 1985, in accordance with art. 53(1). Under the Restatement (Fourth), immunity for special missions is covered by the general provisions of diplomatic immunity.

6. **Representatives to international organizations:** U.N. civil servants are protected under the Convention on the Privileges and Immunities of the United Nations, which generally grants immunities similar to those enjoyed by diplomats and consuls. Two limitations are that U.N. representatives are immune from the legal process only with respect to their official acts, and only their personal luggage is free from customs duties. Protection for international civil servants is provided in the United States under the International Organizations Immunities Act, 22 U.S.C. §258 *et seq.*

7. **Individuals participating in foreign governments:** Individuals that participated in foreign governments are not included in the immunity extended to foreign governments by FSIA. *Enahoro v. Abubakar*, 408 F.3d 877 (7th Cir. 2005).

8. ***Congo v. France*:** The Republic of Congo in 2002 sued France in the ICJ seeking all annulment of French investigation and prosecution of crimes against humanity and torture allegedly committed by the Congolese minister of the interior. Congo objected to France claiming jurisdiction to criminally try a member of its government for actions allegedly committed on Congolese territory. Congo also asserted that France violated the principle of sovereign immunity by issuing a warrant for the questioning of the president of the Congo. France consented to ICJ jurisdiction, and August 11, 2008 was set as the deadline for filing the final rejoinder by France before oral argument. In November 2010, however, the agent for the Republic of the Congo informed the ICJ that his government sought to withdraw its application instituting proceedings and requested the ICJ "make an order officially recording the discontinuance of the proceedings and directing the removal of the case from the list." France presented no objection to such removal.

D. **Immunity of international organizations, their agents, officials, and invitees:** As international organizations become increasingly influential in world affairs, they require some of the same immunities required by states in order to carry out their functions. International organizations, however, have not been established long enough to have enjoyed a prolonged history of immunity similar to sovereign and diplomatic immunity. Consequently, immunity of international organizations has been established by treaty rather than by customary law, and not all states have been eager to extend broad protections. The General Convention of the Privileges and Immunities of the United Nations is an example of such a treaty. It provides the following immunities to the United Nations:

- immunity from ***all legal process***;
- ***inviolability of premises, assets, archives, and official papers***;
- ***exemption from direct taxes*** and customs duties;
- ***exemption for staff from income tax*** on salaries; and
- ***diplomatic immunity for the secretary-general and assistant secretaries-general.*** Other staff members have limited immunities.

Quiz Yourself on *STATE JURISDICTION*

1. A French citizen kills an American in Paris. France clearly has jurisdiction over the murder, but does the United States as well? _______

2. The United States holds a charged terrorist from Egypt, and Egypt is seeking his extradition to be tried for a number of violent crimes committed on Egyptian territory. Attorneys for the defendant are seeking to prevent his extradition to Egypt based on public reports on the widespread use of torture against Egyptian prisoners. Can the defendant be extradited to Egypt? _______

ANSWERS

1. Probably not. The United States does not have either territorial jurisdiction, protective jurisdiction, universal jurisdiction, or jurisdiction based on the nationality of the charged actor, who is French.

Although France has for some time claimed jurisdiction for offenses committed against French citizens, the United States had not recognized the victim's nationality (or passive personality) as a basis for jurisdiction under international law. After 9/11, however, the United States began to be much more receptive to the passive personality doctrine as a basis for jurisdiction under international law, although not as much for ordinary crimes.

2. No, if the defendant can demonstrate that he is likely to be tortured upon his return to Egypt or that he will be discriminatorily prosecuted based on his political opinion or similar grounds. The Torture Convention prohibits a state from turning anyone over to another country where that person may be tortured, and extradition treaties usually contain non-discrimination clauses and provisions that prohibit extradition for political offenses. Increasingly, however, treaties contain an exception to the ban on extradition for political offenses that are also crimes of terrorism to facilitate prosecution for such acts. Even so, the discrimination prohibition and torture prohibition would still apply to preclude extradition.

Exam Tips on STATE JURISDICTION

☛ The most controversial questions of removal of a criminal defendant from one state to another often involve politically motivated offenses, which may as well be acts of terrorism in the sense of inflicting widespread harm on civilians. Aside from the specifics of what a particular extradition treaty between states might provide, most treaties have the standard exceptions for no extradition for discriminatory prosecutions or political offenses, with the political offense exception increasingly subject to its own exception (thus allowing for extradition) for terrorist acts. In such circumstances, the defendant may then resort to the defense of no extradition to a discriminatory state or to a state that may likely engage in torture of the defendant.

☛ Note that all the protections for a defendant in an extradition treaty may be avoided if a state may lawfully engage in extradition by abduction, which the U.S. Supreme Court, in *Sosa v. Alvarez-Machain*, 542 U.S. 692 (2004), held did not preclude the United States from having jurisdiction over the defendant. This decision has been sharply criticized by many international law experts, who contend that extradition by abduction violates the *jus cogens* that treaties must be observed and more generally violates international customary norms of due process.

☛ The issue is complicated by the question of whether or not any treaty or due process violation mandates release of the defendant as opposed to some inter-state remedy.

☛ The Foreign Sovereign Immunities Act (FSIA) is one of the most confusing, incomprehensible pieces of federal legislation you will encounter in this course. The consolation is that there is never a clear answer; so as long as you are familiar with its provisions and the principal cases and can make a reasoned argument on both sides, you will be adequately prepared for any question. Remember the U.S. Supreme Court's 2010 decision in *Samantar v. Yousuf*, in which it held that an *individual* foreign government official is not entitled to immunity from suit as a "foreign state" within the statutory meaning of FSIA for conduct undertaken in his or her official individual capacity.

☛ Much the same can be said for the act-of-state doctrine and the political question doctrine. The precedents are difficult to reconcile, and it may be said that both doctrines have become more of a malleable excuse for a court not to address a politically sensitive case than coherent doctrines. The best advice is just to familiarize yourself with the most significant cases and their differences, if any, argue both sides, and conclude that the decision may ultimately depend more on the court's willingness than its ability to decide the case.

CHAPTER 6

INTERNATIONAL ORGANIZATIONS

International organizations usually refer to public or intergovernmental organizations, in contrast to private or non-governmental organizations (NGOs) such as Amnesty International or the Red Cross. International organizations are established by treaties and governed by international law. *Advisory Opinion on Reparations for Injuries Suffered in the Service of the United Nations*, 1949 I.C.J. 174 (Apr. 11).

I. THE UNITED NATIONS

The United Nations is a public organization of states that was established by intergovernmental cooperation on October 24, 1945. The fundamental purpose of the United Nations was to implement a system of collective security and discourage states from the use of unilateral force. Now, however, much of the United Nation's efforts are directed toward economic and development concerns of impoverished states.

A. The U.N. Charter: The U.N. Charter entered into force on October 24, 1945. The United Nations has 193 members, with most states of the world as members. A few notable exceptions had been Switzerland (full membership in 2002), the Republic of Korea, and the Democratic People's Republic of Korea (full membership as individual members in 1991). Taiwan remains in the United Nations with only observer status after the seat of China was given to the People's Republic of China in 1971.

1. Purposes: The four purposes of the United Nations are described in article 1 as: (1) to "***maintain international peace and security***," which includes using "collective measures for prevention and removal of threats to the peace" and peaceful means for the settlement of international disputes according to international law; (2) to "***develop friendly relations among states***"; (3) to ***achieve international cooperation*** in solving economic, social, cultural, and humanitarian problems; and (4) to be a ***center for states*** to use to attain these common goals. U.N. Charter art. 1 (emphasis added).

2. Principles: Article 2 lists seven guiding principles for the United Nations and its members. First and foremost is the principle of sovereign equality of all member states. Further, members are required to:

- fulfill their ***obligations under the Charter***;
- ***settle disputes by peaceful means***;
- ***refrain from the threat or use of force*** against the territorial integrity or political independence of any state or "in any other manner inconsistent with the Purposes of the United Nations"; and
- give the United Nations "***every assistance***" in any action it takes. U.N. Charter art. 2, ¶¶2-5 (emphasis added).

a. Non-member states expected to conform: The organization will also seek to hold ***non-member states*** to these principles insofar as to maintain international peace and security. U.N. Charter art. 2, ¶6.

b. **Non-intervention in domestic affairs of states:** Finally, the United Nations is ***not authorized to intervene*** in matters that are essentially within the domestic jurisdiction of a state, although this provision does not apply to enforcement measures under Chapter VII. U.N. Charter art. 2, ¶7.

Note: Article 2(7) has had little impact on U.N. action. First, resolutions phrased in general terms and not identifying any specific state or states are not considered "intervention" and, more significantly, many areas once considered "domestic" concerns are now considered matters of international concern (*e.g.*, widespread human rights violations).

3. **Revision of the Charter:** Under article 108, the Charter can be amended by a two-thirds vote of the General Assembly and ratification by the constitutional processes of two-thirds of the members of the United Nations, including all permanent members of the Security Council.

B. **Nature and function of the United Nations:** The United Nations has organizational ***personality*** (legal capacity) and ***immunity*** in the international system.

1. **Legal capacity:** Article 104 specifically states that "the Organization shall enjoy in the territory of each of its Members such legal capacity as may be necessary for the exercise of its functions and the fulfillment of its purposes." The International Court of Justice (ICJ) in an advisory opinion, *Advisory Opinion on Reparations for Injuries Suffered in the Service of the United Nations*, 1949 I.C.J. 174 (Apr. 11), outlined the scope of the legal capacity of the United Nations, filling in the gaps left by the Charter. The court addressed the issue of whether the United Nations can sue a responsible government to obtain reparation for harm done to the organization itself or one of its agents in the performance of his or her duties. The court stated that, without question, the United Nations has the requisite international personality endowing it with the legal capacity to bring international claims for harm done to the organization. It further held that the United Nations can bring claims for reparations for harm done to an agent fulfilling his or her duties, even if the agent is a national of the defendant state, and even if the defendant state is a non-member. The court reasoned that although these powers are not specifically mentioned in the Charter, they are "conferred upon it by necessary implication as being essential to the performance of its duties," and that "the effective working of the Organization—the accomplishment of its task" requires that states strictly adhere to the principle in article 2, ¶5 of the Charter requiring "every assistance" to the United Nations by its members.

2. **Immunity:** The United Nations and its representatives and officials enjoy privileges and immunities in the territory of its members necessary to fulfill its purposes, the same immunity that is normally enjoyed by foreign governments. *See* Chapter 5, §V(C) (discussing immunities granted to foreign government representatives).

C. **Membership:** Membership in the United Nations is governed by provisions in the Charter.

1. **Original and other members:** There were 51 original member states that either participated in the U.N. Conference on International Organization at San Francisco or previously signed the Declaration by United Nations of January 1, 1942, and then signed the Charter and ratified it according to their domestic constitutional procedures. The Charter was signed by a majority of its signatories on October 24, 1945, thereby officially establishing the United Nations. Since its inception, membership in the United Nations has increased dramatically, doubling by 1965 and tripling by 1985. Most new members are former colonies that achieved independence after World War II. As of April 2016, there are 193 member states, with the admission of South Sudan on July 14, 2011.

2. **Admission to membership:** According to article 4, ¶1, membership is open to "all other peace loving states which accept the obligations contained in the present Charter" and are able and willing to carry them out. A state wishing to join must submit a request to the Security Council, which then may submit a recommendation for membership to the General Assembly. The General Assembly then decides by a two-thirds vote whether or not to admit a state. Note, however, that the Security Council is not required to recommend a state for membership and may effectively keep states from joining. Indeed, Russia and the former Soviet Union have kept South Korea from joining the United Nations by vetoing its proposals for membership.

3. **Suspension:** A member state against which preventive or enforcement action has been taken by the Security Council may have its membership suspended by the General Assembly upon recommendation of the Security Council. U.N. Charter art. 5. This provision has never been applied.

4. **Expulsion:** If a member persistently violates the principles of the Charter, it may be expelled from the organization by the General Assembly or upon recommendation by the Security Council. U.N. Charter art. 6. This provision has never been applied.

5. **Withdrawal:** There is no provision in the Charter for voluntary withdrawal by a state.

6. **Credentials:** Which governmental representatives are entitled to represent a member state of the United Nations is a question of credentials. Determination of credentials is considered a procedural question subject to the less demanding voting requirements for procedural questions in the Security Council and General Assembly. *See* §I(E)(1)(d) and §I(E)(2)(c) of this chapter, *infra* (discussing the voting procedures of the General Assembly and the Security Council). Sometimes the question of credentials is difficult to differentiate from admission (*e.g.*, the question of representation/admission of China after the communists gained control of mainland China in 1949).

D. **Charter supremacy and the *Lockerbie* case:** Under article 103, if a Charter obligation conflicts with any other treaty obligation, the Charter prevails. In the *Lockerbie* case (*Libya v. United States*, 1992 I.C.J. 114), Libya, based on the Montreal Convention, resisted extradition requests from the United States, France, and the United Kingdom for Libyan nationals suspected of causing the explosion of a Pan Am flight in 1988 over Lockerbie, Scotland. While Libya's request for provisional relief was pending, the Security Council acting under Chapter VII ordered Libya to comply with the requests. While acknowledging the court's continuing authority despite Security Council action, the court denied Libya's request for provisional relief on the grounds that, whatever the merits of Libya's claims under the Montreal Convention, decisions of the Security Council are binding on U.N. members and under article 103 take precedence over any conflicting treaty obligation.

E. **The U.N. organs:** There are seven principal organs to the United Nations: the *General Assembly*, the *four Councils*, the *Secretariat*, and the *International Court of Justice*.

1. **The General Assembly:** The General Assembly is composed of all member states of the United Nations.

   a. **Sessions:** The General Assembly meets in regular annual sessions and may also meet in special sessions if required. Special sessions are convened by the secretary-general of the General Assembly at the request of the Security Council or of a majority of the members of the United Nations. The General Assembly adopts its own rules of procedure and elects a president for each session.

b. **Functions and powers:** The General Assembly is essentially a ***global forum*** for the exchange and debate of ideas. It may address any questions or matters within the scope of the Charter and may make recommendations to the Security Council or the United Nations on any such questions or matters (U.N. Charter art. 10), except "disputes" or "situations" that the Security Council is considering. U.N. Charter art. 12. Specifically, the General Assembly may consider matters concerning international peace and security and may make recommendations about such matters to the members, concerned states, or the Security Council. The functions of its various commissions and committees include making and considering reports of international events, supervising the Trusteeship Council, approving budgets and applications for membership, participating in the selection of judges for the ICJ, and appointing the secretary-general of the United Nations.

c. **Limitations on its powers:** The most important limitation on the General Assembly's powers is in article 11, ¶2. It provides that any question of international peace and security "on which action is necessary shall be referred to the Security Council. . . ." The ICJ has interpreted article 11, ¶2 to apply only to *enforcement* action. *See* Chapter 9, §I(C)(2).

d. **Voting:** Each member of the General Assembly has one vote. Decisions on "important" questions are made by a two-thirds majority of members present and voting. Important questions according to article 18, ¶2 include recommendations concerning international peace and security; the election of non-permanent members of the Security Council, members of the Economic and Social Council, and members of the Trusteeship Council; admission of new members; suspension and expulsion of members; questions relating to the operation of the trusteeship system; and questions relating to the budget. Decisions on other questions are made by a majority of members present and voting, including determination of which questions other than those in article 18(2) will require a two-thirds majority.

Note: A member that is behind in financial contributions to the United Nations by at least two years may not vote unless the General Assembly has determined that the failure to pay is due to conditions beyond the control of the member. U.N. Charter art. 19.

e. **Legal status of Assembly resolutions:** Although the General Assembly does seek to encourage the progressive development of international law and its codification, its "recommendations" are just that and not legally binding upon members as a matter of Charter law. On the law-making effect of General Assembly resolutions generally under international law, *see* Chapter 2, §III(C).

2. **Security Council:** The Security Council is the U.N. organ with primary responsibility for the maintenance of international peace and security. U.N. Charter art. 24, ¶1.

a. **Composition:** The Security Council consists of 15 member states. The five permanent members are the People's Republic of China, France, the Soviet Union (now Russia), the United Kingdom, and the United States. The other ten member states are rotating members elected by the General Assembly for a term of two years, with due regard to "equitable geographic distribution." U.N. Charter art. 23. Each member of the Council has one representative.

b. **Functions and powers:** The Security Council has primary responsibility for the maintenance of international peace and security. U.N. Charter art. 24. Specifically, the Council's powers include pacific settlement of disputes under Chapter VI; action with respect to threats to the peace, breaches of the peace, and acts of aggression under Chapter VII; using regional arrangements for the maintenance of international peace under Chapter VIII; and certain aspects of the international trusteeship system under Chapter XII. U.N. Charter art. 24, ¶2. Decisions of the Security Council are legally binding upon members. U.N. Charter art. 25. The Council is required to submit annual reports to the General Assembly for its consideration, and special reports when necessary. It adopts its own rules of procedure and selects its president. Unlike the General Assembly, the Security Council is expected to function continuously, with members represented at all times. U.N. Charter art. 28.

c. **Voting:** Under article 27, each member of the Security Council has one vote. Decisions on "procedural" matters require an affirmative vote by nine members. Decisions on "all other matters" require an affirmative vote of nine members, "including the concurring votes of the permanent members…."

It is this requirement of the concurring votes of each permanent member that creates their right to ***veto*** any non-procedural decision brought forth on any non-procedural matter, effectively preventing the decision from passing.

d. **Abstention:** Despite the requirement of the "concurring" votes of the permanent members, in practice a refusal to vote (or abstention) by a permanent member is not treated as a veto. Article 27 also requires that "a party to a dispute" being evaluated by the Council under Chapter VI (for peaceful settlement of disputes) abstain from voting, but in practice, states do not do so even when clearly involved in a dispute under consideration.

e. **"Double veto":** Article 27 gives no guidance on procedural versus non-procedural matters. In the early years of the Council, the Soviet Union treated determination of the procedural/non-procedural nature of a resolution as itself a non-procedural vote subject to a veto, and then would veto the substance of the resolution (thus the "double veto"). This procedural manipulation was soon overcome in practice by another procedural maneuver. The presidency of the Council is held by each member for one month. The president could rule that the procedural/non-procedural issue is itself procedural and not subject to veto; presidential rulings are final unless reversed by a procedural veto (*i.e.*, nine votes, with no state having a veto power).

3. **The Economic and Social Council (ECOSOC):** The ECOSOC is established under Chapter X and consists of 54 members of the United Nations elected by the General Assembly. Each member has one vote and decisions are made by a simple majority. Its primary responsibilities are to make studies and reports on cultural matters and to prepare draft conventions for submission to the General Assembly on matters within its competence. It has established a number of subsidiary organs, including the U.N. Commission on Human Rights.

4. **Trusteeship Council:** The Trusteeship Council under Chapter XII is responsible for administering trusteeship territories that are not yet self-governing. The Council consists of members who administer trustee territories, permanent members of the Security Council, and as many other members as the General Assembly elects as necessary to ensure that the Council is equally divided between members that administer and those that do not. Each member has one vote, and decisions are rendered by a majority of the members present and voting. Its importance has greatly diminished as the trust territories have become independent.

5. **International Court of Justice:** The ICJ is the principal judicial organ of the United Nations, U.N. Charter art. 92, and the successor to the Permanent Court of International Justice for the League of Nations. It functions in accordance with a statute annexed to the Charter. All members of the United Nations are parties to the Statute of the International Court of Justice, and a state that is not a member of the United Nations may become party to the Statute by the General

Assembly upon recommendation by the Security Council. U.N. Charter art. 93. *See* Chapter 7, §VI(A) (discussing non-member states becoming parties to the statute).

6. **Secretariat:** The Secretariat is composed of a secretary-general and any required staff of the organization. U.N. Charter art. 97. The secretary-general is elected by the General Assembly upon recommendation by the Security Council (subject to the veto power), and is the chief administrative officer of the United Nations. The secretary-general is required to submit annual reports to the General Assembly on the work of the organization and may be required to perform other functions as requested by the Security Council, General Assembly, ECOSOC, and the Trusteeship Council. Under article 99, the secretary-general "may bring to the attention of the Security Council any matter which in his opinion may threaten the maintenance of international peace and security." This agenda-setting power is potentially very significant as the basis for more expansive substantive responsibilities for the position.

7. **Human Rights Council:** The Human Rights Council is the newest established organ of the United Nations. It was established in April 2006 by General Assembly Resolution 60/251. The Council grew out of the Human Rights Commission, and was established with the purpose of "promoting universal respect for the protection of all human rights and fundamental freedoms for all." It comprises 47 member states, which are directly elected by the majority of members of the General Assembly. The Council is intended to function as a more authoritative human rights body and respond more efficiently to claims of human rights violations.

F. **Legislative activities of the General Assembly and the International Law Commission:** The General Assembly created the International Law Commission (ILC) in 1947 to assist in fulfilling the Assembly's legislative duties under article 13, ¶1(a) of the U.N. Charter. The ILC is composed of leading international lawyers. The General Assembly has delegated authority to the ILC to research international law and draft conventions. The ILC has drafted many multilateral conventions that codify existing international customary law as well as create new law. When such conventions are adopted by the General Assembly and receive broad support, they often become a generally accepted statement of international law in the area. The legislative activities of the General Assembly, as delegated to the ILC, have contributed significantly to the body of international law.

G. **Specialized agencies:** Specialized agencies are organizations that are related to the United Nations through article 57 of the U.N. Charter.

1. **Defined:** Article 57 defines specialized agencies as those "established by intergovernmental agreement and having wide international responsibilities, as defined in their basic instruments, in economic, social, cultural, educational, health, and related fields. . . ." The Economic and Social Council reaches agreement with qualifying organizations to grant special agency status and coordinates the activities of the special agencies. The agreements differ for each agency but usually involve regular reporting to the ECOSOC and agency consideration of recommendations from the General Assembly.

2. **Examples:** Some of these specialized agencies are the International Monetary Fund (IMF), the International Bank for Reconstruction and Development (World Bank), the U.N. Educational, Scientific, and Cultural Organization (UNESCO), the Food and Agriculture Organization (FAO), World Health Organization (WHO), International Labor Organization (ILO), the Universal Postal Union (UPU), and the International Civil Aviation Organization (ICAO).

3. **Membership:** Membership in specialized agencies is not limited to members of the United Nations. Some organizations admit only U.N. members, but most agencies attempt to expand

their own membership to as many nations as possible. Conversely, a few members of the United Nations are not members in all of the specialized agencies.

4. **Legislative activities:** By making recommendations and drafting conventions, specialized agencies have developed international law in many areas. Like the General Assembly, specialized agencies generally do not have the authority to enact binding legislation. Some agencies, such as the UPU and ICAO, have developed regulations and standards that have been widely accepted. In certain situations, the WHO can enact health regulations that are binding on member states. Other organizations, such as the ILO, have drafted a number of widely adopted treaties. These activities have contributed significantly to the body of international law in newly developing areas.

II. REGIONAL ORGANIZATIONS

Regional organization is a term of art under the U.N. Charter that refers to international associations established under Chapter VIII. Each of these institutions is created through an agreement between the member states that outlines the structure, functions, and authority of the organization. *Regional organization* is not defined in the U.N. Charter. Unlike other international organizations, however, regional organizations are concerned with problems within a specific region. Some handle only specific concerns such as economic, military, or political issues, while others deal with any matter that concerns the nations in that region.

A. **Basic characteristics:** Some regional organizations are loose associations of member states with little or no legislative authority. These organizations may only provide a forum for nations to meet and discuss matters of common interest. Other regional organizations have legislative power and take significant actions in fulfilling their mandates. The organizations with the most legislative authority are supranational organizations, such as the European Union, which have broad legislative authority over their member states.

B. **Major organizations:** Four prominent regional organizations include the Organization of American States (OAS), Arab League, Council of Europe, and African Union (formerly the OAU). In recent times, other regional organizations have coalesced, including the Association of Southeast Asian Nations (ASEAN) and the Asia-Pacific Economic Cooperation (APEC).

1. **The Organization of American States (OAS):** The OAS was created in 1948 to promote unity and cooperation among nations in the Western Hemisphere. One of the primary influences on the formation of the OAS was the Cold War. As a result, its charter emphasized security through a common defense.

2. **The Council of Europe:** The Council of Europe was created in 1949 to promote unity in Europe after World War II.

3. **African Union (formerly the Organization of African Unity [OAU]):** The OAU was formed in 1963 as a loose association of African nations. The many conflicting points of view held by the member states were reflected by the limited power given to the OAU in its charter. Each nation retained autonomy as recognized by the OAU charter. The organization is now known as the African Union.

4. **The Association of Southeast Asian Nations (ASEAN):** ASEAN was preceded by the Association of Southeast Asia, an alliance between the Philippines, Malaysia, and Thailand in 1961. ASEAN proper came into being in 1967, consisting of Indonesia, Malaysia, the Philippines, Singapore, and Thailand. Since then, Brunei, Vietnam, Laos, Myanmar, and

Cambodia have joined. It is now a major trading bloc that frequently meets as ASEAN+3 consisting of the current ASEAN members, China, Japan, and the Republic of Korea after the 1997 Asian financial crisis.

5. **The Asia-Pacific Economic Cooperation (APEC):** APEC was established in 1989 when Australian prime minister Bob Hawke called for more effective economic cooperation across the Pacific Rim. Its purpose is to facilitate trade in the Pacific Rim region, calling for reduction of barriers to trade and investment and building of prosperity through cooperation and coordination.

C. **Functions:** The primary function of each of these regional organizations is to promote cooperation among the member states. The specific areas, methods, and extent of cooperation, however, differ among regional organizations.

1. **The Organization of American States:** The OAS has concentrated its efforts on responding to political developments and furthering political cooperation. The OAS charter outlines the functions of the organization as strengthening security; ensuring peaceful settlement of disputes; coordinating common defense; and promoting economic, social, and cultural development. Although the OAS has drafted a number of treaties, it has been less successful than the Council of Europe in winning the acceptance of those treaties. The OAS has made some progress in the area of regional human rights, including the establishment of the Inter-American Court of Human Rights in 1969.

2. **The Council of Europe:** The Council of Europe has focused on economic cooperation through the European Economic Community (EEC) and human rights and has developed a number of agreements in many areas. These agreements have resulted in significant cooperation between the member states and increased power for the EEC. *See* §III of this chapter, *infra*.

3. **The African Union:** The OAU Charter is primarily concerned with non-interference and peaceful resolution of disputes among member states. The OAU has promoted African unity on issues including human rights, but it has played a limited role in dealing with regional conflicts. However, the OAU has recently been significantly involved in peacekeeping in the war-torn region of Darfur in the Sudan, and, along with the United Nations, it deployed a joint peacekeeping force to the area in 2007 to help implement the peace agreement signed by opposing forces and to protect civilians from further persecution. On the economic front, the OAU adopted the Treaty Establishing the African Economic Community (the Abuja Treaty) in 1991 to promote inter-state cooperation and integration of economic activities among member nations.

4. **The Association of Southeast Asian Nations:** The goals of ASEAN include the acceleration of economic growth, social progress, cultural development, and the promotion of regional peace. One of the primary functions of ASEAN has been to promote nation building because many members became independent after the end of World War II. As a result, non-interference is a key principle and ASEAN processes function through consultation and consensus. Recently, ASEAN has been focused on dialogue with its neighbors, starting with the ASEAN+3 format between ASEAN, China, Japan, and the Republic of Korea, as well as the Asia-Europe Meeting, an informal dialogue between the European Union and the ASEAN+3 format, as well as the East Asia Summit, somewhat controversial because it welcomed Australia and New Zealand but not the United States. ASEAN is also responsible for establishing the ASEAN Free Trade Area agreement.

5. **The Asia-Pacific Economic Cooperation:** APEC is designed to be primarily involved in economic cooperation in the Pacific Rim. It holds annual summits discussing matters such as open markets, structural reform, and trade liberalization. In the 2005 summit in Busan, Republic of

Korea, for example, APEC discussed the Doha round of the World Trade Organization negotiations, with APEC leaders urging the European Union to agree to reduce farm subsidies. APEC has also discussed matters tangentially related to regional economic concerns such as the North Korean nuclear test and missile tests. At a 2009 summit meeting, APEC parties discussed the North Korean nuclear program, indicating a willingness to use the Cooperation as a forum to discuss some regional security issues in addition to economic issues.

D. Relationship to United Nations: Chapter VIII of the U.N. Charter describes the relationship between the United Nations and regional organizations. Article 52, ¶1 in the U.N. Charter allows U.N. members to participate in any regional arrangement with principles consistent with the United Nations. The United Nations encourages its members in regional organizations to attempt to settle "local disputes" in those organizations before referring them to the Security Council. U.N. Charter art. 52, ¶2. Regional organizations have a duty to inform the Security Council of any actions the organization is undertaking or contemplating for the maintenance of international peace and security. U.N. Charter art. 54. Regional organizations must seek Security Council authorization for any enforcement action. U.N. Charter art. 53.

1. **Jurisdictional issues:** Chapter VIII is unclear concerning regional jurisdiction and the often overlapping authority of the Security Council. Although it has been argued that regional organizations have primary or exclusive jurisdiction over regional matters (*see* U.N. Charter art. 52, ¶2), neither of these arguments has been accepted, given the Security Council's "primary" responsibility for the maintenance of international peace and security. *See* U.N. Charter art. 52, ¶4 and art. 24. The U.N. Security Council, however, has chosen to defer to regional organizations in a number of instances. The Security Council may also choose to exercise concurrent jurisdiction, but these decisions are founded more on pragmatic considerations than any legal requirements in the U.N. Charter.

2. **Collective self-defense organizations distinguished:** Occasionally, the term *regional organization* has been loosely applied to collective defense arrangements under article 51 of the U.N. Charter. Collective self-defense refers to the aid of other states coming to the defense of an attacked state, and is discussed in Chapter 9, §I(C)(1)(a)(iv).

III. SUPRANATIONAL ORGANIZATIONS

Supranational organizations are a relatively new development in international law. The concept of supranationality involves an association with its own structures, sovereign rights, and authority independent from the member states. Member states submit themselves and their citizens to the law-making power of the organization through treaties with the other member states. Supranational organizations result in a division of power between the individual member states and the organization in which member states have forfeited some aspects of their sovereignty but still actively participate in the law-making powers of the organization.

Example: The European Union, which resulted from the unification of three organizations, is the quintessential example of a supranational organization. The European Coal and Steel Community (ESCS), formed in 1952, was the first European organization with supranational characteristics. In 1958, the European Economic Community (EEC) and the European Atomic Energy Community (Euratom) were created with similar institutions and powers. These three organizations were subsequently merged into the European Community with common institutional structures, further integrating into the European Union; however, each of the original treaties is still applicable to the three Communities. An attempt has been made to pass a constitution that would override all the treaties with a single document, but it failed to be ratified.

A. **Mandate:** The predecessor to the European Union, the European Community, was established to promote unity and economic integration among the member states. This general goal was accompanied by several specific aims to be achieved by the Community. The Community was to promote free movement of goods and capital and freedom of movement for persons between the member states. Many of the goals desired by the European Community came into fruition with the Maastricht Treaty (entered into force in 1993), which set a 1999 deadline for economic union, a parliament with veto power, and new developments towards political union, defense policy, immigration, and other social issues. The Maastricht Treaty resulted in the formation of the European Union and led to significant developments such as the 1997 Treaty of Amsterdam and the Treaty of Nice in 2001, which revised the Rome and Maastricht treaties to allow the European Union to better cope with further enlargement to the east. It also resulted in the creation of a single currency called the euro, with euro notes and coins replacing the national currencies in 19 of the 28 member states in 2016.

B. **Structure:** The treaties establishing the European Union provide the institutional structure for the organization. These agreements created four institutions to utilize the power held by the European Union: the Commission, the Council of Ministers, European Parliament, and the European Court of Justice. The Commission comprises persons appointed collectively by the member states, and each must be a national of one of the member states. No more than two can be nationals of the same member state. The Commission makes its decisions in private and is not intended to represent the individual interests of the member states. These interests are represented by the Council, which consists of one representative from each of the member states. The European Parliament was created to represent the peoples of the Union and is composed of representatives elected in direct elections. Seats in the Parliament are not allotted according to population but according to party. The European Court of Justice has 28 judges appointed for six-year terms and 11 advocates-general that issue advisory opinions in each case. Every three years a partial replacement of judges and advocates-general takes place. The court ensures compliance with E.U. policies and reviews actions by the other institutions under the treaties that created them.

C. **Community law and domestic law:** The treaties signed by the member states in the European Union are treated as the ***constitution of the Union*** and are ***binding*** on each of the nations and individuals in lieu of the failure to ratify an E.U. constitution. Regulations, directives, and decisions created by the institutions of the European Union in accordance with the treaties are also directly applicable to member states and citizens. The European Court of Justice has held that these Union laws are superior to any conflicting domestic laws. The Court of Justice has made this determination in previous cases and continues to decide questions of Union law and enforcement. The court has used two theories to support this conclusion.

   1. **The institutional theory:** The institutional theory states that member states have given up their sovereignty in certain specified areas in favor of the Union; therefore, they have given up the power to enact conflicting laws in these areas.

   2. **The political theory:** Under the political theory, the states have limited their sovereignty by granting power to the Union, so any laws of an individual member state that contradict Union laws are not valid. This power of the Union to enact laws that supersede the laws of the member states and apply them directly to the citizens is a primary difference between supranational and other regional organizations. The lack of complete control of the legislative process by the individual member states is another important characteristic.

IV. THE WORLD TRADE ORGANIZATION

The World Trade Organization (WTO) came into being in 1995 in order to implement and administer agreements designed to liberalize and regulate international trade. It is a direct successor to the General Agreement on Tariffs and Trade (GATT), which was created in 1947 and operated as a *de facto* organization.

A. **Functions:** WTO, beyond overseeing and implementing WTO agreements, provides a forum for negotiations and more importantly, settling disputes. The WTO, like two other components of the Bretton Woods system, the IMF and the World Bank, reviews national trade policies to ensure transparency of trade policies and global economic policy making, working closely with these other organizations. It also has taken on the task of assisting developing nations adjust to WTO rules.

B. **Structure:** The WTO has four primary levels in its hierarchy, not including special committees:

1. **The Ministerial Conference:** The highest level is the Ministerial Conference, which must meet at least every two years, bringing in all members of the WTO, and can make decisions on all matters under any multilateral trade agreements.
2. **The General Council:** The General Council runs the daily work of the Ministerial Council, regularly meeting in Geneva. It consists of three components: the General Council, the Dispute Settlement Body, and the Trade Policy Review Body.
3. **The Councils for Trade:** The Councils for Trade work under the General Council and consist of three components: the Council for Trade in Goods, the council for Trade-Related Aspects of Intellectual Property, and the Council for Trade in Services. Six other bodies apart from the Councils for Trade report to the General Council.
4. **The subsidiary bodies:** There are multiple subsidiary bodies under the three councils. The Goods Council, a subsidiary under the Council for Trade in Goods, has 11 committees consisting of all member countries dealing with agriculture, market access, subsidies, etc. Some of the constituent committees include the Information Technology Agreement (ITA) Committee and the Textiles Monitoring Body. The Services Council, which is a subsidiary under the Council for Trade in Services, deals with financial services, domestic regulations, etc. There are the Dispute Settlement Panels and the Appellate Body, a subsidiary of the Dispute Settlement Body, to resolve disputes and appeals.
5. **Other committees:** Other committees exist, such as those on trade and the environment, or working groups on accession, trade, debt, and finance.

Quiz Yourself on INTERNATIONAL ORGANIZATIONS

3. The U.N. General Assembly passes a resolution calling on the People's Republic of China to respect the religious beliefs of the residents of Tibet. Does the resolution violate the article 2(7) prohibition on interference in the domestic jurisdiction of a state? _______

4. The U.N. Security Council, acting under Chapter VII, authorizes the use of force in Kosovo. Does this violate the article 2(4) prohibition on states engaging in the use of force against any state? _______

5. Blocked by the veto, the Security Council is unable to act to address genocide in the state of Balhazar. The General Assembly passes a resolution directing all U.N. members to contribute to an armed force to restore order in Balhazar. Is the G.A. resolution authorized and binding? _______

ANSWERS

3. No. Human rights, including the freedom of religion, are considered a matter of international law and not merely domestic matters.

4. No. The article 2(4) prohibition is subject to authorization by the Security Council of the use of force under Chapter VII when there is a breach of peace, a threat to peace, or an act of aggression as found by the Security Council.

5. Possibly. The express provisions of the Charter limit the General Assembly to making non-binding "recommendations." The Uniting for Peace Resolution, passed by the General Assembly itself, seems to give it the authority to engage in enforcement action when the Security Council is unable to act. It is a matter of debate as to whether the General Assembly could give itself enforcement power that the Charter itself seems to preclude. *See* Chapter 9.

Exam Tips on *INTERNATIONAL ORGANIZATIONS*

- An understanding of how the United Nations works and its powers is absolutely fundamental to a grasp of international law. If there is one treaty that you should read or skim in its entirety for the course, it should be the U.N. Charter. Generally, as for any international organization, keep in mind that the overall limit on the organization's authority would be the stated purposes of the organization in its charter, and sometimes these purposes seem to work against each other.

- Another general provision of significant impact is article 103, which states that in the event of a conflict between the Charter and any other treaty obligation, the Charter prevails for U.N. members. A striking example of how this provision might work occurred during the Bosnian war in the 1990s and the embargo on shipment of arms to Bosnia. The Bosnian government contended that it had a right to receive arms to engage in its universally recognized right of self-defense. In Council debates, it was contended that even the right to self-defense had to yield to a binding Security Council resolution passed in accordance with the Charter and binding on U.N. members.

- With respect to the Security Council, it is critical to understand the voting procedures. Only substantive decisions can be blocked by a single veto, but what is or is not a substantive decision can itself be a substantive decision subject to veto. The reality is that how an issue will be addressed and what the vote will be is largely, if not entirely, negotiated before any vote is taken. An abstention, despite the seemingly contrary language of the Charter, is treated as a veto.

CHAPTER 7

INTERNATIONAL DISPUTE SETTLEMENT

I. "DISPUTE" DEFINED

Under international law, *dispute* has a specific meaning that goes beyond a mere difference of views. A dispute is ***a contest of some specificity, the resolution of which has some practical effect on the relations between the parties***. The International Court of Justice (ICJ) accepts only "disputes," which are defined as "a disagreement on a point of law or fact, a conflict of legal views or interests between two persons." *Mavrommatis Palestine Concessions* (*Greece v. Gr. Brit.*) (1924) P.C.I.J. (ser. A) No. 2, at 11.

II. THE ROLE OF THE UNITED NATIONS

The U.N. Charter includes several provisions outlining methods of dispute settlement. Article 2, ¶3 requires members to engage in ***peaceful settlement*** of disputes. Article 33 of the Charter calls for peaceful settlement of disputes through "negotiation, enquiry, mediation, conciliation, arbitration, judicial settlement, resort to regional agencies or arrangements, or other peaceful means of their own choice." Several organs of the United Nations are engaged in dispute settlement. In addition to the ICJ, disputes may be brought before the General Assembly and the Security Council.

A. General Assembly: Articles 10, 11, 12, and 14 deal with the ability of the General Assembly to hear disputes. Any member state, as well as any non-member state that is party to the dispute and agrees to the obligations of pacific settlement imposed by the U.N. Charter, may bring disputes to the General Assembly. The General Assembly is limited to establishing fact-finding missions and making recommendations. Although the actions of the General Assembly may have significant political influence, states are under no legal obligation to cooperate with the fact-finding missions or to follow recommendations.

B. Security Council: Consideration of a dispute by the Security Council may be requested by any member of the United Nations (article 35, ¶1), by any non-member that is party to the dispute and agrees to the obligation of peaceful pacific dispute settlement (article 35, ¶2), by the General Assembly (articles 10, 11, ¶¶2-3), and by the secretary-general (article 99). The Security Council has discretion to deny the request or accede to it by placing the dispute on its agenda. Once it is on the agenda, only the Security Council may remove it. Under Chapter VI, the Security Council has investigative powers and may make recommendations. The recommendations of the Security Council under Chapter VI exert great political influence but create no legal obligations. Recommendations are substantive and subject to veto power.

III. OTHER TREATY OBLIGATIONS OF PEACEFUL SETTLEMENT

Before the U.N. Charter came into force, there were many separate bilateral treaties calling for conciliation and arbitration. Since the entry into force of the U.N. Charter, the treaties calling for peaceful dispute settlements are primarily regional treaties, such as the European Convention on the Peaceful

Settlement of Disputes (1957) and the African states' Protocol on Conciliation and Arbitration. In addition, treaties on everything from opium production to anti-ballistic missiles include provisions for peaceful settlement of disputes, ranging from a simple reference to the obligation imposed by the U.N. Charter to complex schemes outlining varying procedures and methods depending on the nature of the dispute.

IV. NON-JUDICIAL METHODS

Methods of non-judicial dispute resolution are negotiation, inquiry, mediation/good offices, and conciliation. Each method may be used alone or in any combination with the other methods. Many international institutions today provide dispute resolution processes that combine negotiation, inquiry, mediation, and conciliation and, as a final resort, adjudication.

A. **Negotiation:** Negotiation is a face-to-face discussion between the disputing parties. It is a traditional and commonly employed method, and usually the first step in the peaceful resolution of disputes. In fact, international courts such as the ICJ ***require*** parties to enter into "meaningful" negotiations before presenting the matter for adjudication. *See, e.g., Armed Activities on the Territory of the Congo* (*D.R.C. v. Rwanda*), 2006 I.C.J. ¶117. Negotiations are not bound by rules of procedure and are frequently carried out through diplomatic channels or handled by "competent authorities" representing appropriate government departments and ministries. In addition, recurring problems may be addressed by joint commissions specifically created to negotiate.

B. **Inquiry:** Inquiry is the attempt to clarify the facts pertinent to a dispute in the hopes that agreement on factual matters will facilitate a final resolution. A group of individuals or an institution may be designated as impartial fact-finders.

C. **Mediation:** Mediation, unlike negotiation, involves the intervention of an outside party. This method is commonly employed when the negotiations have reached a deadlock and a third party is required to break the impasse and assist the parties in reaching an acceptable solution. Mediation may be sought by the disputing parties themselves or may be offered by outside parties. The third-party mediator becomes an active participant and is expected to informally present proposals for a solution based on information supplied by the disputing parties. The benefit of mediation is that it provides the disputing parties with the possibility of solutions without binding them to the mediator's suggestions. Furthermore, disputing parties may find it politically easier to make necessary concessions through a third party, as opposed to making concessions in the course of direct negotiations.

D. **Good offices:** An outside party is said to contribute "good offices" when the intervention in a dispute is more passive than that of a mediator. A third party contributing "good offices" usually does nothing more than simply encourage a resumption of the negotiations or provide an additional channel of communication.

E. **Conciliation:** This method of dispute settlement also involves the intervention of a third party and is a link between mediation and arbitration. Conciliation has been described as the process of settling a dispute by referring it to a commission of persons whose task it is to elucidate the facts and to make a report containing proposals for a settlement, but without the binding character of an award or judgment. Conciliation is a more formal process than mediation and involves independent investigation of factual matters but does not result in legally binding solutions, as does arbitration. Although 200 or more conciliation commissions have been formed and conciliation is provided for in the Vienna Convention on the Law of Treaties and the Vienna Convention on Succession of States in Respect of Treaties, it is not a commonly employed method of dispute settlement.

V. QUASI-JUDICIAL METHODS/ARBITRATION

Arbitration, unlike any of the five methods discussed above, results in ***legally binding settlements***. The settlement is reached on the basis of law by a group of judges appointed by the parties. Arbitral panels may be used to settle not only disputes between states, but also commercial disputes between a state and a private party or between private parties. Many states have passed domestic legislation to facilitate arbitration and have ratified bilateral treaties and conventions utilizing arbitration as a means of settling disputes.

A. Advantages of arbitration: Arbitration has several advantages over both the other non-judicial means of dispute settlement and adjudication:

- It is ***more conclusive*** than the other forms of non-judicial dispute settlement because the decisions of the arbitral panels are binding upon the parties.
- The disputing parties retain ***greater control*** in the arbitration process than they retain in the judicial process because they appoint the arbitrators. In making such appointments, the parties may select people with specialized knowledge of the matters at issue.
- Parties may ***designate the procedures and the laws*** to be applied. The selected procedures are usually less cumbersome than those applied in the courtroom, and the arbitration process can therefore be less time-consuming.
- Arbitration is ***less formal*** and ***less contentious*** than adjudication. This is especially important for maintaining commercial relationships.
- Both the arbitration proceedings and decisions can be kept ***confidential***, a great advantage in disputes regarding sensitive matters.

B. Disadvantages of arbitration: Arbitration also has its disadvantages:

- If the parties do not specify procedures, arbitration may be a ***very cumbersome*** and ***time-consuming*** process.
- Arbitration panels ***do not have the authority of courts*** to conduct discovery or subpoena witnesses.
- The ***parties themselves pay for the entire cost*** of the arbitration, which includes compensation for the arbitrators as well as administrative costs. However, if the arbitration is conducted efficiently, these costs are often less than the costs of litigation.

C. Types of international arbitral clauses: There are several types of international arbitral clauses:

1. **Clause inserted in treaty:** An arbitration clause may be inserted in a treaty dealing with one or more substantive issues to provide a method of settling disputes arising from the treaty. Such arbitration clauses are common in commercial treaties and in international civil aviation agreements.

2. **Treaty itself establishes settlement method:** The treaty itself may exist solely to establish a method of resolving either certain categories of disputes or all disputes that may arise between the parties. Two well-known examples are the Hague Convention for the Pacific Settlement of International Disputes and the General Act for the Pacific Settlement of International Disputes.

3. **"After-the-fact" arbitral agreements:** Arbitral agreements may be concluded after the dispute has arisen. Such an "after-the-fact" arbitral agreement is often concluded when the parties have been unsuccessful with the other methods of dispute settlement. An example is the Iran-U.S. Claims Tribunal.

D. **Consent to arbitrate and the *compromis*:** Unless the parties to a dispute have previously consented to submit to arbitration through an arbitral clause or arbitration convention, there is ***no international law requirement to arbitrate***. Parties may, subsequent to the rise of a dispute, consent to arbitrate. A single instrument may express this consent and provide details of the arbitration process itself. On the other hand, the consent may be expressed in one document followed by a subsequent agreement dealing with the details of the arbitration. The subsequent agreement is called the *compromis d'arbitrage*, and it outlines the constitution of the arbitral panel, the rules of procedure, the issues to be decided, and the binding nature of the arbitral decision.

E. **Composition of the arbitral tribunal:** An arbitral tribunal may be established on an ad hoc basis or as a continuing institution, and it usually has a tripartite structure. Each party selects a member independently and then the third member is selected by a joint decision of the parties. Should the parties fail to agree on a selection, the final member is chosen by an outside party, such as the secretary-general of the Permanent Court of Arbitration at the Hague. Some arbitral tribunals, such as the Iran-U.S. Claims Tribunal, have nine members, but the tripartite structure is maintained.

F. **Choice of location:** Choice of location can be important because some countries' laws provide that their courts have jurisdiction over arbitration proceedings. Those courts may review arbitral awards reached within their country and may sometimes entertain interlocutory appeals. To avoid the jurisdiction of a party's courts, arbitration in a neutral country is advisable.

G. **Rules of arbitration—ad hoc vs. institutional arbitration:** Parties may choose between the established sets of rules for arbitration or may develop their own ad hoc rules. With the exception of the U.N. Commission on International Trade Law Arbitration (UNCITRAL), the set of rules listed below have accompanying institutions. The institutions may be used to actually conduct the arbitration or may assist by advising on all aspects of the arbitration, such as organization of the panel or the unique problems of conducting arbitration in particular countries. The principal established sets of arbitration rules are:

1. **Rules of the International Centre for the Settlement of Investment Disputes (ICSID):** The ICSID is affiliated with the World Bank and it deals with investment disputes. The United States is a signatory to this Convention.

2. **Rules of Conciliation and Arbitration of the International Chamber of Commerce (ICC):** Both the ICC Rules and the Court of Arbitration are very widely used, especially in the area of trade.

3. **Rules of the U.N. Commission on International Trade Law Arbitration (UNCITRAL):** This set of rules governs the Iran-United States Claims Tribunal.

4. **Commercial Arbitration Rules of the American Arbitration Association (AAA):** The AAA promotes both domestic and international arbitration in many fields.

H. **Applicable law:** The *compromis* usually sets forth the governing rules to be applied by the arbitrators, and those rules in turn stipulate the choice of law. The ICSID, for example, provides for application of the law of the host country, "(including its rules on the conflict of laws) and such rules of international law as may be applicable," unless the parties have agreed otherwise. Arbitral panels look to the decisions of the ICJ and other permanent courts, as well as other contemporary arbitral decisions, for evidence of international law.

I. **Arbitral award:** As a general rule, ***arbitral awards are binding*** on the parties and ***are not subject to appeal***. However, parties to a dispute may derogate from this rule and permit judicial review by a court such as the ICJ. According to the U.N. Convention on the Recognition and Enforcement of Foreign Arbitral Awards, other circumstances providing a ***defense against enforcement*** of the arbitral award are:

- The arbitral tribunal ***exceeded its powers***.
- The enforcement of the award is ***contrary to*** the ***public policy*** of the forum country.
- The award resulted from arbitration of matters considered ***incapable of settlement*** by arbitration under the laws of the forum country.
- The ***defendant*** proves that he was "***not given proper notice***…or was ***otherwise unable to present his case***." (Article V(1)(b)) (emphasis added).
- The award is in "***manifest disregard***" of the law.

The U.N. Model Rules of Arbitral Procedure provide ***additional bases for challenging the validity*** of an arbitral award:

- ***Corruption*** on the part of a member of the arbitral panel.
- ***Failure to state the reasons*** for the award.
- ***Serious departure from a fundamental procedural rule***.
- The agreement to arbitrate or the *compromis* is a ***nullity***.
- The ***tribunal exceeded its powers***.

The New York Convention on the Recognition and Enforcement of Foreign Arbitral Awards provides the following ***defenses to enforcement*** of the arbitral award:

- The parties to the agreement were under some ***incapacity***.
- The ***agreement is invalid*** under the applicable law of the arbitration or under the law of the country where the award is to be made.
- The ***defendant*** was ***not given proper notice*** or was ***otherwise unable to present its case***.
- The award ***exceeds the powers*** of the tribunal.
- The composition of the arbitral tribunal was ***not in accordance with agreement*** of the parties or of the law in the country in which the arbitration took place.
- The award is not binding because it has been ***set aside*** or ***suspended*** by a competent authority in the country in which the award was to be made.
- The subject of the arbitration is ***not capable of settlement*** by arbitration according to the laws of the country where the award is to be recognized and enforced.
- Recognition and enforcement of the award are ***contrary to*** the ***public policy*** of that country.

J. The role of the International Court of Justice (ICJ): Article 36, ¶1 of the Statute of the International Court of Justice sets forth the ICJ's role as a public international arbiter, stating that the court has jurisdiction in "all cases which the parties refer to it." A *compromis* may confer jurisdiction of particular legal questions on the ICJ and indicate the rules of law to be applied by the court. The ICJ, however, differs from other arbitration tribunals in that its membership is preestablished.

VI. THE INTERNATIONAL COURTS

There are a number of recognized international courts. They include the International Court of Justice, Court of Justice of the European Communities, Benelux Court of Justice, European Court of Human Rights, and the Inter-American Court of Human Rights. Newer additions to this list of specialized jurisdictions (discussed *infra*) include the African Court of Human and Peoples' Rights, the International Tribunal for the Law of the Sea, the International Criminal Courts, the International Criminal Tribunals for Rwanda and for the former Yugoslavia, the Special Court for Sierra Leone, and the Special Tribunal for Lebanon.

A. **The International Court of Justice:** The International Court of Justice (ICJ), successor to the Permanent Court of International Justice, is the ***principal judicial organ*** of the United Nations. Its statute is annexed to the U.N. Charter. All members of the United Nations are automatically parties to the ICJ statute, and under certain circumstances, parties that are not members of the United Nations may appear before the court and may also be parties to the statute. U.N. Charter art. 93. Being a party to the statute does not mean that the state has submitted itself to the court's jurisdiction. The ICJ hears relatively few cases because only states may be parties in contentious proceedings before it. Stat. of the ICJ art. 34, ¶1. States must consent to jurisdiction. This limitation is further compounded by the fact that historically, states often have chosen to settle disputes through political and diplomatic channels rather than through the ICJ. Regional international courts, on the other hand, have been more frequently utilized for international law claims of private parties. Nevertheless, the cases the ICJ has decided have had a major impact on the development of international law.

1. **Structure and composition:** Article 3, ¶1 of the statute requires that the court, with its seat in The Hague, be composed of 15 judges elected by both the Security Council and the General Assembly. Judges serve for nine-year periods but may be, and often are, reelected. The terms are staggered so that elections for five of the 15 judges take place every three years. In practice, several considerations, including the following, determine the composition of the court. For instance, members of the Security Council almost always have a judge on the court. Judges are elected with regard for distribution. A balanced distribution, as exemplified in the 1996 court, was four judges from Western Europe, two judges from Eastern Europe, three judges each from Africa and Asia, two judges from Latin America, and one judge from the United States. No more than one national of a state may sit as a judge at any one time. Stat. of the ICJ art. 3, ¶1. If a state appearing before the court does not have one of its own nationals as a judge, it may appoint an ad hoc judge to ensure that its views will be fully considered. This practice is not easily reconciled with the view of judges as impartial decision makers. *See* Stat. of the ICJ art. 20.

2. **Contentious and advisory jurisdiction:** The court may hear only cases ***governed by international law***. Stat. of the ICJ art. 38. The ICJ has two types of jurisdiction: contentious jurisdiction and advisory jurisdiction. Contentious jurisdiction is based on either the express or implied consent of the parties, and only states party to the ICJ statute may be parties in a contentious case. *See, e.g., Legality of Use of Force* (*Serb. & Mont. v. Belg.*), 2004 I.C.J. ¶79. Decisions in contentious cases are binding on the parties. The court may also issue non-binding, advisory opinions at the request of bodies so authorized by the U.N. Charter. Article 36 provides three ways for a state to consent to the jurisdiction of the ICJ. First, states may refer an existing dispute on an ad hoc basis. Second, a treaty may provide that any disputes arising from it be settled by the ICJ. Stat. of the ICJ art. 36. Third, the ICJ may have jurisdiction under the so-called "optional clause" of art. 36, ¶2.

3. **Compulsory jurisdiction under the optional clause:** Article 36, ¶2 provides that states that are parties to the present statute may at any time declare that they recognize as compulsory *ipso facto* and without special agreement, in relation to any other state accepting the same obligation, the jurisdiction of the court in all legal disputes concerning the interpretation of a treaty; any question of international law; the existence of any fact which, if established, would constitute a breach of an international obligation; and the nature or extent of the reparation to be made for the breach of an international obligation. As of 1993, 68 states had made declarations under article 36, ¶2, but only 56 of the declarations were still in force. In 1986, in response to *Nicaragua v. United States, infra*, the United States withdrew its acceptance of the court's compulsory jurisdiction under article 36(2), but remains a party to many treaties conferring jurisdiction to the court under article 36, ¶1.

    a. **Reciprocity:** A state accepting the jurisdiction of the ICJ, under the optional clause of article 36, ¶2, does so only with respect to other states that have made a similar declaration. Thus, a respondent state may assert not only whatever reservations it has declared on the court's compulsory jurisdiction, but also any reservations of the petitioner state. *See Case of Certain Norwegian Loans* (*Fr. v. Nor.*) 1957 I.C.J. 9 (July 6).

    b. ***Nicaragua v. United States:*** In 1946, when the United States accepted the ICJ's jurisdiction under art. 36, ¶2, it accepted jurisdiction for a period of five years and "thereafter until the expiration of six months after notice may be given to terminate this declaration." In 1984, however, the United States sought to amend the declaration to exclude disputes with Central American states, with the amendment to take effect immediately. In *Military and Paramilitary Activities in and Against Nicaragua* (*Nicar. v. U.S.*), 1984 I.C.J. 392 (Nov. 26), the ICJ agreed with Nicaragua and ruled that the United States was bound to its original six-month-notice provision and was thus precluded from escaping the ICJ's jurisdiction on such short notice. The court so held even though Nicaragua's declaration had no advance notice requirement. The court refused to apply reciprocity to excuse compliance with a state's own declaration "whatever its scope, limitation, or conditions." The court appears to require that reasonable notice of withdrawal be given. Moreover, withdrawal precludes future cases but not cases that have already been started. *Nottebohm (Liecht. v. Guat.)* 1953 I.C.J. 111 (Apr. 6).

4. **Duration of declaration under article 36, ¶2:** Some declarations state no time limits, while others remain in effect for specific periods (usually five or ten years) and often include automatic renewal clauses. Many declarations include a right to terminate effective upon receipt by the U.N.'s secretary-general of a notice of withdrawal.

5. **Reservations to compulsory jurisdiction:** Article 36, ¶3 authorizes reservations conditioned on other states accepting the court's compulsory jurisdiction or for a certain time. In fact, a wide variety of reservations have been utilized:

    a. **Disputes to be settled by other means:** The most common reservation is to exclude disputes that the parties had already agreed to settle in other tribunals or by other means. Even when such an agreement exists, in determining jurisdiction, the scope of the reservation can be determined by considering the text of the reservation as well as external factors surrounding the reservation. *See generally* Beatrice I. Bonafé, *Maritime Delimitation in the Indian Ocean,* 111 AM. J. INT'L L. 725 (2017).

    b. **Disputes within domestic jurisdiction:** Another common reservation is the so-called self-judging reservation, such as the "Connally Amendment," a reservation by the United States to the acceptance of compulsory jurisdiction from 1946 to 1986. This reservation excluded from the jurisdiction of the ICJ "disputes with regard to matters which are essentially within the domestic jurisdiction of the United States of America as determined by the United States of America." It has been argued (most notably by ICJ judge and eminent scholar Hersch Lauterpacht) that such clauses violate article 36, ¶6, which provides that the ICJ, rather than domestic courts, shall determine whether or not it has jurisdiction over a dispute.

c. **Disputes under multilateral treaties:** Other reservations exclude disputes arising under a multilateral treaty "unless all parties to the treaty affected by the decision are also parties to the case before the court," or "unless all parties to the treaty are also parties to the case before the court."

d. **Specific disputes:** Also excluded may be specific disputes, such as those concerning law-of-the-sea issues and territorial disputes.

6. **Reservations for national security and self-defense:** A number of states have modified their acceptance of compulsory jurisdiction to exclude matters related to national security and defense. The ICJ itself, however, does not adhere to the view that such matters are *ipso facto* unsuitable for adjudication in its court. In *Oil Platforms* (*Iran v. U.S.*), 2003 I.C.J. 161, U.S. attacks on Iranian oil platforms were not measures necessary to national security because they did not qualify as acts of self-defense.

7. **Effect and enforcement of judgments:** Article 94 of the U.N. Charter and article 59 of the ICJ statute provide that judgments of the ICJ are ***binding*** upon the parties. Article 94 authorizes the Security Council to "make recommendations or decide upon measures to be taken to give effect to the judgment." Recommendations under Chapter VI or enforcement measures under Chapter VII are substantive and subject to the veto power. When Nicaragua sought enforcement of the ICJ decision against the United States, the United States vetoed the proposed resolution. *See* 25 ILM 1352 (1986).

8. **Advisory jurisdiction:** Article 65 of the ICJ Statute authorizes the court to give advisory opinions "on any legal question at the request of whatever body may be authorized by or in accordance with the charter to the United Nations to make such a request." Article 96 of the U.N. Charter authorizes the General Assembly or the Security Council to request advisory opinions, as well as "[o]ther organs of the United Nations and specialized agencies, which may at any time be so authorized by the General Assembly." Examples of other authorized bodies are the International Labor Organization, the World Health Organization, the International Bank for Reconstruction and Development (World Bank), the International Monetary Fund, and the International Atomic Energy Agency.

9. **Legal effect:** Although advisory opinions are legally ***non-binding***, they are, nevertheless, very influential in the development of international law. Some international agreements do provide that disputes arising from the agreement will be submitted to the ICJ for an advisory opinion that will be "accepted as decisive by the parties." The Convention on the Privileges and Immunities of the United Nations is one such example.

10. **Preliminary relief:** The ICJ under article 41 may provide preliminary relief "if the circumstances so require…to preserve the respective rights of either party." Examples include the preliminary prohibition on mining of Nicaraguan harbors in *Nicaragua v. United States*, and the preliminary order against Yugoslavia to take measures to prevent genocide in *Bosnia v. Yugoslavia*, 1993 I.C.J. 3.

B. Other international courts: Since World War II, the number of regional and specialized tribunals has grown, particularly in Western Europe. Three regional courts sitting in Europe are the Court of Justice of the European Communities, the Benelux Court of Justice, and the European Court of Human Rights.

1. European Court of Justice: This court is the ***sole judicial organ of the European Union***, which, as of 2010, includes Austria, Belgium, Bulgaria, Cyprus, Czech Republic, Denmark, Estonia, Finland, France, Germany, Greece, Hungary, Ireland, Italy, Latvia, Lithuania, Luxembourg, Malta, Netherlands, Poland, Portugal, Romania, Slovakia, Slovenia, Spain, Sweden, and the United Kingdom.

a. Functions: The European Court of Justice was established to ensure that the laws of the European Union are enforced, to act as referee between disputing member-states and between E.U. institutions and the member states, and to guard against infringement of individual rights by the E.U. institutions.

b. Structure: The 28 judges are appointed for staggered six-year terms and are eligible for reappointment. Traditionally, there is a judge from each member state. The court may sit in plenary session, the quorum for a full court being 15; or it may sit in chamber of 3 or 5 judges to consider preliminary rulings or actions instituted by individuals. The judges issue a single "judgment of the court" and have been sworn to uphold the secrecy of their deliberations. The judges are thus protected from the pressure of national interests. In addition to the judges, the European Court of Justice has eight advocates general, whose function it is to make "reasoned submissions on cases brought before the Court of Justice, in order to assist the Court…"

c. Jurisdiction: The European Court of Justice has only the jurisdiction conferred on it by the treaties. There is a fundamental division between direct actions, which are those actions initiated in the European Court of Justice, and actions begun in a national court but referred to the Court of Justice for a preliminary ruling. Direct actions begin and end in the European Court of Justice and are usually the result of an agreement between the parties assigning disputes to the Court of Justice. On the other hand, actions begun in national courts also end in national courts, which apply the preliminary ruling obtained from the Court of Justice. The Court of Justice issues preliminary rulings only when requested to do so by a national court seeking clarification of E.U. law before coming to its own decision.

d. Precedence: Although there is no legal doctrine of *stare decisis* in the European Court of Justice, the court often follows earlier decisions. Instances in which prior rulings have not been followed are often the result of changed circumstances or changed opinions among the judges. In such instances, the court does not follow the common law practice of formally overruling the earlier decision, but rather ignores it altogether.

e. Sources of law: The European Court of Justice relies on ***primary legislation***, ***secondary legislation***, and ***international agreements*** concluded by the European Union. Primary legislation includes the European Union's constitutive treaties with all their amendments, protocols, etc. Secondary legislation consists of the laws created by E.U. institutions.

f. The Court of First Instance: The Single European Act called for the addition of this new court to relieve the European Court of Justice of its heavy caseload. It has a more limited jurisdiction than the Court of Justice but otherwise has similar structures and procedures.

2. **Benelux Court of Justice:** This court is modeled after the European Court of Justice and was established by Belgium, the Netherlands, and Luxembourg. Its primary function is to ensure uniformity of the interpretation of the many Benelux treaties.

3. **European Court of Human Rights:** This court, established under the European Convention on Human Rights, enforces European human rights law and is discussed at Chapter 8, §VIII(B)(2).

VII. THE WORLD TRADE ORGANIZATION

The dispute settlement process under the WTO is considered a central pillar in resolving problems in the multilateral trading system and purports to offer stability in the global economy.

A. **The dispute arises:** A dispute arises when one country adopts policies regarding trade or takes action that one or more of the WTO members believe to be breaking WTO agreements or obligations. Instead of taking unilateral action, WTO membership stipulates that members will use a multilateral system of settling disputes.

B. **The Understanding on Rules and Procedures Governing the Settlement of Disputes:** Agreed upon in 1994, the Understanding on Rules and Procedures Governing the Settlement of Disputes (DSU) allows member states to engage in consultations to resolve trade disputes in regard to a "covered agreement" or, if that fails, to have a WTO panel hear the case. Only about 130 of 400-plus cases have reached the full panel process because of a strong preference to settle disputes through consultations. The operation of the dispute settlement process involves parties and third parties to a case and may involve Dispute Settlement Body (DSB) panels, composed of representatives of all WTO members and responsible for administering the DSU, the Appellate Body, the WTO secretariat, arbiters, independent experts, and several specialized institutions.

1. **When consultations fail:** If consultations fail to resolve the dispute within 60 days after the receipt of request for consultations, the complainant state(s) may request the establishment of a panel. Unless the DSB through consensus says otherwise, respondent states cannot prevent or delay the establishment of a panel, which usually consists of three members appointed ad hoc by the secretariat. They receive written and oral submissions of the parties and offer a presentation to the DSB.

2. **The final report:** The final version of the panel's report is distributed to the parties and then to all the members of the WTO. The report is required to be adopted at a meeting of the DSB within 60 days of its circulation unless consensus decides to not adopt the report or a party gives notice of its intention to appeal. A party may then appeal the panel report to the Appellate Body. The Appellate Body may uphold, modify, or reverse the panel's findings and conclusions, normally not lasting more than 60 days and an absolute maximum of 90 days.

C. **Compliance, compensation, retaliation:** Three alternative remedies are available to implement WTO rulings.

1. **Compliance:** In regards to compliance and the DSU, within 30 days of adopting the report, the member concerned is to inform the DSB of its intentions in regard to implementation of the recommendation and rulings. If it is impractical to comply immediately, the member is given a reasonable amount of time to comply. If there is a disagreement, it is dealt with by a panel, if possible the same one that heard the original dispute.

2. **Compensation and retaliation:** Two other possibilities are set out in the DSU if all else fails. If a member fails within the "reasonable period" to carry out the recommendations and rulings, it may negotiate with the complaining state for mutually acceptable compensation. If no agreement or compensation is reached within 20 days of the expiration of the "reasonable period," the prevailing state may require authorization from the DSB to suspend application to the member concerned of concessions or other obligations, but this type of retaliation is not preferred.

Quiz Yourself on INTERNATIONAL DISPUTE SETTLEMENT

6. Under the U.N. Charter, is there anything the organs and members of the United Nations must do before resorting to force? _______

7. Are all members of the United Nations parties to the ICJ statute? _______

8. Is a *compromis* on a case-by-case basis the only way a state may accept the ICJ's jurisdiction over a case? _______

9. May a state request an advisory opinion from the ICJ? _______

10. State *A* accepts the mandatory jurisdiction of the ICJ under Article 36. State *B* does as well, but with an exception for issues relating to its national security. State *B* sues State *A*, and State *A* contends it is not subject to jurisdiction because the case relates to State *A*'s national security. May State *A* assert State *B*'s exception to jurisdiction to avoid jurisdiction? _______

ANSWERS

6. Yes. Under article 2(3), members of the United Nations must attempt peaceful settlement of disputes before resorting to any use of force authorized by the Charter. Similarly, the General Assembly and Security Council are directed by the Charter to use peaceful methods of dispute settlement. Exhaustion of other peaceful and enforcement methods of dispute settlement is particularly important under article 42, which requires a determination by the Security Council that measures short of the use of force would be inadequate before force may be authorized by the Council.

7. Yes, but it is important to understand that a state being a party to the ICJ statute does not make it subject to the court's jurisdiction. A state must separately agree to the court's jurisdiction.

8. No. A state may agree to be subject to the ICJ's jurisdiction in a particular case or agree in a treaty to be subject to the court's jurisdiction in any dispute arising under the treaty. It may also agree to be subject generally to the ICJ's mandatory jurisdiction in any case brought against the state.

9. No. Only designated organs of the United Nations may request an advisory opinion from the ICJ.

10. Yes. Under the reciprocity doctrine of article 36, a state may assert not only its own reservations to jurisdiction, but those of the state suing it as well.

Exam Tips on INTERNATIONAL DISPUTE SETTLEMENT

- There are a number of serious limitations, legal and political, on the reach of the ICJ's jurisdiction, but its decisions continue to be very influential in forming international law. Decisions of the ICJ are binding as well on the parties to the decision. The ICJ's decisions, however, can be enforced only by the Security Council, which is itself a substantive decision subject to veto power.
- Keep in mind that although the United States no longer accepts the general compulsory jurisdiction of the ICJ, it remains subject to its jurisdiction for disputes arising under a number of multilateral treaties (for example, the Vienna Convention on Consular Relations) and whenever it accepts jurisdiction on a case-by-case basis.
- Also keep in mind, however, that the U.S. Supreme Court held in *Medellin v. Texas* in 2008, *see* Chapter 3, §II(C)(2), that decisions of the ICJ were not directly enforceable as federal law in state courts and that neither the relevant provisions of the U.N. Charter, the ICJ statute, nor the Optional Protocol to the Vienna Convention on Consular Relations was self-executing. (The Court assumed without deciding that the provisions of the Vienna Convention on Consular Relations itself were self-executing.)

CHAPTER 8

THE RIGHTS OF INDIVIDUALS—INTERNATIONAL LAW OF HUMAN RIGHTS

I. STATUS OF INDIVIDUALS

Under the modern international law of human rights, ***individuals are protected without regard to their status as nationals or aliens***. This approach is in sharp contrast to the traditional concept of international law governing relations between states. The law governing a state's obligations to an alien was established within this traditional framework of international law regulating the relationship between states, but not the relationship between states and individuals. Thus, an offense to an alien was considered an offense only against the alien's native state. The modern international law of human rights, however, makes nationality irrelevant.

II. BRIEF HISTORY

Historically, a state's treatment of individuals in its territory was considered a domestic affair, not a matter of international law.

A. Traditional concept: An early exception, dating as far back as Roman times, was recognition of a state's obligations to aliens. *See* Chapter 4, §III (discussing the recognition of states and governments). By the late nineteenth century, there were many "minority" treaties concluded by European governments to protect ethnic minorities with which they identified in other states. The only clear early example of an internationalization of individual rights was with respect to slavery. Several major countries abolished slavery in the nineteenth century; the unacceptability of slavery became an international standard; and slave trading became illegal. In a related matter, the doctrines of humanitarian intervention and humanitarian rules of war have roots traceable to the seventeenth and eighteenth centuries.

B. Early twentieth century: A major recognition of an international law of individual human rights came with the establishment of the International Labor Organization (ILO) after World War I. The ILO set forth basic universal standards for labor and social welfare and has since promulgated over a hundred conventions. A number of the peace treaties after World War I provided protection to national, religious, linguistic, and ethnic minorities in Central and Eastern Europe. These treaties focused on group rights—a minority's right to its own schools, language, and religions—and freedom from discrimination. The Covenant of the League of Nations also created a mandate system by which the population of the colonies formerly under German and Turkish control were to be protected.

C. Post–World War II: The modern concept of international human rights law is the result of the world's reaction to the Holocaust and other Nazi atrocities during World War II. Nazi war criminals were tried for violating international law before the Nuremberg tribunal, the establishment of which demonstrated that human rights were a matter of international concern rather than a matter left solely to each state. *See* §IV(I) of this chapter, *infra*. This modern concept of international human rights law was also key to the formation of the United Nations in 1945, having as one of its principal purposes the promotion and protection of human rights. U.N. Charter art. 1, ¶2; art. 3.

D. **Current status:** Although the basic concept of international human rights law is now firmly established, its relatively recent emergence results in a body of law characterized by evolving ideas, institutions, and procedures.

III. HUMAN RIGHTS AND THE UNITED NATIONS

The U.N. Charter in 1945 was a departure from earlier treaties remedying the problems of particular abuses or particular groups because it was the first attempt to provide comprehensive protection for all individuals. In 1946, the United Nations established a Commission on Human Rights to draft human rights treaties, and in 1948, the U.N. General Assembly passed the Universal Declaration of Human Rights. In the decades since its foundation, the United Nations has continued to promote and protect human rights and has drafted treaties for global adoption dealing with many aspects of human rights. In addition to the Charter, the Universal Declaration of Human Rights, together with the subsequent International Covenant on Civil and Political Rights, the International Covenant on Economic, Social, and Cultural Rights, and the two Optional Protocols to the Civil and Political Covenant form the so-called International Bill of Human Rights.

A. **The U.N. Charter:** The two main provisions of the U.N. Charter concerning human rights are articles 55 and 56. These articles are the foundation of modern human rights law.

1. **Article 55:** Article 55 states that "the United Nations shall promote . . . universal respect for, and observance of, human rights and fundamental freedoms for all without distinction as to race, sex, language, or religion."

2. **Article 56:** Article 56 states that "all members pledge themselves to take joint and separate action in cooperation with the Organization for the achievement of the purposes set forth in article 55."

3. **Implementation:** The Commission on Human Rights was established in 1946 to draft treaties implementing articles 55 and 56, and these two articles have been the main source of subsequent human rights treaties. The language of article 56 may suggest that the member states are obliged to a progressive rather than present fulfillment of the goals set forth in article 55. The imprecision of articles 55 and 56 has led one U.S. court to find that they are not self-executing and do not confer any rights on individuals. In *Sei Fuji v. California*, 242 P.2d 617 (1952), the California Supreme Court held that the U.N. Charter lacked the mandatory quality and precision required to create enforceable rights as a matter of U.S. law.

   In April 2006, General Assembly Resolution 60/251 upgraded the status of the Commission on Human Rights to the Human Rights Council. Changing the status of the commission resulted in the creation of a standing body that now operates under the mandate of the General Assembly instead of the mandate of the Economic and Social Council. The council is intended to function as a more authoritative human rights body and respond more efficiently to claims of human rights violations. The creation of this council was opposed by the United States. *See* Human Rights Council, G.A. Res. 60/251, U.N. Doc. A/RES/60/251 (April 3, 2006); Yvonne Terlingen, "The Human Rights Council: A New Era in U.N. Human Rights Work?" ETHICS AND INTERNATIONAL AFFAIRS (2007), *available at* https://www.carnegiecouncil.org/publications/ journal/21_2/essay/001.html/_res/id=sa_File1/EIA_21_2_Terlingen.pdf (last accessed April 10, 2016).

B. The Universal Declaration of Human Rights: In 1948, the U.N. General Assembly passed the Universal Declaration of Human Rights. The rights delineated fall into two general categories: ***civil and political rights***, and ***economic, social, and cultural rights***. This declaration was intended to define the rights protected by articles 55 and 56 of the U.N. Charter. As a resolution of the General Assembly, it is not per se legally binding. At the time of its passage, many of the 48 states that voted to pass the declaration regarded it as a statement of aspirations rather than a legal obligation. There is, however, an argument to be made that since 1948, it has become ***binding as a new rule of customary international law***. Those finding a legal obligation point to a 1968 U.N. resolution proclaiming the Declaration to constitute "an obligation for the members of the international community." Clearly, some of the rights listed have evolved into customary international law.

1. **Civil and political rights:** The provisions dealing with civil and political rights include the prohibition of slavery and torture; discrimination on grounds of race, gender, religion, language, political opinion, nationality, ethnicity, birth, or other status; and arbitrary arrests or interferences with privacy. Protected are the rights to a fair trial, to marry, to own property, and to political asylum. In addition, the freedoms of religion, expression, movement, and peaceful assembly and association are to be respected. Also called for are the establishment of free elections and equal access to public positions. Political and civil rights are the ***foundation of democratic political systems*** and have been the focus of human rights development in those countries.

2. **Economic, social, and cultural rights:** Communist and developing countries have pushed for greater recognition of these rights, which include the right to social security, full employment, fair work conditions, education, health care, an adequate standard of living, and participation in the community's cultural life.

3. **Limitations on human rights:** Most human rights documents contain exceptions to the protections provided as necessary to maintain public order and preserve the security of the state. Accordingly, the Universal Declaration allows limitations "for the purpose of securing due recognition and respect for the rights and freedoms of others and of meeting the just requirements of morality, public order, and the general welfare in a democratic society." U.N. Charter art. 29, ¶2. Such limitations are uncertain in scope and often subject to abuse.

C. The U.N. human rights covenants: The two groups of rights set forth in the Universal Declaration of Human Rights were the basis for the General Assembly's adoption of two treaties in 1966: the International Covenant on Civil and Political Rights (with the Optional Protocol to the Civil and Political Covenant) and the International Covenant on Economic, Social, and Cultural Rights. Both entered into force in 1976 after ratification by 35 states.

1. **The International Covenant on Civil and Political Rights (ICP):** This instrument deals, in greater detail, with the same political and civil rights protected by the Declaration of Human Rights. The ICP has approximately 167 states parties.

   a. **Rights protected:** In addition to the many individual rights protected by the Declaration, the Covenant includes two "rights of peoples" or group rights: the ***right of self-determination*** and the ***right of all peoples to freely dispose of their natural wealth and resources***. Article 27 also provides that ethnic, religious, and linguistic minorities "shall not be denied the right, in community with the other members of their own group, to enjoy their own culture, to profess and practice their own religion, or to use their own language." Interestingly, neither Covenant includes the right to property included in the Universal Declaration.

b. **Limitations:** *See* §VII(A) of this chapter, *infra* (discussing and listing the limitations under this covenant).

2. **The International Covenant on Economic, Social, and Cultural Rights:** This covenant, with 160 states parties, like the one on civil and political rights, amplifies the rights set forth in the Universal Declaration.

a. **Rights protected:** In addition to elaboration on the economic, social, and cultural rights in the Universal Declaration, the covenant also guarantees two collective rights: the ***right of self-determination*** and the ***right of all peoples to freely dispose of their natural wealth and resources***.

b. **Limitations:** The legal obligations of the Covenant are much less precise and demanding than those in the Covenant on Civil and Political Rights. Article 2 requires a state only to "take steps . . . to the maximum of its available resources . . . with a view to achieving progressively" the rights in the Covenant. Moreover, the state may limit rights "for the purpose of promoting the general welfare in a democratic society." U.N. Charter art. 4.

c. **Review of compliance:** Review of compliance is also more limited than in the other covenant. Implementation is limited to review of state reports by the Economic and Social Council, which has established an expert committee to review reports.

d. **Recent U.N. Conventions: Some recent U.N. Conventions are as follows:**

1. The Convention on the Protection of the Rights of All Migrant Workers and Members of Their Families went into force on July 1, 2003; it mainly seeks to protect the human rights of migrant workers by calling attention to the fact that they are humans. It calls for sanctions against entities that violate these rights by luring migrant workers with false information and also against those that traffic in human beings.

2. The Convention on the Rights of Persons with Disabilities went into force on May 3, 2008. This Convention is designed to provide persons with disabilities the same rights and access to information as those without disabilities. Some of the rights specifically protected in the Convention include the right to live independently; the right to personal mobility; and the right to access roads, buildings, and information.

3. The Convention for the Protection of all Persons from Enforced Disappearance went into effect on December 23, 2010. The Convention calls for states parties to investigate claims of enforced disappearance and bring the perpetrators to justice, to cooperate with other states parties to bring people involved in the enforced disappearance of people to justice, and to ensure that victims of enforced disappearance receive adequate compensation.

D. **The role of specialized agencies of the United Nations:** A number of specialized agencies, particularly U.N. commissions, the International Labor Organization (ILO), the U.N. Economic and Social Council (ECOSOC), and the Commission on Human Rights, have been active in the area of developing human rights law.

IV. FUNDAMENTAL HUMAN RIGHTS

Many of the rights discussed below are addressed by specific U.N. treaties and resolutions. Although those instruments are emphasized here, support for these fundamental rights can often be found in other international agreements, as well as regional human rights conventions.

A. The right of peoples to self-determination: The principle of self-determination is the ***right of people in a territory to decide the political and legal status of that territory***. The concept has its political origins in the American Declaration of Independence (1776) and has been invoked throughout the nineteenth and twentieth centuries and beyond by nationalist movements as the basis for their right to establish independent states. In 1945, the concept of self-determination was incorporated into the U.N. Charter. In 2017, Catalonia declared independence from Spain following the success of the "referendum." Spain brought a suit against the Catalan government declaring that the right of self-determination was not extended within States with entirely democratic systems. The Spanish Constitutional Court determined that (1) the Catalan government did not have the constitutional authority to issue a referendum and (2) the Spanish Constitution had supremacy over inferior laws, including the ones created by the Catalan government.

1. **The U.N. Charter:** Although the U.N. Charter incorporates the concept of self-determination, the general principles of "self-determination of peoples" referred to in the Charter lack concrete definition. The main provisions referring to self-determination are in articles 1, ¶2; 55; 73; and 76, ¶b. Article 1, ¶2 states one purpose of the Charter is the promotion of "equal rights" and "self-determination of peoples." Article 55 states that the United Nations promotes solutions to international economic, social, health, and related problems with a view to creating stability and friendly relations among nations "based on the respect for the principle of equal rights and self-determination of peoples." Article 73 is aimed at U.N. members assuming responsibility for the administration of non-self-governing territories. Such members are to assist in the development of self-government through the establishment of free political institutions. Chapter XII states that a basic objective of the international trusteeship system established for the trust territories after World War II is to promote "progressive development towards self-government or independence as may be appropriate to the particular circumstances of each territory and its peoples and the freely expressed wishes of the peoples concerned." U.N. Charter art. 76, ¶b.

2. **Other U.N. documents:** The U.N. General Assembly has contributed to the development of the principle of self-determination. In 1960, the U.N. General Assembly adopted the Declaration on the Granting of Independence to Colonial Countries and Peoples, viewed as the basis for the U.N. policy of decolonization. As discussed in §III(B) of this chapter, *supra*, the International Covenants on Civil and Political Rights and on Economic, Social, and Cultural Rights also provided for the right of all peoples to self-determination. The most comprehensive and authoritative treatment of the principle of self-determination is the U.N. Declaration on Principles of International Law Concerning Friendly Relations and Cooperation Among States.

B. Defining a "people": For a group to be characterized as a "people," there must exist the proper objective and subjective elements. The objective element is the existence of an ***ethnic group*** linked by some ***common history***. The common history is often, but not always, expressed by a common language, religion, or territory. The subjective element is the group's ***own identification of itself as a "people."*** The group maintains the desire to live together and uphold common traditions.

C. **Legal status of principle of self-determination:** Despite its inclusion in several U.N. documents, the principle of self-determination is subject to some uncertainty as a result of its lack of concrete definition, as well as its conflict with the well-established principle of sovereignty. The law of decolonization and the right of the inhabitants of an established state to determine their own government are well accepted, but there is little or no agreement on the right of groups to secede from states of which they form a part, the reunification of peoples in divided states, or the right of minorities to preserve their own separate identities within a state.

D. **Rights of indigenous peoples:** Indigenous peoples have asserted a right to self-determination to prevent their complete absorption into states dominated by non-aboriginal populations. Indigenous peoples may be seeking to secede to form their own states or to retain control over their own communities and land. Recognition of such a right of self-determination for indigenous peoples presents conflicts with respect to territorial claims and competition between the sovereignty of the state and the traditional institutions of the indigenous people. The emphasis on integration and assimilation in the Convention Concerning the Protection and Integration of Indigenous and Other Tribal and Semi-Tribal Populations in Independent Countries is disfavored by many indigenous leaders. The U.N. General Assembly approved a Declaration on the Rights of Indigenous Peoples on September 13, 2007. This document affirmed the rights discussed above and many others, including the right to practice traditional medicine and education. GA Res. 61/295, U.N. Doc A/61/295 (Oct. 2, 2007). Additionally, in 2015 the Inter-American Court of Human Rights "assert[ed] that under the American Convention on Human Rights indigenous peoples are entitled, as collective entities, to recognition of their legal personality." Lucas Lixinski, *Case of the Kaliña and Lokono Peoples v. Suriname*, 111 AM. J. INT'L L. 147, 147-148 (2017).

E. **Civil and political rights:** These rights are defined and protected under the International Covenant on Civil and Political Rights, discussed at §III(C) of this chapter, *supra*.

F. **Economic, social, and cultural rights:** These rights are defined and protected under the International Covenant on Economic, Social, and Cultural Rights, discussed at §III(C) of this chapter, *supra*.

G. **Prohibition of slavery:** An early development in the internationalization of human rights was the widespread prohibition against slavery. During the nineteenth century, major countries abolished slavery, resulting in the development of an international standard prohibiting slavery and outlawing the slave trade. This antislavery movement eventually led to the adoption of the Slavery Convention of 1926 and the protocol amending that convention. The prohibition against slavery is a ***fundamental norm as a matter of customary international law***, and the norm is recognized as *jus cogens*, from which no derogation is permitted.

H. **Genocide:** The 1948 Convention on the Prevention and Punishment of the Crime of Genocide was adopted by the General Assembly in response to the atrocities of the Holocaust in World War II. Genocide is a crime for which individuals are punishable under international law. Convention on the Prevention and Punishment of the Crime of Genocide, Dec. 9, 1948, 78 U.N.T.S. 277.

1. **Definition:** Article 2 defines genocide as acts "committed with the intent to destroy, in whole or in part, a national, ethnic, racial, or religious group, as such." Prohibited acts include killing members of the group, inflicting serious mental or bodily harm, inflicting living conditions calculated to destroy the group, imposing birth control measures to prevent births within the group, and forcibly transferring children of the group to another group.

Under both the Convention and customary international law, genocide is a crime that states undertake to prevent and to punish.

a. **Definition:** In the case concerning the massacre at Srebrenica, the ICJ ruled that the state of Serbia had not committed genocide but had nonetheless violated the Geneva Convention by failing to prevent genocide and failing to punish those who committed genocide or surrender them to the International Criminal Tribunal for the Former Yugoslavia (ICTY). Many commentators have argued against courts affixing state responsibility for crimes of genocide because judgments of collective guilt undermine efforts to prevent future genocides by not holding individuals accountable for their actions. *Application of the Convention on the Prevention and Punishment of the Crime of Genocide (Bosn. & Herz. v. Serb. & Mont.)* (Judgment of Feb. 26, 2007), *available at* http://www.icj-cij.org/docket/index.php?p1=3&p2=3&case=91&p3=4 (last visited April 10, 2016).

2. **Punishable acts:** Article 3 makes punishable the following: genocide, conspiracy to commit genocide, direct and public incitement to commit genocide, complicity in genocide, and attempt to commit genocide.

3. **Elements of genocide:** The International Criminal Tribunal for Rwanda found that a conviction for "complicity in genocide" requires proof that the defendant actually participated in the killing. It also held that "direct, public incitement to commit genocide" is a crime that carries personal criminal liability. *Prosecutor v. Akayesu*, Case No. ICTR-96-4-T, Judgment (Sept. 2, 1998).

4. **Jurisdiction:** Given the absence of an established international tribunal for genocide or criminal court, punishment is left to the domestic courts of states. Genocide is generally acknowledged as a ***universal crime punishable in any state***. In the United States, the Second Circuit determined that the Alien Tort Claims Act serves to give federal courts jurisdiction over any claim of a violation of the law of nations, *i.e.*, a universal crime. *Kadic v. Karadzic*, 70 F.3d 232 (2d Cir. 1995).

I. **Crimes against humanity:** The Nuremburg Tribunal was established after World War II to punish Nazi leaders in accordance with international law. *See* Chapter 13, §IV(A). The Nuremberg Charter, charging Nazi leaders with "crimes against humanity," invoked the customary law of human rights and was an important step in the development of international human rights law.

1. **Definition:** "Crimes against humanity" were defined as "murder, extermination, enslavement, deportation, and other inhumane acts committed against any civilian population, before or during the war, or persecutions on political, racial, or religious ground . . . whether or not in violation of the domestic law of the country where perpetrated." Agreement for the Prosecution and Punishment of the Major War Criminals of the European Axis (Nuremberg Charter), art. 6, 59 Stat. 1544, 1547-1548. Crimes against humanity can be committed in peacetime as well as war. *See* Chapter 9, §II(E)(4).

2. **Rape and sexual enslavement:** In *Prosecutor v. Kunarac, Kovac and Vukovic*, Case No. IT-96-23, Judgment on Appeal (June 12, 2002), the ICTY based conviction of crimes against humanity on incidences of rape and sexual enslavement. The Trial Chamber found that rape was used by members of the Bosnian Serb armed forces as an instrument of terror that they were given free rein to apply whenever and against whomever they wished. The decision sets an important precedent for expanding the definition of a "crime against humanity." The Council

of European Convention on Action against Trafficking in Human Beings focuses on protecting victims of human trafficking while prosecuting traffickers. States are to prevent human trafficking and aid victims, which includes making offers of medical and psychological treatment and even accommodation. It was adopted on May 16, 2005, and entered into force on February 1, 2008.

a. **Rome Statute of the International Criminal Court:** In 1998 the international community gathered in Rome, Italy, and created the Rome Statute. The statute took effect in July 2002, establishing an International Criminal Court. The statute designated many crimes, including rape and sexual enslavement, as "crimes against humanity." For the rape or enslavement to be a "crime against humanity," it must occur "as part of a widespread or systematic attack directed against any civilian population, with knowledge of the attack." Rome Statute Article 7. Specifically, the requirements include both *actus reus* and *mens rea.* The *actus reus* requirement includes (1) the "widespread or systematic attack against members of a civilian population"; (2) the nexus between the specific crime and the attack; (3) an attack against a civilian population; and (4) an attack "on a widespread or systematic basis." The *mens rea* requirement includes " 'actual' or 'constructive' knowledge" of the greater systematic attack. United Nations, Rome Statute of the International Criminal Court (2003), *available at* https://treaties.un.org/Pages/ViewDetails.aspx?src=TREATY&mtdsg_ no=XVIII-10&chapter=18&lang=en; Vincent-Joel Proulx, *Rethinking the Jurisdiction of the International Criminal Court in the Post-September 11th Era: Should Acts of Terrorism Qualify as Crimes Against Humanity?* 19 AM. U. INT'L REV. 1009, 1060, 1061 (2004).

J. **Prohibitions of discrimination:** Racial, sexual, and religious discrimination have been prohibited in certain international treaties.

1. **Racial discrimination:** The principal treaties are the International Convention on the Elimination of All Forms of Racial Discrimination and the International Convention on the Suppression and Punishment of the Crime of Apartheid. The first convention entered into force in 1969, and the Apartheid Convention entered into force in 1976.

a. **International Convention on the Elimination of All Forms of Racial Discrimination:** This convention defines "racial discrimination" as "any distinction, exclusion, restriction, or preference based on race, colour, descent of national or ethnic origin which has the purpose or effect of nullifying or impairing the recognition, enjoyment or exercise, on an equal footing, of human rights and fundamental freedoms in the political, social, cultural or any other field of public life." International Convention on the Elimination of All Forms of Racial Discrimination, opened for signature Mar. 7, 1966, art. 1, 660 U.N.T.S. 195 [hereinafter *Race Convention*]. States parties must eliminate racial discrimination (art. 2), and are permitted in some circumstances to take special measures to secure advancement of racial or ethnic groups. art. 1. States are also obligated to prevent, prohibit, and eradicate the practice of apartheid in their territories. art. 3. The enforcement machinery of this Convention goes beyond the usual reporting mechanisms for implementation. A Committee on the Elimination of Racial Discrimination has jurisdiction to hear complaints by one state against another, as well as individual petitions if the state has agreed to be subject to such petitions. arts. 11, 14. The action it can take, however, is limited to reports and recommendations.

b. **The International Convention on the Suppression and Punishment of the Crime of Apartheid:** This convention defines apartheid as a ***crime against humanity***, involving "inhuman acts committed for the purpose of establishing and maintaining domination by one racial group of persons over any other racial group of persons and systematically oppressing them." "Inhuman acts" include denial of life and liberty through murders, infliction of serious bodily or mental harm, and arbitrary arrests and imprisonment; certain suppressive or divisive legislative measures; and forced labor. International Convention on the Suppression and Punishment of the Crime of Apartheid, Nov. 30, 1973, art. II, 13 I.L.M. 50 (1974). Liability extends to conspiracy to commit, aiding and abetting, and direct incitement of the inhuman acts listed in article II. A person charged with the offense may be tried by any state party or before an international penal tribunal yet to be established, and implementation consists of periodic reports to a group of experts.

2. **Sexual discrimination:** The first international document to recognize equal rights without regard to sex was the U.N. Charter. The International Convention on the Elimination of All Forms of Discrimination Against Women, which was adopted by the General Assembly in 1979 and entered into force in 1981, focuses on the status of women and provides an extensive bill of rights for women, including the right to equal education, health care, and equality before the law.

   a. **General protections:** "Discrimination against women" is defined as "any distinction, exclusion, or restriction made on the basis of sex which has the effect or purpose of impairing or nullifying the recognition, enjoyment or exercise by women, irrespective of their marital status, on a basis of equality of men and women, of human rights and fundamental freedoms in the political, economic, social, cultural, civil, or any other field." Convention on the Elimination of All Forms of Discrimination Against Women, Dec. 18, 1979, art. 1, U.N.G.A. Res 34/180 (xxxiv) [hereinafter *Sex Discrimination Convention*].

   Under article 3 of the Sex Discrimination Convention, "State Parties shall take in all fields, in particular in the political, social, economic, and cultural fields, all appropriate measures, including legislation to ensure the full development and advancement of women, for the purpose of guaranteeing them the exercise and enjoyment of human rights and fundamental freedoms on a basis of equality with men." Special measures designed to achieve equality between men and women shall not be considered discrimination but shall be discontinued when the objective of equality has been achieved. Sex Discrimination Convention, art. 4, U.N.G.A. Res 34/180 (xxxiv). States parties must take all "appropriate measures" "(a) To modify the social and cultural patterns of conduct of men and women, with a view to achieving the elimination of prejudices and customs and all other practices which are based on the idea of the inferiority or the superiority of either of the sexes or on stereotyped roles for men and women. (b) To ensure that family education includes a proper understanding of maternity as a social function and the recognition of the common responsibility of men and women in the upbringing and development of their children." Sex Discrimination Convention, art. 5, U.N.G.A. Res 34/180 (xxxiv).

   b. **Review of compliance:** Implementation is reviewed through submission of periodic reports by states parties to the Committee on the Elimination of Discrimination Against Women. Sex Discrimination Convention, U.N.G.A. Res 34/180 (xxxiv).

3. **Religious discrimination:** Of more recent origin than the other discrimination prohibitions, the prohibition against discrimination on religious grounds is embodied in the 1981 U.N. General Assembly resolution entitled Declaration on the Elimination of All Forms of Intolerance and of Discrimination Based on Religion or Belief. Passed in accordance with the U.N. Charter, it affirms the fundamental freedom of all thought, conscience, and religion; the elimination of discrimination; and the right of children to have religious education. Freedom of religion is subject only to "such limitations as are prescribed by law and are necessary to protect public safety, order, health, or morals or the fundamental rights and freedoms of others." art. 1, ¶3. States have an affirmative duty to enact or rescind legislation in order to prevent or eliminate discrimination based on religious beliefs. art. 4. Among other specific rights, the Declaration acknowledges the right of parents to have access to religious education and the right to teach a religion or belief in suitable places. arts. 5, 6. Nothing in the Declaration, however, is to restrict or derogate from any right in the Universal Declaration on Human Rights or the International Covenants on Human Rights. art. 8.

K. **Freedom from torture:** There are ***no justifications for torture*** or exceptions to its prohibition. Convention Against Torture and Other Cruel, Inhuman, or Degrading Treatment or Punishment, entered into force June 26, 1987, art. 2, ¶¶2, 3, U.N. Doc. E/CN. 4/1984/72, 23 I.L.M. 1027 [hereinafter *Torture Convention*]. States must adopt measures to prevent torture in their jurisdictions and ensure that torture, complicity, and attempts to commit torture are criminal offenses. art. 2, ¶1; art. 4.

1. **Definition of torture:** The Torture Convention, which entered into force in 1987, defines torture as ". . . any act by which severe pain or suffering, whether physical or mental, is intentionally inflicted on a person for such purposes as obtaining from him or a third person information or a confession, punishing him for an act he or a third person has committed or is suspected of having committed, or intimidating or coercing him or a third person, or for any reason based on discrimination of any kind, when such pain or suffering is inflicted by or at the instigation of or with the consent or acquiescence of a public official or other person acting in an official capacity. It does not include pain or suffering arising only from, inherent in, or incidental to lawful sanctions." Torture Convention, art. 1, ¶1.

2. **Committee for the Prevention of Torture (CPT):** The implementation of articles 2(1) and 4 is monitored through periodic state reports to a Committee for the Prevention of Torture. If a state consents, the committee can hear inter-state complaints and individual complaints. Torture Convention, arts. 21, 22. If no solution is reached, the committee issues a report to the parties involved. The committee also has the unusual power to initiate inquiries unless a state has declined to recognize this committee function at the time of its signature on ratification. arts. 20, 28.

3. **Rape as torture:** The International Criminal Tribunal for Rwanda found that rape committed during interrogation amounted to torture. *Prosecutor v. Furundzija*, Case No. IT-95-17/1-T, Judgment (Dec. 10, 1998).

4. **Other means of torture and prohibited conduct:** The European Court of Human Rights held that the "five techniques" of sensory deprivation and disorientation employed by the United Kingdom during detention and interrogation of suspected Irish terrorists were violations of article 3 of the European Convention on Human Rights. The court ruled that use of techniques like "hooding" and sleep deprivation did not amount to torture per se, but it found that the techniques were prohibited inhumane and degrading treatment. In response to the judgment, the

attorney general of the United Kingdom announced that the techniques would never again be used by the government as interrogation aids. *Republic of Ireland v. United Kingdom*, 2 Eur. Ct. H.R. 25 (1978).

5. **Torture and inadmissible evidence:** Under Article 15 of the Convention Against Torture, the European Convention on Human Rights, and also the common law of England, courts can never hear evidence obtained by torture. Consequently in England, the burden of proving the evidence was not obtained through torture in cases before the Special Immigration Appeals Court (SIAC) must be placed on the government. *A and Others v. Sec'y of State for the Home Dep't (No. 2),*[2005] UKHL 71; *see Abbasi and Anor v. Sec'y of State for Foreign and Commonwealth Affairs*, [2002] EWCA Civ. 1598, 126 ILR 685.

6. **Asylum and torture:** There is conflicting international law regarding the granting of asylum in the case of torture that is incidental to conflict conditions such as civil war. In regard to minority discrimination and killings and tortures arising from clan and sub-clan based civil war in Somalia, the English House of Lords explains that, unlike France or Germany, Britain recognizes the persecution by non-state agents as the basis of the asylum claim and overturned a previous decision that the secretary of state had the right to deport because an asylum claim did not arise from the 1951 Geneva Convention in cases where the asylum seeker was *at no greater risk* of such ill treatment by reason of his clan or sub-clan membership than other people generally at risk. In contrast, the Australian courts decided in a similar case that in the context of the Somali civil war, asylum arises from clan and sub-clan based civil war if the dominant group involved in targeting the asylum-seeker's minority group exercises de facto control. *See Adan v. Sec'y of State for the Home Dep't*, [1999] 1 A.C. 293; *Elmi v. Australia*, U.N. Committee Against Torture (2007) 7IHRR 603.

L. **Rights of refugees:** The principal international instruments concerning refugees are the 1951 Geneva Convention Relating to the Status of Refugees, the 1957 Hague amendments to that convention, and the 1967 Protocol Relating to the Status of Refugees. At present, customary international law ***does not appear to recognize a right to asylum***, although this rule has been the subject of much criticism.

1. **Definition of a refugee:** The 1951 Geneva Convention defines a refugee as a person who "owing to well-founded fear of being persecuted for reasons of race, religion, nationality, membership of a particular social group or political opinion, is outside the country of his nationality and is unable or, owing to such fear, is unwilling to avail himself of the protection of that country; or who, not having a nationality and being outside the country of his former habitual residence as a result of such events, is unable, or owing to such fear, is unwilling to return to it." Geneva Convention Relating to the Status of Refugees, July 28, 1951, art. 1, §A, ¶2, 189 U.N.T.S. 137. In *INS v. Elias-Zacarias*, 502 U.S. 478 (1992), the Supreme Court held that a Guatemalan native had failed to show persecution on account of political opinion based on his resistance to recruitment by a guerilla movement because he was afraid the government would retaliate against him or his family.

   a. **Compare:** In *In re Fauzia Kasinga*, Bd. of Immig. Appeals, File A73 476 695 (June 13, 1996), the Board of Immigration Appeals held (for the first time) that a well-founded fear of female genital mutilation can be the basis for a grant of asylum. In granting asylum, the board found the applicant to be a member of a "particular social group," consisting of young women of her tribe who had not been subjected to female genital mutilation and who opposed the practice, with a well-founded fear of countrywide persecution.

In 2004, the court reversed a Board of Immigration Appeals decision that denied asylum to a nine-year-old Ethiopian girl and her mother. The court ruled that fear of female genital mutilation that might occur if the girl were deported to Ethiopia was a valid basis for an asylum claim and refugee status in the United States. *Abay v. Ashcroft*, 368 F.3d 634 (6th Cir. 2004).

b. **Expanded definition:** In *Aguirre-Cervantes v. INS*, 242 F.3d 1169 (9th Cir. 2001), the court held that a Mexican woman was eligible for asylum because she and her family were subjected to severe physical abuse that amounted to "persecution" by her father in Mexico. The court expanded the definition of persecution against a particular social group by concluding that the woman's immediate family constituted a "particular social group."

2. **State's obligation to refugees:** The Convention aims to secure the best possible treatment of refugees lawfully within a state, and its provisions address many topics, including access to courts, employment, housing, and education. Refugees illegally within a state must be given a reasonable time to resettle. The Convention and subsequent instruments do not, however, guarantee any right of entry into a country or impose any duty on the state to admit refugees. The ***state has a right to grant asylum***, but the ***individual has no right to demand asylum***. Articles 13 and 14 of the Universal Declaration of Human Rights and the General Assembly's 1967 Declaration on Territorial Asylum recognize the "right to leave any country, including [one's] own" and the "right to seek and to enjoy in other countries asylum from persecution." Those rights, however, are not coupled with a corresponding state obligation to grant asylum. The principle of *nonrefoulement* prohibits return of the refugee to the state of persecution, and an admitted refugee may be deported only for reasons of state security.

3. **The *Haitian Refugees* case:** In *Sale v. Haitian Centers Council,* 509 U.S. 155 (1993), the U.S. Supreme Court held that neither domestic immigration law nor article 33 of the Refugee Convention, prohibiting return of a refugee to the state of persecution, applied extraterritorially to interception upon the high seas.

4. **Diplomatic asylum:** Diplomatic asylum is the ***granting of refuge by a state in its embassies, ships, or aircraft in the territory of another state***. Once diplomatic asylum is granted, there is a right of safe conduct from the foreign state. Beyond that, the rules of asylum are generally based on treaty rather than customary international law.

V. NEWLY EMERGING RIGHTS AND FUNDAMENTAL RIGHTS RECOGNIZED AS CUSTOMARY INTERNATIONAL LAW

Many of the rights recognized in international agreements above are also recognized as customary international law. An early invocation of human rights as part of customary international law was found in the Nuremberg Charter, charging Nazi leaders with "crimes against humanity." A more recent acknowledgment of the rights recognized in customary law is found in *Filartiga v. Pena-Irala*, 630 F.2d 876, 884, 890 (2d Cir. 1980) ("we conclude that official torture is now prohibited by the law of nations."). "[T]he torturer has become—like the pirate and slave trader before him—*hostis humani generis*, an enemy of all mankind."

A. **Restatement (Fourth) of the Foreign Relations Law of the United States §702:** The comments following this section indicate that it is a list of human rights generally accepted as customary law.

The comments further state that the list is neither complete nor closed, and other rights may have also reached the status of customary law. "A state violates international law if, as a matter of state policy, it practices, encourages or condones genocide, slavery or slave trade, the murder or causing the disappearance of individuals, torture or other cruel, inhuman, or degrading treatment or punishment, prolonged arbitrary detention, systematic racial discrimination, or consistent patterns of gross violations of internationally recognized human rights."

B. Creation of customary human rights law: The Reporter's Notes to Restatement §701 suggest that customary human rights law is established in a manner different from other customary law, because, historically, human rights have been a matter between a state and its own individuals. According to the notes, customary human rights law may be established through virtually universal adherence to the U.N. Charter; virtually universal adherence to the Universal Declaration of Human Rights; widespread participation of states in preparation and adoption of international human rights agreements; widespread support for U.N. General Assembly resolutions applying international human rights principles; and frequent invocation and application of international human rights principles in both domestic practice and diplomatic practice.

C. The evolution of new rights: Human rights law is constantly evolving from recognition of rights in treaties, U.N. resolutions, and domestic state practice to the level of custom and *jus cogens*. Many protections originate in internal domestic law, with gradual recognition as general principles of international law if common to most legal systems. For example, recently developed rights were recognized in:

- The 1989 Convention on the Rights of the Child (in force since 1990);
- The 1986 General Assembly Resolution on the Right to Development;
- The Declaration on the Rights of Persons Belonging to National or Ethnic, Religious and Linguistic Minorities (adopted by the General Assembly in 1992);
- The 1994 proposal to the United Nations for a Declaration of Principles on Human Rights and the Environment;
- The Convention on the Protection of the Rights of All Migrant Workers and Members of Their Families (in force since 2003);
- The Convention on the Rights of Persons with Disabilities (in force since 2008); and
- The Convention for the Protection of All Persons from Enforced Disappearance (in force since 2010).

VI. ENFORCEMENT OF HUMAN RIGHTS LAW IN THE U.S. COURTS

A. Generally: The United States has ratified six comprehensive human rights treaties: the Protocol Relating to the Status of Refugees; the Convention on the Political Rights of Women; the Convention on the Prevention and Punishment of the Crime of Genocide; the Convention Against Torture and Other Cruel, Inhuman, or Degrading Treatment or Punishment; the International Covenant on Civil and Political Rights; and the International Convention on the Elimination of All Forms of Racial Discrimination.

1. **Treaties not yet ratified by the United States:** The United States has not ratified the International Covenant on Economic, Social, and Cultural Rights, the American Convention on Human Rights, the Apartheid Convention, the Convention on Elimination of All Forms of Discrimination Against Women, the Convention on the Rights of the Child, or the Optional Protocols to the International Covenant on Civil and Political Rights.

2. **No implementing legislation for Civil and Political Rights Treaty:** In 1992, the United States ratified the International Covenant on Civil and Political Rights, after signing with five reservations, five understandings, and four declarations by the Senate. No implementing legislation has been passed, and the Senate has explicitly declared the treaty to be non-self-executing.

B. Incorporation by custom: Because the United States has failed to ratify so many human rights treaties or to implement non-self-executing treaties, enforcement of human rights law in U.S. courts is largely dependent on ***incorporation of custom by courts into U.S. law*** (*see* Chapter 2, §III(A-B), and ***specific legislative provisions***, such as the Alien Tort Claims Act (also known as the Alien Tort Statute) (28 U.S.C. §1350). The Alien Tort Claims Act (ATCA) confers district court jurisdiction over any "civil action by an alien for a tort only, committed in violation of the law of nations or a treaty of the United States."

Example: In *Filartiga v. Pena-Irala*, 630 F.2d 876 (2d Cir. 1980), the Second Circuit Court of Appeals held that *freedom from torture was part of customary international law* for which §1350 provides federal jurisdiction. *See also Trajano v. Marcos*, 978 F.2d 493 (9th Cir. 1992) (reaffirming the *Filartiga* approach); *Kadic v. Karadzic*, 70 F.3d 232 (2d Cir. 1995), *cert. denied*, 518 U.S. 1005 (1996) (noting that a broad reading of the Alien Tort Claims Act (ATCA) was established in *Filartiga* in the grant of federal jurisdiction and later codified by Congress in the Torture Victim Protection Act [TVPA] of 1991). *But see Saleh v. Titan Corp.*, 580 F.3d 1 (D.C. Cir. 2009) (affirming the dismissal of plaintiff-detainees' claim under ATCA for alleged infliction of torture, filed against American companies that contracted to provide military interrogators to the U.S. military in Iraq; the Circuit Court noted that while torture committed by a state is "recognized as a violation of international norm, that cannot be said of private actors").

Additionally, in *Mushikiwabo v. Barayagwiza*, 1996 WL 164496 (S.D.N.Y. 1996), the District Court for the Southern District of New York allowed a suit against a leading Rwandan political figure. The court awarded damages, under the ATCA and the TVPA, to plaintiffs whose families were massacred during the Rwandan genocide. Following the Second Circuit opinion in *Kadic v. Karadzic*, the court found jurisdiction under both the ATCA and the TVPA.

Example: In *Abebe-Jira v. Negewo*, 72 F.3d 844 (11th Cir.), *cert. denied*, 519 U.S. 830 (1996), the Eleventh Circuit awarded damages to plaintiffs who alleged that the defendant had been an Ethiopian government official who had personally supervised their torture during the "Red Terror" in the 1970s. The court held that there was a private action to sue under the ATCA because the act required only an allegation of a violation of the law of nations. Further, the court held that the court's own precedent precluded any reliance on the political question doctrine simply because foreign relations were implicated. *See also Linder v. Portocarrero*, 963 F.2d 332 (11th Cir. 1992) (holding that the political question doctrine did not bar a tort action instituted against Nicaraguan contra leaders).

Example: Additionally, in *In re Cincinnati Radiation Litigation*, 874 F. Supp. 796 (S.D. Ohio 1995), a group of low-income and African American cancer patients who were subjected to medical experiments between 1960 and 1972 were allowed to bring suit in federal court. Based upon the principles articulated by the Nuremberg Tribunal, the court held that the prevailing law required voluntary consent to bodily invasion. It stated, "[t]he Nuremberg Code is part of the law of humanity. It may be applied in both civil and criminal cases by the federal courts in the United States." *Id.* at 821.

Example: In contrast, the D.C. Circuit Court of Appeals in *Tel-Oren v. Libya Arab Republic*, 726 F.2d 774 (D.C. Cir. 1984), took a much more restrictive approach to §1350. In *Tel-Oren*, the plaintiffs sued the alleged perpetrators of an attack on a civilian bus in Israel. The three-judge court dismissed the case with three separate opinions. Judge Robb held the case involved a non-justiciable political question. Judge Edwards endorsed *Filartiga*, but he concluded that non-state, politically motivated acts of terrorism were not prohibited by customary international law. Judge Bork concluded that the ATCA provided jurisdiction only over alien tort suits for which ***international law*** recognizes an individual cause of action (such as violation of safe conducts, piracy, and infringement of the rights of ambassadors).

After these and other Alien Tort Statute cases, it remained unclear whether the statute itself provides a cause of action or whether the question arises under international law or under §1331 as a federal question. It is also not clear what torts are encompassed by the statute, federal common law, or international law.

C. *Sosa v. Alvarez-Machain:* In the landmark *Sosa v. Alvarez-Machain* decision, the U.S. Supreme Court was confronted with the Bush administration's position that the ATCA provided no cause of action for human rights violations beyond those explicitly provided elsewhere in U.S. legislation, and the position of human rights advocates that it provided a cause of action for any violation of human rights law. The Court rejected both positions.

1. ***Sosa* decision:** In the landmark *Sosa* decision, 542 U.S. 692 (2004), the U.S. Supreme Court held that the ATCA does not itself provide a cause of action, but that a cause of action for which the act provides jurisdiction may be found in treaties or customary international law in addition to in U.S. legislation. Less clarity was provided by the Court on how clearly established the international norm must be for a cause of action to be recognized under the ATCA, stating that it must "rest on a norm of international character accepted by the civilized world and defined with a specificity comparable to the features of the eighteenth-century paradigms we have recognized."

2. **Corporate liability:** In *Doe v. Unocal Corporation*, 110 F. Supp. 2d 1294 (C.D. Cal. 2000), several Burmese villagers sued under the ATCA, alleging that the corporation had aided and abetted the military government of Myanmar in using the plaintiffs as forced laborers and that members of the military had killed, tortured, and raped villagers. These human rights violations were designed to discourage opposition to a pipeline project in the Tenasserim region. Myanmar had granted Total S.A., a French oil company, a license to explore coastal gas deposits. The project involved building the Yadana Gas Pipeline Project from the coast through the Tenasserim region to Thailand. Unocal acquired 28 percent of the project from Total.

   The court cited the Second Circuit's decision in *Kadic v. Karadzic*, *supra*, for the proposition that ATCA liability may attach to non-state actors. The ATCA, according to the court, not only confers jurisdiction, but also creates a cause of action against non-state actors in some circumstances. As to Unocal's liability for knowingly aiding the violations, the court adopted the reasoning of the International Criminal Tribunal for the former Yugoslavia in *Prosecutor v. Furundzija*, Case No. IT-95-17/1-T, Judgment (Dec. 10, 1998), that the *actus reus* of aiding and abetting in international criminal law requires practical assistance, encouragement, or moral support that substantially affects the criminal behavior. The court concluded that there were genuine issues of fact as to whether Unocal, as a non-state actor, satisfied the *actus reus* and *mens rea* required under the ATCA for aiding and abetting the state's alleged commission of forced labor, murder, and rape. The court found insufficient evidence, however, to support the torture claims against dismissal. The Ninth Circuit Court of Appeals granted a rehearing *en banc*, vacating the panel decision.

Following the Ninth Circuit Court of Appeals decision to vacate and rehear *en banc Doe v. Unocal Corporation* in February 2003, Unocal encountered major setbacks in what it hoped would be a dismissal of the case against it. The first major setback was the U.S. Supreme Court decision in *Sosa v. Alvarez-Machain* to uphold the ATCA. The second major setback came in September 2004, when Unocal's appeal for dismissal was rejected, thus urging the case into the beginning stages of a jury trial. Rather than stand trial, Unocal decided to settle out of court in December 2004.

The Second Circuit considered *Khulumani v. Barclay National Bank, Ltd.*, 504 F.3d 254 (2d Cir. 2007). The plaintiffs, South Africans, sued some 50 corporate defendants, alleging that they "aided and abetted" the government in maintaining the apartheid regime. The district court had dismissed the action, but the appellate court reversed. The panel held that Alien Tort Statute plaintiffs "may plead a theory of aiding and abetting liability." *Id.* at 260. But the panel could not determine whether international law or federal common law should be applied to determine the scope of this liability.

This aiding and abetting theory is difficult to satisfy. In *Presbyterian Church of Sudan v. Talisman Energy, Inc.*, 582 F.3d 244 (2d Cir. 2009), *cert. denied*, 131 S. Ct. 79, 122 (2010), 131 S. Ct. 122 (2010), the Second Circuit declined to hold a Canadian company liable for aiding and abetting acts of genocide and other crimes against humanity in the Sudan. A litigant seeking to hold a corporation liable under the ATCA for crimes against humanity "must show that the [corporation] provided substantial assistance with the purpose of facilitating the alleged offenses." *Id.* at 247. That standard was not met in this case because the plaintiffs presented no evidence that the Canadian company had the purpose of furthering international war crimes.

Following an attack on an offshore oil rig off the coast of Nigeria, in which Nigerian government forces shot and killed two striking oil rig workers, several Nigerian citizens filed suit in California under the ATCA and the TVPA. *Bowoto v. Chevron Corp.*, 621 F.3d 1116 (9th Cir. 2010). The Nigerian government had acted at the behest of Chevron. The Ninth Circuit determined that the TVPA does not apply to corporations and, therefore, affirmed a jury verdict for the oil company.

The Second Circuit determined in *Kiobel v. Royal Dutch Petroleum Co.*, 621 F.3d 111 (2d Cir. 2010), *reh'g denied*, 2011 U.S. App. LEXIS 2200 (2d Cir. 2011), that jurisdiction and liability under the ATCA must be judged by customary international law. The plaintiffs alleged that the corporate defendants aided and abetted the Nigerian government in suppressing resistance to oil exploration. The court reasoned that no court had ever held a corporation liable for international crimes. Additionally, customary international law had rejected corporate liability for international crimes. The plaintiffs were alleging violations of international crimes against corporate defendants. Thus, the court rejected these claims. The ATCA would not serve to give the court jurisdiction over a corporate defendant alleged to have committed crimes against the law of nations. The Second Circuit determined that the ATCA does not apply to foreign corporations and, therefore, dismissed the action for lack of subject matter jurisdiction.

In direct response to *Kiobel,* the D.C. Circuit held in *Doe v. Exxon Mobil Corp.*, 654 F.3d 11 (D.C. Cir. 2011), that the Second Circuit had ignored "the plain text, history, and purpose of the [ATCA]." Indonesian villagers brought suit against Exxon Mobil Corporation and its subsidiaries arguing that Exxon's security forces committed murder, torture, sexual assault, battery, and false imprisonment. The court reasoned that the ATCA is broad and does not distinguish among classes of defendants. The court reviewed the "historical context" of the statute and the principle of corporate liability in U.S. tort law. Additionally, the court held that although in order to have a cause of action under ATCA the violation must be "specific, universal, and obligatory" in the norm of international law under *Sosa*, the remedy is governed by the law of the United States and not the law of nations.

A few days later the Seventh Circuit ruled in *Flomo v. Firestone Natural Rubber Co.*, 643 F.3d 1013 (7th Cir. 2011), a case brought by Liberian children against Firestone for allegedly using child labor in its rubber plantation. The court criticized the Second Circuit's reliance on the fact that no corporation has been charged for violating customary international law, stating that at the end of World War II the allied powers dissolved German corporations. Additionally, the court noted that there is always a first time for litigation to enforce a norm. The Ninth Circuit had a similar holding to *Flomo and Doe v. Exxon Mobil* in *Sarei v. Rio Tinto, PLC*, 2011 WL 5041927 (9th Cir. 2011).

However, the Supreme Court granted certiorari for *Kiobel*, originally on the issue of corporate liability under ATCA, and then sought further briefing regarding under what circumstances courts may recognize a cause of action under the ATCA for violations of the law of nations occurring within the territory of a sovereign other than the United States. *Kiobel v. Royal Dutch Petroleum Co.*, 133 S. Ct. 1659 (2013). The Court stated first that there was a presumption against extraterritoriality that must be overcome in order for the federal courts to have jurisdiction. That extraterritoriality is generally overcome only when there is a clear indication of an extraterritorial application, and the ATCA has no such indication. The Court reviewed the legislative history of the ATCA and found that there was no intent in the first Congress to allow extraterritoriality, and further that the word "any" in reference to "any tort" does not lend itself to weighing against the claims of extraterritoriality. Additionally, the Court stated that at the time of the ATCA's passage there were only three principal offenses against the law of nations: violation of safe conduct, infringement of rights of ambassadors, and piracy. The first two offenses have no requirement of extraterritoriality, whereas the third does. Piracy occurs on the high seas, which has been recognized as if it were a foreign sovereign in extraterritoriality cases. The Court reasoned that since there was no actual sovereignty involved with matters occurring on the high seas, it carries less foreign policy consequences than a tort on foreign soil. In a final statement, the Court held that a corporation's presence in both the United States and another sovereignty does not overcome the presumption against extraterritorial application. Although the Court dismissed the action because "all the relevant conduct took place outside the United States" it did not determine whether foreign corporations could be sued under the ATCA. *Id.* at 1669.

D. ***Jesner v. Arab Bank, PLC*:** In the landmark *Jesner v. Arab Bank, PLC* decision, 138 S. Ct. 1386 (2018), the U.S. Supreme Court reaffirmed the Second Circuit's decision in *Kiobel* that foreign corporations cannot be sued under the ATCA. The Court reasoned that holding otherwise would create a new precedent that would deter American corporations from investing in developing nations because they could be dragged into foreign courts for violating international law. Furthermore, the Court determined that if the ATCA permitted suits against foreign corporations, this could lead to diplomatic strife with foreign nations, which the First Congress hoped to avoid by enacting the ATCA. The Court concluded that Congress must determine whether victims of human rights violations could sue foreign corporations in U.S. federal courts because the legislative, rather than the judicial, branch is best equipped to address foreign policy concerns.

E. ***Medellín v. Texas*:** The state of Texas convicted José Ernesto Medellín, a Mexican national, of murder and sentenced him to death. Texas officials did not inform him of his right under article 36 of the Vienna Convention on Consular Relations to report his detention to the Mexican consulate. The International Court of Justice (ICJ) determined that because the United States failed to inform him, and others in his position, of the Vienna Convention, he was entitled to a review of his state court conviction. President George W. Bush issued an executive order calling for compliance with the ICJ's ruling. The Supreme Court, however, held otherwise. The Court determined that Medellín was not entitled to review because the Optional Protocol of the Vienna Convention does not displace state procedural rules. Additionally, the Vienna Convention has not received implementing legislation from Congress, and it is not self-executing. *Medellín v. Texas*, 552 U.S. 491 (2008).

   1. **Backlash:** Following the Court's decision, human rights advocates have expressed concerns. First, the Court determined that the federal government could not require a state to meet a national obligation under international law. Second, some find concern in the Court's presumption against self-execution in the requirement of a "clear and express statement" of the intent to be bound in the treaty. Third, the Court seemed to imply that even when treaties are self-executing, they do not provide a private cause of action in domestic courts. Finally, the Court also implied that international treaties are not domestically enforceable federal law.

VII. DEROGATION FROM PROTECTION OF RIGHTS

Agreements ensuring protection of fundamental human rights often allow derogation from the rights in times of ***public emergencies***. A wide margin of appreciation is given to countries to determine whether such a "public emergency" exists in their state. Human rights conventions with derogation clauses include the International Covenant on Civil and Political Rights (article 4), Convention Relating to the Status of Refugees (article 9), Convention Relating to the Status of Stateless Persons (article 9), European Convention for the Protection of Human Rights and Fundamental Freedoms (article 15), and the European Social Charter (article 30). The derogation provisions of the Covenant on Civil and Political Rights and the European Convention serve as key examples, demonstrating the necessary circumstances and limitations to derogation.

A. **The International Covenant on Civil and Political Rights:** There are limitations on, and procedures regulating, derogation under this Covenant.

   1. **Requirements for derogation:** Article 4 provides derogation from the Covenant's obligations under the following circumstances: It must be a "time of public emergency which threatens the

life of the nation." The existence of such dire circumstances must be "officially proclaimed." Derogation is permitted "only to the extent strictly required by the exigencies of the situation." The measures may not be "inconsistent with their other obligations under international law." The measures may not "involve discrimination solely on the ground of race, colour, sex, language, religion, or social origin."

2. **Limitations to derogation under the Covenant:** Certain rights may not be derogated from, even in times of public emergency. Article 4, ¶2 states that no derogation is permitted from the rights accorded by articles 6, 7, 8 (¶¶1 and 2), 11, 15, 16, and 18.

   a. **Article 6:** Article 6 protects the inherent right to life, prohibits genocide, restricts the death penalty to only the most serious crimes, requires rights to seek pardon or commutation of the death penalty, and prohibits the death penalty for persons under 18 and pregnant women.

   b. **Article 7:** Article 7 prohibits torture and cruel, inhuman, or degrading treatment or punishment.

   c. **Article 8:** Article 8, ¶1 prohibits slavery and slave trading. Paragraph 2 prohibits holding anyone in servitude.

   d. **Article 11:** Article 11 prohibits imprisonment for failure to fulfill a contractual obligation.

   e. **Article 15:** Article 15 prohibits conviction for any act or omission that was not a criminal offense under either national or international law at the time it was committed. It also prohibits imposition of a heavier penalty than was applicable at the time the crime was committed.

   f. **Article 16:** Article 16 guarantees each person everywhere a right to recognition as a person before the law.

   g. **Article 18:** Article 18 protects the rights of religious freedom and prevents the imposition of religion.

3. **Procedure:** Article 4, ¶3 requires a state availing itself of the right of derogation to follow specific steps. For instance, a state must immediately inform other states parties to the Covenant of the provisions from which it has derogated, using the U.N. secretary-general as intermediary; it must provide the reasons for derogation; and it must communicate the date on which it terminates the derogation.

B. **European Convention for the Protection of Human Rights and Fundamental Freedoms:** The derogation provision of the European Convention is similar to that of the Covenant on Civil and Political Rights.

1. **Requirements for derogation:** Article 15, ¶1 permits derogation: "[i]n time of war or other public emergency threatening the life of the nation"; "[o]nly to the extent strictly required by the exigencies of the situation"; and "[p]rovided such measures are not inconsistent with its other obligations under international law." European Convention for the Protection of Human Rights and Fundamental Freedoms, Nov. 4, 1950, art. 15, ¶1, Europ. T.S. No. 5 [hereinafter *European Human Rights Convention*]. The European Court of Human Rights has given states a wide "margin of appreciation" in determining whether the first condition exists, but it has been more demanding in determining whether the second condition has been satisfied.

2. **Limitations to derogation:** Article 15, ¶2 prohibits derogation from articles 2, 3, 4 (paragraph I), and 7.
   a. **Article 2:** Article 2 protects the right to life, except for executions resulting from conviction of a crime for which the death penalty is provided by law. Deprivation of life does not violate this article if it occurs as a result of self-defense; in the course of attempts to make a lawful arrest or prevent escape from lawful detention; or from lawful action taken to quell riots or insurrections.
   b. **Article 3:** Article 3 prohibits torture or inhuman or degrading treatment or punishment.
   c. **Article 4:** Article 4 prohibits slavery or servitude.
   d. **Article 7:** Article 7 prohibits *ex post facto* criminal law.
3. **Procedure:** Article 15, ¶3 requires the derogating party to fully inform the secretary-general of the Council of Europe of measures taken and the reasons therefor and further inform the secretary-general when derogation has ceased and provisions of the Convention are once again fully executed.
4. **Clauses of limitation:** A number of the rights enumerated in the European Convention on Human Rights also have their own clauses of limitation, which allow restrictions on the right as necessary to protect national security, safety, and health or morals.

VIII. REGIONAL HUMAN RIGHTS LAW AND INSTITUTIONS

Regional human rights regimes operate in Western Europe, the Americas, and Africa. Asia has a small regional system in the Association of South-East Asian Nations (ASEAN), established on August 8, 1967, but ASEAN has only ten member states. The Permanent Arab Commission on Human Rights has focused mostly on the rights of Palestinian Arabs in Israeli-occupied territories, and the League of Arab States has endorsed an Arab Charter on Human Rights, which incorporates many of the international human rights treaties. However, it also condemns Zionism and retains a section about the positive discrimination against women in sharia law. The significance of the regional regimes, particularly the European system, is attributed to three factors. First, the relative homogeneity of socioeconomic, cultural, political, and juridical characteristics permits the members of a regional system to act in concert with one another, thus facilitating the promotion and protection of human rights. Second, the geographic proximity of states within a region results in more or less common interests and an interdependence between them. Third, the relative homogeneity and geographic proximity facilitate the actual process of investigating and remedying human rights violations.

A. **The European system of human rights law:** European human rights law is contained primarily in the European Convention for the Protection of Human Rights and Freedoms and subsequent protocols for civil and political rights, and the European Social Charter for Economic and Social Rights.

1. **The European Convention on Human Rights:** The organization and content of the European Convention is similar to the International Covenant on Civil and Political Rights. There are 47 states bound by the Convention's terms, including every member of the Council of Europe that has ratified the Convention. The European Convention and its protocols include the right to life; freedom from torture and inhuman treatment; freedom from

slavery, servitude, or forced labor; rights to a fair and public hearing to determine civil rights and criminal charges; freedom of expression and religion; rights of privacy; rights of assembly and association; and freedom from discrimination. Protocols that have entered into force in the last decade prohibit capital punishment in time of peace and double jeopardy. The Convention differs from the International Covenant by failing to recognize a people's right of self-determination or make any reference to the rights of people belonging to ethnic, religious, or linguistic minorities. The Convention also differs by not making any reference to the rights of the child or to prohibitions on war propaganda or propaganda inciting discrimination. This convention is sometimes supplemented by additional conventions, such as the European Convention on Human Rights and Biomedicine, in force since 1999.

a. **Includes protection of the right to a private and family life:** The European Convention also includes the protection of the right to a private and family life. art. 8. In one case, a Spanish national filed an application with the European Commission of Human Rights, asserting that she was unable to obtain relief under Spanish law from the noxious emissions of a water treatment and purification plant located near her home. The Commission and the European Court of Human Rights held that serious consequences of environmental degradation may affect an individual's well-being so as to deprive her of the enjoyment of a private and family life, and they ordered public authorities to take the necessary measures to protect those rights. *Lopez Ostra v. Spain*, 303-C Eur. Ct. H.R. (ser. A) (Judgment of Dec. 9, 1994).

b. **Migrant protection under the ECHR shifted during the immigration crisis**

The case of *Khlaifia v. Italy*, App. No. 16483/12 Eur. Ct. H.R. (2016), changed the interpretation of the European Convention on Human Rights by strengthening procedural protection, flipping the burden of proof for expulsion, and reversing precedent on defining cruel and inhumane treatment.

In *Khlaifia*, a group of Tunisian migrants were held in overcrowded and unsanitary "hotspots" under constant police supervision and without access to legal aid or counsel. They were eventually transported to holding ships off of Palermo, Italy, before being deported.

The Grand Chamber of the European Court of Human Rights strengthened article V of the European Convention on Human Rights (the requirement of procedural guarantees to detainees) by holding that states must base the detention of an immigrant on a specific domestic law, and allow those detained access to legal services. However, the court also overturned precedent and weakened article III protections against cruel and inhumane treatment, by holding there was no violation of article III, because the interpretation of "cruel and inhumane" could be evaluated in light of the migrant crisis, and the court could take into account that the migrants detained were not asylum seekers, or members of a protected class.

The decision notably shifted the burden of proof under Article IV, Protocol IV (the prohibition on collective expulsion) from the state to the migrant, and eliminated the requirement of individual interviews prior to deportation.

2. **The European Social Charter:** In addition to the European Convention's protection of political and civil rights, there is promotion and protection of economic and social rights

under the European Social Charter, which has been ratified by approximately half of the states in the Council of Europe. The Charter's recognition of economic, social, and cultural rights includes the right to work, the right to fair compensation, the rights of children, the rights of employed women to protection, and the right to social and medical assistance. States have some latitude in selecting which of the enumerated rights they will accept. European Social Charter, Oct. 18, 1961, art. 20, Europ. T.S. No. 35. The Charter's lack of adjudicative machinery (implementation is through a reporting system like many human rights treaties) makes it less prominent than the Convention in the enforcement of human rights in Europe.

3. **The European Convention on Human Rights and Biomedicine:** Also known as the Oviedo Convention, this Convention went into effect on December 1, 1999. It represents an intersection of human rights law and health law. The convention bans all forms of discrimination based on genetic makeup and allows for predictive genetic testing for medicinal purposes only. The Convention also states that all patients have a right to be informed about their health, including the results of predictive genetic testing, but the patient also has the right to refuse the knowledge. The Convention also prohibits the removal of organs and tissues that are non-regenerative from people that are unable to give consent. Additionally, the Convention calls for certain rules and conditions for medical testing and research.

4. **The European Convention on Action Against Trafficking in Human Beings:** This Convention entered into force on February 1, 2008. The European Council has a Web site fully devoted to this Convention at http://www.coe.int/en/web/anti-human-trafficking (last accessed August 2, 2016). The Convention recognizes that human trafficking is an international problem and calls on states parties to cooperate in stopping this practice and bring violators to justice. Specifically, the Convention calls for states parties to strengthen their borders, to criminalize human trafficking, and to assist the victims of trafficking to seek compensation. Interestingly, the Convention's Web site has a comic strip devoted to raising awareness about the problem of human trafficking.

B. **The original institutions of the European regime:** The European Convention of Human Rights has established an effective human rights regime, enforcing rights originally through the European Commission of Human Rights, the European Court of Human Rights, and the Committee of Ministers of the Council of Europe.

1. **European Commission of Human Rights:** The Commission was composed of a number of members equal to the number of states parties to the Convention. As of April 2016, there were 47 states bound by the terms of the Convention. The Commission was vested with both compulsory and optional jurisdiction.

   a. **Compulsory jurisdiction:** It could hear cases filed by one state against another state so long as both states had ratified the Convention. European Human Rights Convention, art. 24, Europ. T.S. No. 5.

   b. **Optional jurisdiction:** The Commission had optional jurisdiction with respect to individual petitions. The optional jurisdiction was invoked only if a state had ratified the Convention and declared its acceptance of the Commission's right to hear individual petitions. European Human Rights Convention, art. 25, Europ. T.S. No. 5. Most states made such a declaration.

2. **European Court of Human Rights:** The court comprises a number of members equal to the number of states parties to the Convention. Originally, cases could be referred to the court by states, the Commission, or individuals, and the court's judgments are final and binding. The court is vested with the power to award damages. The court also has limited authority to issue advisory opinions. Decisions of the court were originally enforced by the Committee of Ministers.

3. **Merger of the European Commission and the Court of Human Rights:** The European system under the European Convention of Human Rights has merged their commission and the court into one body after the adoption of Protocol 11 (Permanent Single Court) in May 1994. Protocol 11 entered into force in 1998. The merger was recommended because the commission and the court have become full-time bodies in recent years and the system and the users began to question the necessity of a decision from both bodies, as the decisions were often considered redundant or contradictory, therefore confusing jurisprudence within the system. *See* §VIII(C)(3) of this chapter, *infra*.

4. **Committee of Ministers of the Council of Europe:** The committee was made up of one representative for each member state of the Council of Europe. It appointed the members of the Human Rights Commission and decided those cases that the commission failed to settle and were not referred to the European Court within three months after the commission's report.

C. **The process of implementation and enforcement:** The process discussed below is the adjudicative process under the European Convention as modified by Protocol 11, followed by a brief description of the reportorial system under the European Social Charter.

1. **Court cases:** Prior to the entry into force of Protocol 9, adopted in 1990, individual claims could come before the court only through submission by the commission because only states or the commission could bring cases before the court. Today, the court may address cases brought to it by either a state party or individuals claiming to be victims of a violation of the Convention or one of its protocols. The commission has been abolished.

   The European Court of Human Rights is the judicial organ of the Council of Europe, an organization distinct from the European Union. Every state that is a party to the European Convention has accepted the jurisdiction of this court. The member most frequently before the court has been the United Kingdom, which has no constitution and no formal domestic guarantee of individual rights, and this often forces individuals to seek protection for individual rights in this forum. There are 46 judges, one for each of the states that are parties to the Convention and members of the Council of Europe, which has its seat in Strasbourg, France. No 2 judges can be nationals of the same state. Judges serve for staggered six-year terms. The court sits in chambers of 7 judges and a Grand Chamber of 17 judges.

2. **The European Social Charter:** The Charter does not provide an adjudicative process similar to that of the European Convention. Rights are promoted and protected primarily by reportorial means. European Social Charter, arts. 21-29, Europ. T.S. No. 35. States parties "undertake to consider the economic, social and cultural rights enumerated [in the Charter]" and to pursue such aims with appropriate measures. States report on their progress in annual reports submitted to the Council of Europe's secretary-general. The reports are on a

four-year cycle because countries report on four thematic areas. Thus, every country reports on one particular theme once every four years. The reports are examined by the Committee of Experts; then passed on with the Committee of Expert's conclusions to the Governmental Social Committee and finally to the Council's Consultative Assembly. The Committee of Ministers may, on the basis of reports and consultation with the foregoing bodies, make necessary recommendations to the state.

3. **Reform of the European Convention:** In 1994, the Council of Europe proposed Protocol No. 11 to the Convention. Protocol 11 involved a massive restructuring of the human rights institutions of the European regime and called for the European Court of Human Rights to be a full-time body. Protocol 11 required unanimous consent by all member states, and it entered into force as of 1998. The merger was proposed to resolve the considerable backlog of cases before the commission. *See* §VIII(B)(3) of this chapter.The expansion of membership of the Council of Europe and acceptance of the European Convention by a number of former communist states has made the human rights jurisprudence of the court even more significant.

D. **Inter-American system—human rights law:** Outside Europe, the most developed regime of human rights law is in the Americas. The primary sources for human rights law in the Americas are the Charter of the Organization of American States (OAS) and the 1969 American Convention on Human Rights.

1. **OAS Charter:** The original OAS Charter itself made little mention of human rights and provided no machinery for the protection of human rights. An enumeration of substantive rights was embodied in the American Declaration of the Rights and Duties of Man, but until 1960, the Declaration served only as a non-binding resolution of the OAS. In 1960, however, the OAS formed the Inter-American Commission on Human Rights to promote respect for human rights. In 1970, the commission was elevated to the status of an organ of the OAS in order to further implementation of the American Declaration. The American Declaration is similar to the European Convention on Human Rights and includes the rights to life, liberty, security of one's person, equality before the law, religious freedom, freedom of expression, special protection for pregnant women and children, freedom of movement, and the right to an education.

   Numerous cases have been brought to the attention of the commission challenging U.S. adherence to human rights law. In some cases, the commission dismissed the petitions for failing to exhaust local remedies or for failure to establish a violation of rights. *See e.g., Walker v. United States,* Case 12.049, Inter-Am. C.H.R., Report No. 62/03 (2003); *Lares-Reyes v. United States,* Case 12.379, Inter-Am. C.H.R., Report No. 19/02 (2002). For examples of cases where the petition was accepted by the commission, see *Beazley v. United States,* Case 12.412, Inter-Am. C.H.R., Report No. 101/03 (2003); *Dann v. United States*, Case 11.410, Inter-Am. C.H.R., Report No. 75/02 (2002).

2. **The American Convention on Human Rights:** The second source of Inter-American human rights law is the 1969 American Convention on Human Rights, which entered into force in 1978 and has been signed but not ratified by the United States. The American Convention is similar to the European Convention and has a similar institutional structure. Until 1988, the American Convention focused on protection of political and civil rights such as the right to life, freedom from torture and inhumane treatment, prohibition of *ex post facto* criminal laws, freedom of association, right to participate in free elections, etc. In 1988, an additional protocol

was adopted addressing economic and social rights. The additional protocol entered into force in 1999. Prior to the additional protocol coming into force, economic and social rights were achieved "progressively by legislation or other appropriate means." American Convention on Human Rights, Nov. 22, 1969, art. 26, 9 I.L.M. 673 (1970). The Inter-American Commission, established originally under the OAS Charter, has also been incorporated into the institutional framework established by the American Convention. In 2016, the Inter-American Court of Human Rights held that the American Convention on Human Rights only applies to natural persons, not legal persons. The Court also held that indigenous and tribal communities are protected by the Convention and that labor union organizations are protected by the Protocol of San Salvador.

E. Institutions of the Inter-American system: The two organs responsible for supervising implementation and enforcement of human rights are the Inter-American Commission on Human Rights and the Inter-American Court of Human Rights.

1. Inter-American Commission on Human Rights: The Inter-American Commission is an organ of both the OAS and the American Convention on Human Rights. It consists of seven members elected for four-year, once-renewable terms by the OAS General Assembly to "represent all member countries."

a. Functions under the OAS Charter: Its principal function under the OAS is to ensure compliance by OAS member states to their obligations under the OAS Charter. Note that states, such as the United States, which have not ratified the Convention are nevertheless obliged under the Charter to promote human rights. In addition to receiving individual communications, preparing country studies, and reporting on the status of human rights in various states, the commission may investigate human rights conditions without awaiting formal individual or interstate complaints.

b. Functions under the Convention: The commission's principal function under the Convention is to consider charges of violations of the rights guaranteed by the American Convention on Human Rights. The American Convention differs from other international human rights regimes by making the right of individual petition mandatory and interstate petitions optional. Thus, the commission has authority to deal with individual petitions against any state that has ratified the Convention, but it may consider interstate claims only if both states have made a special declaration in addition to ratification.

c. OAS Conventions:

1. The OAS gives jurisdiction regarding human rights issues to the Inter-American Commission on Human Rights and Inter-American Court of Human Rights. The OAS has developed a number of conventions since its creation. In 1987, its Inter-American Convention to Prevent and Punish Torture became effective.

2. In 1994, the OAS General Assembly adopted the Inter-American Convention on Forced Disappearances. This Convention designated forced disappearance as a crime. In the Convention, the states parties agreed not to allow this practice, to hold those persons who commit these acts responsible for their actions, and to work together with the other states parties to prevent forced disappearances.

3. Another convention, called the Inter-American Convention on the Prevention, Punishment, and Eradication of Violence Against Women, was adopted in 1994. This Convention includes a definition of the phrase "violence against women." In the Convention, the states parties agreed to denounce violence against women, including physical, sexual, and psychological harm; to hold persons committing these acts accountable; and to work to prevent this violence from occurring.

2. **Inter-American Court of Human Rights:** The court was inaugurated in 1979, a year after the American Convention entered into force. By 1991, 12 states had recognized the jurisdiction of the court. The court is composed of seven judges elected by states parties to the American Convention to six-year, once-renewable terms. The judges are not elected by the OAS General Assembly because the court was not established under the OAS Charter, unlike the commission. Only states parties and the commission have the right to bring cases before the court, which has both contentious and advisory jurisdiction.

   a. **Contentious jurisdiction:** Under its contentious jurisdiction, the court has authority to decide claims that a state party violated rights guaranteed by the American Convention. Contentious jurisdiction is optional and cases may be filed by or against only those states that have accepted such jurisdiction.

   b. **Advisory jurisdiction:** The court's authority is broader under its advisory jurisdiction than under its contentious jurisdiction. It may render opinions interpreting not only the American Convention, but also other human rights treaties of the inter-American regime. All OAS member states and all OAS organs may invoke the advisory jurisdiction of the court.

   c. **Human rights and the environment:** In a 2017 advisory opinion on the Environment and Human Rights requested by Colombia, the Inter-American Court of Human Rights (IACtHR) tied environmental harms to human rights and was the first court to link extraterritorial jurisdiction to the obligation to prevent transboundary environmental harms. In their opinion, the court became the first international tribunal to hold a fundamental autonomous human right to a clean and healthy environment.

   c. **The right of autonomy:** In a landmark 2017 advisory opinion on Gender Identity and Equality, the Inter-American Court of Human Rights rejected the doctrine of the margin of appreciation, and held that autonomy is a pillar of international human rights law that embraces one's name, sex, sexual orientation, and gender identity. Strikingly, the IACtHR split from the approach of the European Court of Human Rights, holding that any states not striving for recognition of same-sex marriage are acting in contravention of the American Convention.

F. **Process of implementation and enforcement:** As in the European system, claims of human rights violations are first considered by the commission and then referable to the court.

1. **The commission:** Claims of violations may be brought before the commission by individuals or organizations, and the complainant need not have been a victim of the violation. All domestic remedies must have first been exhausted, and the complaint must state a *prima facie* case. Rejections by the commission at this stage are not appealable. Following admission of a case, the commission investigates the facts of the case and encourages negotiation of a friendly settlement. If the parties fail to reach a settlement, the commission then prepares a report with its factual findings and recommendations and submits it to the parties. During the three months following submission of the report, the commission's recommendations

may be accepted or the case may be referred to the court. If neither occurs, the commission is then authorized to make final determinations and require the defendant state to adopt certain measures by established deadlines. Compared to its European counterpart, however, the commission's reports and subsequent resolutions have thus far shown little legal effectiveness.

2. **The court:** Either the commission or states parties to the Convention that have accepted the court's jurisdiction may refer cases to the court. The court issues final and binding judgments on the parties and also has the authority to award damages, render declaratory decrees, and occasionally enter preliminary injunctions.

G. **African regional system—human rights law:** The primary source of law is the African Charter of Human and Peoples' Rights, which entered into force in 1986. The Charter differs significantly from the European and American human rights regimes. It guarantees economic, social, and cultural rights, as well as political and civil rights; it is concerned with the rights of "peoples" as well as individuals; and it proclaims the duties as well as the rights of individuals. The recent emergence of the African human rights system means that many provisions of the Charter have yet to be interpreted and applied. The Charter also differs significantly from the European and American human rights regime because it does not provide a human rights court. The Charter does, however, establish an African Commission on Human and People's Rights to consider state and individual petitions. The Charter places a relatively strong emphasis on friendly settlements and negotiations.

1. **African Charter on Human and Peoples' Rights:** In July 2008, the protocol to the African Charter on Human and Peoples' Rights on the Establishment of an African Court on Human and Peoples' Rights and the Court of Justice of the African Union was created. The protocol developed as a result of the integration of the African Court of Human and Peoples' Rights and the African Court of Justice. The African Union Executive Council elected 16 judges to this court. The court will become effective once 15 member states have ratified the protocol. As of 2016, 24 countries had ratified it. When the protocol takes effect, states parties to the protocol, the AU Assembly, the Parliament, and other organizations that the Assembly designates, will be able to bring cases before the court. Specifically, human rights cases will be brought by states parties, the African commission, the African Committee of Experts on the Rights and Welfare of the Child, African intergovernmental organizations, and national human rights organizations.

2. **Complaints:** The African Charter adopted in 1981 allows for a system of complaints. Under this system, the African Commission on Human and People's Rights (Commission), a non-governmental organization, a state party, an African intergovernmental organization, or an individual pursuant to article 34(6) of the protocol that finds that another state party has failed to follow the Charter may bring this either to the attention of the state party or to the Commission. One complaint was brought in October 2014 by Ingabire Victoire Umuhoza against Rwanda. *Umuhoza v. Rwanda*, No. 003/2014, Judgment, African Court on Human and Peoples' Rights [Afr. Ct. H.P.R.] (Nov. 24, 2017), http://www.african-court.org/en/images/Cases/Judgment/003-2014-Ingabire%20Victoire%20Umuhoza%20V%20Rwanda%20-%20Judgement%2024%20November%202017.pdf. The complaint alleged that Rwanda violated Umuhoza's freedom of expression and her right to a fair trial. The court, in November 2017, determined that Rwanda violated these human rights and ordered Rwanda to fully restore them.

3. **African Charter on Democracy, Elections, and Governance:** The African Charter on Democracy, Elections, and Governance was established by the African Union in 2007. It emphasizes topics such as elections, state institutions, democratic culture, and ways to stop unconstitutional changes of government. As of April 2016, the Charter has been signed by 38 countries and ratified by 10 countries. More information can be found at http://www.au.int.

4. **Court of Justice of the Economic Community of West African States (ECOWAS):** Under a 2005 protocol, individuals can present human rights claims to this judicial body. The court has heard 33 cases to date, the vast majority of them from Nigeria. For more information on this court and the difficulties it faces, see its Web site: http://www.ihrda.org/court-of-justice-of-the-economy-community-of-west-african-states.

H. **League of Arab States and Human Rights:** The League of Arab States adopted an Arab Charter on Human Rights in 1994. This Charter was revised in 2004. The League attempted to modernize the Charter, *i.e.*, to bring it into line with international standards. However, the Arab Charter still includes several troubling provisions: a condemnation of Zionism; a recognition of the equal right of dignity of men and women but an embrace of the positive discrimination against women in Sharia law; and an allowance of the death penalty in many cases. A seven-member Arab Human Rights Committee reviews periodic state reports on the implementation of the Charter, but the committee cannot hear state or individual complaints.

I. **ASEAN:** ASEAN is the only regional human rights system on the largest continent in the world, yet ASEAN is composed of only ten countries. ASEAN was established in 1967, and the members finally adopted a constituting treaty in 2007. The Charter specifies that the states parties should adhere to the principles of democracy and the protection of human rights. Article 2 of the Charter provides that member states should "respect fundamental freedoms, the promotion and protection of human rights, and the promotion of social justice." To this end, ASEAN established the ASEAN Intergovernmental Commission on Human Rights (AICHR) in October 2009. The AICHR is merely a consultative body, though. Each member state has a representative on the AICHR, and there is also a high-level panel (HLP) that reports to the representatives on a regular basis. The AICHR ensures that member states adhere to a number of human rights declarations, including those for the protection of migrant workers and another against the trafficking of human beings. In 2012, AICHR drafted the ASEAN Human Rights Declaration, and the member states unanimously adopted it. This declaration has come under criticism for its caveats based on cultural relativism, subordination of universal principles to domestic law, novel or unique limitations to universal rights, and group veto over individually held rights. Regardless of the criticism, the declaration is a significant step forward in the human rights framework of the region.

IX. INTERNATIONAL HUMANITARIAN LAW

International humanitarian law attempts to place limitations upon the conduct of warfare in order to prevent unnecessary suffering of civilians and combatants. This topic is more fully discussed in Chapter 9, §II.

Quiz Yourself on THE RIGHTS OF INDIVIDUALS—INTERNATIONAL LAW OF HUMAN RIGHTS

11. Assume that a plaintiff is seeking to enforce in U.S. federal court a claim of unconstitutional race discrimination under state law. Can the plaintiff also allege a violation of the human rights provisions of articles 55 and 56 of the U.N. Charter, to which the United States is a party? ________

12. Human rights organizations allege that the practice of "waterboarding," in which an individual is subjected to treatment that simulates drowning, is a violation of the human rights convention to which the United States is a party. Is this contention correct? ________

Answers

11. Possibly. In *Sei Fujii v. California*, the California Supreme Court held that these provisions of the Charter were not self-executing, and therefore they were not directly enforceable in federal court. The analysis failed to acknowledge, however, that either as a non-self-executing treaty or as evidence of customary international law, such federal law might prevail over a conflicting discriminatory state law. The court's conclusion that articles 55 and 56 are non-self-executing has also been questioned.

12. Yes, it is definitely a violation of the ICP prohibition on torture or cruel, inhuman, or degrading treatment or punishment. More important is the question of whether it constitutes torture under the Torture Convention, as opposed to cruel or unusual treatment or punishment. The difference in legal consequences is that torture is a universal crime punishable by any state, and the forceful protections of the Torture Convention (non-extradition to a country where there are substantial grounds for believing there is a danger of torture, the obligation to arrest, prosecute, and extradite for prosecution any person accused of torture) would apply.

Exam Tips on THE RIGHTS OF INDIVIDUALS—INTERNATIONAL LAW OF HUMAN RIGHTS

- The 2006 creation of the Human Rights Council was a major innovation in the U.N. procedures for protection of human rights. It is likely for several years to come that the reasons for the change and the future actions of the Council, effective or otherwise, will be the object of many exam questions and paper assignments.

- It is also important to be fully versed in the issues of the legal status of the provisions of the Universal Declaration of Human Rights under international law and U.S. law for exam purposes. Under international law, the Declaration is a resolution of the General Assembly, which according to the Charter is a recommendation only and not per se binding, even on the U.N. members who have voted for it. Some scholars have suggested, however, that a resolution like the Declaration that receives unanimous or near unanimous support is "quasi-binding" at the very least. Alternatively, many, if not most, of the rights protected by the Declaration are recognized as protected by customary international law or general principles of international law, and are binding through those sources of international law. Under U.S. law, although the United States voted for the resolution, it is not a treaty and not binding as a treaty obligation. The enforceability of the rights in it depends then on the enforceability of the custom or general principle of international law in U.S. federal court. This, of course, depends on the particular circuit in which the case arises: the Second Circuit said that the Alien Tort Claims Act serves to give federal courts jurisdiction over any claim of a violation of the law of nations, *i.e.*, a universal crime, in *Kadic*. The United States is a party, however, to the International Covenant on Civil and Political Rights, which includes many of the rights contained in the Declaration. The Senate, however, has declared that the International Covenant on Civil and Political Rights is non-self-executing, and therefore it is not directly enforceable in federal court without implementing congressional legislation (of which there has been none). This declaration has been criticized as incorrect, so the question then becomes whether a federal court would consider itself bound by the Senate's determination. Keep in mind in this regard the Supreme Court's presumption in *Medellin v. Texas* in 2008 that treaties are non-self-executing unless demonstrated to be otherwise. After *Medellin*, one must ponder how Congress and the Supreme Court will view the plethora of new international treaties, declarations, and covenants springing to life in recent years, covering a wide variety of issues, including migrant workers, indigenous populations, and the prevention of human trafficking.

☛ Another useful tip in exam preparation is to be aware of the somewhat unique responsibilities of a state under the Genocide Convention. Under most human rights treaties, if a state is in violation, other states have no legal obligation to act upon the violation. The Genocide Convention, however, compels every party explicitly to "prevent and to punish" genocide. This obligation is partially the reason that states are sometimes reluctant to recognize genocide officially, as in Darfur. The demanding intent requirement for genocide, "intent to destroy," facilitates state avoidance of a genocide determination. As an analytical alternative, consider the possibility that what might be genocide may satisfy the legal requirements for a finding of a crime against humanity, another universal crime. This affirmative obligation to punish also appears in the Torture Convention.

CHAPTER 9

THE LAW OF ARMED CONFLICT

I. ARMED CONFLICT GENERALLY

The law of armed conflict is that area of international law governing the circumstances under which a state may use military force as a means of coercion. In addition, once armed hostilities have commenced, the humanitarian law of armed conflict attempts to minimize human suffering by placing limitations upon the means by which force may be exerted and the targets against which such force may be directed. Early international legal scholars referred to this area of law as the law of war, and divided it into two sections—*jus ad bello*, the law leading up to war, and *jus in bello*, the law during war. This section addresses only hostilities of an international character. The law relating to civil conflict is addressed in §III of this chapter, *infra*.

A. Definition of war and armed conflict: The terms *war* and *armed conflict* are extremely difficult to define. Some scholars define war narrowly, reserving it for circumstances in which one or more of the states involved in hostilities has actually declared war. Others define the term more broadly, to encompass any armed hostilities carried on between states or even between citizens in the same state. *Armed conflict* is an equally elusive term. Some scholars use the term *armed conflict* to refer to hostilities that in some fashion fall short of an all-out, formally declared war, while others use it to refer to any state of armed hostilities, including declared wars. For the purposes of this text, the two terms will be used interchangeably to mean any armed conflict beyond isolated and sporadic acts of violence between the armed forces of states.

Note: This definition excludes armed hostilities of an internal nature, or civil wars, which will be dealt with in the final section of this heading. During the nineteenth century, a state had to declare war before international law would recognize its existence. As late as 1907, the Hague Convention provided that a nation should not begin hostilities without "previous and explicit warning" in the form of a declaration of war or an ultimatum. However, in recent years, many states have engaged in hostilities without a formal declaration of war. In any event, whether war is formally declared is a question of decreasing importance because since 1949, article 2 of the Geneva Conventions applied the conventions to any armed conflict between states, even if there is not a recognized state of war between them. For example in the 1982 conflict between Argentina and Great Britain over the Falkland Islands, the servicemen captured were prisoners of war, even though neither side formally declared or acknowledged a state of war. Also, the U.N. Charter speaks in terms of the use of force, rather than in terms of war.

B. Legal prohibitions against international armed conflict: During the nineteenth century, every sovereign state was considered to have the right to wage war. After the devastation of World War I, the Charter of the League of Nations provided for a three-month "cooling off" period before a state could commence hostilities, as well as imposing certain other limitations on the ability of a state to wage war. In the Kellogg-Briand Pact of 1928 (or Treaty of Paris) the signatory states ***renounced war*** as an instrument of national policy and agreed that disputes were to be settled only by pacific means.

1. **The U.N. Charter's requirements of first resort to peaceful means:** The U.N. Charter requires members to settle their disputes by ***peaceful*** means. U.N. Charter, art. 2, ¶3; art. 33,

discussed in Chapter 7, §II. If settlement fails, the parties to any dispute that is a threat to peace must refer it to the Security Council. art. 37.

a. **U.N. peacekeeping functions:** The Security Council has very broad powers to carry out its peacekeeping functions. *See Advisory Opinion on Namibia*, 1971 I.C.J. Rep. 16. The General Assembly also has the authority to recommend peaceful settlement. *See* U.N. Charter, arts. 11, 12. The Security Council has the primary responsibility for maintaining international peace and security. art. 24. When the veto has prevented the Security Council from acting, the General Assembly has used its secondary authority to maintain peace.

b. **Peacekeeping forces and the *Certain Expenses* case:** In 1956, the General Assembly under the Uniting for Peace Resolution (discussed *infra*) sent troops (United Nations Emergency Forces I, or UNEF I) to supervise a cease-fire after Israel, France, and the United Kingdom had attacked Egypt. In 1960, the Security Council sent troops (the U.N. force in the Congo, or ONUC [Opération des Nations Unies au Congo]) to the Congo to restore order after Belgium deployed troops in the Congolese civil war. UNEF I was deployed in Egypt with its consent; ONUC was deployed with the consent of the Congolese government (although it was far from clear who the government was). Several countries, including the Soviet Union and France, refused to pay the expenses of the forces, arguing that these "peacekeeping forces" were unauthorized under the Charter and, thus, their expenses were not expenses of the United Nations within the meaning of article 17. In an advisory opinion requested by the General Assembly, the International Court of Justice (ICJ) concluded that both deployments were not "enforcement actions" within the meaning of Chapter VII because the troops had been deployed with consent. *Advisory Opinion on Certain Expenses of the United Nations*, 1962 I.C.J. 151 (July 20). Despite the decision, several countries continued to refuse to pay and were threatened (but not sanctioned) with loss of voting privileges under article 19. Expenses of peacekeeping forces, as well as of enforcement actions, continues to be a troublesome issue.

c. **Enforcement action distinguished:** Enforcement actions within the meaning of Chapter VII, involving deployment of troops, differ from peacekeeping forces in that an enforcement action is imposed without the consent of the state against which such action is directed.

2. **The U.N. Charter prohibition against the use of force:** Article 2, ¶4 of the U.N. Charter provides that:

> All Members shall refrain in their international relations from the threat or use of force against the territorial integrity or political independence of any state, or in any other manner inconsistent with the purposes of the United Nations.

Article 2, ¶4 is recognized as ***customary international law***. It should be noted that article 2, ¶4 bans not only the ***use of force***, but the ***threat of force***. While it is clear that this provision bans most uses of force, there has been considerable debate as to whether article 2, ¶4 constitutes an absolute ban on the use of force except as expressly permitted by the Charter. The viewpoints summarized below represent the two extremes of this debate; many scholars have adopted views somewhere in between these extremes.

a. **The restrictive reading:** Scholars supporting the restrictive reading argue that the words of article 2, ¶4 must be given their plain, commonsense meaning. Under this approach, article 2, ¶4 prohibits only the use of force that is directed against the territorial integrity or political independence of any state. This interpretation would allow a state to use force against another state for other purposes—for example, to protect itself against possible attack or protect the lives of its nationals, to promote democracy, to further self-determination, or to protect its property in another state because in all these instances, the primary purpose would not be to impinge on the territorial integrity or political independence of the second state. This interpretation also opens the door to recognition of humanitarian intervention, by which a state may forcibly intervene in the domestic affairs of another state in order to rectify gross deprivation of human rights. For example, there is still a debate over whether the forcible humanitarian intervention in Kosovo in 1999 was permitted under article 2, ¶4. Even assuming that the restrictive reading is appropriate, the final phrase of article 2, ¶4, which limits the use of force to actions that are consistent with the purposes of the United Nations, may impose limits on a state's ability to use force. Critics of this view point to this last phrase as indicating that any use of force not expressly authorized by the Charter is inconsistent with the Charter's purpose to promote and maintain international peace and security.

b. **The expansive reading:** Scholars supporting the expansive reading contend that the language in article 2, ¶4 should be interpreted in light of the *travaux prèparatoires*, which indicate that the phrase "use of force against the territorial integrity or political independence of a state" was not intended to be restrictive but, on the contrary, was intended to provide more specific guarantees to small states. Additionally, they point out that the provision must be viewed in light of the presumption against self-help and use of force that underlies the Charter, as indicated in the final phrase of the article. Under this view, article 2, ¶4 should be given an expansive reading, prohibiting all use of force except as expressly permitted by the U.N. Charter.

The decision of the ICJ in the *Corfu Channel case* (*U.K. v. Alb.*), 1949 I.C.J. 4 (Apr. 9), lends support to this reading of article 2, ¶4. After British warships were struck by mines while engaging in innocent passage through Albanian territorial waters, the United Kingdom sent warships to sweep the waters for mines, a form of intervention into Albanian territory. In response to the United Kingdom's asserted justifications of self-help, necessity, or anticipatory self-defense, the court concluded:

> The Court can only regard the alleged right of intervention as the manifestation of a policy of force, such as has, in the past, given rise to most serious abuses and such as cannot, whatever be the present defects in international organization, find a place in international law. Intervention is perhaps still less admissible in the particular form it would take here; for, from the nature of things, it would be reserved for the most powerful States, and might easily lead to perverting the administration of international justice itself. The United Kingdom's agent, in his speech in reply, has further classified "Operation Retail" among methods of self-protection or self-help. The Court cannot accept this defense either. Between independent states, respect for territorial sovereignty is an essential foundation of international relations. The Court recognizes that the Albanian Government's complete failure to carry out its duties after the explosions, and the dilatory nature of its diplomatic notes, are extenuating circumstances for the action of the United Kingdom Government. But to ensure respect for international law, of which it is the organ, the Court must declare that the action of the British Navy constituted a violation of Albanian sovereignty.

The decision of the ICJ in the *Nicaragua v. United States* case also lends support to an expansive reading. There, the court interpreted the meaning of the ban on the use of force to encompass indirect measures, such as supplying an insurgent force in another country with weaponry, training, and intelligence, although it excluded supplying financial assistance. *Nicaragua v. United States*, 1986 I.C.J. 92.

C. **Threat or use of force authorized by the U.N. Charter:** Even within the U.N. Charter, the article 2, ¶4 ***prohibition on the use of force is not absolute***. There are only a few instances in which non-consensual use of force is expressly authorized by the Charter.

1. **Article 51 self-defense:** Article 51 of the U.N. Charter provides in part that:

Nothing in the present Charter shall impair the inherent right of individual or collective self-defense if an armed attack occurs against a Member of the United Nations, until the Security Council has taken measures necessary to maintain international peace and security.

a. **Scope of article 51:** As with the prohibition against the use of force, the exclusivity of the right of self-defense as defined by article 51 has been the subject of considerable debate.

i. **Exclusivity:** There is disagreement as to whether article 51, with its apparent requirement that an armed attack already have occurred, provides the exclusive justification for self-defense or whether states retain some customary right to self-defense that might be broader in scope than that contained in article 51. Proponents of exclusivity argue that allowing states to define broadly what may trigger a right of self-defense undermines the purpose of the Charter to maintain peace. They also argue that because self-defense is an exception to the restriction on the use of force, it should be interpreted narrowly.

ii. **Anticipatory self-defense:** There is disagreement as to whether or not a state may, under article 51 or under customary international law, justify the use of force in anticipatory self-defense when an attack is imminent. Assuming such a right exists, there is great uncertainty as to how imminent the attack must be. The requirements for a valid act of self-defense are discussed at §I(C)(1)(b) of this chapter, *infra*.

Example: In 1981, when Israel attacked a nuclear reactor under construction in Iraq that it claimed would be used to make nuclear weapons, Israel's justification was anticipatory self-defense. The Security Council condemned Israel's action but imposed no sanctions. In 1986, the United States asserted anticipatory self-defense to justify the bombing of Libya after an attack against U.S. soldiers in West Berlin that the United States claimed was sponsored by Libya.

iii. **Self-defense against terrorism:** The terrorist attacks on the World Trade Center and Pentagon on September 11, 2001, raised issues of self-defense to the forefront of international discussions. The military action by the United States against the government of Afghanistan in response was justified on the basis of self-defense, and it received widespread international support as a valid exercise of self-defense from the previous terrorist attacks.

More controversial was the development of a new national security strategy in September 2002 by the United States, with the assertion that anticipatory self-defense may be lawful even when an armed attack is not necessarily imminent, as previously required. A U.N. high-level panel accepted a right of anticipatory self-defense in its Report of December 2004, but the issue of how imminent the threat must be remains controversial and unsettled.

In 2010, President Barack Obama overhauled the foci of America's national security strategy and removed the references to preemptive attacks against other nations or sub-national organizations that defined President Bush's 2002 strategy, which was forged in the wake of 9/11. In particular, President Obama emphasized a desire to garner international support prior to taking action, the need for careful weighing of costs and risks of both action and inaction, and the expansion of the concept of national security beyond the more limited scope of counterterrorism. However, Obama's 2010 strategy does retain language that explicitly reserves the ultimate right of the United States to act unilaterally to defend and protect American interests, although it does not expressly adopt the language of his predecessor in office.

In 2018, the Israeli Supreme Court held that the Israel Defense Forces (IDF) were justified in using lethal force against rioters at the Gaza Strip border because they acted in self-defense and properly followed Israel's Rules of Engagement. HCJ 3003/18 Yesh Din v. IDF Chief of Staff (2018). The court determined that the IDF used lethal force only as a last resort, when non-lethal means to control the crowd were ineffective, against a crowd of terrorists, specifically members of Hamas, who were threatening to infiltrate into Israel.

iv. **Right of collective self-defense:** If a state is entitled to use force in self-defense under article 51, other states are entitled to come to the defense of the attacked state in collective self-defense. NATO invoked the right to assist the United States in its operations against Afghanistan under article 51. There is some question as to whether a state may exercise the collective right of self-defense without an explicit request for assistance from the state on whose behalf the right is being exercised. In *Nicaragua v. United States*, the ICJ concluded that the United States was not entitled to come to the defense of El Salvador, Honduras, and Costa Rica because at the time, it had not been requested to do so.

v. **Duration of right of self-defense:** It is unclear whether the right of a state to act in self-defense comes to an end as soon as the Security Council has taken action. It is clear that self-defense does not justify reprisals; once the threat has been terminated, the state may not continue to use force to retaliate for the attack. The proper duration of the right of self-defense has become more complicated with the indefinite nature of the current war against terrorism being waged by the United States and others. The United States removed its troops from Iraq in December 2011, ending the Iraqi War and transitioning to a governing structure run entirely by Iraqi leaders. However, throughout the withdrawal from Iraq, the conflict in Afghanistan raged on. President Obama declared the war likely to last until at least 2014. In June 2010, the Afghan war became the longest-running conflict in U.S. history. The United States removed the majority of its troops in 2014 and as of 2016 has left a small force in the country to be removed at the end of that year. The uncertainty regarding the duration of these two wars highlights the importance of the necessity and proportionality requirements for self-defense discussed below.

vi. **Targets for which a state may assert self-defense:** An attack triggering self-defense may be upon a state's territory, its armed forces, or state vessels or aircraft. Attacks upon a state's nationals or private property abroad may justify counterattack only if protection of nationals is recognized under international law. *See* §I(D)(2) of this chapter, *infra* (discussing protection of nationals and property).

b. **Necessity and proportionality requirements for self-defense:** The requirements for a valid act of self-defense were stated by Daniel Webster over 150 years ago in the *Caroline* case and reaffirmed in *Nicaragua v. United States*, 1986 I.C.J. 14. These requirements apply whether a nation is acting in self-defense against an attack that has already occurred or acting in anticipatory self-defense. First, there must be a "***necessity of self-defense, instant, overwhelming, leaving no choice of means, and no moment of deliberation***." Second, the actions justified by the necessity of self-defense "***must be limited by that necessity and kept clearly within it***." These two requirements are often referred to as the ***requirements of necessity*** and ***proportionality***.

c. **What constitutes an armed attack:** The concept of an "armed attack" prerequisite to the exercise of self-defense is clarified by three U.N. General Assembly resolutions: the Resolution on the Definition of Aggression, the Declaration on the Inadmissibility of Intervention in the Domestic Affairs of States and the Protection of Their Independence and Sovereignty, and the Declaration on Principles of International Law Concerning Friendly Relations and Cooperation Among States in Accordance with the Charter of the United Nations. The Declaration on the Inadmissibility of Intervention and the Declaration on Principles of International Law prohibit armed intervention against another state and reaffirm the Charter's requirement that international disputes be resolved by peaceful means, the use of force being a last resort. The Definition of Aggression clarifies the meaning of "aggression" for purposes of Chapter VII enforcement action, but is helpful in determining what constitutes an armed attack. The resolution is discussed at §I(C)(2) of this chapter, *infra*.

Example: In the *Oil Platforms* case (*Iran v. U.S.*), 2003 I.C.J. 161 (Nov. 6), Iran sued the United States seeking reparations for the destruction of three offshore oil complexes by the U.S. Navy in 1987 and 1988. The ICJ decided that mine and missile attacks aimed at U.S. flagged military ships were armed attacks, but that attacks on U.S.-owned ships did not amount to attacks on the state.

Example: It has been argued that the September 11, 2001, terrorist attacks on the World Trade Center and Pentagon have expanded the definition of armed attacks to include force by terrorist organizations. The Security Council called the events a "threat to the peace" rather than "armed attacks," but it did pronounce the right to self-defense in the preambles to Resolutions 1368 and 1373, which condemned the attacks.

Example: The *Israeli Wall* advisory opinion of the ICJ, however, suggests that an armed attack by a state is a prerequisite to article 51, although several judges rejected this position in separate opinions from the majority Advisory Opinion on Legal Consequences of the Construction of a Wall in the Occupied Palestinian Territory, 2004 I.C.J. 136.

2. **Enforcement actions by the United Nations:** Chapter VII of the U.N. Charter sets forth the authority of the Security Council to act with respect to "threat[s] to the peace, breach[es] of the peace, or act[s] of aggression." U.N. Charter, art. 39. These critical terms are not defined in the Charter. If the Security Council finds that such circumstances exist, it may take enforcement action in accordance with articles 41 and 42 of the Charter in order "to maintain or restore international peace and security." Before resorting to such measures, the Security Council may take provisional measures. art. 40. All member states are bound by such decisions. art. 25. Action taken under Chapter VII is subject to the veto power.

a. **Definition of aggression:** The General Assembly Resolution on the Definition of Aggression is a clarification of the U.N. Security Council's jurisdiction over "any threat to the peace, breach of the peace, or act of aggression." Article 1 defines aggression as "the use of armed force by a State against the ***sovereignty, territorial integrity, or political independence*** of another State, or in any other manner inconsistent with the Charter of the United Nations. . . . " Article 2 provides that the first use of armed force by a state in contravention of the U.N. Charter is *prima facie* evidence of an act of aggression, defined in article 3 to include the invasion by armed forces of another state. Article 3 lists some acts that qualify as acts of aggression and includes the sending of armed bands to carry out acts of armed force against a state of sufficient gravity to be tantamount to an invasion or attack against the state itself. Finally, article 5 adopts the Nuremberg Principles of the Charter of the International Military Tribunal at Nuremberg (Nuremberg Charter), which make armed aggression a "crime against peace" and prohibit territorial acquisition by virtue of such aggression.

b. **Article 41 measures short of armed force:** This provision authorizes the Security Council to call upon member states to implement measures not involving the use of armed force to give effect to its decisions. They have been imposed on states and non-state actors such as the Bosnian Serbs and UNITA in Angola. Such measures may include "complete or partial interruption of economic relations and of rail, sea, air, postal, telegraphic, radio, and other means of communication, and the severance of diplomatic relations."

Example: In 1965, a white minority regime in Southern Rhodesia (now Zimbabwe) declared independence from the United Kingdom and control of the government. In 1966, the Security Council imposed economic sanctions against Southern Rhodesia. The sanctions were terminated in 1979 when majority rule was accepted. Although this was the first time economic sanctions were imposed, they have been imposed in a number of cases, for example, against Yugoslavia, Iraq, and, more recently, against Iran and North Korea for their persistence in pursuing the development of nuclear power and ballistic missiles. Such measures include embargoes of materiel related to missile programs and other smaller arms embargoes.

i. **International Criminal Tribunal for the Former Yugoslavia:** The U.N. Security Counsel established the Tribunal to implement decisions of the Security Council. The legality of the establishment of the Tribunal was questioned in *Prosecutor v. Tadic* (Oct. 2, 1995) 35 I.L.M. 31 (1996). The Appeals Chamber concluded that Chapter VII of the U.N. Charter, particularly article 41, gives the Security Council ***broad discretion*** in determining measures to secure and maintain peace, including the creation of an international tribunal. Further, the Appeals Chamber rejected the challenge to the primacy of the Tribunal's jurisdiction and held that a state's power to exercise jurisdiction over an alleged offense does not preclude the establishment of an international tribunal with jurisdiction over the same offense. The jurisdiction of a state to try offenses committed in the state's territory may be an aspect of its sovereignty and within its domestic jurisdiction, but both are subject to the authority of the Security Council, to which member states submitted by adhering to the U.N. Charter. In addition, the Appeals Chamber ruled that Tadic's alleged crimes were committed in the context of an armed conflict and that the Tribunal has jurisdiction whether such conflict is deemed internal or international.

c. **Article 42 use of armed force:** Should the Security Council consider that peaceful measures "would be inadequate or have proved to be inadequate, it may take such action by air, sea, or land forces as may be necessary to maintain or restore international peace and security. Such action may include demonstrations, blockade, and other operations by air, sea, or land forces of Members of the United Nations." It should be noted that the Security Council is not required to take peaceful measures under article 41 before proceeding under article 42; the Security Council need only find that peaceful measures would be inadequate.

d. **Provision of forces for enforcement:** Article 43 provides that a state is not required to take part in military operations authorized under article 42 unless it has concluded a special agreement with the United Nations. At this time, no such agreements have been concluded. However, article 43 generally is not considered to prohibit the Security Council from assembling military forces by other means. The Security Council may not order states to take part in military operations, but it can authorize them to do so.

e. **Specific enforcement actions involving the use of force:** There have been only a few instances in which such enforcement action has been taken, but the breaking up of the Soviet Union has led to a recent upsurge in Security Council enforcement. Since October 2003, several major new operations have been deployed in Liberia, Cote d'Ivoire, Burundi, Haiti, Timor-Leste, the Sudan, and the Democratic Republic of the Congo. Some additional examples follow.

   i. **The Korean conflict:** In 1950, when the Soviet Union walked out of the Security Council over the issue of which government represented China, the Security Council passed resolutions recommending that member states furnish assistance to the Republic of Korea against North Korea, and placing forces there under a unified command to be appointed by the United States. The legal authority for the Korean forces is unclear. They flew the U.N. flag and were awarded U.N. medals, but the commander took orders from the United States, and the allied side of the peace conference consisted only of states that had sent troops. The forces may be considered an enforcement action, or an exercise by the states of collective self-defense with Security Council recognition of such right.

   ii. **Iraq:** In 1990, the Security Council, "acting under Chapter VII," gave Iraq until January 15, 1991, to withdraw from Kuwait or be subject to military action. As with the Korean conflict, the question has been raised whether the military action taken against Iraq was an enforcement action or Security Council authorization of collective self-defense under article 51.

   iii. **Somalia:** In 1992, the Security Council acting under Chapters VII and VIII and regional arrangements authorized member states to contribute to a U.S.-led military operation "to establish as soon as possible a secure environment for humanitarian relief operations in Somalia."

   iv. **Bosnia:** In 1993, the Security Council authorized the NATO allies to enforce a ban on military flights over Bosnia.

   v. **Haiti:** In July 1994, acting under Chapter VII, the Security Council authorized a multinational force under unified command to use all necessary force to help with the evacuation from Haiti of the military leadership and the reinstatement of the elected president and legitimate authorities.

vi. **Zaire (Democratic Republic of Congo):** In 1996, the Security Council unanimously adopted Resolution 1080 that determined the situation in Zaire to constitute a threat to international peace and security in that region and, under the authority of Chapter VII, authorized the member states to achieve, by all necessary means, the humanitarian objectives that it set out. In 1998, a complex conflict involving five other African states broke out again, but the Security Council would not deploy a force until there was commitment to a peace settlement, delaying the deployment of a substantial-sized force until 2004.

f. **General Assembly enforcement action under the Uniting for Peace Resolution:** In 1950, the General Assembly passed the Uniting for Peace Resolution, which provides in part:

> [I]f the Security Council, because of lack of unanimity of the permanent members, fails to exercise its primary responsibility for the maintenance of international peace and security in any case where there appears to be a threat to the peace, breach of the peace, or act of aggression, the General Assembly shall consider the matter immediately with a view to making appropriate recommendations to Members for collective measures, including in the case of a breach of the peace or act of aggression the use of armed force when necessary, to maintain or restore international peace and security.

Whether the General Assembly can take enforcement action is highly debatable. Article 11, ¶2 says that "any . . . question on which action is necessary shall be referred to the Security Council by the General Assembly." In upholding the legality of a peacekeeping force placed in Egypt by the General Assembly with Egypt's consent, the ICJ in the *Certain Expenses* case interpreted "action" to mean "enforcement action."

g. **Implied authorization of force?** The United States, United Kingdom, and other nations formed a coalition and undertook the disarmament of Iraq and the ousting of Saddam Hussein in March 2003. The United States and its supporters invoked preemptive self-defense as well as pointing to two Security Council resolutions as the basis for the legality of the operations. Resolution 1441, which was passed in November 2002, gave Iraq a final opportunity to comply with its disarmament obligations imposed under Resolution 687, the cease-fire agreement from 1991. The United States was unable to get an express authorization of force from the Security Council, but it argued that Resolution 1441 did not require a new resolution authorizing force and that it revived the authority to use force given in Resolution 687. Opponents of this theory argue that the United States relied on the resurrection of a ten-year-old resolution to make its case, and that the United States and coalition forces did not have the authority to determine that Iraq was in material breach of its obligations. The Security Council did subsequently confer legitimacy on the operation, while at the same time reaffirming Iraq's territorial integrity and stressing the right of the Iraqi people to choose their political future. Secretary-General Kofi Annan later expressly stated that he believed the original invasion in 2003 was not in conformity with the U.N. Charter. The United States declared an end to its military mission in Iraq in August 2010, but U.S. troops remained in the nation to assist with stabilization and the facilitation of a new Iraqi government.

3. **Enforcement actions by regional organizations under article 53:** Article 53 of the Charter provides that the Security Council can utilize regional arrangements or agencies for enforcement action, but that "no enforcement action shall be taken under regional arrangements or by regional agencies without the authorization of the Security Council."

4. **Actions against former enemy states under articles 53, ¶¶1 and 107:** Article 107 of the U.N. Charter provides:

> Nothing in the present Charter shall invalidate or preclude action, in relation to any state which during the Second World War has been an enemy of any signatory to the present Charter, taken or authorized as a result of that war by the Governments having responsibility for such action.

Article 53, ¶1 specifically waives the requirement of Security Council authorization for actions taken by regional defense organizations pursuant to article 107. While these provisions have been invoked in the past, the view of most scholars is that article 107 and, less clearly, article 53, ¶1 are now obsolete.

D. **Non-Charter justifications of self-help or necessity for the use of armed force:** Assuming that the explicit Charter authorizations for force are not exhaustive and that article 2, ¶4 should be given a narrow reading, a number of justifications for force have been advanced under customary international law. All or most of these justifications are forms of self-help, the pre-Charter custom of absolute sovereignty, allowing a state to take action against another state for a violation of international law.

1. **Humanitarian intervention:** Some scholars argue that military actions undertaken for humanitarian purposes in response to ***gross violations of human rights*** (a term that itself is controversial) are permissible under a narrow reading of article 2, ¶4. Although scholars have proposed many criteria for "legitimate" humanitarian intervention, it is generally agreed that the state using force would have to act from humanitarian motives (not against "the territorial integrity or political independence" of the target state), act proportionally, and cease military operations as soon as the humanitarian objective was achieved.

Example: In 1976, Israel staged a raid on the Entebbe airport to free Israelis and other nationals being held hostage on a hijacked plane. However, in *Nicaragua v. United States*, the ICJ stated that the "use of force could not be the appropriate method to . . . ensure . . . respect" for human rights.

Example: The issue of whether the use of military action was justified for humanitarian purposes was also debated in the *Legality of Use of Force* case (*Serbia and Montenegro v. Belgium*) brought by Yugoslavia against NATO in the ICJ. The United Kingdom in particular argued that the 78-day air campaign in 1999 to help ethnic Albanians in the Kosovo region was intended to prevent a humanitarian disaster and was not directed against the territorial integrity or political independence of Yugoslavia. The ICJ did not overturn its decision of the above *Nicaragua* case, and the legal doctrine of humanitarian intervention is still unclear.

Recently, there has been greater interest within the international community in creating a detailed framework for humanitarian intervention within the United Nations for easier intervention in situations like that occurring in Darfur, Sudan. In 2007, the United Nations and the African Union created and deployed a hybrid operation in Darfur charged with protecting civilians and monitoring the ongoing implementation of agreements among the region's conflicting groups. The operation consists of military and police personnel from countries around the world working to keep ongoing negotiations peaceful. The impetus for action came collectively from the United Nations, however, rather than unilaterally from individual nations.

2. **Protection of nationals and property:** Protection of nationals is distinguished from humanitarian intervention based on the nationality of the victims. It is legally distinguishable because

advocates of the right have asserted that attacks on a state's nationals triggers a right of self-defense under a broad reading of article 51 or as self-help under customary international law.

3. **Reprisals:** The term *reprisal* means an otherwise illegal act committed by one state against a second state, in order to remedy a prior violation of international law by the second state, to protect its interests, or to achieve some other objective. Often, the illegal act involves the use of force. A state that engages in a reprisal in retaliation for past acts is presumably in violation of international law. Prior to 1945, reprisals were an accepted institution in international law, provided that a state acted within the bounds of necessity and proportionality. Such self-help is now presumably prohibited under the U.N. Charter. The Geneva Conventions of 1949 also prohibit specific types of reprisals (such as reprisals against wounded or sick combatants) during times of armed conflict. Although it is generally acknowledged that reprisals are prohibited by international law, it has been argued that such actions may be justified in limited situations. Reprisals must be distinguished from retorsion, which is an action taken by a state against another state in response to an injury arising from a violation of international law or an unfriendly act by the second state. Retorsions themselves must not amount to a violation of international law. Retorsions do not generally involve the use of military force; instead the use of economic force, such as trade sanctions, embargoes, or boycotts, is frequently employed. Other measures include breaking off diplomatic relations, expulsion of nationals, and strict passport regulations. Depending upon the measures taken, retorsions within general limitations of necessity and proportionality may be lawful. The principal issue with the legality of retorsions is whether article 2, ¶4's prohibition on the use or threat of force is limited to armed force.

II. THE HUMANITARIAN LAW OF ARMED CONFLICT

The humanitarian law of armed conflict attempts to place limitations upon the conduct of warfare to prevent unnecessary suffering of civilians and combatants without undermining the effectiveness of military operations. It applies to international armed conflict and, to a more limited degree, internal conflicts or civil wars.

A. **Sources of the law of armed conflict:** Customary law and international treaties are the primary sources of armed conflict law. Many treaties, including the Hague and the four Geneva Conventions, reflect or have evolved into customary law. Whether a treaty reflects custom becomes very important when the treaty limits its coverage to certain conflicts or parties to a conflict.

1. **Customary law:** The humanitarian laws of war were articulated by some of the earliest scholars, such as Grotius and Emrich von de Vattel, among others. Many of the principles laid down by these scholars have entered into customary international law and are the foundation of the landmark treaties of the twentieth century.

2. **International treaties:** Many international treaties regulate the conduct of warfare. Among the most important of these treaties still in force are:

   a. **International treaties:** *The Hague Conventions and Declarations of 1907,* especially the Convention Respecting the Law and Customs of War on Land (Hague Convention IV), with Annex of Regulations (referred to as the Hague regulations).

   b. **International treaties:** *The Nuremberg Charter of 1945,* the inter-allies agreement for the prosecution and punishment of Nazi leaders.

c. The Geneva Conventions of 1949, including:

- Convention for the Amelioration of the Condition of the Wounded and Sick in Armed Forces in the Field;
- Convention for the Amelioration of the Condition of Wounded, Sick, and Shipwrecked Members of Armed Forces at Sea;
- Convention Relative to the Treatment of Prisoners of War; and
- Convention Relative to the Protection of Civilian Persons in Time of War.

d. The Protocols Additional of 1977, including:

- Protocol Additional to the Geneva Conventions of August 12, 1949, and Relating to the Protection of Victims of International Armed Conflicts, and
- Protocol Additional to the Geneva Conventions of August 12, 1949, and Relating to the Protection of Victims of Non-international Armed Conflicts.

B. Protections provided by the Hague and Geneva Conventions: Certain protections are provided to specific categories of people and property.

1. Protection of the individual: The degree of protection the laws of armed conflict extend to any given individual depends largely upon that individual's characterization under the Hague and Geneva Conventions.

a. Protections extended to combatants: The primary source of protection to combatants is the Annex to the Hague Convention IV of 1907. Under the laws of armed conflict, a combatant is ***any individual legally entitled to take part in hostilities.*** Combatants include not only members of the armed forces of a state involved in a conflict, but also citizens who rise in a *levee en masse* (a spontaneous, mass uprising) and members of organized resistance groups who fulfill the criteria of being commanded by a responsible superior, wearing some type of uniform, carrying arms openly, and obeying the laws and customs of war. Under the laws of armed conflict, a combatant is ***subject to attack at any time.*** The protections extended to active combatants are minimal; in general, the only protections consist of the limitations on weapons and tactics discussed at §II(F) of this chapter, *infra.* The laws of armed conflict also extend certain additional protections against attack to medical personnel, clergy, and the like.

b. Protections extended to wounded, sick, and shipwrecked combatants: While an active combatant is accorded minimal protection, a combatant who is wounded, sick, or who has surrendered is ***accorded considerable protection*** under international law; he or she may not be subjected to further attack. The primary sources of protection to these individuals are the Hague Convention IV, the Geneva Convention for the Amelioration of the Condition of the Wounded and Sick in Armed Forces in the Field, and the Geneva Convention for the Amelioration of the Condition of Wounded, Sick and Shipwrecked Members of Armed Forces at Sea. An individual who is injured or sick is not only protected from further attack but ***must be provided with medical care.*** Information about the wounded individuals must be forwarded to the central prisoner-of-war information agency.

c. Protections extended to prisoners of war (POWs): Any lawful combatant who falls into the hands of the enemy is entitled to prisoner-of-war status. These protections are extended whether or not the detaining power recognizes the authority of the organization or group that they represent. The primary source of international law relating to the treatment of POWs is the 1949 Geneva Convention Relative to the Treatment of Prisoners of War. Essentially, the Convention provides for the ***humane and decent treatment*** of POWs and expressly forbids torture, biological experimentation, and other invasions of personal dignity. POWs may be used as a labor force, but non-commissioned officers may be employed only in supervisory roles and commissioned officers cannot be forced to work at all. If POWs are employed as a labor force, they must be compensated, the tasks may not be unhealthy or unreasonably dangerous, and due regard must be given to their physical capabilities. POWs are subject to the disciplinary regulations of the detaining power, and they may be tried, within limits set forth in the Convention, for violations of such regulations. The protecting power may oversee all trials and punishments. During a conflict, POWs must be repatriated if they have suffered substantial mental or physical impairment or if they need medical attention that will last more than one year. Upon the conclusion of active hostilities, all POWs must be released and repatriated without delay.

d. **Protections extended to civilians:** In the nineteenth century, the protection of civilians was not a major concern of the laws of war. The Hague Convention provided protection to some civilians and undefended areas. With the advent of the concept of total war (involvement of both the military and civilian populace in the conflict) in World War II, and developments in military technology, the protection of civilians became a prime concern. This concern is reflected in the fourth Geneva Convention of 1949, the Convention Relative to the Protection of Civilian Persons in Time of War. This Convention protects civilians both during active hostilities and during time of enemy occupation of a state by providing for the creation of various protected zones in which hostilities may not be carried out. An occupying power may take security measures, but torture, murder, corporal punishment, and the like are prohibited, as are collective punishments and hostage-taking. While internment of civilians is permitted, the Convention requires that internees be provided treatment that roughly corresponds to that of POWs. Perhaps most importantly, while an occupying power may set up a government, the rights of the people under occupation are delineated.

i. ***Rasul v. Bush***: In *Rasul v. Bush*, 542 U.S. 466 (2004), the U.S. Supreme Court held that foreign nationals seized in Pakistan and Afghanistan shortly before or during the U.S. invasion of Afghanistan and transferred to Guantanamo Bay, Cuba, were entitled to challenge their detention in U.S. federal court through habeas corpus. In so holding, the Court concluded that the United States had sufficient sovereign control of Guantanamo Bay to extend habeas corpus jurisdiction.

ii. ***Hamdi v. Rumsfeld***: The U.S. Supreme Court held that constitutional due process protections require the Defense Department to provide a U.S. citizen captured in Afghanistan pursuant to military operations and detained within the territory of the United States an opportunity to challenge his classification as an "enemy combatant" before a neutral decision maker. *Hamdi v. Rumsfeld*, 542 U.S. 507 (2004); *see also In re Guantanamo Detainee Cases*, 355 F. Supp. 2d 443 (D.D.C. 2005). Four of the Justices relied on the Geneva Convention in finding some due process rights to challenge status and detention for any alleged "enemy combatant," a classification not otherwise found within the express terms of the Geneva Convention.

iii. ***Hamdan v. Rumsfeld*:** In *Hamdan v. Rumsfeld*, 548 U.S. 557 (2006), the Court held that the special military commission that was to try a detainee was unlawfully constituted because Congress had not clearly authorized the President to establish the commission and because the commission's rules deviated substantially from evidentiary and appellate procedures required by the Uniform Code of Military Justice and the Geneva Convention.

iv. ***Boumediene v. Bush*:** In *Boumediene v. Bush*, 553 U.S. 723 (2008), foreign nationals held at Guantanamo Bay challenged their status as enemy combatants and detention through habeas corpus under U.S. constitutional law, federal law, treaty obligations including the Geneva Conventions, and customary international law. The Military Commissions Act of 2006 (MCA), passed by Congress after the *Hamdan* decision, operated to preclude federal courts' jurisdiction to hear habeas corpus actions of detained aliens determined to be enemy combatants. A divided Court held that the aliens detained at Guantanamo Bay were entitled to the privilege of habeas corpus to challenge the legality of their detention, and that the provision in the MCA that denied such jurisdiction effected an unconstitutional suspension of the writ. The Court also held that the statutory protections afforded in the MCA's combatant status review tribunals fell short of those procedures that would eliminate the need for habeas review.

2. **Protection of property:** As with individuals, the degree of protection extended to any particular piece of property depends largely upon its nature. As a general rule, under both the Hague Conventions of 1907 and the Geneva Conventions of 1949, the destruction or confiscation of enemy property is forbidden except for situations of military necessity. In no event is looting of enemy property permissible, although enemy military equipment may be seized as war trophies.

a. **Military installations:** All military installations, including industries and facilities that directly contribute to the war effort, are ***subject to attack.*** Article 26 of the Annex to Hague Convention IV provided that the commander of attacking forces must attempt to notify the enemy before such an attack. While often impracticable, this rule still applies, especially if civilians may be at risk.

b. **Civilian structures:** The 1907 Hague Conventions provided that undefended buildings, towns, and the like were ***not to be attacked.*** However, with the increasing involvement between civilian personnel and military industries, this provision is becoming increasingly difficult to enforce or obey.

c. **Areas with special protection:** The 1949 Geneva Conventions extended special protections to ***medical facilities*** (both military and civilian) and provided for the establishment of hospital, neutralized, and safety zones in which attacks are forbidden. ***Works of art*** are also entitled to special protection from attack under both the Annex to Hague Conventions IV and the 1954 Hague Convention on the Protection of Cultural Property in the Event of an Armed Conflict. Cultural property includes both movable and immovable property having special cultural significance.

C. **Conflicts encompassed by the Geneva Conventions and Protocols:** Which provisions of the Geneva Conventions and protocols apply depends upon whether the conflict is an international conflict, civil war, or a war of self-determination.

1. **International conflicts:** Under common article 2, the Geneva Conventions in their entirety apply to ***international conflicts***. Protocol I of 1977 also applies to international conflicts.

2. **Civil wars:** For an "armed conflict not of an international character," only common article 3 of the Geneva Convention applies. The protection that it provides is general and ***much more limited*** than the protection provided in international conflicts. Article 3 requires all parties to the conflict to treat humanely "persons taking no active part in the hostilities, members of armed forces who have laid down their arms and those placed *hors de combat* by sickness, wounds, detention, or any other cause. . . . " Discrimination on the basis of race, color, religion or faith, sex, birth or wealth, or similar criteria is prohibited. Specifically prohibited are:

   - violence to life and person, in particular murder of all kinds, mutilation, cruel treatment, and torture;
   - taking of hostages;
   - outrages upon personal dignity, in particular humiliating and degrading treatment;
   - the passing of sentences and the carrying out of executions without previous judgment pronounced by a regularly constituted court affording all the judicial guarantees that are recognized as indispensable by civilized peoples.

   Because governments and opposing factions alike had resisted application of common article 3 to civil wars, Protocol II relating to "non-international armed conflict" was adopted in 1977. It contains detailed provisions for humane treatment in conflicts between a state's armed forces and dissident armed forces or other organized armed forces that meet a specified level of control and command. Article 1 states, however, that the protocol supplements article 3 without modifying the existing conditions of application for article 3. Some civil wars that fall under the broad coverage of common article 3 will not qualify for coverage under the more restrictive conditions for coverage in Protocol II. The protocol also does not apply to "internal disturbances and tensions, such as riots, isolated and sporadic acts of violence and other acts of a similar nature. . . . " Under this provision, the issue is at what point hostilities reach an intensity that qualifies for coverage under Protocol II. Many countries as of 2016, including the United States, have refused to ratify Protocol II.

3. **Wars of self-determination:** Protocol I applies not only to international conflicts, but also to "armed conflicts in which people are fighting against colonial domination and alien occupation, and against racist regimes in the exercise of their right of self-determination, as enshrined in the Charter of the United Nations and the Declaration on Principles of International Law concerning Friendly Relations. . . . " Protocol I also makes the four Geneva Conventions applicable to such conflicts. Many countries as of 2016, including the United States, have refused to ratify Protocol I for this reason.

D. Applicability of general human rights obligations during armed conflict: *See* §II(A) of this chapter, *supra* (discussing the humanitarian law of armed conflict).

E. Sanctions and enforcement: Several treaties and conventions contain sanctions and enforcement provisions.

1. **The Hague Conventions of 1907:** The Hague Conventions of 1907 provided that a state might be required to pay reparations if it, or any member of its armed forces, violated the Convention. However, the Conventions established no procedural framework through which a nation might

press its claims that a violation had occurred. The Hague Conventions by their terms were binding only as between parties to the Conventions, and then only if all of the states involved in a conflict were also parties to the Convention. The International Military Tribunal at Nuremberg concluded that the provisions of the Hague Conventions are ***customary international law.***

2. **The Geneva Conventions of 1949:** Parties have a general obligation to ensure respect for the Geneva Conventions in all circumstances. The Conventions provide that once a violation has been established, the parties shall "put an end to it and repress it with the least possible delay." The Geneva Conventions also contain provisions allowing a state to subject any individual, regardless of nationality, to ***criminal*** prosecution for violations of the Conventions. Unlike the Hague Conventions, the Geneva Conventions are not entirely self-administered; the Conventions provide that the interests of each party to the conflict are to be safeguarded by a neutral "protecting power." *See* §II(A)(2)(c) of this chapter, *supra* (discussing the Geneva Conventions and the additional protocols). By their terms, the Geneva Conventions apply to "all cases of declared war or of any other armed conflict" between contracting states. The parties to the convention are bound to apply its terms between themselves, even if not all of the states involved in the conflict are contracting parties. In addition, if a non-party state accepts and applies the provisions of the Conventions, the contracting parties are required to abide by the Conventions as they pertain to that state. The Geneva Conventions are generally regarded as ***custom.*** States are liable for grave breaches by its nationals for whom they are responsible. With respect to prosecution and enforcement against individuals, the Conventions provide:

   > The High Contracting Parties undertake to enact any legislation necessary to provide effective penal sanctions for persons committing, or ordering to be committed, any of the grave breaches of the present Convention defined in the following Article. Each High Contracting Party shall be under the obligation to search for persons alleged to have committed, or to have ordered to be committed, such grave breaches, and shall bring such persons, regardless of their nationality, before its own courts. It may also, if it prefers, and in accordance with the provisions of its own legislation, hand such persons over for trial to another High Contracting Party concerned, provided such High Contracting Party has made out a *prima facie* case. Each High Contracting Party shall take measures necessary for the suppression of all acts contrary to the provisions of the present Convention other than the grave breaches defined in the following Article.

   Grave breaches that are listed under each Convention are generally recognized as ***war crimes*** under international law. The Conventions provide for enforcement by the states, although the parties are not precluded from conferring jurisdiction upon an international tribunal over those grave breaches that constitute war crimes under international law.

3. **The Protocols Additional of 1977:** Protocol II does not establish any methods of implementation or enforcement. Protocol I does establish a fact-finding commission to investigate grave breaches if its jurisdiction to do so is recognized by the parties to the conflict. Protocol I expands upon the substantive rules and procedural mechanisms of the Convention for repression of breaches.

4. **The Nuremberg Principles:** The Charter of the International Military Tribunal at Nuremberg, which was later recognized as custom by the General Assembly of the United Nations, provided for individual ***criminal*** responsibility for "crimes against peace," "war crimes," or "crimes against humanity":

- **Crimes against peace:**

  Namely, planning, preparation, initiation or waging of a war of aggression, or a war in violation of international treaties, agreements or assurances, or participation in a common plan or conspiracy for the accomplishment of any of the foregoing;

- **War crimes:**

  Namely, violations of the laws or customs of war. Such violations shall include, but not be limited to, murder, ill-treatment, or deportation to slave labor or for any purpose of civilian population of or in occupied territory, murder or ill-treatment of prisoners of war or persons on the seas, killing of hostages, plunder of public or private property, wanton destruction of cities, towns, or villages, or devastation not justified by military necessity;

- **Crimes against humanity:**

  Namely, murder, extermination, enslavement, deportation, and other inhumane acts committed against any civilian population, before or during the war; or persecutions on political, racial, or religious grounds in execution of or in connection with any crime within the jurisdiction of the Tribunal, whether or not in violation of the domestic law of the country where perpetrated.

  Leaders, organizers, instigators, and accomplices participating in the formulation or execution of a common plan or conspiracy to commit any of the foregoing crimes are responsible for all acts performed by any persons in execution of such plan.

  Example: In 1996, the International Criminal Tribunal for the Former Yugoslavia indicted eight Serbs, who were members of the military, paramilitary, and police, charging them with the rape of 14 Muslim women. *Indictment of Gagovic & Others*. This was the first time that rape had been considered a separate indictable war crime. The indictment details the acts of sexual assault and, mainly on the basis of such acts, charges the perpetrators with crimes against humanity, grave breaches of the Geneva Conventions, and violations of the laws or customs of war. *See also Prosecutor v. Furundzÿa*, in Chapter 13.

  Example: In *Application of Yamashita*, 327 U.S. 1 (1946), General Yamashita of Japan was tried by a special U.S. military commission applying the international laws of war as incorporated into U.S. domestic law. Yamashita was charged with war crimes, including the massacre of civilian populations in the Philippines, which was also a crime against humanity under the Nuremberg Principles. The gist of the charge was that Yamashita failed as commander to control the troops in his command and thereby prevent the alleged atrocities. In holding Yamashita responsible for the alleged war crimes, the Court established that an official or commander who, through reports received by him or through other means, learns that troops or other persons subject to his control are about to commit or have committed war crimes, and fails to take the necessary and reasonable steps to ensure compliance with the law of war, is responsible for such crimes.

5. **War crimes tribunals and an international criminal court:** The Nuremberg Tribunal is an example of an international tribunal with jurisdiction conferred by agreement of the parties. In 1993, the Security Council authorized the establishment of tribunals for Yugoslavia and Rwanda. There is now an international criminal court with jurisdiction over war crimes and other crimes under international law. *See generally* Chapter 13.

F. **Limitations on the methods of warfare:** The limitations on the methods of warfare are complex and detailed. The following summary is intended only to give a general outline of the limitations, primarily for weaponry.

1. **Limitations on weaponry:** As ever-more-destructive weapons have been developed, there have been many specific treaties and declarations to limit the human suffering caused by these weapons. Perhaps the most important agreement in this area is the Treaty on Conventional Armed Forces in Europe, Nov. 19, 1990, *S. Treaty Doc.* No. 102-8 (1991), 30 I.L.M. 1. Thereunder, North American and European states set specific limits for each party on a range of conventional weapons, such as tanks and aircrafts.

   More recently, states worldwide have been concerned with the international small arms trade. On July 21, 2001, several states adopted a voluntary, politically binding program of action calling upon states to pursue a variety of national, regional, and global measures against the illicit international trade in small arms.

   In general, use of the following weapons is at least arguably ***prohibited by customary law***:

   a. **Explosive projectiles under 400 grams:** The St. Petersburg Treaty of 1868 prohibited the use of explosive projectiles weighing under 400 grams.

   b. **"Dum-dum" bullets:** The Third Hague Declarations of 1899 banned the use of expanding bullets and projectiles.

   c. **Poisons and poisonous weapons:** These weapons were prohibited by article 23(a) of the Annex to Hague Convention IV of 1907.

   d. **Chemical and bacteriological weapons:** The Geneva Protocol of 1925 prohibits the use of poisonous and asphyxiating gases and the use of bacteriological (biological) methods of warfare. In addition, the 1972 Convention on the Prohibition of the Development, Production, and Stockpiling of Bacteriological (Biological) and Toxin Weapons and on Their Destruction not only prohibited the use of such weapons, but also their development and production. In January 1993, the Chemical Weapons Convention was signed by more than 100 countries. The Convention, which bans chemical weapons, prevents states from producing and selling materials or facilities that can be used to manufacture chemical weapons. It is the first treaty intended to eliminate an entire class of weapons.

   e. **"Arms, projectiles, or materials calculated to cause unnecessary suffering":** Weapons that cause needless suffering are prohibited by article 23(e) of the Annex to Hague Convention IV of 1907.

   f. **Nuclear weapons:** Although several U.N. General Assembly declarations state that use of nuclear weapons is illegal, the 2017 Treaty on the Prohibition of Nuclear Weapons, prohibiting the development, possession, transfer, stationing, use, and threat of use of nuclear weapons is the first adopted treaty to prohibit use of nuclear weapons. Although none of the nine states in possession of nuclear weapons have signed it, 122 states have voted in favor of the treaty. Views on whether the use of nuclear weapons violates custom are widely divergent. Because of the degree of "unnecessary suffering" nuclear weapons cause, it has been argued that their use violates a customary prohibition on weapons that cause unnecessary suffering, even if custom does not specifically prohibit the use of nuclear weapons *per se*. It has also been argued that the nuclear arms race itself violates the Charter's prohibitions on the threat of force.

i. **Review of the Treaty on the Non-Proliferation of Nuclear Weapons (NPT):** In 1995, a conference was convened to review the Treaty on the Non-Proliferation of Nuclear Weapons (NPT). A majority of the 175 states that have subscribed to the NPT supported its indefinite and unconditional extension. In addition, the conference adopted documents to strengthen the NPT's review process and establish a set of common principles for the non-proliferation and disarmament of nuclear weapons. United Nations: Final Document on Extension of the Treaty on the Non-Proliferation of Nuclear Weapons, 34 I.L.M. 959 (1995).

ii. **NPT's ruling on use of nuclear weapons:** In July 1996, the ICJ issued an advisory opinion on the question presented by the U.N. General Assembly of whether the threat or use of nuclear weapons in any circumstance is permitted under international law. The ICJ found that the threat or use of nuclear weapons would generally be contrary to the rules of international law applicable in armed conflict. However, the ICJ did not conclude definitively on whether the threat or use of nuclear weapons would be lawful in extreme circumstances of self-defense in which the survival of a state would be at stake. In addition, the ICJ found that in neither customary nor conventional law is there any specific authorization or prohibition of the threat or use of nuclear weapons. The ICJ concluded that there exists an obligation of good faith to bring to a conclusion negotiations leading to nuclear disarmament. Legality of the Threat or Use of Nuclear Weapons, I.C.J. Reports, 1996, p. 226.

iii. **Legality of the Use by a State of Nuclear Weapons in Armed Conflict Opinion (1996):** The ICJ found that it was not able to give the advisory opinion requested by the World Health Organization (WHO) on this issue. The court concluded that there are three conditions which must be satisfied in order to found the jurisdiction of the court when an advisory opinion is requested by a specialized agency: (1) the agency requesting must be duly authorized, under the Charter, to request opinions from the court; (2) the opinion requested must be on a legal question; and (3) this question must be one arising within the scope of the requesting agency's activities. The court found that the WHO satisfied the first two conditions, but not the third. ***Legality of the Use by a State of Nuclear Weapons in Armed Conflict*, General List No. 93 (Advisory Opinion of July 8, 1996).**

iv. **Other agreements:** Various other agreements—for example, the Strategic Arms Limitation Talks (SALT) agreements, the Strategic Arms Reduction Talks (START) agreements, and the Intermediate Nuclear Forces (INF) Treaty—were all designed to freeze, reduce, or eliminate different types of nuclear weapons during the Cold War. While not all of these agreements were actually entered into force and others have been questioned in the post–Cold War period, the United States and Russia built upon these treaties in May 2002 by concluding a Strategic Offensive Reductions Treaty—in which they agreed to reduce warheads on launchers to a range of 1,700 to 2,200 warheads. In 2010, the United States and Russia further cemented their commitment to the reduction of strategic arms by signing the New START treaty, which, among other provisions, limited each nation to 1,550 warheads, a total 30 percent below the limit established in 2002.

2. **Limitations on tactics:** The Hague Convention IV of 1907 makes it illegal to "kill or wound treacherously individuals belonging to the hostile nation or army." Although the Convention

provides no definition of treachery, it has been interpreted to mean such tactics as disguising soldiers as civilians and the like. Similarly, the Convention also prohibits the improper use of a flag of truce, the national flag or uniform of the enemy, or such symbols as the red cross. Tactics of this nature must be distinguished from "ruses of war," which are expressly permitted by the Convention. Ruses, although enabling an army to gain the advantage of surprise or position, do not involve deceit. Spying is also permitted, but if not in uniform, a captured spy is not entitled to the protections given a prisoner of war.

3. **Limitations on the region of armed conflict:** The region of war is that area in which the combatant states may prepare and execute military operations. In general, the region of war may not be extended to neutral states or areas under their jurisdiction, demilitarized zones, international neutralized zones, or the waterways, territorial seas, or airspace of such areas.

III. CIVIL WARS

International law does not prohibit civil war. Article 2, ¶4 of the U.N. Charter prohibits only force against states. Civil wars may be fought for control of the government of the state, for the creation of a new state through succession, or to gain independence from colonial rule.

A. **Generally:** Throughout this section, the parties seeking control of the government or creation of a new state are referred to as the ***insurgents***, and the opposing parties previously in control as the ***governing authorities***.

1. **Categories of conflicts:** Traditionally, internal conflicts are classified into three categories:

a. **Rebellion:** This is a sporadic, isolated act of violence against the governing authorities, deemed to be a domestic matter subject to the control of the state.

b. **Insurgency:** An insurgency is more severe than a rebellion but less intense than a belligerency.

c. **Belligerency:** This state of affairs refers to a full-scale, widespread conflict between the governing authorities and the parties opposing them.

B. **Traditional rule regarding intervention:** Under the traditional rule, states could support the governing authorities ***until a belligerency was recognized***, at which point they had to remain neutral or be prepared to justify under international law their intervention for whichever side they supported. This rule was easily manipulated by states wanting to intervene, and recognition of a belligerency rarely occurred during the civil wars of the twentieth century. Therefore, analysis of the legality of intervention in civil wars now focuses on the general norms of non-intervention and self-determination, the prohibitions on force, and the limited justifications for force in international law after promulgation of the U.N. Charter.

C. **The concept of non-intervention:** One of the purposes of the post-Charter legal system is promotion of self-determination. U.N. Charter, art. 1, ¶2; art. 55. There is a customary norm of non-intervention in the domestic affairs of other states generally, and in civil wars more specifically, because any foreign intervention in a civil war inhibits self-determination. This norm of non-intervention is based on the sovereign equality of states in article 2, ¶1 of the Charter, several General Assembly resolutions (*e.g.*, Declaration of International Law Concerning Friendly Relations and Cooperation Among States, U.N.G.A. Res. 2625 (xxv), 25 U.N. GAOR, Supp. (No. 28) 121, U.N. Doc. A/8028 (1971), Declaration on the Inadmissibility of Intervention in the Domestic Affairs of the States, U.N.G.A. Res. 2131 (xx) (1966)), and by implication from the prohibition in article 2, ¶7 on U.N. intervention in the domestic affairs of states. In *Military and Paramilitary Activities in and Against Nicaragua* (*Nicar. v. U.S.*), 1984 I.C.J. 392, the ICJ concluded that the ***principle of non-intervention is part of customary international law.***

D. Acts constituting intervention: To remain neutral in a conflict, a state must not engage in any acts constituting intervention.

1. Clear acts of state intervention: The following acts by a state are clearly acts of intervention when done to support either side of a civil war:

- ***Sending armed forces,*** military instructors, or technicians;
- ***Drawing up*** **or** ***training regular or irregular forces***;
- ***Supplying weapons*** or other war material; and
- ***Allowing the state's territory to be used*** as a base for operations, supplies, refuge, or for passing of forces or war material.

2. Acts of a state's nationals as intervention: It is unclear whether a state must prohibit its nationals from raising contingents, collecting equipment, or crossing the border as mercenaries or volunteers for either side in a civil war. *See* Resolution on the Principle of Non-intervention in Civil Wars of the Institut de Droit International, art. 2, ¶1, 56 Ann. Inst. Dr. Int'l 544 (1975); Resolution on the Definition of Aggression, U.N.G.A. Res. 3314 (xxix) (1974). There are often, however, treaties and domestic legislation that prohibit a state's nationals from supporting the overthrow of the government of another state with which the state is not at war. *See, e.g.,* Neutrality Act of 1914. It is also unclear whether a state must prohibit its nationals from selling or providing weapons or other war material in order to remain neutral.

Example: In *Military and Paramilitary Activities in and against Nicaragua* (*Nicar. v. U.S.*), 1986 I.C.J. 14, the ICJ held that Nicaragua was not liable for allowing weapons to be transported across its territory to insurgents in El Salvador because Nicaragua was unable to stop the flow of weapons. The court did not appear to find relevant whether the weapons were being sent by private individuals or by another state.

E. Acts not constituting intervention: A state may ***provide humanitarian aid*** for food and medical supplies without violating an obligation of neutrality. Although it has been argued that it is not intervention to provide humanitarian aid to one side only, the decision of the ICJ in *Nicaragua v. United States, supra,* suggests otherwise. ("[I]f the provision of 'humanitarian assistance' is to escape condemnation as an intervention in the internal affairs of Nicaragua, not only must it be limited to the purposes hallowed in the practice of the Red Cross, namely to 'prevent and alleviate human suffering,' and to 'protect life and health and to ensure respect for the human being,' it must also, and above all, be given without discrimination to all in need in Nicaragua, not merely to the contras and their dependents." 1986 I.C.J. at 115.). It does not constitute intervention for a state to express its support for one side over another, so long as such expressions are not accompanied by acts constituting intervention.

F. Wars of national liberation as an exception to the norm of non-intervention: There is one possible exception to the post-Charter norm of non-intervention. Several General Assembly resolutions suggest that insurgents engaged in a war of national liberation not only have a right of self-determination to do so, but that outside states may aid the insurgents in overthrowing the governing authorities. *See, e.g.*, Declaration of International Law Concerning Friendly Relations and Cooperation Among States, U.N.G.A. Res. 2625 (xxv), 25 U.N. GAOR, Supp. (No. 28) 121, U.N. Doc A/8028 (1971) ("In their actions against and resistance to such forcible action [depriving peoples of their right to self-determination], such peoples are entitled to seek and to receive support in accordance with the purposes and principles of the Charter of the United Nations."). In *Nicaragua v. United States, supra*, the ICJ noted that it was not addressing the "process of decolonization" in evaluating prohibited intervention; the judge from the United States in his dissent criticized the court for "appearing to justify foreign intervention in furtherance of 'the process of decolonization.'"

G. **Justifications for intervention in civil war:** There have been several justifications put forward by states for intervention in civil wars, but the legal validity of most is questionable in the post-Charter system of international law.

1. **Consent of the governing authorities:** States have agreed that aiding the governing authorities is ***always legal*** or, at the least, legal until a belligerency is recognized (which rarely occurs). Whether seen as independent justification for intervention or simply a restatement of the traditional rule for intervention discussed above, this justification is difficult to reconcile with the post-Charter norm of non-intervention and general prohibition on use of force. It is also impractical in that there are no objective criteria for identifying who qualifies as the government in a full-scale civil war.

2. **Collective and individual self-defense:** In general, the use of force in self-defense has always been recognized as legitimate in international law. The justification of collective self-defense may arise in two contexts—when State *A* is aiding the governing authorities in State *B* to resist insurgents allegedly supported by State *C*, or when State *A* is aiding insurgents against the governing authorities of State *B* because the authorities of State *B* are aiding insurgents in State *D*. In the second scenario, State *D* itself may be aiding the insurgents against the governing authorities of State *B* on grounds of self-defense. The second scenario is that which the United States claimed in *Nicaragua v. United States* (the United States was aiding the contras in Nicaragua because Nicaragua was allegedly aiding the rebels in El Salvador). The ICJ found that Nicaragua was not even responsible for the transport of weapons across Nicaraguan territory to the insurgents in El Salvador, and therefore, the U.S. support of the contras could not be justified as a response to an ***armed attack.*** Nevertheless, the ICJ went on to say that self-defense was triggered only by an armed attack, and that the supplying of weapons did not constitute an armed attack. The court did not address the legality or illegality of El Salvador's aid to the contras based on self-defense. The court did note that an armed attack was not limited to action by regular armed forces across an international border but would also include under the Resolution on the Definition of Aggression "the sending by or on behalf of a state of armed bands, groups, irregulars, or mercenaries, which carry out acts of armed force against another state of such gravity as to amount to . . . an actual armed attack . . . or its substantial involvement therein." Therefore, in both scenarios above, the legality of State *A*'s intervention on grounds of collective self-defense depends upon whether it is responding to an armed attack and, as always, the force must be proportional.

   Example: Recent state practices suggest that the initial "armed attack" need not be made by a government. Al Qaeda, an Afghanistan-based terrorist organization, orchestrated a series of airplane hijackings in the United States on September 11, 2001, which led to the collapse of the World Trade Center and damage to the Pentagon. The United States then exercised its right to self-defense by pursuing a military campaign in Afghanistan against both the terrorist organization and the Taliban. The global community reacted in a largely supportive way to the U.S. resort to self-defense in this instance. In fact, prior to the U.S. military response, the Security Council passed two resolutions, expressly recognizing the right of self-defense in this context. U.S. military operations are likely to continue, as coalition armed forces suppress insurgency movements and root out remaining Taliban strongholds in the quest to establish a stable, democratic government in Afghanistan.

The sometimes elusive legal distinctions in the use of force in self-defense are illustrated by the NATO bombing of Libya and the killing of Osama Bin Laden by the United States, both in 2011. The only expressly authorized use of force in the U.N. Charter by a state or group of states is the authorization of force in self-defense in article 51. Although frequently asserted as a legal justification, humanitarian intervention without Security Council authorization is questionable as by its very definition it is forcible intervention on behalf of another population, not in defense of the state using force or its population. NATO's bombing of Libya was authorized by Security Council Resolution 1973, which authorized member states "acting nationally or through regional organizations . . . to take all necessary measures . . . to protect civilians." The Security Council can authorize force whenever there is a threat to peace, breach of peace or act of aggression, which has been interpreted to include widespread human rights violations. Although thus authorized to protect civilians and take other measures, no state or group of states is authorized to use force simply to remove Qaddafi from power in Libya for regime change.

With respect to Bin Laden, assassination even of a self-confessed international criminal is an unlawful extrajudicial killing under international law and an arguable violation of the U.S. presidential executive order 12333 (1981) prohibiting assassinations. Nevertheless, when effectuating an arrest as a matter of international and domestic criminal law, deadly force may be utilized to effectuate an arrest in certain circumstances, including when necessary in self-defense for those effectuating an arrest. This raises a factual question of whether the operation was to kill Bin Laden or to arrest him if possible. In addition, it is not an extrajudicial killing or assassination to kill an individual military authority in self-defense (which might turn on Bin Laden's active planning of continuing attacks on the United States and its citizens, with additional line-drawing of imminent self-defense versus problematic anticipatory self-defense) or as part of an ongoing armed conflict (the "war" on terror?). Most problematic legally is that it appears the United States did not inform Pakistan and obtain its consent for the operation, which would constitute the illegal use of force against the territorial sovereignty of Pakistan.

3. **Anticipatory self-defense:** Although not as often invoked in the context of intervention in civil wars, anticipatory self-defense could arise in the two contexts described above in response to another state's imminent intervention. Some states and scholars assert that a right of "anticipatory" self-defense must exist today—in the age of weapons of mass destruction, they argue that it would be unreasonable to expect a state to refrain from responding to a potentially devastating imminent attack. However, others doubt the ability of a state to predict a future armed attack and view the concept of anticipatory defense as undesirable.

   For more on the question of the doctrine's validity under international law (which is even more questionable after the *Nicaragua* case), *supra*.

4. **Counterintervention:** The term is used here to mean intervention by a state in response to another state's illegal intervention in a civil war that falls short of an armed attack. Although the United States did not claim counterintervention as a justification for its use of force, the ICJ in *Nicaragua v. United States*, discussed *supra*, stated that no state may justify the use of armed force on grounds of counterintervention even when it is responding to illegal intervention by another state. The court also rejected any right of counterintervention, with or without force, in support of a particular ideology or political movement.

H. **Humanitarian rules of war in civil wars:** The Geneva Conventions and protocols govern the humanitarian rules of war in civil conflicts and are discussed *supra*.

Quiz Yourself on THE LAW OF ARMED CONFLICT

13. Under the Uniting for Peace Resolution, the General Assembly directs U.N. members to use armed force against a state in violation of numerous Security Council resolutions that the Council has been unable to enforce due to the veto power. Can the General Assembly authorize the use of armed force?_ ______

14. Under article 2(4), can a state engage in a military exercise off the coast of a country in reaction to a dispute between the two states?_______

15. Because of widespread executions and persecutions of an ethnic minority in State *A*, State *B* sends in armed forces to stop the violence. Is this use of armed force lawful under the U.N. Charter?_______

16. Civil war within State *A* has caused a mass exodus of refugees into politically unstable State *B*. Can the Security Council under Chapter VII send armed forces into State *A* without its consent?_______

ANSWERS

13. Possibly. The General Assembly's Uniting for Peace Resolution seemingly authorizes it to direct the use of force if the Security Council fails to act when there has been a threat to peace, a breach of peace, or an act of aggression, but the provisions of the Charter speak only in terms of the General Assembly making non-mandatory "recommendations." If a state consents to the placement of armed forces on its territory, it is not an "enforcement action," which is any action taken without the consent of a state under the *Certain Expenses* decision of the ICJ.

14. No. Article 2(4) prohibits force or "the threat of force" directed against the territorial integrity or political independence of any state. The question would be whether the exercise was intended ("directed") against the other state because of the dispute, or just a routine exercise that would otherwise be lawful so long as it takes place in accordance with the restrictions on such activities under the law of the sea.

15. Possibly. Article 2(4) prohibits the use of force by one state against another. The issue is whether the prohibition should be given an expansive reading, by which only express authorization under the Charter of unilateral or multilateral force by a state or states is allowed, or whether custom might

recognize other permissible uses of armed force by states. The only explicit authorization of a state's use of force is in article 51 for self-defense, which does not include humanitarian intervention on behalf of another state's ethnic minority. Under a more restrictive reading of article 2(4), however, there has been a long-standing practice arguably under custom of humanitarian intervention. Resorting to the overall purposes of the U.N. Charter for guidance is not very helpful, insofar as those purposes include both protection of human rights and prohibition on state use of armed force.

16. Yes. The Security Council may take progressively more forceful actions, without a state's consent, whenever it finds that there is a "threat to peace, breach of peace, or an act of aggression." These terms are not defined in the Charter, and they are as expansive as they seem, particularly "threat to peace." The precedents set in Somalia and Haiti in particular indicate that a refugee crisis in an unstable area may constitute a threat to peace, allowing for the use of armed force under article 43.

Exam Tips on *THE LAW OF ARMED CONFLICT*

- Many of the most controversial issues of international law revolve around permissible uses of armed force by states without U.N. authorization. The only clear justification for the use of armed force is the article 51 authorization of self-defense against "an armed attack" against a state. It is a definite authorization, but the parameters of what constitutes an "armed attack" and how preventive the use of force may be are subject to much debate. Alternatively, it may be argued that there are a number of customary law justifications for the use of armed force outside of the Charter, such as humanitarian intervention, anticipatory self-defense, and self-help. These justifications have gained more of a foothold in the international arena with recent U.N. intervention in the Sudan and Libya, among other nations. The decisions of the ICJ in the *Nicaragua* case and the *Corfu Channel* case, however, suggest that authorization for force must be found in the confines of the Charter's provisions. Today's debate over the use of force to prevent terrorism turns largely on this long-standing legal debate. In addition, the shift in U.S. national defense policy precipitated by the election of President Obama could alter the U.S. reaction to any future terrorist acts.

- Frequently overlooked, but important to any exam analysis of the use of force, are the requirements of resort to peaceful means first under article 2(3) and the proportionality requirement for self-defense. If a state resorts to force without demonstrating that peaceful means were exhausted or ineffective, or uses more force than necessary to redress the threat, that is in itself a violation of international law even if the use of force is otherwise justifiable.

- In a course that delves into the Geneva Conventions, the Supreme Court cases of *Rasul*, *Hamdan*, *Hamdi*, and *Boumediene*, with the ongoing issue as to the procedural rights of foreign nationals detained in Guantanamo Bay, raise multiple, complex issues of constitutional law and international humanitarian law. Essentially, the overriding questions concern what procedures are an adequate substitute for habeas corpus given Congress's attempt to strip the courts of habeas jurisdiction over the detainees' challenges to their detention, and what procedures are required to determine their status and thus the legality of their detention under due process and the requirements of the Geneva Convention.

CHAPTER 10

THE LAW OF THE SEA

I. GENERALLY

The law of the sea is ***one of the oldest subjects in international law***.

A. Historically: Until the 1950s, the law of the sea was based almost entirely on custom. In 1958, under the auspices of the United Nations, four treaties were promulgated: the Convention on the Territorial Sea and Contiguous Zone, the Convention on the High Seas, the Convention on Fishing and Conservation of the Living Resources of the High Seas, and the Convention on the Continental Shelf. These conventions, widely adopted in subsequent years, codified the customary law of the sea but also introduced some new developments, which themselves became custom as more and more states accepted the provisions.

B. The U.N. Law of the Sea Convention: In 1982, again under the auspices of the United Nations, a comprehensive law of the sea treaty was promulgated. It incorporated much of the 1958 treaties, but it also addressed issues unresolved in the earlier treaties—such as breadth of the territorial sea, exclusive economic zones, deep seabed regulation, and preservation of the marine environment. The 1982 U.N. Convention on the Law of the Sea did not meet with universal acceptance, in large part because of its controversial deep-seabed provisions. As a result, controversies in the law of the sea often turn on determining whether the applicable law is that in the 1982 treaty, the 1958 treaties, or custom—which may or may not be consistent with the 1958 or 1982 treaty approaches.

II. NATIONALITY OF VESSELS

Three basic principles are fundamental to the law of the sea: (1) ***a ship of any state can navigate the oceans freely;*** (2) ***the state of the ship's nationality has exclusive jurisdiction over the ship on the high seas;*** and (3) ***no other state can exercise jurisdiction over that ship absent some affirmative rule authorizing concurrent jurisdiction.***

A. Introduction: The nationality of a ship is that of the state whose flag it is authorized to fly. Other terms used to refer to a ship's nationality are its "***flag state***" or its state of "***registration***" or "***documentation***." A ship may fly the flag of only one state. Convention on the High Seas, Apr. 29, 1958, art. 6, ¶1, 450 U.N.T.S. 82 [hereinafter *High Seas Convention*]; U.N. Convention on the Law of the Sea, Oct. 7, 1982, art. 92, ¶1, 21 I.L.M. 1261 (1982) [hereinafter *LOS Convention*]. A ship without nationality may be prevented from engaging in international trade or commerce, or navigation of any sort on the high seas. LOS Convention, art. 110, ¶1, cl. d. A ship without nationality also does not benefit from any treaties that confer rights on ships when entering foreign ports.

B. The right of states to confer nationality upon a ship: In order to confer its nationality on a ship, a state usually must register the ship, authorize it to fly the state's flag, and issue documents indicating that the ship's nationality is that of the issuing state.

1. General principle: The U.S. Supreme Court has recognized the well-established rule that "[e]ach state under international law may determine for itself the conditions on which it will grant its nationality to a merchant ship." *Lauritzen v. Larsen*, 345 U.S. 571, 584 (1953). This principle has been included in many international agreements and treaties.

2. **Limitations:** The general principle that states are free to set the conditions for nationality is subject to two basic limitations.

   a. **One-flag limitation:** A state may ***not*** grant its nationality to a ship that is already authorized to fly the flag of another state, except if necessary to transfer the ship from one state's registry to another. High Seas Convention, art. 6, ¶1; LOS Convention, art. 6, ¶1; LOS Convention, art. 92, ¶1.

   b. **Genuine link necessary:** A state must have a "***genuine link***" to a ship in order for a state to confer its nationality upon it. High Seas Convention, art. 5, ¶1; LOS Convention, art. 91, ¶1. The requirement of a sufficient connection between a flag state and its ships is premised upon a belief that a state can carry out its obligations to exercise effective control over its ships only if such a link exists. ***Proof of a genuine link*** between a flag state and a ship may be based on one or more of the following: (1) ***ownership by nationals;*** (2) ***national officers;*** (3) ***national crew;*** and (4) ***national build.***

      i. **"Flags of convenience":** The requirement of a "genuine link" was in response to the use of "flags of convenience," now known as open registries. After World War II, many shipowners had transferred their ships to the registries of countries such as Panama and Liberia to avoid increasingly restrictive regulation in other states.

      ii. **Procedure when genuine link questioned:** A state "which has clear grounds to believe that proper jurisdiction and control with respect to a ship has not been exercised may report the facts to the flag State." The flag state then has an obligation to investigate the matter. LOS Convention, art. 94, ¶6.

C. **Documentation and registration:** A state that authorizes ships to fly its flag must (1) maintain a register of ships containing the name and description of each ship so authorized; and (2) issue documents to the registered ships evidencing authorization. High Seas Convention, art. 5, ¶2; LOS Convention, art. 91, ¶2. A ship may change its flag during a voyage or while in a port of call only when there is a real change in registry. High Seas Convention, art. 6, ¶1; LOS Convention, art. 92, ¶1. If a ship's owner fraudulently obtains registration of a ship by misrepresenting fulfillment of conditions for registration or by registering a ship with no genuine link to the flag state, the vessel may be liable to seizure and forfeiture by the flag state.

D. **Duties of the flag state:** Under international law, each state has a duty to "effectively exercise its jurisdiction and control in administrative, technical, and social matters over ships flying its flag." High Seas Convention, art. 5, ¶1. Article 94 of the LOS Convention further specifies that each flag state has the obligation to:

- ***Maintain a register of ships authorized to fly its flag***;
- ***Govern the internal affairs*** of such ships;
- ***Ensure the safety*** at sea of such ships with regard to their construction, equipment, and seaworthiness, and with regard to the labor conditions and the training of their crews, the maintenance of their means of communication, and the prevention of collisions;
- ***Ensure that each ship is surveyed*** by a qualified surveyor of ships and has on board appropriate charts, nautical publications, and navigational equipment;

- ***Ensure that each ship is manned*** by a qualified master, officers, and crew; and
- ***Ensure that the master, officers, and, to the appropriate extent, the crew are fully conversant with and are required to observe applicable international regulations*** regarding the safety of life at sea; the prevention of collisions; the prevention, reduction, and control of marine pollution; and the maintenance of radio communications.

III. BASELINE DETERMINATIONS FOR MEASURING COASTAL ZONES

Maritime delimitation negotiations often fail, and as a consequence, there is a large body of arbitral and adjudicatory decisions. Marine delimitation disputes have accounted for nearly one-fifth of the ICJ's docket since 1969. Usually, a line equidistant from the coast of each country is used as the delimitation, but there are other rules and exceptions, such as the "equidistance/special circumstances" rule set out in article 15 of the 1982 LOS Convention, which is used in unique island and archipelagic situations. *See Maritime Delimitation and Territorial Questions (Qatar v. Bahr.)*, 2001 I.C.J. 40 (Mar. 16).

A. **Purpose of the baseline:** The baseline is the ***starting point from which a coastal state's coastal zones are measured***. Waters on the landward side of the baseline are considered internal waters of the state. Convention on the Territorial Sea and Contiguous Zone, Apr. 29, 1958, art. 5, ¶1, 516 U.N.T.S. 205 [hereinafter Territorial Sea Convention]; LOS Convention, art. 8. There has been a growing trend of favoring a simple, single maritime boundary for the water column, the seabed, and the extended continental shelf (ECS).

B. **Validity of baselines:** Validity of baseline delineations and maritime jurisdiction is determined by international law. *Fisheries* (*U.K. v. Nor.*), 1951 I.C.J. 116 (Dec. 18).

C. **Delineation of the baseline:** The baseline is the ***low-water mark along the coast***. Territorial Sea Convention, art. 3; LOS Convention, art. 5; *see also Fisheries* (*U.K. v. Nor.*), 1951 I.C.J. 116 (Dec. 18).

1. **Rivers:** If a river flows directly into the sea, the baseline is drawn straight across the mouth of the river between the low-water points of its lands. Territorial Sea Convention, art. 13; LOS Convention, art. 9.

2. **Bays:** A bay is considered to be internal waters of a state when the bay's area is as large or larger than that of the semicircle for which the diameter is a line drawn across the mouth of the bay. The line between the natural entrance points of the bay may not exceed 24 nautical miles. If it does exceed this limit, a straight baseline of 24 nautical miles can be drawn so as to enclose the maximum area of water possible with a baseline of that length. Territorial Sea Convention, art. 7; LOS Convention, art. 10.

a. **Exception for "historic bays":** Historic bays are considered internal waters even if they do not meet the above requirements. Territorial Sea Convention, art. 7, ¶6; LOS Convention, art. 10, ¶6. The International Court of Justice (ICJ) has defined "historic waters" as internal waters "which would not have that character were it not for the existence of an historic title." *Fisheries* (*U.K. v. Nor.*), 1951 I.C.J. 116, 130 (Dec. 18). Three factors have been suggested for evaluating historic title over coastal waters: (1) whether the state ***exercises sovereign authority*** over the waters; (2) whether the authority has been exercised regularly for a ***considerable time***; and (3) whether ***other states have acquiesced*** in the exercise of that authority. U.N. Secretariat, *Judicial Regime of Historic Waters, Including Historic Bays*, U.N. Doc.A/CN.4/143 (1962), [1962] 2 Y.B. Int'l L. Comm'n 13.

   b. **Gulf of Sidra incident:** In 1986, when U.S. warships engaged Libyan forces in the Gulf of Sidra, the United States claimed it was exercising a right of innocent passage for its warships in the waters of the Gulf beyond the 12-nautical-mile limit. Libya claimed that the Gulf of Sidra was a historic bay and part of its internal waters. A baseline drawn across the mouth of the bay would exceed 24 nautical miles.

3. **Islands:** An island is "a naturally formed area of land, surrounded by water, which is above water at high tide." Territorial Sea Convention, art. 10; LOS Convention, art. 121. Every island is entitled to claim rights in a territorial sea, contiguous zone, exclusive economic zone, and continental shelf.

4. **Indented coastlines and island fringes:** "In localities where the coastline is off the mainland deeply indented and cut into, or if there is a fringe of islands along the coast in its immediate vicinity, the method of straight baselines joining appropriate points may be employed in drawing the baseline from which the breadth of the territorial sea is measured." Territorial Sea Convention, art. 4, ¶1; LOS Convention, art. 7, ¶1; *see also Fisheries* (*U.K. v. Nor.*), 1951 I.C.J. 116 (Dec. 18). A number of limitations on the use of straight baselines have been incorporated into the 1958 Convention on the Territorial Sea and the LOS Convention.

   a. ***Fisheries* case:** In the *Fisheries* case, the ICJ imposed limitations on the use of straight baselines: they "must not depart to any appreciable extent from the general direction of the coast"; the "areas lying within these lines" must be "sufficiently closely linked to the land domain to be subject to the regime of internal waters"; and account should be taken of "certain economic interests peculiar to a region, the reality and importance of which are clearly evidenced by a long usage," in determining the appropriateness of straight baselines in a particular area. *Fisheries* (*U.K. v. Nor.*), 1951 I.C.J. 116, 133 (Dec. 18). These limitations have been incorporated into the Territorial Sea Convention, art. 4, ¶2; LOS Convention, art. 7, ¶¶3, 5.

   b. **Low-tide elevations:** Straight baselines may not be drawn to and from low-tide elevations unless lighthouses or similar installations, which are permanently above sea level, have been built on them. Territorial Sea Convention; LOS Convention, art. 7, ¶4.

   c. **Cutting off territorial sea:** The system of straight baselines may not be applied by a state in such a manner as to cut off the territorial sea of another state from the high seas or an exclusive economic zone. Territorial Sea Convention, art. 4, ¶5; LOS Convention, art. 7, ¶6.

   d. **Innocent passage:** Where the establishment of a straight baseline encloses areas that had not previously been considered internal waters, the coastal state must grant other states a right of innocent passage. LOS Convention, art. 8, ¶2.

5. **Archipelagic states:** Straight baselines joining the outermost points of the outermost islands may be drawn. Baselines of archipelagic states may not exceed 100 nautical miles and are subject to other limitations. LOS Convention, art. 47, ¶2.

6. **Low-tide elevations:** Low-tide elevations situated wholly or partly within a territorial sea may be used as the baseline. Territorial Sea Convention, art. 11; LOS Convention, art. 13.

7. **Harbors and roadsteads:** The outermost permanent harbor-works, which form an integral part of the harbor system, are regarded as forming part of the coast for determining the baseline. Territorial Sea Convention, art. 8; LOS Convention, art. 11. Roadsteads do not influence the baseline from which the areas of coastal jurisdiction are measured. Territorial Sea Convention, art. 9; LOS Convention, art. 12.

D. **Demarcation of baseline with adjacent and opposite states:** If the coasts of two states are opposite or adjacent to each other, neither state is entitled to extend its territorial sea beyond the median line, defined as every point of which is equidistant from the nearest points on the baseline from which the breadth of the territorial sea is measured. Historic title or special circumstances may require a different division. Territorial Sea Convention, art. 12; LOS Convention, art. 15. The delimitation of the continental shelf and economic zone between states is determined by agreement. Convention on the Continental Shelf, Apr. 29, 1958, art. 6, 499 U.N.T.S. 311 [hereinafter *Continental Shelf Convention*]; LOS Convention, arts. 74, 83. In the absence of agreement or special circumstances, the 1958 Convention states that the boundary will be the median line, where opposite states are involved; and an equidistant line, where adjacent states are involved. *Continental Shelf Convention*, art. 6. In 1969, the ICJ refused to find that the "equidistant/special circumstances" rule had become custom in continental delimitation between adjacent states absent agreement. *North Sea Continental Shelf*, 1969 I.C.J. 3. Articles 74 and 83 of the LOS Convention states that "[t]he delimitation of the exclusive economic zone [or continental shelf] between states with opposite or adjacent coasts shall be effected by agreement on the basis of international law, as referred to in article 38 of the Statute of the International Court of Justice, in order to achieve an equitable solution." This formulation fails to mention equidistances and emphasizes equitable considerations in delimitation.

Example: In 2009, the ICJ settled a dispute between Romania and the Ukraine regarding the establishment of a maritime boundary delimiting the continental shelf and the EEZ (exclusive economic zone) between the two nations in the Black Sea. The ICJ determined that a rocky Ukrainian island, called Serpent's Island, was too small to affect the delimitation line in this case and its existence would not permit Ukraine exclusive jurisdiction over the entire disputed zone. After considering other factors potentially affecting the equality of the result, the line the ICJ delineated set a single maritime boundary delimiting the continental shelf and EEZ for both Romania and Ukraine. The final placement of the line was therefore based primarily on the provisional equidistance line between the nations' adjacent coasts. The ICJ's holding was significant because it gave Romania access to 80 percent of gas and crude oil in the disputed zone beneath the Black Sea. *Maritime Delimitation in the Black Sea (Romania v. Ukraine)* (I.C.J. 2009).

Example: As demonstrated in *Ghana v. Ivory Coast* (2017), there has been a growing trend of favoring a simple, single maritime boundary for the water column, the seabed, and the extended continental shelf (ECS). Dispute Concerning Delimitation of the Maritime Boundary Between Ghana and Côte d'Ivoire in the Atlantic Ocean (Ghana v. Côte d'Ivoire), Case No. 23, Judgment of Sept. 23, 2017. A special Tribunal of the International Tribunal on the Law of the Sea resolved a seabed oil exploitation dispute after 3 years of litigation. Ghana prevailed on its view for an equidistance-based single maritime boundary in the territorial sea, in the Exclusive Economic Zone (EEZ), and in the continental shelf within two hundred nautical miles. The boundary beyond two hundred nautical miles should, according to Ghana, extend on the same azimuth as the boundary within two hundred nautical miles, up to the limit of national jurisdiction (para. 63). Ghana also maintained that the equidistance-based single maritime boundary had been recognized and applied by Ivory Coast, but the Tribunal rejected that there was a tacit agreement between the parties which estopped the Ivory Coast from objecting to the boundary, which Ghana called a "customary equidistance boundary."

IV. INTERNAL WATERS AND PORTS

A coastal state has ***full sovereignty*** over its internal waters and ports.

A. **General definition:** Internal waters are the waters of lakes, rivers, and bays ***landward of the baseline*** of the territorial sea. Territorial Sea Convention, art. 5; LOS Convention, art. 8. A port is a place for loading or unloading a ship.

B. **Freedom of access to ports:** Freedom of access to ports by foreign merchant vessels is a rule of custom ***conditioned on reciprocity.***

1. **Landlocked nations:** Landlocked nations may not be denied freedom of access to ports solely because of their inability to reciprocate. High Seas Convention, art. 3; LOS Convention, art. 131.

2. **Closing of ports:** "[P]orts of every state must be open to foreign vessels and can only be closed when the vital interests of a State so require." *Saudi Arabia v. Arabian American Oil Company (ARAMCO)*, Award of August 23, 1938, 27 Int'l L. Rep. 117, 212 (1963).

3. **Regulation:** A coastal state may condition a foreign ship's access to a port upon compliance with laws and regulations governing the conduct of the business of the port, such as pollution and safety controls. Such laws and regulations may not be discriminatory against or among foreign vessels.

C. **Inland waters:** If a state within the United States may claim submerged lands based on the area's status as historic inland waters, it must demonstrate that the United States exercises authority over the area, has done so continuously, and has done so with the acquiescence of foreign nations. The exercise of sovereignty must have been an assertion of power to exclude all foreign vessels and navigation. Nations may exclude from inland waters even vessels engaged in so-called innocent passage. *See Alaska v. United States*, 545 U.S. 75 (2005).

D. **Jurisdiction over foreign vessels:** A foreign merchant ship that enters the ports of a state is subject to the ***administrative, civil,*** and ***criminal jurisdiction of that state***. Even warships must comply with laws relating to navigation, safety, health, and post administration.

1. **Matters internal to a ship:** Jurisdiction over a ship's internal matters, which do not involve the "peace or dignity" of the coastal state or "tranquility of the port," are generally left to the flag state. *Wildenhus' Case*, 120 U.S. 1, 11 (1887); *see also Benz v. Compania Naviera Hidalgo, S.A.*, 353 U.S. 138 (1957) (withholding application of jurisdiction absent clear congressional intent).

2. **Seeking refuge:** Foreign vessels are not subject to a coastal state's jurisdiction when the vessel is seeking refuge because of distress or *force majeure*.

E. **Jurisdiction of flag state:** If the coastal state does not assert jurisdiction over an offense in its ports or internal waters, "it is the duty of the courts of the [flag state] . . . to apply its own statutes." *United States v. Flores*, 289 U.S. 137, 158-159 (1933).

F. **Enlarged port state jurisdiction under the LOS Convention:** A port state may investigate and institute proceedings in respect of any discharge from a ship "voluntarily within a port or at an offshore terminal" in violation of international standards, even if the discharge occurred outside the internal waters, territorial sea, and exclusive economic zone of the state. If the discharge occurred in the waters of another state, proceedings may be instituted only by the port state or at the request of that state, the flag state, or the state damaged or threatened by the discharge. LOS Convention, art. 218, ¶¶1-4, art. 220, ¶1, art. 228.

V. THE TERRITORIAL SEA AND CONTIGUOUS ZONE

A coastal state has full sovereignty over its territorial sea subject primarily to a right of innocent passage in other states.

A. Coastal state sovereignty over the territorial sea: A state has the ***same sovereignty over its territorial sea, airspace, seabed, and subsoil thereof*** as it has with respect to its land. Territorial Sea Convention, arts. 1-2; LOS Convention, art. 2.

B. Breadth of the territorial sea: For many years under the so-called cannon-shot rule, a three-mile territorial sea was recognized as customary under international law. After World War II, many states made claims to a more extensive territorial sea, in some cases up to 200 miles. As a result, no agreement could be reached in the 1958 Convention on the Territorial Sea and Contiguous Zone on the breadth of the territorial sea, although a 12-mile contiguous zone was incorporated. According to the LOS Convention, every state has the right to establish the breadth of its territorial sea ***up to 12 nautical miles*** as measured from the baseline. LOS Convention, art. 3. The United States still adheres to a three-mile territorial sea for domestic law purposes. For international relations, however, the United States has extended its territorial sea to 12 nautical miles to be consistent with the LOS Convention. *Proclamation No. 5928*, 54 Fed. Reg. 777 (1988).

C. The right of innocent passage: The right of ships of all states to innocent passage through the territorial sea of any coastal state is an exception to the sovereignty of a state over its territorial sea. Territorial Sea Convention, art. 14; LOS Convention, art. 17.

1. **General definition of passage:** *Passage* means navigation through the territorial sea for the purpose of either traversing that sea without entering internal waters, or proceeding to or from internal waters. Passage must be continuous, but a ship may anchor if this is incidental or necessary to assist persons in distress. Territorial Sea Convention, art. 14, ¶3; LOS Convention, art. 18, ¶2.

2. **Meaning of innocent passage:** Innocent passage ***must not be prejudicial to the peace, good order, or security*** of the coastal state. Territorial Sea Convention, art. 14, ¶4; LOS Convention, art. 19, ¶1. The LOS Convention specifies which circumstances do ***not*** qualify as "innocent passage," including: (1) threat or use of ***force***; (2) exercise or practice with ***weapons***; (3) collecting ***information that prejudices the defense or security*** of the coastal state; (4) ***propaganda affecting the defense or security*** of the coastal state; (5) ***aircraft*** activity; (6) any activity involving a ***military device***; (7) loading or unloading of any commodity, currency, or person ***in violation of the coastal state's customs, fiscal, immigration, or sanitary laws and regulations***; (8) willful and serious ***pollution*** in contravention of international law; (9) ***fishing***; (10) ***research*** or surveying; (11) ***interfering with communications*** of the coastal state. LOS Convention, art. 19, ¶2.

3. **Coastal state's rights:** Within the territorial sea, the coastal state may not interfere with innocent passage, subject to very limited exceptions.

   a. **Verification:** The coastal state has the unilateral right to verify the innocent character of passage, and it may take the necessary steps in its territorial sea to prevent passage that it determines to be not innocent. Territorial Sea Convention, art. 16, ¶2; LOS Convention, art. 25, ¶2.

   b. **Suspension of right of innocent passage:** The coastal state may temporarily suspend the right to innocent passage if essential for protection of the state's security. Suspension may take effect only after due publication. Territorial Sea Convention, art. 16, ¶3; LOS Convention, art. 25, ¶3.

c. **Regulation of right of innocent passage:** Under the LOS Convention, the coastal state may also adopt regulations relating to innocent passage with regard to: (1) safety of navigation and the regulation of maritime traffic; (2) the protection of navigational aids and facilities and other facilities and installations; (3) the protection of cables and pipelines; (4) the conservation of living resources; (5) the preservation of the environment of the coastal state and the prevention, reduction, and control of pollution thereof; (6) marine scientific research; and (7) the enforcement of fishing, customs, fiscal, immigration, and sanitary regulations. LOS Convention, art. 21, ¶1. Any regulation of design, construction, manning, or equipment must be in conformity with generally accepted international rules and standards. art. 21, ¶2. The coastal state may also establish sea lanes and traffic separation schemes for passage through its territorial sea, where they are necessary to ensure the safety of navigation. art. 22. Included in the above regulations is the right of the coastal state to require high-risk ships, such as large tankers, nuclear-powered ships, and ships carrying inherently dangerous substances, to confine their passage to identified sea lanes. art. 22, ¶2.

d. **Exercising criminal jurisdiction:** A coastal state may exercise criminal jurisdiction on board a foreign ship passing through the territorial sea for the purpose of arresting a person or conducting an investigation only in the following circumstances: (1) the consequences of the crime extend to the coastal state; (2) the crime is of a kind that disturbs the peace of the country or the good order of the territorial sea; (3) the assistance of the local authorities has been requested by the master of the ship or by a diplomatic agent of the flag state; or (4) such measures are necessary for the suppression of illicit traffic in narcotic drugs. Territorial Sea Convention, art. 19, ¶1. LOS Convention, art. 27, ¶1. The coastal state may not take any steps on board a ship in connection with any crime committed before the ship entered the territorial sea, if the ship is only passing through the territorial sea without entering internal waters. LOS Convention, art. 27, ¶5.

e. **Exercising civil jurisdiction:** The coastal state may not exercise civil jurisdiction over foreign ships passing through the territorial sea, except for obligations assumed in the course of, or for the purpose of, the ships' voyage through the waters of the coastal state. However, a coastal state may levy execution against or arrest for civil proceedings a foreign ship lying in the territorial sea or passing through the territorial sea after leaving internal waters. Territorial Sea Convention, art. 20; LOS Convention, art. 28.

f. **Jurisdictional limitations:** The coastal state may not exercise civil jurisdiction over foreign ships despite the ability to detain a foreign ship for violations of laws under article 73 of the Convention of the Sea. The International Tribunal for the Law of the Sea (ITLOS) determined that excessive force and endangerment of human life in the capture of a ship may result in a violation of the rights of the flag state of the captured ship. Furthermore, ITLOS rejected the inclusion of non-monetary conditions in the bond release of a captured vessel. *See St. Vincent v. Guinea*, 27 I.L.M. 360 (Int'l Trib. L. of the Sea 1998); *Russia v. Australia (Volga)*, 126 I.L.R. 433.

4. **Warships:** The LOS Convention does not require prior notification or authorization for innocent passage of a warship through a territorial sea. The United States takes the position that no prior notification is required. A warship that does not comply with the laws of the coastal state and disregards any request for compliance may be required to leave the territorial sea immediately. LOS Convention, art. 30. Submarines must navigate on the surface and show their flag. Territorial Sea Convention, art. 14, ¶6; LOS Convention, art. 20.

D. Transit passage: Transit passage is navigation or overflight for the purpose of ***continuous and expeditious transit***. LOS Convention, art. 38, ¶2. Under the 1958 Territorial Sea Convention, straits that are used for international navigation between one part of the high seas and another part of the high seas or the territorial sea of a foreign state are subject to a right of transit passage. Territorial Sea Convention, art. 16, ¶4. The LOS Convention grants the right between two areas of the high seas on two exclusive economic zones. LOS Convention, art. 38, ¶2. The right does not exist where a strait is broad enough to allow navigation through a high seas route in its middle. LOS Convention, art. 36. *Contra Corfu Channel* (*U.K. v. Alb.*), 1949 I.C.J. 4 (holding that the Corfu Channel was an international strait even though it was not a necessary route between two areas of the high seas).

1. **Distinguished from innocent passage:** The LOS Convention established a regime governing transit passage through straits that is separate from innocent passage through territorial seas. LOS Convention, arts. 34-35. Unlike innocent passage, transit passage ***extends to aircraft and submarines***. Also, states may not unilaterally suspend transit passage. art. 42, ¶5. The fields in which a state bordering a strait may regulate transit passage are more limited than those for innocent passage. A state may regulate for pollution control, fishing, and enact customs, fiscal, immigration, and sanitary regulations. art. 42. These laws may not discriminate against foreign ships or in any way act to impede transit passage. art. 42.
2. **Archipelagic sea lanes passage:** Under the LOS Convention, all ships also have a right of archipelagic sea lanes passage. LOS Convention, art. 53.

E. Contiguous zone: The coastal state may exercise the control necessary to prevent infringement of its customs, fiscal, immigration, or sanitary laws and regulations in a zone contiguous to its territorial sea. Territorial Sea Convention, art. 24, ¶1; LOS Convention, art. 33, ¶1. Under the 1958 Convention, the contiguous zone may not exceed 12 nautical miles. Under the LOS Convention, the contiguous zone may not extend beyond 24 nautical miles from the baseline. LOS Convention, art. 33, ¶2. The United States has claimed such a contiguous zone.

VI. EXCLUSIVE ECONOMIC ZONE

The exclusive economic zones (EEZs) established in the LOS Convention give states exclusive economic rights in expanded zones contiguous to their coasts.

A. High seas to fishery zones to exclusive economic zone: No state had jurisdiction over waters beyond the territorial sea and contiguous of the state until the middle of the twentieth century.

1. **Early coastal management:** In the 1940s, increased exploitation of fisheries in waters contiguous to coastal states led many states to enter into conservation and management agreements for fisheries. In 1945, the United States asserted the right to claim jurisdiction over the natural resources contained in the subsoil and seabed of its continental shelf. *See* §VII(A) of this chapter, *infra*. Additionally, the United States proclaimed sole fishery conservation and management authority in areas where its nationals historically had fished. Following the U.S. assertion of sole jurisdiction of its coastal waters, a number of South American states asserted exclusive fishing rights over their own coastal waters. The South American proclamations established zones that extended up to 200 nautical miles. The United States and 33 other nations signed the 1958 Fishing on the High Seas Convention. The Convention granted coastal states special rights to conserve, manage, and exploit fisheries in areas contiguous with their coasts without specifying any zone within which such rights might apply. The ICJ

subsequently recognized that a coastal state has preferential rights to exploit fisheries around its coasts, but the coastal state must consider the fishing rights of those states that have traditionally fished in the same waters. Both parties must negotiate in good faith to find an equitable solution to their differences. *Fisheries Jurisdiction* (*U.K. v. Ice.*), 1974 I.C.J. 3 (July 25).

2. **The 200-mile exclusive economic zone (EEZ):** The 200-mile EEZ was adopted at the Third U.N. Conference on the Law of the Sea in 1982. The LOS Convention established ***exclusive rights*** for coastal states to explore, exploit, conserve, and manage ***all living and non-living resources within the zone***. The Convention also allows coastal states to exercise limited jurisdiction in establishing and using artificial islands, installations, and structures. LOS Convention, arts. 55-75. Aside from the coastal state's exclusive right to exploit the zone's resources, the waters are otherwise treated like the high seas. All states are free to operate ships and aircraft and to lay submarine cables and pipelines within an EEZ. They may also engage in other internationally lawful uses of the sea that are part of high seas freedoms. In exercising these freedoms, all states must give due regard to the rights and duties of the coastal state and obey all lawful regulations of the coastal state. Reciprocally, the coastal state must give the same due regard to the rights and duties of the other states operating lawfully in the EEZ. The United States, in 1983, adopted the 200-mile EEZ set forth in the LOS Convention. The United States and other major maritime states agree that the EEZ continues to be part of the high seas, although subject to the special rights of exploitation of coastal states. Other states insist that the EEZ is a special zone of the coastal state, subject only to the freedoms of navigation and overflight. Conflicts are to be resolved based upon equity in light of all relevant circumstances, taking into account the respective importance of the interests of the states involved as well as the interests of the entire international community. LOS Convention, art. 59.

B. **Management and conservation of the living resources within the EEZ:** The coastal state has several responsibilities in the management of the resources within the EEZ.

1. **Duty of the coastal state to prevent overexploitation of living resources in the EEZ:** Coastal states must maintain levels of fishing that produce a "maximum sustainable yield," a level at which the maximum amount of fish can be harvested without depleting the stock. LOS Convention, art. 61, ¶¶2-3. Maximum sustainable yield is calculated based upon scientific data, but the coastal state must also consider the economic needs of its coastal fishing communities and those of developing states in the region.

2. **Duty of coastal state to promote optimum utilization of the living resources within its EEZ:** "Optimum utilization" is a flexible concept by which a coastal state determines the allowable catch of the living resources within its EEZ and its own capacity to harvest the allowable catch. Although a coastal state may not set an allowable catch that would cause overexploitation of living resources, the state may set the allowable catch at the same level as its own capacity to harvest. This prevents foreign states from harvesting the surplus that the coastal state cannot harvest. However, if the allowable catch exceeds the capacity of the coastal state to harvest, the coastal state must grant access to other states to harvest the surplus taking into account "all relevant factors." LOS Convention, art. 62, ¶2.

C. **Right of geographically disadvantaged states and landlocked states in the EEZ:** Geographically disadvantaged states are coastal states that can claim no EEZ of their own or whose geographic locations make them dependent upon exploitation of the EEZ of other coastal states in the region. LOS Convention, art. 70, ¶2. Landlocked states do not border coastal waters.

1. **Rights:** Landlocked and geographically disadvantaged states have the right to participate, on an equitable basis, in the exploitation of any fishery surplus in the EEZs of coastal states in the region. These equitable rights take into account the relevant economic and geographic circumstances of all states concerned. LOS Convention, arts. 69, ¶1, 70, ¶1. This includes the need to minimize detrimental effects on states whose citizens have habitually fished in the EEZ.

2. **Terms of participation:** In establishing terms of participation, the states involved must consider the following factors: (1) the need to avoid detriment to fishing communities or industries of the coastal state; (2) the extent to which the disadvantaged state participates in the exploitation of other states' EEZs; (3) avoidance of a particular burden on any single coastal state; and (4) the nutritional needs of the populations concerned. LOS Convention, arts. 69, ¶2, 70, ¶2. When a coastal state raises its capacity to harvest to the point where it could harvest its entire allowable catch, the coastal state must establish equitable arrangements to allow developing geographically disadvantaged states in the region to exploit living resources in the EEZ.

3. **Special access of developing states to limited surplus:** When a coastal state is near a point of being able to harvest the entire allowable catch, it must cooperate with *developing* landlocked and geographically disadvantaged states in the region to establish equitable arrangements for participation. LOS Convention, arts. 69, ¶3, 70, ¶4.

D. **Species subject to special rules:** Several species have been singled out for special treatment within EEZs.

1. **Species extending beyond a single EEZ:** Coastal states must cooperate to enact conservation and management measures for the same stock of species that occur within the EEZs of more than one coastal state, or "straddling stocks." This obligation also applies when the species stock is in an EEZ adjacent to an area of high seas frequented by foreign fishermen (LOS Convention, art. 63), and for highly migratory species such as tuna. art. 64.

2. **Marine mammals:** Exploitation of marine mammals may be more strictly regulated by the coastal state than fish stocks. LOS Convention, art. 65; *see also* the Marine Mammal Protection Act of 1972, 16 U.S.C. §1361-1362, 1371-1384, 1401-1407 (1972).

3. **River stocks:** Anadromous and catadromous species are the primary responsibility of the states in whose rivers the species originate or spend the greater part of their life cycles. The coastal state must cooperate with other states outside its EEZ in whose waters the river species migrate. Coastal states must also cooperate with other states when their nationals fish the anadromous or catadromous stocks outside their EEZ. LOS Convention, arts. 66, 67.

4. **Sedentary species:** Sedentary species exploitation is not governed by the LOS Convention. Sedentary species are immobile or under the seabed at their harvesting stage. They are considered part of the natural resources of the continental shelf. *See* §VII(D) of this chapter, *infra*.

E. **Enforcement of conservation and management measures:** Enforcement of conservation and management measures of the EEZ depends upon whether the violation occurred within the EEZ or beyond it. A coastal state has more enforcement rights within the EEZ.

1. **Within the EEZ:** A coastal state has the right to ***enforce all laws enacted*** to conserve and manage living resources. The coastal state authorities may board and inspect a ship, impound the ship and arrest its crew, and institute judicial action against them. Punishment for violators

may not include imprisonment or corporal punishment under the LOS Convention. Upon arrest, the enforcing coastal state must notify the flag state of the seized vessel.

2. **Outside the EEZ:** Enforcement of regulation of anadromous species, highly migratory stocks, and straddling stocks beyond the EEZ are allowed if all states concerned agree. Arrest for violations that occur in the EEZ may occur outside the EEZ in cases of "hot pursuit." *See* §IV(C)(4) of this chapter, *infra.*

F. **U.S. legislation relating to conservation and exploitation of the living resources in the EEZ:** In the 1976 Fishery Conservation and Management Act, the United States established a 200-mile fishery conservation zone to counteract overexploitation of certain fishery stocks. The Act places regulatory planning authority in regional fishery management councils. The plans must prevent overexploitation of the fisheries while promoting the harvest of an "optimum yield" from each area. 16 U.S.C. §1851-1855 (1976). The Act defines "optimum yield" as a yield that provides the maximum overall benefit to the United States. The Act also allows control of foreign access to the fishery zones. Foreign fishing is authorized only if an existing treaty requires access or if the foreign state entered into a fishery agreement with the United States that acknowledged U.S. fishery conservation and management jurisdiction in the zone. 16 U.S.C. §1821(a)-(b) (1977). If there is no surplus, no foreign fishermen may harvest. Amendments in 1980 set a new method for determining the allowable level of foreign fishing that may result in the United States phasing out foreign fishing. Until phase-out occurs, "market access" gives preferential allocation of fishery surpluses to nations that give preferential access to their surpluses to the United States. Highly migratory species regulation is left to international agreement but anadromous species regulation is allowed. The United States has also claimed a more general 200-mile EEZ.

G. **Non-living resources of the EEZ:** A coastal state may also exploit non-living resources in its EEZ, such as production of energy from water, currents, or winds.

H. **Marine scientific research:** Coastal states may regulate, authorize, and conduct marine scientific research within their EEZs. Other states must obtain consent to conduct marine scientific research in the EEZ of another coastal state. If the proposed scientific research is for peaceful purposes for the scientific benefit of all mankind, the coastal state must consent. A coastal state may refuse consent, however, if the research directly involves exploration and exploitation of natural resources; involves drilling or the use of explosives and other dangerous materials; involves the construction of artificial islands; or contains inaccurate information; or if the applicant has outstanding obligations to the coastal state. LOS Convention, art. 246. The coastal state has a right to be informed of the nature and progress of the research project.

I. **Artificial islands and installations:** The coastal state has the exclusive right to construct and regulate construction, operation, and use of any artificial islands, and of installations and structures built for economic purposes in its EEZ. The coastal state also has exclusive jurisdiction over such artificial islands, installations, and structures. LOS Convention, art. 60, ¶¶1, 2, 7.

VII. CONTINENTAL SHELF

The 1958 Continental Shelf Convention recognized the principle of sovereign rights of exploration and exploitation for coastal states over the natural resources of their continental shelves. Continental Shelf Convention, art. 2. The rights do not affect the freedoms of the high seas in the waters above the continental shelf. These basic principles were elaborated on in the LOS Convention in 1982.

A. Early claims: In 1945, the United States proclaimed its control over the natural resources of the seabed and subsoil on the continental shelf surrounding its territory. This proclamation, however, recognized the freedoms of the high seas in the seas above the continental shelf. Other states soon asserted various claims to the shelf and the superadjacent waters.

B. Definition and delimitation: Geologically, the continental shelf ***begins at the shore and ends where the continental slope to the deep seabed begins***.

1. **The 1958 Continental Shelf Convention:** The 1958 Continental Shelf Convention defines the continental shelf as the seabed and subsoil of submarine areas adjacent to the coast but outside the limits of the territorial sea to a depth of 200 meters, or to where the water depth allows exploitation of natural resources. The first criteria came to be considered as too arbitrary and the second as too vague. The concept of an economic zone also necessitated revision of the delimitation in the LOS Convention.

2. **The LOS Convention:** The LOS Convention establishes two alternative measures for continental shelves. The first is the geological definition, which recognizes the continental shelf as running to the edge of the continental margin. The second delineation allows a coastal state to claim a continental shelf 200 nautical miles from the baseline. If the continental margin extends beyond 200 nautical miles, the outer limit of the shelf may not exceed 350 nautical miles from the baseline, or 100 nautical miles from the point at which the depth reaches 2,500 meters. LOS Convention, art. 76.

C. Rights and duties of the coastal state over the continental shelf: The coastal state has ***limited obligations*** in managing the continental shelf and has ***extensive rights*** in the resources of the shelf.

1. **Extent of sovereign rights:** The coastal state has ***exclusive sovereignty*** over its continental shelf for the purpose of exploring and exploiting "natural resources." Natural resources are minerals and other non-living resources of the seabed and subsoil, as well as sedentary living plant and animal species. Continental Shelf Convention, art. 2, ¶4; LOS Convention, art. 77, ¶4. Shipwrecks and lost cargo on the shelf are not natural resources. If a coastal state does not exercise its rights to explore and exploit, no one else may do so without the express consent of the coastal state. LOS Convention, arts. 77, 81. The coastal state's rights over the continental shelf do not extend to the superadjacent waters and airspace. Thus, the coastal state may not unjustifiably interfere with the high seas freedoms of navigation, overflight, fishing, laying of submarine cables and pipelines, and the right to conduct scientific research. LOS Convention, arts. 78, 87. However, the course of submarine cables or pipelines is subject to the coastal state's consent.
2. **Duties:** When a coastal state exploits non-living resources on its continental shelf beyond the 200-mile limit, the coastal state must pay a fee to the deep-seabed mining authority established under the LOS Convention. LOS Convention, art. 82.

D. Sedentary fisheries: The coastal state has sovereign rights over all sedentary fisheries on its continental shelf. Unlike fishery zones, sedentary fisheries are not subject to "optimum yield" regulations. Therefore, the coastal state need not grant access to any portion of its sedentary fisheries to other states.

E. Marine scientific research on the continental shelf: The same rules apply to research in the continental shelf as apply to the EEZ. *See* §VI(H) of this chapter, *supra*. For research on a shelf more than 200 nautical miles from the baseline, a coastal state may not withhold consent to a research project if it will be conducted in an area where the coastal state has not or will not begin exploitation or exploration activities within a reasonable time. LOS Convention, art. 246.

F. **U.S. practice and legislation relating to the continental shelf:** In the United States, control over the continental shelf area is divided between the federal government and its coastal states.

1. **Federal sovereignty:** The U.S. government has "paramount rights in, and full dominion and power over, the lands, minerals and other things" beyond the low water mark. *United States v. California*, 332 U.S. 19 (1947).

2. **The Outer Continental Shelf Lands Act (OCSLA):** This Act establishes a federal regulatory system for the resources of the outer continental shelf (generally the area more than three miles from the baseline). The Submerged Lands Act granted states full jurisdiction and rights over the inner continental shelf area. 43 U.S.C. §1331. The U.S. federal government reserved its powers to regulate commerce, navigation, defense, and international affairs within the inner shelf. 43 U.S.C. §1214.

VIII. EXPLOITING THE MINERAL RESOURCES OF THE DEEP SEABED

International law pertaining to exploitation of mineral resources of the deep seabed, despite its uncertainty, will continue to grow in importance as resources become scarce and technology improves. Potential conflicts may arise over conflicting claims to mineral resources until there is more widespread agreement on the legal principles governing exploitation of the deep seabed.

A. **Current status of the legal regime of the deep seabed:** There is no universally agreed upon legal regime governing exploitation of the mineral resources of the deep seabed. Ever since scientists in the 1960s discovered vast resources in the form of manganese nodules on the deep ocean floors, the legal status of the deep seabed has been highly disputed. Three views have developed regarding the legal status of the deep seabed.

1. **"Common heritage of mankind" view:** The "common heritage of mankind" view is that the mineral resources of the deep seabed may be exploited only by or under the auspices of an ***international authority acting on behalf of all countries*** to assure equitable division. No state or person may claim, explore, or exploit these resources until the establishment of such an authority. This view is adhered to mostly by developing states and is premised on the theory that the seabed belongs to every member of the international community in common (*res communis*). It differs from the pure *res communis* view, which is that what belongs to everyone can be exploited by no one.

   a. **Declaration of Principles Governing the Seabed . . . beyond the limits of the national jurisdiction:** In 1970, the U.N. General Assembly adopted this measure by a unanimous vote. The Declaration states in part that the deep seabed and its natural resources "are the common heritage of mankind," and that all will benefit from its exploitation. The Declaration envisions an international treaty that will set up a regime to govern the resources of the deep seabed, but it did not prohibit exploitation of resources before the establishment of a "generally agreed upon" international regime. The earlier, so-called Moratorium Resolution, which prohibited exploitation until such time, was voted against by the United States and other developed countries.

b. The LOS Convention: In 1982, the LOS Convention established a deep-seabed mining regime. Whether the regime of the Convention will become customary international law, binding upon non-parties, is troublesome given the opposition of many developed countries, including the United States. The principal objections to the regime focus on the methods of distribution of profits from exploitation to the international community and of sharing technology. The Convention regime would be clearly established as custom only if a majority of all regional groups, of both developed and developing states, accepts it and conforms mining practices to it.

2. **Freedom of the high seas view:** The freedom of the high seas view is that the right to explore and exploit the mineral resources of the deep seabed is a ***freedom of the high seas***. A state may authorize or engage in the exploration and exploitation of deep-seabed mineral resources, provided that such activities are conducted with reasonable regard for the rights of other states to do similar activities. ***No state may claim or acquire exclusive rights*** over any part of the deep seabed or its mineral resources. This view, at least pending an agreed upon regime, is asserted by the United States and most other developed nations.

3. ***Res nullius* view:** The *res nullius* view is that the seabed belongs to no one (*res nullius*), and that the seabed, as well as its mineral resources, may be explored and exploited to the exclusion of all others by the first state that claims it. This view has been adopted by some legal scholars but has not gained widespread acceptance.

B. Seabed mining under the LOS Convention: No state may claim, exercise sovereign rights over, or appropriate any part of the deep seabed or its resources because the mineral resources of the seabed are the common heritage of mankind. LOS Convention, arts. 136, 137, ¶1.

1. **The International Seabed Authority:** The Convention establishes an authority, known as the International Seabed Authority, which will act on behalf of mankind in governing the deep seabed. LOS Convention, arts. 137, ¶2, 153, 156-157. The Authority consists of an assembly, a council, and a secretariat. Arts. 156, ¶2, 158.

2. **The Assembly:** The Assembly is the "supreme organ" of the Authority and establishes its policies. The Assembly's membership consists of one representative from each member of the Authority. LOS Convention, arts. 159, ¶1, 160, ¶1.

3. **The Council:** The Council is the "executive organ" of the Authority and establishes "specific policies" and approves "plans of work" for each mining project. The Council's membership consists of 36 members of the Authority, chosen to represent the following interests: (1) consumers of minerals to be produced by deep-seabed mining; (2) investors in deep-seabed mining activities; (3) terrestrial producers of the same minerals; (4) developing states; and (5) a geographic distribution of the members. LOS Convention, arts. 160, 161.

4. **The Enterprise:** The Enterprise is the separate legal entity that will carry out mining activities on behalf of the Authority. LOS Convention, art. 170.

5. **Regulation of mining:** Annex III provides the basic guidelines for exploring and exploiting the deep seabed. Applicants who apply for a license to explore or exploit the deep seabed must either be a citizen or be controlled by a state party to the LOS Convention. LOS Convention, art. 153. Each applicant must submit a "plan of work" with the following conditions: (1) payment

of $500,000 application processing fee; (2) description of the activity; (3) two sites of estimated equal commercial value, one for the Enterprise (which may turn it over to a developing country) and the other for the applicant's use; and (4) full disclosure to the Authority of equipment, non-proprietary technology, and methodology to be used. LOS Convention, Annex III, arts. 13, ¶2, 8, 9, 5, ¶1. If the permit is granted, the contractor must pay an annual fixed fee of $1 million until the date of commencement of commercial production. LOS Convention, Annex III, art. 13, ¶3. Thereafter, the contractor shall pay the greater of $1 million or the "production charge"—calculated either as 5 percent of the market value of the processed metals during the first ten years of commercial production and at a 12 percent market value thereafter, or calculated as a fixed fee of 2 percent of the market value of the processed metals during the first period of commercial production, rising to 4 percent in the second period of production. LOS Convention, Annex III, art. 13, ¶¶3-6. After the contractor has recovered its development costs, it shall pay a share of its net proceeds to the Authority on a graduated scale of 35 to 70 percent. LOS Convention, Annex III, art. 13, ¶6, cl. c. The Enterprise's exploration activities are in part financed by assessments against states parties to the Convention, and a Seabed Disputes Chamber is established for resolution of disputes under the regime.

6. **The 1994 implementing agreement:** In response to the objections of the major developed countries, a 1994 implementary agreement made extensive changes to the treaty's deep-seabed regime. Under the agreement, only a minimal seabed authority is established in Jamaica with responsibilities yet to be developed. Important decisions are to be made by the Council largely by consensus. The Enterprise will not be established until the Council decides that it should be, and it will not operate independently.

C. **U.S. legislation:** The 1980 Deep Seabed Hard Mineral Resources Act establishes an interim program to regulate U.S. citizen exploration for and commercial recovery of hard mineral resources of the deep seabed pending establishment of an international regime. 30 U.S.C. §1401 (1980). Applicants must obtain a license for initial exploration activities and a permit for commercial recovery of resources.

IX. FREEDOM OF THE HIGH SEAS

Since the seventeenth century, it has been recognized that all states, whether coastal or landlocked, may exercise certain freedoms of the seas. Under the 1958 High Seas Convention and the LOS Convention, these freedoms include, but are not limited to: (1) ***freedom of navigation***; (2) ***freedom of overflight***; (3) ***freedom of fishing***; and (4) ***freedom to lay submarine cables and pipelines***. The LOS Convention also lists freedom to construct artificial islands, installations and structures, and freedom of scientific research.

A. **General principles:** These freedoms must be exercised with due regard for the interests of other states. All states are bound to refrain from acts that unreasonably interfere with the high seas freedoms of other states. LOS Convention, art. 87. No state may exercise its jurisdiction over any part of the high seas.

B. **Reservation of the high seas for peaceful purposes:** The high seas must be used for ***peaceful purposes***. Naval forces may use the high seas, but use or threat of force violates the LOS Convention and article 2, ¶4 of the U.N. Charter absent other justification of international law (*e.g.*, self-defense).

C. Freedom of navigation: Every state has the right to sail ships on the high seas bearing its national flag. LOS Convention, art. 90. With this right comes the obligation to give due consideration to the interests of others. This includes: (1) observing rules relating to safety of navigation; (2) protecting life at sea; and (3) preventing and reducing pollution. Absent a state of war, warships and state-owned ships have complete immunity from jurisdiction of any other state than the flag state when on the high seas. arts. 95, 96. The flag state of merchant ships has exclusive jurisdiction in terms of arrest or any other physical interference over a merchant ship on the high seas. There are, however, a number of exceptions to this exclusive jurisdiction by which a warship may interfere with another state's merchant ship.

1. **Treaty exception:** A flag state may expressly provide by international agreement to allow another state to exercise jurisdiction over its ships on the high seas. High Seas Convention, art. 6, ¶1; LOS Convention, art. 92, ¶1. A government ship of a foreign state may board, search, and, in some instances, seize a ship on the high seas if a treaty so provides or a flag state has consented. Specifically, the LOS Convention provides that a state that has reasonable grounds to believe a ship flying its flag is engaged in illegal drug traffic may request the cooperation of other states to suppress such traffic. LOS Convention, art. 108.

2. **Collision cases:** When conduct on the flag state's ship on the high seas has effects on a foreign ship or foreign territory, the foreign state has concurrent jurisdiction based on the territoriality principle. *See The S.S. Lotus* (*Fr. v. Turk.*), P.C.I.J. Ser. A, No. 10 (1927), discussed in Chapter 5, §I(B). In collision cases, jurisdiction is now limited to the flag state of the vessel alleged to be responsible and to the state of nationality of the accused. High Seas Convention, art. 11; LOS Convention.

3. **Right of visit:** A warship is entitled to board another ship when there are reasonable grounds for suspecting that the ship is engaged in piracy, slave trading, or (under the LOS Convention) unauthorized broadcasting. High Seas Convention, art. 22, ¶1; LOS Convention, art. 110. Piracy is defined in both Conventions as:

   a. **Right of visit:** Any illegal acts of violence, detention, or any act of depredation, committed for private ends by the crew or the passengers of a private ship or a private aircraft, and directed:

      i. **Right of visit:** On the high seas, against another ship or aircraft, or against persons or property on board such ship or aircraft;

      ii. **Right of visit:** Against a ship, aircraft, persons, or property in a place outside the jurisdiction of any State;

   b. **Right of visit:** Any act of voluntary participation in the operation of a ship or of an aircraft with knowledge of facts making it a pirate ship or aircraft;

   c. **Right of visit:** Any act of inciting or of intentionally facilitating an act described in sub-paragraph [a] or sub-paragraph [b] of this article. High Seas Convention, art. 15; LOS Convention, art. 101.

   A government ship may also board a ship when it has reason to suspect that, though flying a foreign flag, the ship has the same nationality as the government ship. High Seas Convention, art. 22, ¶1, cl. e; LOS Convention, art. 110, ¶1, cl. e. A stateless ship or a ship flying the flag of more than one state has ***no protection*** against boarding and search on the high seas. High Seas Convention, art. 6, ¶1; LOS Convention, art. 92, ¶2. Depending upon the nature of the violation suspected, search and arrest may follow.

Example: In 2009, the U.N. Security Council adopted Resolution 1897 as a result of the expanding dangers presented by pirates off the coast of Somalia. The Resolution renewed its earlier call upon member states and regional organizations to fight Somali pirates by "deploying naval vessels, arms, and military aircraft" and also by seizing boats suspected of piracy off the Somali coast. For several years prior to the Resolution, Somali pirates were increasingly disruptive of international commercial trade and humanitarian aid efforts and had become notoriously violent in their ransom collection methods for captured boats and their hostages. In 2010, another U.N. Resolution expressly noted that 1897's authorizations applied only to the situation in Somalia and would not be considered to establish customary international law. This later Resolution also called on member states to criminalize piracy in their domestic legal systems and incarcerate those convicted for crimes of piracy as part of the overall strategy to combat the pernicious effects of Somali pirate outfits.

4. **"Hot pursuit":** The "right of hot pursuit" allows a warship to engage in pursuit of a foreign ship continuing into the high seas if the state has good reason to believe the ship has violated its laws. The right of hot pursuit ceases as soon as the ship pursued enters the territorial waters of another state. The pursuit must begin in the internal waters, territorial sea, contiguous zone, exclusive economic zone, or continental shelf of the pursuing state. For pursuit convening in or beyond the contiguous zone, the pursuit must be for a violation of the coastal state's rights in that zone.

5. **Necessity:** The LOS Convention provides that nothing in the section on preservation of the marine environment prejudices the right of states pursuant to custom and treaty law to take proportional measures to protect their coasts and related waters from pollution or the threat of pollution from a maritime casualty that may reasonably be expected to result in major harmful consequences. LOS Convention, art. 221.

   Example: In 1967, when a Liberian oil tanker, the *Torrey Canyon*, ran aground on a reef in the English Channel, the United Kingdom bombed the tanker to minimize the pollution of its coasts.

6. **Self-defense:** The rules governing the threat or use of force in self-defense are governed by the U.N. Charter, and are discussed in Chapter 9, §I(C).

7. **Action authorized by the United Nations:** The role of the United Nations is discussed at Chapter 9, §I(C)(2).

D. **Freedom of overflight:** All civilian and military aircraft have the right to fly over the high seas.

E. **Freedom of fishing and conservation measures:** All states have the right to fish the high seas. This right is limited by treaties and by the rights of coastal states to regulate their continental shelves. The LOS Convention includes a section on conservation and management of the living resources of the high seas that requires states to cooperate in the conservation and management of resources. LOS Convention, art. 118. Coastal states acting in cooperation and international organizations may also regulate to protect marine mammals. art. 120.

   1. **The Central Arctic Ocean Agreement:** An example of an agreement limiting this freedom is the Agreement to Prevent Unregulated High Seas Fisheries in the Central Arctic

Ocean (CAO) (ratified 2018), a legally binding agreement between the United States, the E.U., Canada, China, Denmark, Iceland, Japan, Norway, Russia, and South Korea. The agreement bans unregulated high seas fishing in the 2.8 million square kilometers of the central Arctic Ocean and establishes a cooperative scientific program to monitor fish stocks in the region.

2. **U.N. Negotiations for the First Conservation Treaty for the High Seas:** The first formal negotiations to develop a formally binding instrument to protect biodiversity on the high seas started in 2018 and planned through 2020. Negotiating parties have agreed to develop a deal that addresses marine genetic resources, marine spatial planning tools, environmental impact assessments, and capacity building.

F. **Freedom to lay submarine cables and pipelines:** The route of cables and pipelines is subject to coastal state regulations on the continental shelf. LOS Convention, arts. 79, 112.

G. **Freedom to construct artificial islands:** Construction and operation of artificial islands, installations, and structures is subject to coastal state regulations involving such activities on the continental shelf or in the EEZ.

H. **Freedom of scientific research:** All states and competent international organizations have the right to conduct scientific marine research outside EEZs. LOS Convention, art. 257.

X. PRESERVATION OF THE MARINE ENVIRONMENT

Prior to the 1960s, there was very little protective regulation of the marine environment. The limited provisions of the 1958 High Seas Convention contemplated future action. In the 1970s, general rules for the preservation of the global environment imposed a few limitations on pollution of the seas. Growing concern with marine pollution led to the inclusion of extensive provisos in the LOS Convention for protection and preservation of the marine environment. A crucial issue is whether these provisions can be said to reflect customary international law or whether they are binding only on parties to the Convention.

A. **The 1958 High Seas Convention:** The only provisions of the 1958 High Seas Convention specifically addressed to preservation of the marine environment are articles 24 and 25. Article 24 requires states to regulate to prevent pollution of the seas by oil discharge from ships, pipelines, or deep-seabed activities. Article 25 calls on states to take measures to prevent pollution of the seas from radioactive materials.

B. **The Stockholm Declaration and general obligation to preserve the environment:** In 1972, the Stockholm Declaration of the United Nations Conference on the Human Environment was adopted at the U.N. Conference on the Human Environment. Principle 7 of the Declaration requires states to take "all possible steps" to ***prevent pollution*** of the seas. Principle 21 provides that states must ensure, in exercising their sovereign rights to exploit their resources, "that activities within their jurisdiction or control do not cause damage to the environment or other states or of areas beyond the limit of national jurisdiction." Principle 21 expanded upon the international law principle that no state could use or permit its territory to be used in a manner injurious to another state's territory. *See, e.g., The Trail Smelter Case* (*U.S. v. Can.*), 3 R.I.A.A. 1905 (1941). Principle 22 further requires states to cooperate to develop international law for liability and compensation for damage caused by states to areas beyond their jurisdiction.

C. **Third U.N. Conference on the Law of the Sea:** Article 192 of the LOS Convention outlines the general obligations of states to ***protect and preserve the marine environment***. States are required to meet this obligation by taking all measures necessary to prevent pollution of the marine environment from any source. LOS Convention, art. 194, ¶1. All sources of pollution of the marine environment must be considered, such as: (1) the release of toxic, harmful, or noxious substances from land-based sources, from or through the atmosphere, or by dumping; (2) pollution from vessels; (3) pollution from installations and devices used in the exploration or exploitation of the natural resources of the seabed and subsoil; and (4) pollution from other installations operating in the marine environment. art. 194, ¶3. The provisions apply to commercial ships; states have only to ensure that warships, as far as practicable, act consistently with international rules and standards. art. 236. In 2013, the U.N. General Assembly, in the Resolution on Oceans and the Law of the Sea, decided to establish a process for taking a decision on the development of an international instrument under the LOS Convention to address the conservation and sustainable use of marine biological diversity of areas beyond national jurisdiction.

1. **Regional standards adopted:** States are required to harmonize their policies on a regional level with regard to pollution from land-based sources and from seabed activities within zones of national jurisdiction. LOS Convention, arts. 207, ¶3, 208, ¶4.

2. **Global standards adopted:** States are requested to harmonize their policies on a global level with regard to pollution from land-based sources, seabed activities subject to national jurisdiction, pollution from dumping, and pollution of the marine environment through or from the atmosphere. LOS Convention, arts. 207, ¶4, 208, ¶5, 210, ¶4, 212, ¶3.

D. **Vessel source pollution:** States are required to establish international guidelines governing vessel-source pollution through international organizations, such as the International Maritime Organization or through general diplomatic conferences. LOS Convention, art. 211.

1. **Flag state jurisdiction:** Flag states are required to adopt laws and regulations for the prevention of pollution of the marine environment from ships flying their flag or of their registry. Areas of regulation include: (1) the design, construction, equipment, operation, and manning of vessels; (2) accident prevention; (3) emergency procedures; (4) operations of sea safety standards; and (5) prevention of intentional and unintentional discharges. LOS Convention, arts. 194, ¶3, cl. b, 211.

2. **Coastal state regulation in ports, in internal waters, and in the territorial sea:** Coastal states may adopt laws and regulations for the prevention, reduction, and control of marine pollution from foreign vessels within their territorial seas, but they may not hamper innocent passage. States may set standards for pollution prevention as a condition for entrance into their ports or for internal waters. LOS Convention, art. 211, ¶¶3-4.

3. **Coastal state jurisdiction in the EEZ:** States may regulate vessel-source pollution in the EEZ in accordance with generally accepted rules and standards through a competent international organization or diplomatic conference. Coastal states may request a competent international organization to authorize the states to adopt additional regulations if the reviewing organization finds that the international rules and standards are inadequate to protect an area of their EEZs. LOS Convention, art. 21, ¶6.

4. **North American Emission Control Area:** In effect since August 1, 2012, states are mandated to reduce allowable emissions of nitrogen oxides, sulfur oxides, and particulate matter from

ships. The covered area includes most Atlantic and Pacific coastal waters and waters extending seaward 200 nautical miles.

E. Pollution from land-based sources: All states must adopt laws or regulations to prevent pollution of the marine environment from land-based sources. LOS Convention, art. 207.

F. Ocean dumping: States are required to adopt laws and regulations to prevent pollution of the marine environment by the dumping of sewage, sludge, and other waste materials into the ocean. LOS Convention, art. 210. These laws must be no less stringent than global standards. Dumping in the territorial sea, EEZ, or continental shelf of a state requires permission from the proper state authorities. The 1972 Convention on the Dumping of Wastes at Sea sets forth regulations regarding three categories of waste. The Convention prohibits the dumping of materials listed in Annex I: (1) high-level radioactive wastes; (2) materials produced for biological and chemical warfare; and (3) non-biodegradable synthetic materials. Dumping of wastes in the second category, which includes low-level radioactive wastes, requires a special permit. The third category of waste materials requires only a general prior permit. Annex III to the Convention specifies terms and conditions upon which general and special permits are issued.

G. Pollution from seabed activities subject to national jurisdiction: States are required to adopt all laws and regulations necessary to prevent pollution of the marine environment arising from or in connection with their exploration and exploitation of the seabed and subsoil, or from artificial islands, installations, and structures under their jurisdictions, taking into account any internationally agreed upon standards. LOS Convention, art. 194, ¶3, cl. e, art. 208.

H. Pollution from deep-seabed mining: Part XI of the LOS Convention authorizes the Authority to adopt appropriate rules and regulations to prevent pollution of the marine environment from deep-seabed activities. *See* §VII(B) of this chapter, *supra*.

I. Pollution from or through the atmosphere: All states are required to adopt laws and regulations to prevent pollution of the marine environment from or through the atmosphere, taking into account internationally agreed upon rules. All vessels flying a state's flag or aircraft under the state's registry must abide by the regulations. LOS Convention, art. 212.

J. Protection of fragile ecosystems: States are obligated specifically to take measures necessary to protect and preserve rare or fragile ecosystems as well as the habitat of depleted, threatened, or endangered species and other forms of marine life. LOS Convention, art. 194, ¶5, 211. A coastal state also may adopt and enforce non-discriminatory laws and regulations for the prevention, reduction, and control of marine pollution from vessels in ice-covered areas within its EEZ, where severe climatic conditions and the presence of ice for most of the year create obstructions or exceptional hazards to navigation. art. 234.

K. Fisheries: Recently, despite jurisdictional challenges offered by Japan, the International Tribunal for the Law of the Sea (ITLOS) ordered Japan to refrain from conducting an experimental fishing program, concluding that an arbitral tribunal would have *prima facie* jurisdiction under the Law of the Sea Convention. The Tribunal implicitly applied a precautionary approach to fisheries, a principle that has found strong application in international environmental law recently, although its status as customary international law is still disputed. *See Southern Bluefin Tuna Cases (N.Z. and Austl. v. Japan)*, 38 I.L.M. 1624 (Int'l Trib. L. of the Sea 1999). Parties to the Convention on the Conservation of Migratory Species of Wild Animals have agreed to implement a Memorandum of Understanding on the Conservation of Migratory Sharks through information sharing, research, cooperation through regional fisheries management organizations, and regulations requiring sharks to be landed with fins naturally attached.

L. **Liability:** A state that fails to fulfill its obligations to protect and preserve the marine environment is liable in accordance with international law. States must ensure recourse is available for prompt and adequate relief for damage caused by pollution, such as through compulsory insurance or compensation funds. LOS Convention, art. 235.

1. **Liability for nuclear accidents:** Article 2 of the 1962 Nuclear Ships Convention provides that the operator of a nuclear ship "shall be absolutely liable for any nuclear damage upon proof that such damage has been caused by a nuclear incident involving the nuclear fuel of, or radioactive products or waste produced in, such ship." The licensing state is obligated to ensure that payments are made for the claims for compensation for injuries resulting from a nuclear accident.

2. **Liability for oil pollution:** The 1969 Convention on Civil Liability for Oil Pollution Damage governs injuries caused by oil pollution in a state party's territory or territorial sea. Because this Convention did not provide full compensation for victims of oil pollution injuries, the 1971 Convention concerning an International Fund for Compensation for Oil Pollution Damage was promulgated. It is important to note that these Conventions apply only to oil pollution damage resulting from oil spills from *tankers*. Thus, they would not provide a remedy for any eventual damages caused by oil pollution that resulted from the April 20, 2010, explosion of a British Petroleum (BP) oil-drilling rig in the Gulf of Mexico. Those outside the United States suffering from the after effects of the catastrophic BP oil spill must devise alternative methods of recovery because these Conventions do not provide remedies for oil pollution from offshore wells, including the Deepwater Horizon rig that exploded off the Gulf Coast. In 2011, the Court of Federal Claims found that a government contract can recover the costs of cleanup resulting from Corrective Order on World War II–era defense contracts. *See Exxon Mobil Corp. v. United States*, 101 Fed. Cl. 576 (2011).

M. **Enforcement:** Flag states, coastal states, and port states may enforce rules and regulations relating to the marine environments. The extent of their enforcement powers varies, depending on the source of pollution, the location of the violation, and the degree of harm to the environment.

1. **Flag state enforcement:** Flag states are obligated to ensure that all ships flying their flags or listed on their registries comply with international rules and standards established by the competent international organization or diplomatic conference, and state laws adopted in accordance with the Convention. LOS Convention, art. 217, ¶1. Flag states must inspect ships to issue and periodically verify certificates of compliance with the laws of the state. Other states must accept these certificates as evidence of the condition of the ship. art. 217, ¶¶2-3. Flag states must establish penalties harsh enough to discourage violations by their ships. art. 217, ¶8. In the event a ship violates international rules and standards, the flag state must investigate immediately and institute proceedings if appropriate. art. 217, ¶4.

2. **Coastal state enforcement:** When a ship is in port, a coastal state may institute proceedings against it for violation of its laws adopted under the Convention or any international standards if the violation occurred on its territorial sea or EEZ. When a ship is in the territorial sea of

a state, the state may undertake physical inspection if it has clear grounds for suspecting a violation and institute proceedings if the violation occurred during its passage through the territorial sea. When a ship is in the EEZ or territorial sea, the coastal state may require it to provide relevant information if it has clear grounds for believing that the ship committed a violation in the EEZ. Whether the coastal state may take further steps for violations in the EEZ depends upon the extent of damage caused or threatened by the violation. LOS Convention, art. 220.

3. **Port state enforcement:** If a ship in a foreign port is responsible for a discharge beyond the port state's EEZ in violation of international standards, the port state may investigate and, if warranted, institute enforcement proceedings. If the discharge occurred within the EEZ, territorial sea, or internal waters of another state, the port state cannot institute proceedings unless so requested by that state, the flag state of the ship, or another state damaged by the discharge, unless the waters of the port state itself have been or are likely to be polluted by the discharge. As far as practicable, the port state is obligated to investigate or institute proceedings if so requested by the flag state of the ship, any state whose coastal waters are damaged by the discharge, or any state within whose waters the discharge occurred. LOS Convention, art. 218.

4. **Liability for wrongful enforcement:** A state is obligated to compensate the flag state for any injury or loss attributable to unlawful or excessive measures taken against a foreign ship. The legal systems in all states must provide for private actions in respect to such injury or loss. LOS Convention, art. 232. Also, under the 1973 International Convention for the Prevention of Pollution from Ships (MARPOL), a ship "shall be entitled to compensation for any loss or damage suffered" from a state's measures that cause the ship to be unduly delayed or detained. International Convention for the Prevention of Pollution from Ships, art. 7, ¶2, 12 I.L.M. 1319 (1973).

N. **Notification and cooperative action:** As soon as a state is aware that injury to the marine environment has occurred or is imminent, it must ***notify*** immediately the appropriate global or regional international organizations and all states likely to be affected. LOS Convention, art. 198. To eliminate or minimize the effect of an accident causing marine pollution, neighboring states have a duty to develop contingency plans to respond to pollution. art. 199.

O. **Government non-commercial ships:** Ships that are used by governments for non-commercial purposes are not subject to the international rules, standards, and enforcement procedures discussed above. Each state must adopt measures to ensure that such ships follow the international rules and standards as far as practical. LOS Convention, art. 236.

P. **ITLOS:** The ITLOS was constituted in 1996 upon the election of 21 judges with the court seat in Hamburg, Germany. Under Annex VI to the LOS Convention, the Tribunal may interpret the treaty (as can the ICJ and certain designated arbitral tribunals). The Tribunal has exclusive jurisdiction over certain specified matters under the treaty, including release and detention of vessels, and deep-seabed mining (which is exercised by the 11-judge Deep Seabed Chamber of the Tribunal).

Quiz Yourself on THE LAW OF THE SEA

17. Does the 1982 U.N. Law of the Sea Convention govern the United States rather than the earlier law of the sea treaties to which the United States is a party? _______

18. As a result of global warming, many ice-bound Arctic areas are seasonally melted and navigable. As a result, northern states have been claiming more extensive continental shelves. Do they have a basis for asserting extended claims, even though they have not bothered to in the past because of inaccessibility? _______

19. Can a military submarine pass through the territorial sea of another state? _______

20. Are the freedoms of the high seas listed in article 87 the exclusive freedoms allowed?_______

ANSWERS

17. Yes, although more as customary international law rather than as a treaty. The United States is still not a party to the 1982 LOS Convention treaty, although the overwhelming majority of states are. The United States has acknowledged that many of the provisions of the 1982 treaty have become customary international law. The U.S. claims to coastal zones reflect the 1982 treaty's provisions, and the United States generally follows the treaty's substantive provisions, but it remains outside the treaty system for the purposes of participating in its development and administration of its organs, such as the treaty's tribunals.

18. Yes. The continental shelf is considered a natural prolongation of a state's territory, albeit under the sea. Under the 1982 LOS Convention treaty, the shelf may be defined by either a 200-nautical-mile limit from the baseline or to the edge of the continental margin where the deep seabed begins. There is, however, an outermost limit of 350 nautical miles from the baseline or 100 nautical miles from the point of 2,500 meters depth.

19. Possibly. There is a right of innocent passage even for military vessels, but they may not be engaging in military exercises, gathering information, or otherwise engaging in any activities "prejudicial to the peace, good order, or security of the coastal state."

20. No. It is important to realize that both the 1958 Convention on the High Seas and the 1982 LOS Convention treaty list these four freedoms of the high seas "inter alia," or as being among other unspecified rights, which are important as more uses of the seas develop.

Exam Tips on *THE LAW OF THE SEA*

- The continuing failure of the United States to ratify the LOS Convention treaty, while following most of its provisions, lends itself to exam essay questions concerning the deep-seabed regime. To prepare for such a question, review the reasons why the United States initially refused to ratify the treaty relating to exploitation of the resources of the seabed, whether such justifications are still valid, and what advantages/disadvantages generally the United States might have under the treaty were it to ratify. Many different constituencies of many different political bents have now urged the United States to ratify, so that the failure to do so may have more to do with administrative deadlock rather than any principled objections to the treaty that could not be rectified with a few reservations. A few of the advantages that have been cited for U.S. ratification are extended claims within the coastal zones, more security from expanded passage rights for military vessels and aircraft, and influence in the organs of the LOS Convention system in which the United States cannot now participate as a non-state-party.

- Consider, as in the case *Maritime Delimitation in the Black Sea*, how the ICJ's involvement in disputes over seabed territory will affect the distribution of resources discovered in that territory; also consider how such disputes over unclaimed deep-sea resources will affect the general relations between neighboring states as industrializing nations pursue access to minerals and fuel sources.

CHAPTER 11

AIR AND SPACE LAW

I. DEFINING STATE SOVEREIGNTY OVER AIRSPACE

A. **Common law view:** Common law doctrine held that a state's control over airspace ***extended to the end of the universe***.

B. **Balancing free airspace with states' self-preservation:** Early attempts to define states' sovereignty over airspace balanced the inherent nature of airspace as free from sovereign control against the need of the sovereign to provide for self-preservation and the defense of its citizens.

C. **Exclusive control:** With the increased use of aircraft during World War I came the need to reach an international agreement regarding states' control of airspace. In 1919, the international community resolved at the Paris Convention to establish each state's ***exclusive control over its superincumbent airspace***.

1. **Territory limited by territorial waters:** States retained this exclusive control of the airspace above only the territory of the state itself and above its territorial waters.
2. **No control over high seas:** Airspace above the high seas has long been considered ***free from state control*** and remained so under the Paris Convention.

D. **The "five freedoms" and accommodation of international air travel:** During World War II, the international community witnessed a dramatic rise in international air traffic. The need arose to establish some general principles to govern international air travel.

1. **The "five freedoms":** At this time in the development of the law of international aviation, free airspace had been broken down into five components. These so-called ***five freedoms*** became the basis of the international agreements of this era. The five freedoms are as follows:
   a. **Overflight:** The privilege to fly across a state's territory without landing.
   b. **Non-traffic landing:** The privilege to land for non-traffic purposes.
   c. **Putting down traffic:** The privilege to put down passengers, mail, and cargo in the state whose nationality the aircraft possesses.
   d. **Picking up traffic:** The privilege to take on passengers, mail, and cargo destined for the state whose nationality the aircraft possesses.
   e. **International traffic:** The privilege to take on or put down passengers, mail, and cargo destined for or coming from any contracting state.
2. **The Chicago Convention:** The most important of the World War II era agreements was the Chicago Convention on International Civil Aviation. The Chicago Convention took place in 1944 and created the International Civil Aviation Organization (ICAO) and the International Air Services Transit Agreement. The Chicago Convention extends all five freedoms to non-scheduled international air service.
   a. **Aircraft must follow prescribed safe routes:** For safety reasons, states reserved the right to prescribe routes that aircraft must follow when flying over regions that are inaccessible or without adequate navigation facilities.

b. **Right to refuse intra-state traffic:** States also reserved the right to refuse to allow aircraft from other states to take on traffic in their territory that is destined for another point within their territory.

c. **Applies only to civil aircraft:** The Chicago Convention governs only civil aircraft and does not apply to state aircraft, including military aircraft.

d. **Discrimination based on nationality prohibited:** States may promulgate regulations regarding air travel within their airspace, but such regulations must be applied identically to all aircraft without regard to nationality. A state or entity in that state may promulgate rules that, when applied evenly, impact some states adversely but not others. A court will not view such an impact as a violation of applicable international anti-discrimination standards.

Example: The Port Authority of New York had established a set of noise regulations for Kennedy Airport. France and Great Britain wished to begin supersonic transport (SST) service to Kennedy, but the Port Authority placed an ad hoc ban on SSTs at the site even though the SSTs complied with the existing noise regulations. The Port Authority claimed the ban was necessary to study further the environmental effects of the SSTs' unique low-frequency sound. Great Britain and France sued the Port Authority, claiming discrimination. The court held that the disparate impact of the ban on Great Britain and France did not render it discriminatory or unlawful. Anti-discrimination principles do not require the Port Authority to "blind itself to significant differences in the noise characteristics of aircraft, merely because they are operated by foreign carriers." *British Airways v. Port Authority of New York*, 558 F.2d 75 (2d Cir. 1977).

3. **International Air Services Transit Agreement extends limited freedoms to scheduled air service:** Only the first two freedoms, *i.e.*, overflights and non-traffic landings, are generally available under the International Air Services Transit Agreement for scheduled air service.

a. **No general agreement on the remaining three freedoms:** The International Air Transport Agreement extended the final three freedoms to scheduled international air service. However, very few states have signed this agreement. Because of this lack of agreement, the United States withdrew from the agreement in 1947.

b. **Scheduled air service governed by bilateral agreement:** Because no single agreement has satisfied the needs of the international aviation community with regard to scheduled air service, states have entered into a complex web of bilateral arrangements to govern international air traffic.

4. **Definition of "scheduled international air service":** Because the rules governing scheduled and non-scheduled international air service differ, the International Civil Aviation Organization promulgated the following definition. A "scheduled international air service" is a series of flights that possesses all of the following characteristics:

a. **Overflies more than one state:** It passes through the airspace of more than one state;

b. **Open to the public:** It is performed for the transport of passengers, mail, or cargo for remuneration, in such a manner that each flight is open to members of the public; and

c. **Regular service:** It serves traffic between the same two or more points, either

- according to a published timetable; or
- with flights so regular or frequent that they constitute a recognizable, systematic series.

5. **Prescriptive jurisdiction for international air travel:** When an aircraft engages in international air travel, it will at all times be traveling either in airspace governed by a state's domestic regulations or in airspace above the high seas. Regulations regarding air travel differ by jurisdiction.

   a. **Domestic regulation applies over subjacent state:** When the aircraft is in airspace above a state or its territorial waters, the regulations of that state apply. In airspace other than over the high seas, ICAO rules apply, but only to the extent they do not conflict with rules published by the subjacent state in Annex 2 of the Chicago Convention.

   b. **ICAO regulation applies over high seas:** When the aircraft is in airspace above the high seas, rules promulgated by the ICAO under article 12 of the Chicago Convention apply.

      i. **Flight information regions:** The global airspace is divided into flight information regions (FIRs). The ICAO allocates responsibility for administering navigational duties and dispensing weather information in each FIR to local states.

      ii. **Air defense identification zones:** Some states maintain air defense identification zones (ADIZs) in global airspace. An ADIZ is a region of airspace where ready identification, location information, and control of a civil aircraft are required to further national security.

      Example: The United States requires that aircraft operating in its ADIZs (1) file a flight plan with the appropriate aeronautical facility, and (2) enter the United States from the ADIZ only after having given its position between one hour's and two hours' cruising distance from the United States.

      (a) **Legal under the Chicago Convention:** The Chicago Convention is silent on the subject of ADIZs. Thus, states are not precluded from maintaining ADIZs.

      (b) **No effect on entry:** When an aircraft complies with the requirements of the ADIZ, the ADIZ does not preclude any aircraft from entering the airspace of the state.

6. **Aircraft has nationality of state of registration:** Article 17 of the Chicago Convention defines the nationality of any aircraft as the state in which it is registered.

7. **Bilateral agreements:** States have implemented article 6 of the Chicago Convention with a complex network of bilateral agreements given the lack of any widely accepted multilateral treaty.

II. LIABILITY OF AIR CARRIERS

A. **Limitations on liability needed to foster airline industry:** The original purpose for placing limits on the recovery from airlines for damages was to assist the growth of the fledgling airline industry. In 1929, the Warsaw Convention for the Unification of Certain Rules Relating to International Carriage by Air limited liability for death or personal injury to approximately $8,300. In 1975, the limitation was increased by the Montreal Convention for the Unification of Certain Rules Relating to International Carriage by Air to $75,000.

   1. **Need to attract capital:** The airline industry needed capital to assist its growth, and it was hoped that a limitation on costs for damages would further that cause.

2. **Need to obtain insurance:** The limitations also served to make the airlines more attractive to insurance carriers that would otherwise not extend policies to the airlines because of the prospect of a catastrophic accident causing heavy losses.

3. **Need to (1) achieve uniformity of rules and (2) balance the interests of passengers seeking recovery for personal injuries with the air carrier's interests of limiting liability.**

   The primary purpose of the Warsaw Convention was to achieve uniformity of rules governing claims arising from international air transportation, while a secondary purpose was to balance the interests of passengers seeking recovery for personal injuries and the interests of air carriers seeking to limit potential liability. *El Al Israel Airlines, Ltd. v. Tsui Yuan Tseng*, 525 U.S. 155 (1999).

4. **Limitations narrowly construed:** Many U.S. courts construe the limitation of liability provisions very strictly against air carriers on the theory that the original purpose behind the provisions is no longer valid.

B. **Standard of liability:** In exchange for the limitation on liability, the Warsaw Convention provided a stricter standard of liability for the airlines. A carrier will be liable for death or personal injury unless it can prove that it or its agents have taken ***all necessary measures to avoid the damage*** or that it was ***impossible for the carrier to take such measures***. This creates a presumption that the carrier must rebut in order to escape liability. In cases where a plaintiff can prove willful misconduct on the part of the carrier, the carrier cannot take advantage of the liability cap.

1. **Requirement of delivery of ticket:** Under the Warsaw Convention, if the carrier accepts a passenger without a passenger ticket having been delivered, the carrier cannot avail itself of the liability limitation. Courts in the United States are split as to how strictly to interpret this provision.

   a. **Liberal interpretation:** Because courts in the United States dislike the liability limitation, they have often construed the delivery requirement very liberally to allow full recovery. These courts require that delivery of the ticket must be made in such a manner as to provide adequate notice to the passenger of the limitations in order to allow the passenger the opportunity to obtain further protection for himself or herself against injury or death.

   b. **Strict interpretation:** Other courts have held that the delivery requirement merely demands that the passenger physically possess a ticket before boarding. These courts do not read the Warsaw Convention or the Montreal Agreement as requiring adequate notice.

   Example: The plaintiffs sued the airline for damages caused when the airline's plane was destroyed in flight. The plaintiffs argued that delivery of the ticket was invalid because the limitation was printed in 8-point size type, which is smaller than the 10-point size required by the Montreal Agreement. The court held that neither the Warsaw Convention nor the Montreal Agreement require that the limitation be held invalid because the type size is smaller than that specified in the Montreal Agreement. *In re Korean Air Lines Disaster of September 1, 1983*, 829 F.2d 1171 (D.C. Cir. 1987), *aff'd sub nom. Chan v. Korean Air Lines*, 490 U.S. 122 (1989).

2. **Limitation not applicable to certain flights:** The limitation on liability applies only to two types of international travel. The limitation applies to travel that *initiates and terminates in*

different states, both of which are parties to the Convention. The limitation also applies to travel that *initiates and terminates in a single state that is a party to the Convention*, even if the travel involves stops abroad.

C. Jurisdiction: The Warsaw Convention specifies when a state has jurisdiction for actions brought under its terms. Under article 28, there is jurisdiction in the state of:

- the carrier's ***domicile***;
- the carrier's ***principal place of business***;
- the ***location at which the ticket was purchased***; and
- the passenger's ***destination***.

Also note: When a personal injury suit does not satisfy the conditions for liability under the Warsaw Convention, a passenger is barred from bringing his or her claim under local law as an alternative remedy. *El Al Israel v. Tsui Yuan Tseng*, 525 U.S. 155 (1999).

Also note: Tort suits against foreign carriers are compensable under the Convention only when a passenger has suffered a "bodily injury" that was the result of an "accident." The detention and search of a passenger during boarding is not an "accident" for the purposes of the treaty; therefore, recovery is barred under local law. *Id.*

III. VIOLATIONS OF AIRSPACE

Under the various international conventions and bilateral agreements governing international aviation, an aircraft normally needs authorization to enter a state's airspace and is required to follow certain procedures while operating in that airspace.

A. The *Powers* case: In the well-known *Powers* case, Powers, a citizen of the United States, violated the airspace of the Soviet Union in a U2 plane equipped for espionage. Soviet military shot down Powers's aircraft. The Soviet government tried and convicted Powers for espionage, and he was sentenced to confinement for ten years in the Soviet Union. *Powers Case*, 30 Int'l L. Rep. 69 (1966). Note that Powers was not tried for violation of airspace under international law but was found guilty of a crime under the laws of the Soviet Union.

B. Use of force to terminate a trespass: By analogy to the law of the sea, states may use only "necessary and reasonable force" in response to intruding aircraft. *See The I'm Alone*, 3 R.I.A.A. 1609 (1935). The ICAO has taken the position that force should never be used against civilian aircraft.

Example: In 1983, the Soviet Union shot down a Korean Air Lines passenger jet that had violated Soviet airspace, killing everyone on board. The secretary-general of the United Nations concluded that the magnitude of the deviation into Soviet territory was difficult to explain but found no evidence that the pilots were aware of the deviation or intentionally flew off course. In contrast, the Soviet Union attempted to use evidence that the flight passed directly over sensitive military installations to support its contention that the aircraft was on a spy mission and was mistaken for a military aircraft. The ICAO condemned the Soviet Union's use of armed force.

IV. OFFENSES COMMITTED ABOARD AIRCRAFT

A. **Jurisdiction generally:** Article 17 of the Chicago Convention provides that an aircraft takes on the nationality of the flag state, thus ***giving the flag state jurisdiction*** over offenses committed on board the aircraft. In addition, the ***subjacent state over which the aircraft flies may assert concurrent jurisdiction*** based on territoriality. Other states may also assert jurisdiction for offenses committed based on other aircraft principles, such as the nationality of the defendant, universality, or the nationality of the victim. *See* Chapter 5, §II.

B. **Hijacking and sabotage:** Hijacking involves the use or threat of force to exercise control over an aircraft. Sabotage generally addresses efforts to place the safety of the aircraft in jeopardy. The international community has established conventions to govern both of these offenses. The Convention for the Suppression of Unlawful Seizure of Aircraft (Hague Convention) governs hijacking, and the Convention for the Suppression of Unlawful Acts Against the Safety of Civil Aviation (Montreal Convention) deals with sabotage. Many of the articles of the two conventions are identical.

1. **Duty to extradite or prosecute:** Both conventions place upon the state in which the alleged offender is found the duty to either prosecute or extradite the offender.

2. **Jurisdiction:** The Hague and Montreal conventions (as well as the International Convention for the Taking of Hostages) recognize hijacking and sabotage as universal crimes. *See* Hague Convention art. 4, §2; Montreal Convention art. 5, §2; art. 7 in both.

   Example: The Montreal Convention allowed the United States to prosecute individuals who attacked U.S. airlines in Southeast Asia. *United States v. Yousef*, 327 F.3d 56 (2d Cir. 2003).

V. OUTER SPACE

A. **Definition of "outer space":** Two fundamental issues arise in the context of delimiting the border of outer space. First, is a definition even necessary? Second, if a definition is necessary, how shall that definition be derived?

1. **Necessity of a definition debatable:** States disagree on whether a definition is even necessary.

   a. **Definition not necessary:** The United States, among other states, takes the position that there is no need to define where outer space begins.

      i. **No complaints:** Throughout the history of space exploration, no state has ever complained that another state has violated their airspace during the launch or landing of a space vehicle.

      ii. **Definition would be arbitrary:** Science is not yet able to define exactly where outer space begins, so any attempt to set a definition would be arbitrary.

      iii. **Definition not of practical importance:** The minimum height at which satellites can remain in orbit is far beyond the maximum height at which aircraft can fly.

   b. **Definition is necessary:** Other countries assert that a definition should exist for the following reasons:

      i. **Future applications of international law:** A definition is necessary for applying the international law of air and space as technology develops.

ii. **Secure state sovereignty:** Lack of a definition invites states to violate the sovereignty of other states.

iii. **Basis for domestic law:** A definition serves as the basis for enacting domestic law to provide for a state's defense and for the full exercise of state sovereignty.

2. **Scientific versus contrived definition:** A definition can be based on scientific principles or be based on the needs of the international community.

   a. **Scientific definition:** Some states that argue for a definition of outer space contend that a scientific determination of the line between airspace and outer space is possible.

   b. **Contrived definition:** Scholars note that the "indivisibility principle" supports the notion that airspace and outer space are merely different degrees of one another. Thus, if a definition is necessary, it should be arrived at through traditional decision-making processes that take into account social, cultural, economic, historical, and political needs.

3. **Possible definitions:** At least seven possible definitions have been supported over the years:

   - the ***limit of the atmosphere***;
   - the ***limit of air flight***;
   - the ***point at which the atmosphere will no longer sustain human life***;
   - the ***lowest point at which a satellite can orbit***;
   - the ***point at which centrifugal forces replace aerodynamic forces***;
   - the ***limit of a state's effective control over its airspace***; and
   - the ***current orbital minimum*** (approximately 100-110 km).

B. **Control of outer space:** The widely adopted Treaty of Principles Governing the Activities of States in the Exploration and Use of Outer Space, Including the Moon and Celestial Bodies (hereinafter *Outer Space Treaty*) generally provides for ***free access to outer space and celestial bodies by all nations***. The Outer Space Treaty prohibits states from appropriating by claim of sovereignty any part of outer space, the Moon, or any other celestial body by any means. A state's activities must be conducted in accordance with international law and must not interfere with the activities of other states in outer space.

C. **Liability for damage caused by space objects:** Under the Outer Space Treaty and the more detailed Convention on International Liability for Damage Caused by Space Objects (hereinafter *Liability Convention*), a state that launches or authorizes launching of an object, or from whose territory an object is launched, can be held liable for damages caused by the object.

1. **Standards of liability:** The standard of liability varies depending upon where and how the damage occurs.

   a. **Strict liability:** A state will be held strictly liable for damage caused by its space object on the surface of the Earth or to aircraft in flight.

   b. **Fault-based liability:** If a state's space object causes damage to another state's space object that is not on the surface of the Earth, the former state will be held liable only if the damage is due to its fault or the fault of persons for whom it is responsible.

c. **Joint and several liability:** States will be jointly and severally liable in two situations:

i. **Previous damage:** States *A* and *B* will be jointly and severally liable to State *C* when, elsewhere than on the surface of the Earth, a space object of State *A* causes damage to a space object or the persons or property on board a space object of State *B* and damage is thereby caused to State *C* or its natural or juridical persons.

ii. **Joint mission:** When two or more states jointly launch a space object, they will be held jointly and severally liable for any damages. A state from whose territory a space object is launched is considered a participant in a joint mission.

2. **Measure of damages:** Damages are determined in the Liability Convention by the amount needed to return the injured party, whether that party is a person, state, or international organization, "to the condition which would have existed if the damage had not occurred."

3. **Defenses:** Only one affirmative defense is available under the Liability Convention. An otherwise-liable state is not liable if the damage at least partially results from "gross negligence or from an act or omission done with intent to cause damage on the part of the claimant."

4. **Obligation to consider rendering assistance:** In cases in which the damage caused "presents a large scale danger to human life or seriously interferes with the living conditions of the population or the functioning of vital center," the responsible state shall examine the possibility of rendering assistance to the damaged state.

5. **Responsibility for activities in outer space:** Under the Outer Space Treaty, states bear international responsibility for national activities in outer space regardless of whether the activity is carried out by governmental or non-governmental entities. For activities in outer space conducted by an international organization, the international organization bears responsibility.

6. **State retains jurisdiction over objects it launches into space:** States retain jurisdiction over objects launched into space that are registered to it. This applies to component parts and objects landed or constructed on a celestial body. Objects registered to a state that are found outside the territory of that state are to be returned to the state of registration.

D. **Military applications in outer space:** The Outer Space Treaty bans military use of outer space and celestial bodies but permits some military use of orbiting spacecraft.

1. **Ban on weapons of mass destruction:** The Outer Space Treaty prohibits nations from placing nuclear weapons or other weapons of mass destruction ***in orbit***, ***on celestial bodies***, or ***in outer space*** in any other manner. Other military uses of spacecraft orbiting the earth are implicitly permitted.

2. **Ban on non-peaceful use of celestial bodies:** In contrast to the rules for orbiting spacecraft, the Moon and other celestial bodies can be used only for ***peaceful purposes***. The Outer Space Treaty specifically prohibits states from erecting military fortifications, bases, or installations, or undertaking military maneuvers on celestial bodies. The Treaty does not, however, prohibit the use of military personnel in the conduct of research or for other peaceful purposes.

E. **Geostationary orbits:** A satellite in a geostationary orbit remains over the ***same position*** on the Earth. Such orbits occur only over the equator.

1. **Valuable resource:** Geostationary orbits are valuable because satellites occupying these orbits are always within reception range and require little tracking. Furthermore, because satellites

must be spaced apart to avoid interference, the available orbital lots are limited in number, enhancing their value.

2. **Not controlled by any particular state or states:** Although some states along the equator claim special rights to geostationary orbits, the prevalent view is that such orbits are properly considered "outer space" and therefore are under no state's control.

   Example: In 1976, eight equatorial nations signed the Bogota Declaration, ITU Broadcasting Satellite Conference, which declared their sovereignty over the superjacent segments of the geostationary orbit. The Declaration did not receive widespread acceptance and regulation of the geostationary orbits have been generally recognized as the province of the International Telecommunications Union (ITU) of the United Nations.

3. **Regulated use of geostationary orbits:** Because geostationary orbits are so valuable and are limited in number, the international community has sought agreement on their use.

   a. **Squatter's rights rule:** Formerly, a practice of squatter's rights applied to geostationary orbits—that is, any country that had the technology to launch such a satellite could pick any available orbital slot. Developing states objected to this practice because they would not have the means to place a satellite in a geostationary orbit until after the orbit was saturated.

   b. **ITU approach:** The participants at the World Administrative Radio Conference of the ITU in 1989 agreed to guarantee all states at least one satellite position and an associated block of frequencies.

F. **Remote sensing:** Remote sensing occurs when one state obtains, for example, through satellite photography, information about another state from a remote location, such as a satellite in outer space. Some states object to being observed without their consent. The U.N. General Assembly has adopted a set of principles that govern remote sensing. Principle 12 requires that a sensed state shall have immediate access, on a non-discriminatory basis and at reasonable cost, to all primary, processed, and analyzed data concerning territory under its jurisdiction.

VI. CELESTIAL BODIES

A. **Territory not subject to state control:** Under the Outer Space Treaty, *no state may exercise any claim of right to the Moon or any other celestial body*. The Moon and other celestial bodies may be used only for peaceful purposes.

B. **Control of resources on the Moon and other celestial bodies:** Only a few states (not including the United States or Russia) have signed the Agreement Governing the Activities of States on the Moon and other Celestial Bodies, which addresses exploitation of the Moon's resources. The Agreement provides, *inter alia*:

1. **Development of a governing regime:** Parties to the Agreement shall develop a regime to govern the exploitation of the Moon's resources. The regime shall address the following activities:

   a. **Development of resources:** The orderly and safe development of the natural resources of the Moon;

   b. **Management of resources:** The rational management of those resources;

c. **Expansion of opportunity:** The expansion of opportunities in the use of those resources; and

d. **Equitable sharing of benefits:** The equitable sharing of those resources, giving special consideration to the interests and needs of developing states.

2. **Common heritage:** The treaty also provides that the Moon and its resources are the common heritage of mankind. Lack of U.S. support for the treaty has been attributed to this provision.

Exam Tip on AIR AND SPACE LAW

- In an introductory international law course, exam questions in this very specialized area of international law frequently focus on either hijacking or uses of outer space. With respect to hijacking, the multitude of treaties criminalizing the offense have now given hijacking and sabotage the status of international crimes, with universal jurisdiction in every state, for such offenses. For outer space, exam questions often test the status as law of the Outer Space Treaty and whether a particular state activity in space is permissible as peaceful. For example, when the United States shot down a malfunctioning spy satellite in February 2008, questions were raised as to whether the action was necessary, or whether it was a pretext for testing of military weapons in space.

CHAPTER 12

INTERNATIONAL ENVIRONMENTAL LAW

I. EMERGENCE OF INTERNATIONAL ENVIRONMENTAL LAW

Several international organizations, including the United Nations, have played a fundamental role in developing general principles of international environmental law. The modern development of international environmental law is marked by the 1972 Stockholm Conference on the Human Environment, followed by the 1992 "Earth Summit" in Rio, and culminating in the 2002 Johannesburg World Summit on Sustainable Development.

A. Stockholm Conference: In 1972, the United Nations sponsored the first global conference on the environment in Stockholm. The 113 parties to the Stockholm Conference adopted the Stockholm Declaration on the Human Environment and an Action Plan for the Human Environment.

1. Stockholm Declaration on the Human Environment: In this declaration, the Stockholm Conference parties set forth 26 principles that addressed the major environmental themes of the time, and established a global approach to the problem of environmental protection.

a. Principle 1: Principle 1 recognizes a "fundamental right to freedom, equality, and adequate conditions of life, in an environment of a quality that permits a life of dignity and well-being. . . ."

b. Principle 21: This principle provides that although states have the ***right to exploit their own resources***, states must ensure that "activities within their jurisdiction or control do not cause damage to the environment of other states or of areas beyond the limits of national jurisdiction."

c. Principle 22: This principle affirms that states should cooperate in developing international law regarding liability and compensation ***for victims of pollution and other environmental damage*** produced outside boundaries.

2. Action Plan for the Human Environment: In this plan, the parties to the Conference adopted 109 resolutions that addressed the following items: a global environmental assessment program, environmental management activities, and supporting measures.

B. U.N. Environment Program (UNEP): Partly as a result of the Stockholm Conference, the U.N. General Assembly created UNEP in 1973, a specialized subsidiary organ of the United Nations that coordinates environmental protection activities for the United Nations as a whole.

1. Structure of UNEP: UNEP has a Governing Council of 58 members, a Secretariat based in Kenya, and an Environment Fund.

2. Functions of UNEP: These functions include gathering information on environmental problems and existing efforts to solve them, recommending and initiating environmental protection programs, and funding chosen environmental protection programs through utilization of UNEP's Environment Fund.

3. **UNEP's legal activities:** UNEP plays a lead role in the formulation of international environmental law and sponsored major international environmental agreements including, ***inter alia***, the Vienna Convention for the Protection of the Ozone Layer, the Montreal Protocol on Substances that Deplete the Ozone Layer, and the Convention on Biological Diversity.

C. **World Charter for Nature:** Drafted by the World Conservation Union (IUCN) in 1982, the World Charter sets forth global environmental principles. The Charter contains a preamble and 24 articles divided into three sections: general principles, functions, and implementation.

1. **General principles:** These principles state that ***nature shall be respected*** (Principle 1), and that unique areas of the globe should receive special protection (Principle 3).
2. **Functions:** These principles stress the importance of integrating nature conservation into social and economic development planning (Principle 7), and the necessity of avoiding destruction of natural resources through either waste, pollution, natural disaster, or other adverse processes (Principles 10-11).
3. **Implementation:** These principles focus on the importance of incorporating the U.N. Charter principles into the law and practice of each state. Of particular importance, Principle 21 provides that states and other entities shall . . .
   - Cooperate through common activities, such as information exchanges, to conserve nature,
   - Establish standards for products and manufacturing processes with adverse effects on nature,
   - Implement international legal provisions for nature conservation and environmental protection,
   - Ensure that their own activities do not harm the natural systems of other jurisdictions or those areas beyond national jurisdiction, and
   - Safeguard and conserve natural areas beyond national jurisdiction.

D. **Articles on State Responsibility:** The International Law Commission (ILC) has drafted various articles focusing on state responsibility and liability for ***transboundary pollution*** and other environmental damage. Since 1978, it has separately addressed state responsibility for activities not otherwise prohibited by international law.

1. **Article 1:** Article 1 states that "every internationally wrongful act of a state entails the international responsibility of that state."
2. **Article 3:** Article 3 states that an intentionally wrongful act occurs when (1) conduct is an act or omission "attributable to the state under international law," and (2) "that conduct constitutes a breach of an international obligation of the state."
3. **Article 19(3)(d):** In this article, the ILC listed among international crimes "a serious breach of an international obligation of essential importance for the safeguarding and preservation of the human environment, such as those prohibiting massive pollution of the atmosphere or of the seas."
4. **Articles 29, 30, and 31:** These articles describe three circumstances that preclude a state's liability for an otherwise wrongful act under international law:
   1. The affected state has consented to the act.

2. The act was a response to an internationally wrongful act of the other state.

3. The act was due to "an irresistible force or to an unforeseen external event beyond its control."

An act consented to by the affected state that is not in conformity with an existing obligation to that state is not wrongful "to the extent that the act remains within the limits of that consent." This defense, however, "does not apply if the obligation arises out of a peremptory norm of general international law." An act done in response to a wrongful act of another state is not wrongful only if the act also "constitutes a measure legitimate under international law against that other state, in consequence of . . . [the] wrongful act of the other state." Finally, the "***force majeure*** and fortuitous event" defense requires that the extraordinary event made it "materially impossible" for the state to act in conformity with its international obligations, and that the state in question "has [not] contributed to . . . the situation of material impossibility."

E. **Restatement (Fourth) on the Foreign Relations Law of the United States:** The American Law Institute has also addressed state responsibility for environmental damage in the Restatement on Foreign Relations Law. Section 601 provides:

1. A state is obligated to take such measures as may be necessary, to the extent practicable under the circumstances, to ensure that activities within its jurisdiction or control

   a. conform to generally accepted international rules and standards for the prevention, reduction, and control of injury to the environment of another state or of areas beyond the limits of national jurisdiction; and

   b. are conducted so as not to cause significant injury to the environment of another state or of areas beyond the limits of national jurisdiction.

2. A state is responsible to all other states

   a. for any violation of its obligations under Subsection (1)(a), and

   b. for any significant injury, resulting from such violation, to the environment of areas beyond the limits of national jurisdiction.

3. A state is responsible for any significant injury, resulting from a violation of its obligations under Subsection (1), to the environment of another state or its property, or to persons or property within that state's territory or under its jurisdiction or control.

F. **The 1992 Rio Earth Summit:** On the twentieth anniversary of the Stockholm Conference, the United Nations sponsored the U.N. Conference on Environment and Development (UNCED) in Rio de Janeiro, Brazil, the largest global conference on the environment, also known as the "Earth Summit."

1. **Summit Documents:** The Earth Summit produced five major documents: the Convention on Biological Diversity, the Framework Convention on Climate Change, the Declaration of Principles on Forest Conservation, the Rio Declaration on Environment and Development, and Agenda 21.

2. **The Rio Declaration:** The modern equivalent of the 1972 Stockholm Declaration, the Rio Declaration is a non-binding declaration of 27 principles adopted by the Conference and endorsed by the U.N. General Assembly. It is a result of compromise between developed and developing nations and reflects a balance of the goals of each, including the "right to development" insisted upon by developing countries. Important principles include:

a. **Principle 2:** This principle is a revision of Principle 21 of the Stockholm Declaration with greater emphasis on ***states' right to develop their own resources***. It provides:

> States have, in accordance with the Charter of the United Nations and the principles of international law, the sovereign right to exploit their own resources pursuant to their own environmental and developmental policies, and the responsibility to ensure that activities within their jurisdiction or control do not cause damage to the environment of other States or of areas beyond the limits of national jurisdiction.

b. **New elements:** New concepts not encompassed in the Stockholm Declaration include the precautionary approach to environmental management (Principle 15), the right to development (Principle 2), and an obligation to undertake environmental impact assessments of proposed activities likely to have a significant adverse impact on the environment (Principle 17).

c. **Other key environmental principles:** A number of other concepts address problems associated with transboundary pollution: notification of environmental emergencies or disasters (Principle 18), notification and consultation with states regarding transboundary effects of proposed activities (Principle 19), liability and compensation for pollution victims (Principle 13), and warfare (Principle 24).

3. **Agenda 21:** Agenda 21 is an 800-page comprehensive program of action for sustainable development and environmental preservation. It includes a set of priority actions and means for accomplishing the priority actions. There are six priorities:

    1. ***Achieving sustainable growth***, through integrating environment and development in decision making;
    2. ***Fostering an equitable world***, by combating poverty and protecting human health;
    3. ***Making the world habitable***, by addressing issues of urban water supply, solid waste management, and urban pollution;
    4. ***Encouraging efficient resource use***, a category that includes management of energy resources, care and use of fresh water, forest development, management of fragile ecosystems, conservation of biological diversity, and management of land resources;
    5. ***Protecting global and regional resources***, including the atmosphere, oceans and seas, and living marine resources; and
    6. ***Managing chemicals and hazardous and nuclear wastes***.

    A Commission for Sustainable Development, which reports to UNESCO, is established to monitor and review the implementation of Agenda 21.

G. **The 2002 World Summit on Sustainable Development:** Held in Johannesburg, South Africa, the 2002 World Summit on Sustainable Development was the most important world conference on sustainable development since the 1992 Earth Summit in Rio de Janeiro.

1. **Emphasis and global targets:** The Summit emphasized the growing gap between rich and poor; participating nations attempted to address the problem by setting global targets in poverty reduction, clean water and sanitation, and infant mortality.

2. **Johannesburg Declaration on Sustainable Development:** The Summit concluded with adoption of the Johannesburg Declaration on Sustainable Development, which reaffirmed

participants' commitment to Agenda 21, the plan created ten years earlier in Rio de Janeiro. It also stated that the benefits and opportunities created by globalization, while numerous, were not evenly distributed.

II. TRANSBOUNDARY POLLUTION

As a general matter, no state may use its territory in a manner that injures another state, but the exact nature of that liability under customary international law is not well defined. There are many difficulties in enforcing this liability, particularly in domestic courts. As a result, many environmental problems have been addressed by multilateral treaties; the approach has varied depending upon the nature of the problem and how it might best be controlled.

A. General rule: As indicated in several of the sources above, no state may use or permit the use of its territory in a manner that is injurious to another state, or that other state's persons or property.

1. *Pulp Mills on the River Uruguay* case: *Pulp Mills on the River Uruguay (Argentina v. Uruguay)*, 2010 I.C.J. (April 20), emphasized the significance of advance notification in the resolution of transboundary pollution disputes.

In 2010, the International Court of Justice (ICJ) ruled that Uruguay violated its procedural obligations to notify Argentina of its plans to build several pulp mills along the River Uruguay, which serves as part of the boundary between the two neighboring countries. In 1975, the two nations established a statute to govern the joint utilization of the river in future projects, and stipulated that disputes would be resolved by the ICJ. The ICJ's opinion reinforces the notion that states are obligated to inform adjacent states regarding their proposed plans that will significantly affect the environment of the region. Importantly, the ICJ ruled that Uruguay breached its notification requirements even though it simultaneously decided that it did not breach any *substantive* obligations to protect the environment under the statute.

2. *Trail Smelter* case: The *Trail Smelter* case (*U.S. v. Can.*), 3 R.I.A.A. 1911 (1949), established two fundamental principles of liability for transboundary pollution under international law: (1) a state must show material damage and causation to be entitled to legal relief, not merely that emissions or releases from one state have crossed into the territory of another state, and (2) a state has a duty to prevent, and may be held responsible for, pollution by private parties within its jurisdiction if such pollution results in demonstrable injury to another state.

In *Trail Smelter*, a smelter near Trail, British Columbia, Canada, emitted 300-350 tons of sulfur dioxide daily. The United States contended that these emissions were harming forests vital to Washington State's lumber industry. The United States and Canada submitted the dispute for arbitration. An arbitration tribunal found that fumes from the smelter had already caused $78,000 in damage to the forests and would continue to cause damage there in the future. The Tribunal held that Canada was legally responsible for the actions of the smelter, ordered Canada to pay damages, and required the smelter to refrain from causing further damage to the United States.

3. *Corfu Channel* case: The *Corfu Channel* case (*U.K. v. Alb.*), 1949 I.C.J. 4, established the principles that every state has an obligation not to knowingly allow its territory to be used for acts contrary to the rights of other states, and every state has a duty to notify states of any imminent danger that might harm another state.

In *Corfu Channel*, the United Kingdom sued Albania in the ICJ for physical damage and loss of life sustained by two British warships that ran into moored contact mines in the Straits of

Corfu. The ICJ determined that the laying of the minefield could not have been done without Albania's knowledge, and that Albania did not notify the United Kingdom of the minefield's existence or warn the approaching warships. The ICJ recognized that permitting extraterritorial damage from intrastate activity that is in and of itself lawful may, nevertheless, render a state responsible for the damage inflicted, and held Albania responsible for the damages caused to the United Kingdom.

4. ***Lake Lanoux Arbitration*:** The *Lake Lanoux Arbitration* (*Fr. v. Spain*), 12 R.I.A.A. 281 (1957), held that downstream states do not have a right of veto over an upstream state's use of water, but the panel also stated that an upstream state must consider the counterproposals of a downstream state offered to it.

5. ***Nuclear Test* cases:** In the *Nuclear Test* cases (*Austrl. v. Fr.*), 1973 I.C.J. 99, and (*N.Z. v. Fr.*), 1973 I.C.J. 135, Australia and New Zealand claimed that atmospheric nuclear testing by France was causing them to incur risks and damages. The ICJ enjoined France from further testing until final judgment. The merits of the case were never reached, however, because the French government unilaterally decided to halt its testing, thus rendering the case moot according to the ICJ. *See also Advisory Opinion on Legality of Threat or Use of Nuclear Weapons*, Chapter 9, §II(F)(1)(f)(iii).

6. ***Gabcikovo-Nagymaros Project*:** In this 1993 case, which was the first time the ICJ ruled on an environmental dispute, both Hungary and Slovakia claimed that the other had breached a treaty for constructing a system of dams on the Danube River. Although concluding that both states had breached their obligations, the court found that Hungary's breach was not justified by its claim of "ecological necessity." In so holding, the ICJ acknowledged that a balance between economic development and environmental protection, or sustainable development, was an expanding area of international law. *Gabcikovo-Nagymaros Project* (*Hung. v. Slov.*), 1997 I.C.J. 7.

7. ***Question of Compensation* case:** The case *Question of Compensation (Costa Rica v. Nicar.)*, Judgment, 2018 I.C.J. 150 (Feb. 2) marked the International Court of Justice's (ICJ) first adjudication on compensation for environmental damages. The judgment established that damage to the environment itself is compensable under international law, as distinct from compensation for expenses incurred by environmental damage.

   Question of Compensation is a follow-up case from *Along the San Juan River (Nicar. v. Costa Rica)*, Judgment, 2015 I.C.J. 665 (Dec. 16), in which the ICJ ruled that Nicaragua had incurred, occupied, and used Costa Rican territory. The court gave the parties a year to agree on compensation, but after an impasse, the ICJ was asked to step in. The court awarded compensation based on an "Overall Valuation" evaluating the impairment, or loss of environmental goods and services, as well as the time the area might take to recover. The court separately awarded Costa Rica expenses. The court left no clear damages calculation precedent, however; the court claimed to follow the *Chorzów* formula (putting the injured party in the place they would have been in had no wrong been committed), but remained opaque on specific methodology.

B. **Possible theories of liability for transboundary pollution under international law:** Such theories include: (1) an absolute duty to protect against harm from ultrahazardous activities, which, if violated, results in a state being held strictly liable; (2) responsibility for negligent or intentional acts ("abuse of rights"); and (3) liability for a state that permits transboundary pollution to exceed that which its neighbors can reasonably be expected to endure ("good neighborliness"). Of these theories, the least clearly established in customary international law is strict liability for ultrahazardous activities.

1. **Specific treaties focusing on transboundary pollution:** Treaties in this area take a variety of approaches, such as agreeing to try to reach agreement ("framework conventions"), establishing substantive standards, "freezing" pollution at current levels, providing for notification and consultation, and authorizing an international organization to establish applicable rules.

   a. **Acid rain treaties:** Various treaties and agreements have been negotiated in response to the growing problem of acid rain. Acid rain is caused by gases, such as sulfur oxides and nitrogen oxides, dissolving into water carried in the air. These gases form acids in the atmosphere, and the acids descend to the Earth through precipitation.

      i. **Convention on Long-Range Transboundary Air Pollution of 1979 (LRTAP):** This Convention was adopted in Geneva and went into force March 16, 1983. As of November 2010, 51 states (including the United States) were parties to the Convention. The purpose is to "limit, and as far as possible, gradually reduce and prevent air pollution including long-range transboundary air pollution." The Convention provides for enforcement through research, exchange of information, and an interim executive body (IEB). The IEB was established to carry out a cooperative program for monitoring pollution in Europe. The Convention also includes notice and consultation requirements. The original Convention's weakness is the absence of ceilings and timetables to achieve reduction in acid rain, a common omission in a framework convention.

         (a) **Protocol on the Reduction of Sulfur Emissions:** This Protocol went into force in 1987. Using 1980 levels as a basis, the Protocol requires the reduction of sulfur emissions or their transboundary fluxes by 30 percent by 1993. The Protocol also requires annual reporting of sulfur emissions. Several major sulfur producers—including the United States and the United Kingdom—did not ratify this Protocol. An additional protocol in 1994 for further reductions went into effect in 1998 and governed until 2010. Further developments on the future of the Protocol have not occurred. The United States was not a party to the 1994 protocol.

         (b) **Nitrogen oxides protocol:** This Protocol requires the stabilization of nitrogen dioxide emissions or their transboundary fluxes at 1987 levels by 1994. The Protocol covers major stationary sources and vehicle emissions. The Protocol also requires use of the best available technology for national emissions standards and eventual negotiation of internationally accepted "critical loads." Unlike the sulfur emissions protocol, these minimal decreases by 1994 have not even been fully met. As the United States is the only significant developed country outside these requirements, its sulfur dioxide emissions have been controlled on the international level primarily by the 1991 U.S.-Canada Air Quality Agreement.

         (c) **Subsequent developments:** Since the 1979 Convention, the LRTAP regime has added eight protocols. In addition to the two sulfur emissions protocols in 1985 and 1994, and the nitrogen oxide protocol in 1998, it has formulated a 1991 protocol (which took effect in 1997) for volatile organic compounds (VOCs), a 1998 protocol for heavy metals (in effect in 2003), a 1998 protocol for persistent organic pollutants (POPs) (which took effect in 2003), and a 1999 protocol for ground level ozone (which took effect in 2005). The LRTAP protocol on POPs has been overtaken by the Stockholm Convention on POPs (*see* §V(E) of this chapter, *infra*), which is open globally for adoption, and went into effect in 2004.

III. OZONE DEPLETION AND GLOBAL WARMING/ CLIMATE CHANGE

The Montreal Protocol mandating reduced emissions of chlorofluorocarbons and other substances is considered a success story of international environmental law. Its basic approach of a timetable for increasing reductions from a baseline-year level of air emissions was greatly facilitated by the development of substitute chemicals for the regulated pollutants. Climate change, however, is in large part attributable to air pollutants from fossil fuels burned for energy, for which there is no obvious alternative.

A. **Protection of the ozone layer:** Several treaties address the problem of the depletion of the ozone layer. The ozone layer in the atmosphere filters out harmful ultraviolet radiation from the sun. Chlorofluorocarbons (CFCs) are primarily responsible for the depletion of the ozone layer. CFCs are used in air conditioning, aerosols, styrofoam, and refrigerators. As more radiation reaches the Earth due to the depletion of the ozone layer, the incidence of cancer, smog, and eye disease increases.

1. **Vienna Convention for the Protection of the Ozone Layer 1985:** This framework convention, formulated by the U.N. Economic Commission for Europe on a regional basis, primarily focuses on information exchange and cooperation among states in research and scientific assessments on the depletion of the ozone layer. The Convention's goal is to develop appropriate measures to protect human health and the environment against adverse effects resulting from or likely to result from activities that modify or are likely to modify the ozone layer. The Convention also allows the parties to the Convention to adopt protocols to implement the goals of the Convention.

2. **Montreal Protocol on Substances that Deplete the Ozone Layer:** This Protocol to the Vienna Convention was originally adopted in 1987, with major amendments in 1990 and ongoing amendments at the Conferences of the Parties.

a. **1987 Protocol:** This Protocol was in force in 1989. The Protocol sets forth a timetable for the reduction in use of CFCs—50 percent by 1999. The Protocol also bans CFC imports of non-parties unless the non-parties meet the reductions of the Protocol. The Protocol freezes halons at 1986 levels.

b. **1990 amendments:** These amendments place a total ban on CFCs by the year 2000 (by the year 2010 for developing countries). The amendments provide for graduated reduction in CFCs: 20 percent by 1993, 50 percent by 1995, and 85 percent by 1997 (based on 1986 levels). The amendments also establish a 14-member executive committee, and a $240 million fund to assist developing countries in the transition to technology free of CFCs. Additional amendments have added other chemicals such as methyl bromide to list of controlled chemicals, created new deadline timetables, and in some instances accelerated established timetables. The most recent agreement was in Beijing in 1999. It is believed that if the international agreement is adhered to, the ozone layer is expected to recover by 2050.

c. **Recent developments:** In 2011, the parties met and reached an agreement on the following issues: (1) $450 million replenishment of the Multilateral Fund (MLF) for the period of 2012-2014 to help developing nations adopt alternatives to ozone-depleting substances (ODS); (2) certain essential use exemptions; (3) mitigation of ODS emissions from feedstock and process-agent uses; and (4) treatment of ODS used to service ships. In 2012, the parties approved a critical use nomination by the United States for methyl bromide. At the 25th meeting of the Parties to the Protocol in 2013, Canada, Mexico, and the United States urged parties to adopt a proposal to phase down the production and consumptions of CFCs and hydrofluorocarbons (HFCs).

d. **Noncompliance:** Under article 8 of the Montreal Protocol, a party concerned about its ability or the ability of another state to comply may report its concern to an implementation committee. The committee may gather information and issue a report to the Conference of the Parties, which in turn may decide on measures to bring the state into compliance. Failure to comply can result in suspension of a state's rights and benefits under the Protocol.

B. **Protection of the climate:** Another serious environmental problem is climate change due to the ***greenhouse effect***. The greenhouse effect results when gases in the air, such as carbon dioxide, methane, CFCs, and nitrogen dioxide, trap infrared radiation near the surface of the Earth, preventing the radiation from escaping into the atmosphere and thus elevating global temperatures.

1. **U.N. resolutions on climate change:** Two resolutions passed in 1989 recognize climate change as a common concern of humankind and a topic to be given high priority by U.N. organizations and programs. These resolutions emphasize the need for governmental and intergovernmental efforts to prevent detrimental effects on the climate. The resolutions also review possible elements that may be included in an international convention on climate change.

2. **The U.N. Framework Convention on Climate Change:** This Convention was signed at the Earth Summit held in Rio de Janeiro during June 1992. The Convention emphasizes the concern over changes in the Earth's climate, especially those changes caused by greenhouse gases, and has as its objective the stabilization of greenhouse gas concentrations in the atmosphere. No specific controls or deadlines are set, although the Convention had an implicit goal of returning to 1990 levels of emissions by the year 2000.

a. **Commitments of the parties:** The parties to the Convention commit themselves to the following goals: periodic national inventories of anthropogenic emissions and removal of greenhouse gases by sinks; mitigation programs on a national and regional level; the development of technology to control emissions; the consideration of climate change in various decision-making processes; and cooperation in the exchange of information, education, and public awareness. In addition, developed countries commit to the adoption of national policies and mitigation measures; the use of the best available scientific technology for calculation; and the financing of developing countries to help them meet their obligations under the Convention. The 1997 Kyoto Protocol to the United Nations Framework Convention on Climate Change, which entered into force in February 2005, commits developed countries to an additional reduction in greenhouse gas emissions of at least 5 percent from 1990 levels during the period from 2008-2012. The Protocol was created after extensive negotiations and remains controversial; notably, the United States has indicated it will not ratify the Protocol. In a 2009 summit in Copenhagen, the participating countries reached an accord in which major developed nations planned to further reduce global emissions while also beginning to send financial resources to less developed nations to aid in the latter's emission reduction plans. However, these nations specifically determined that the commitments made in the accord were not legally binding and that each country would simply "take note" of the accord's provisions. In 2011, the parties met and agreed to a second commitment period of the Protocol.

b. **Structure of the Convention:** The Convention establishes a Conference of the Parties to review implementation of the Convention and to adopt protocols, amendments, and annexes as needed. A Secretariat is also established to arrange for sessions of the Conference and to prepare reports on climate change. The Convention also provides for two subsidiary bodies, one for implementation and another for scientific and technological advice. A financial mechanism is included in the Convention to enable developing countries to meet the demands of the Convention.

3. **Asia-Pacific Partnership on Clean Development and Climate:** In 2005, the United States partnered with Australia, China, India, Japan, and the Republic of Korea to attend to climate change issues and invest in new technologies to address these concerns. These countries represent approximately half of the world's economy and population, as well as half of the world's greenhouse gas emissions. *See* Asia-Pacific Partnership on Clean Development and Climate. In 2011 the Asia-Pacific Partnership was quietly ended and its remaining projects were cancelled.

4. **Climate change before the U.S. Supreme Court—international applicability of U.S. statutes:** Recently, environmental groups have been able to gain standing for causes of action arising under the National Environmental Policy Act (NEPA) and the Clean Air Act (CAA) based on complaints of ***global*** climate change. It is uncertain whether courts will be willing to open the door to litigation to force the preparation of an Environmental Impact Statement (EIS) for every federal agency action that may affect the global climate. Most courts have taken the position that climate change issues are better left to the political arenas of government. In *Connecticut v. Am. Elec. Power Co.*, 406 F. Supp. 2d 265 (S.D.N.Y. 2005), the court refused to allow a cause of action based on the "public nuisance" of global warming. The court conclusively stated that "Congress has recognized that carbon dioxide emissions cause global warming," but it added that "the EPA has ruled that the CAA does not authorize carbon dioxide regulation." 406 F. Supp. 2d at 268.

   Change may be on the horizon. In *Massachusetts v. EPA*, 549 U.S. 297 (2007), the Supreme Court said that the EPA not only could but must regulate carbon dioxide and other greenhouse emissions from mobile sources such as cars if it were to find on remand that they endanger the public health and welfare. The 5-4 decision by the Court was a departure from the judiciary's tradition of deferring to the political branches of the government where climate control issues are concerned. The case came before the Court when 12 states joined environmental groups, several cities, and the government of American Samoa to bring suit against the EPA for its consistent refusal to regulate carbon dioxide emissions. Petitioners asked the court to determine whether the EPA has a statutory duty to regulate greenhouse gas emissions from new automobiles as an air pollutant. If such a duty to regulate existed, the petitioners asked the Court to determine whether the EPA's stated reasons for non-regulation were permitted by the statute.

   The EPA's first contention was that the petitioners lacked standing to invoke the Supreme Court's jurisdiction under article III. A litigant must demonstrate that it has suffered a particularized injury (either actual or imminent), that the injury is traceable to the defendant, and that redress of the injury is possible through litigation. Justice Stevens, writing for the majority, was not persuaded by the EPA's argument that global warming was such a widespread problem that none of the petitioners could show the "particularized injury" necessary for standing. Focusing on Massachusetts, the Court reasoned that the state owned a great deal of land allegedly affected by global warming and thus had a concrete and personal stake in the outcome of the case. Massachusetts offered that it had lost hundreds of miles of coastal lands to rising waters—a condition it alleged to be the result of global warming. The Court found that the EPA's refusal to regulate emissions presented a risk of harm to Massachusetts that satisfied both the actual and imminent criteria, as its stance of refusing to regulate greenhouse emissions "contribute[d]" to the state's injury. Furthermore, the matter was properly a "controvers[y]" within the meaning of article III's jurisdictional language, as it dealt with the construction of a congressional statute. The Court also pointed to the fact that Congress had expressly authorized challenges of this kind to EPA actions. *See* 42 U.S.C. §7607(b)(1).

In the alternative, the EPA argued that its failure to regulate contributed too little to the problem of climate change to satisfy the standing requirement of a particularized injury and redressability. If Massachusetts was injured by global warming, this injury was not traceable to the EPA, and the state could not hope to reverse or remedy the problem by bringing suit against the EPA. The Court concluded, however, that even though developing countries like China and India were predicted to increase their own emissions in the coming years, the EPA was not relieved of its duty to curb the emission of carbon dioxide in the United States if that emission was harmful to the public health and welfare.

Determining that the Supreme Court did indeed have jurisdiction to answer the questions posed by the petitioners, the Court held that greenhouse gases easily fit within the Clean Air Act's definition of "air pollutants" and that, as such, the EPA has a statutory duty to regulate these emissions as air pollutants from new motor vehicles. *See* 42 U.S.C. §7602(g) (defining the EPA's grant of regulatory authority as covering "any air pollutant . . . including any physical, chemical . . . substance" emitted into the air that has been found to endanger the public health and welfare). The agency could not rely on congressional action since the enactment of the Clean Air Act to support its decision not to regulate greenhouse gases. In the Court's view, post-enactment legislative history could not provide a basis for abdicating a duty clearly imposed by statute.

The EPA put forth several policy reasons that regulation of greenhouse gases was unwise, including the fact that the executive branch had voluntary programs for addressing global warming, and the concern that ill-timed regulation would impair the power of the President in negotiations with foreign countries. Characterizing these reasons as impermissible policy judgments, the Court held that under the statute, the EPA could avoid rulemaking only if it determined that greenhouse gases clearly did not contribute to climate change or if the agency could provide some other reasonable explanation of why it could not or should not exercise its discretion to determine whether they do. Basing its refusal to regulate on concerns that were beyond the reach of the Clean Air Act was "arbitrary" and "capricious," according to the Court. The majority remanded the case with directions to the EPA to ground its reasons for inaction in the statute.

The decision produced two dissents. In the dissent by Chief Justice Roberts, which Justices Scalia, Thomas, and Alito joined, the Chief Justice took issue with the majority's holding that Massachusetts had standing to bring suit. "The very concept of global warming seems inconsistent with" the particularized injury requirement, wrote the Chief Justice. Furthermore, the majority strayed from precedent in interpreting the "availability of redress" criteria. The majority focused on the loss of coastal lands as the injury to Massachusetts, yet broadly spoke of reducing emissions as a means of redress of the state's injury. "What must be likely to be redressed is the particular injury in fact," Roberts argued, and the majority did not say how or why reducing emissions would help redress the loss of coastal lands. In Roberts's view, the majority had created a new doctrine of state standing diluting the standing requirement under the law, and opening the door for courts to litigate issues that were better left to the executive and legislative branches. Scalia agreed that the petitioners lacked standing, but his dissent, which was joined by the Chief Justice, as well as Justices Thomas, and Alito, proceeded to attack the majority's decision on the merits. For Justice Scalia, the majority had read out of the statute all discretion reserved to the agency, and would compel it to rulemaking where the agency had not yet formed a judgment. The statute requires action once a judgment has been formed about the harmful effects of a substance, but in Scalia's view, the statute did not limit the agency's ability to defer making a judgment about an issue, leaving it to be dealt with at another time. The EPA had formed no judgment about emissions as related to new motor vehicles, which was what was at stake in the present case. There was no basis in the text or precedent, argued Scalia, for so narrowing what constitutes a valid, reasonable justification for non-action. Without the formation of a judgment about greenhouse gases in the particular context of new motor vehicles, there was no statutory compulsion for the EPA to act.

The majority's decision is significant both with respect to standing and with respect to when the EPA must regulate an air pollutant under the Clean Air Act. As to standing, the majority rejects the notion that an injury common to all cannot be specific injury to any party sufficient for standing. As to regulation of pollutants (and greenhouse pollutants in particular), the decision stands for the proposition that whenever a substance falls within the broad statutory definition of an air pollutant, the EPA must regulate it if the pollutant endangers the public health and welfare. The agency may not fail or refuse to regulate for any reason not found within the statutory provisions.

5. **Future regulation of greenhouse gases—the Paris Agreement and beyond:** On December 12, 2015, at the U.N. Climate Change Conference, the Paris Agreement was adopted as the consensus of the 196 Parties to the U.N. Framework Convention on Climate Change. The Agreement has three stated goals to enhance the implementation of the Convention: (a) holding the average global temperature to well under 2 °C above pre-industrial levels while pursuing efforts to further limit average global temperature to 1.5 °C above pre-industrial levels; (b) increasing the global ability to adapt to the negative repercussions of climate change; (c) creating "finance flows" consistent with lowering greenhouse gas emissions and improving climate resilience. In accordance with these goals, the Parties agreed to seek global peaking of greenhouse gas emissions as soon as possible.

   The Parties to the Agreement will work toward this goal by making nationally determined contributions (NDCs), which will be individually determined by each country according to its differentiated responsibilities and capabilities. Countries may also act jointly in deciding their NDCs, allowing for greater international cooperation and ambition. At least every five years, countries will indicate a new, ambitious NDC, which will represent a progression beyond their original contribution. As these NDCs are not legally binding and there is no enforcement method or punishment for not meeting intended targets, the Agreement states that contributions will be publicly recorded. Thus, a system of "name and encourage" may be used to hold Parties to their pledges.

On April 22, 2016, the Agreement opened for signatures. As this book goes to press, only a handful of the signatories have ratified the Agreement. The Agreement will only go into effect a month after at least 55 countries accounting for 55 percent of total global greenhouse gas emissions have ratified, accepted, or approved it. In the United States, the Paris Agreement is a contentious issue. Some critics argue that it too harshly restricts American industry when compared to other high-emission states, such as India or China. On the other side, some argue that the Agreement lacks teeth since each nation picks its own levels of NDCs and there is no enforcement mechanism.

Concomitantly, the imposition of mandatory controls on greenhouse gases through a cap-and-trade system (similar to that which has been used to control sulfur dioxide under the U.S. Clean Air Act) is losing support in Congress. It remains to be seen exactly how such a system will be established given competing legislative proposals.

IV. WILDLIFE PRESERVATION

The general provisions for protection of wildlife and nature have been supplemented with global, multilateral treaties to protect specific populations and habitat, to preserve biodiversity, to prevent trade in endangered species, and to limit transboundary movement of living modified organisms.

A. **Provisions under the Stockholm Declaration and the World Charter of Nature:** Both the Stockholm Declaration and the World Charter for Nature contain provisions focusing on the preservation of wildlife.

1. **Stockholm Declaration:** In Principle 4, the Declaration states that the plants and animals of the Earth are a world heritage, and that humans have a special responsibility to safeguard nature. Principle 4 also states that nature conservation should receive a place of importance in economic development planning.

2. **World Charter for Nature:** In Principle 2, the World Charter stresses the need to safeguard necessary habitats so that the genetic viability of the Earth is not compromised, and the necessity of maintaining population levels of all life forms sufficient for survival. In Principle 3, the World Charter states that all areas of the Earth are subject to conservation, and that special protection should be provided for unique areas.

B. **International Convention for the Regulation of Whaling:** The International Whaling Commission was established by the International Convention for the Regulation of Whaling of 1946. The original intent of the Convention's framers was to negotiate a fishing treaty to regulate the whaling industry. Implementation of the Convention has increasingly been directed to conservation of whales.

1. **Structure of the Commission:** The Commission has one member from each contracting government, with slightly over 40 members, including the United States. The Commission holds annual sessions to analyze information about the whaling industry and adopt recommendations for regulation. Three standing committees are the technical, scientific, and finance and administration committees.

2. **Functioning of the Convention:** A schedule with whaling regulations is published annually. The Commission has the power to modify the schedule. The Convention also contains an opt-out provision—any member may exempt itself from compliance with any regulation by

objecting. The Commission adopted a three-year moratorium on commercial whaling in 1982 and extended that moratorium in 1990 for ten more years. In 1994, the Commission established a working group to work toward a revised management scheme (RMS), which would consist of a phased-in approach to resumption of commercial whaling, arrangements for observation and inspection of whale catches, and registers of whaling statistics and whale DNA. The working group has met several times, most recently in 2007, but it has had difficulty establishing consensus on issues such as a code of compliance and enforcement measures.

C. **Convention on International Trade in Endangered Species of Wild Fauna and Flora (CITES):** With over 100 parties, this Convention sets up a complex system of import and export permits and regulations to safeguard endangered species from overexploitation.

1. **Structure of the Convention:** The Convention establishes a Secretariat operated under UNEP that prepares scientific and technical studies. The Secretariat also coordinates the national record keeping and reporting required by the Convention. The Convention establishes a Conference of States Parties that meets every two years to adapt the Convention to evolving conditions. For instance, in 2011, the CITES Parties met and identified measures to reduce the impact of the illegal trade in rhinoceros horns and to conserve the species.

2. **Functioning of the permit system:** The import and export permits required under the Convention are nationally administered and are keyed to categories of endangered species. Exemptions from the permit system exist, and states are permitted to take stricter measures if they wish. The categories of endangered species are contained in the appendices to the Conventions. Appendix I contains all species threatened with extinction that are or may be affected by trade; Appendix II contains those species that are not currently threatened but may become so; and Appendix III contains species states designate as "locally endangered." No permit may be issued for commercial use of an Appendix I species or a recognizable part or derivative of such a species.

D. **U.N. Convention on Biological Diversity:** This Convention was signed at the Earth Summit held in Rio de Janeiro in June 1992. The objectives of the Convention include conserving biological diversity and the sustainable use of its components, and the equitable sharing of benefits of utilizing genetic resources.

1. **Commitments of the parties:** The parties of the Convention obligate themselves to the following: developing national strategies for the conservation of biological diversity; integrating conservation into sectoral or cross-sectoral plans; developing identification and monitoring schemes; establishing a system of protected areas; adopting incentive measures; cooperating in the establishment of research and training programs; public education and awareness programs; and impact assessment procedures.

2. **Structure of the Convention:** The Convention establishes a Conference of the Parties to review implementation and to adopt protocols, amendments, and annexes. A Secretariat is also established to arrange meetings of the Conference and prepare reports on biological diversity. The Convention sets up a subsidiary body to provide scientific, technical, and technological advice to the Conference. The Convention also contains an arbitration mechanism and the opportunity for a conciliation commission.

E. **Cartagena Protocol on Biosafety to the Convention on Biological Diversity:** This protocol adopted in 2000 seeks to regulate and control the risks that the transboundary movements of living modified organisms (LMOs) pose to human health and biodiversity.

1. **Commitments of the parties:** The parties of the Protocol will provide information when exporting LMOs to other party countries so that they might make an informed decision prior to importation; communicate domestic agricultural use of LMOs, importation, or release of LMOs and any national laws designed to implement the Protocol; provide the proper documentation when transporting LMOs to or from a party nation; and ensure that risk assessment and management will occur for all LMOs.

V. HAZARDOUS WASTE, RADIOACTIVE POLLUTION, AND ENVIRONMENTAL EMERGENCIES

Treaties regulating transboundary movement of hazardous waste have progressed from restrictions on such movement (the Basel Convention) to regional bans on importation (the Banako Convention). With radioactive pollution, conventions imposing private actor liability have not gained widespread acceptance. In environmental emergencies, there is a general, customary obligation to notify other states of the emergency and an even less definite obligation of states to provide assistance.

A. Early conventions on civil liability for nuclear damage: These conventions include the Paris Convention of Third Party Liability in the Field of Nuclear Energy of 1960, the Brussels Convention Supplementary to the Paris Convention, the Vienna Convention on Civil Liability for Nuclear Damage of 1963, and the Joint Protocol Relating to the Application of the Vienna Convention and the Paris Convention of 1988.

1. **Vienna Convention on Civil Liability for Nuclear Damage 1963:** Based on the Paris Convention and its Brussels Supplementary Convention, this Convention gives jurisdiction to the courts of the state in whose territory the damage occurred. The operator of a nuclear installation is absolutely liable for nuclear damage, but exemptions exist. A victim of nuclear damage must present a claim within ten years from the date of the accident or else the claim is barred by the Convention. The Convention also requires the installation state to insure payment of the claim against the operator. Few states are parties to the Convention, and none of the parties are major nuclear powers.

2. **Joint Protocol Relating to the Application of the Vienna Convention and the Paris Convention 1988:** This Protocol was negotiated by the International Atomic Energy Agency (IAEA) in cooperation with the Nuclear Energy Agency (NEA) of the Organization for Economic Cooperation and Development (OECD). The purposes of the Protocol are to eliminate conflicts of law when both conventions apply, and to require the parties of each convention to grant each other a right of compensation under each instrument.

B. The Chernobyl accident and resulting conventions: On April 26, 1986, an explosion occurred in a reactor at the Chernobyl nuclear power plant in the Soviet Union. The accident raised questions about the inadequacy of international law in compensating victims of nuclear accidents, in utilizing international law to prevent such accidents in the future, and in informing states when such accidents occur. As a result of the accident, two conventions were negotiated.

1. **The Convention on Early Notification of a Nuclear Accident:** This Convention was signed by 58 states on September 26, 1986. The Convention provides for notification "forthwith" and information regarding a nuclear accident "which has resulted or may result in an international transboundary release that could be of radiological safety significance for another state." States are also required to notify the IAEA of the authority responsible for the accident.

2. **Convention on Assistance in the Case of a Nuclear Accident or Radiological Emergency 1986:** Also signed on September 26, 1986, this Convention provides that parties should cooperate in coordinating emergency response and assistance in the event of a nuclear accident that could involve transboundary radiological release. Under this treaty, any exposed state can claim assistance. The Convention focuses on efforts prior to and after nuclear accidents. Prior to accidents, the Convention requires the identification of experts, equipment, materials available, financial assistance, and elaboration of emergency plans. After accidents, states that require assistance are required to indicate the scope and type of assistance needed. The IAEA has a central role under the Convention in facilitating cooperation among the parties, receiving and dispersing information about accidents, and coordinating emergency response to nuclear accidents.

3. **Emergency notification and obligation to assist:** The growing number of treaties, including those above, that require notification in the event of an environmental emergency and obligate other states to assist (if able to do so) arguably has created a norm of customary international law requiring such notification and assistance.

   Example: In May 2008, Myanmar experienced a disastrous cyclone that killed as many as 100,000 people. The refusal of the Myanmar regime to allow full access for humanitarian aid was condemned by U.N. officials and other members of the international community.

C. **Basel Convention on the Control of Transboundary Movements of Hazardous Wastes and Their Disposal:** This Convention seeks to limit and regulate international traffic in hazardous waste products.

1. **Obligations of the parties:** General obligations include prohibiting the export of hazardous waste without prior approval of the importing country and proof that the importing country has adequate facilities to dispose of the waste; prohibiting trade with non-parties; minimizing the generation of hazardous waste; managing exported waste in an environmentally sound manner; labeling and packaging shipments of waste in accordance with generally accepted international rules and standards; and cooperating in training of technicians, the exchange of information, and the transfer technology. In 2011, the Parties to the Convention met and agreed to allow a "Ban Amendment" that bans the export of hazardous waste for final disposal and recycling to developing countries.

2. **Structure of the Convention:** The Convention establishes a Conference of the Parties to review implementation and to adopt protocols, amendments, and annexes. The Convention also establishes a Secretariat to arrange meetings of the Conference and to prepare reports.

3. **The 1991 Bamako Convention on the Ban of Import into Africa and the Control of Transboundary Movement and Management of Hazardous Wastes Within Africa:** The Bamako Convention prohibits African countries from importing any banned or restricted chemicals from non-parties. An African country may be party to both the Bamako Convention and the Basel Convention.

D. **Rotterdam Convention on the Prior Informed Consent Procedure for Certain Hazardous Chemicals and Pesticides in International Trade:** The Rotterdam Convention, which entered into force on February 24, 2004, seeks to protect human health and the environment by promoting shared responsibility among nations that import and export specified hazardous chemicals.

1. **Obligations of the parties:** The Convention creates legally binding obligations for signatory states to exchange information about chemical bans and restrictions; trade in hazardous

chemicals, based on the principle of prior, informed consent; and meetings of the Conference; and to prepare reports.

E. **Stockholm Convention on Persistent Organic Pollutants (POPs):** Adopted in 2001 and entered into force on May 17, 2004, the POPs Convention seeks to eliminate or restrict the use or release of 12 POPs, toxic chemicals that travel great distances and infiltrate the food chain. Signatory countries agree to develop and implement national plans to comply with the Convention. The Convention also seeks to prevent development of new POPs and sets forth criteria for expanding the list of restricted substances.

VI. ANTARCTICA

Antarctica comprises about 10 percent of the Earth's land and water mass and is the ***only continent that has not been economically exploited***. The principal mechanisms for protection of the Antarctic environment are described below.

A. **Antarctic Treaty of 1959:** The Antarctic Treaty was the first international agreement governing the use of Antarctica. Its goal was to assure continued scientific research while suspending the right of states to claim "sectors" of the continent.

1. **Antarctic Treaty Consultative Parties (ATCPs):** The ATCPs include 48 states. Primary among them are the 12 original signatories (the Antarctic Directorate) and 17 other states that have demonstrated their interest in Antarctica by conducting substantial scientific research activity there (the Consultative Parties). The remaining 19 signatories are referred to as non-consultative parties or acceding states.
2. **Environmental provisions:** Two provisions are environmentally important: article 5 prohibits nuclear explosions and disposal of radioactive waste material; and article 9(1) requires the original signatories to meet regularly to exchange information, consult on matters of common interest, and, if necessary, formulate measures to further the objectives of the Treaty that may concern preservation and conservation of living resources in Antarctica. State representatives have adopted several measures designed to protect living organisms on the continent, including the establishment of a "special conservation zone" within the boundaries of the treaty and "specially protected areas" within that zone.

B. **Convention for the Conservation of Antarctic Seals:** This Convention, signed in 1972, recognizes the necessity to protect Antarctic seals, which had almost disappeared because of excessive hunting. The Treaty does not ban hunting, but instead it establishes a regulatory system to prevent overexploitation. Some species are totally protected by the Treaty.

C. **Convention on the Conservation of Antarctic Marine Living Resources:** This Convention, signed in 1980, covers conservation of Antarctic marine resources within the entire Antarctic marine ecosystem. This zone, called the Antarctic Convergence, extends beyond the original Antarctic Treaty area to the physical boundaries of the Antarctic Ocean. Its objectives, described in article II(3), reflect its ecological perspective: maintenance of the levels of population sufficient to ensure their viability, protecting ecological relations, and prevention of changes that could have irreversible effects. The "rational use" of resources is permitted within this context. The Convention has created two organs to implement the Treaty: the Commission for the Conservation of Antarctic Marine Living Resources, which must meet at least once a year, and a Scientific Committee to assist the Commission.

D. **Agreed Measures for the Conservation of Antarctic Fauna and Flora:** The ATCPs adopted these measures in 1964. The most significant provision is the declaration of the Antarctic Treaty area as a "Special Conservation Area." It establishes a regulatory permit system for the killing or harming of mammals or birds and requires states to take steps to minimize habitat interference and water pollution. Areas of outstanding scientific interest are designated as "Specially Protected Areas" subject to special regulatory protections.

E. **The 1991 Protocol on Environmental Protection to the Antarctic Treaty (Madrid Protocol):** The Madrid protocol provides the ***first comprehensive protection of the Antarctic environment***.

1. **Specific protection:** Article 3 establishes the basic environmental principle underlying the Protocol, with paragraph 1 stating that protection of the Antarctic environment "shall be the fundamental consideration in the planning and conduct of all activities in the Antarctic Treaty Area." In furtherance of this principle, paragraph 2 of article 3 provides, for the first time, a basis for a uniform standard to assess all human activity on Antarctica. It states that all activities "shall be planned and conducted so as to limit adverse impacts on the Antarctic environment...[and] on the basis of information sufficient to allow prior assessments of...their possible impacts on the Antarctic environment." Subparagraph (d) of article 3(2) provides for "regular and effective monitoring...to allow assessment of impacts...including the verification of predicted impacts." Article 11 establishes a Committee for Environmental Protection, an independent body meant to oversee compliance with the Protocol. Under article 9 of the Protocol, the annexes constitute an integral part of the agreement. They include Annex 1 (establishing procedures for environmental impact assessment, including a provision for public notice and comment), Annex II (conservation of wild flora and fauna), Annex III (procedures on waste disposal and management that aim to reduce and remove waste "to the maximum extent possible"), Annex IV (prevention of marine pollution), and Annex V (area protection and management). The most controversial aspect of the Protocol is that it effectively bans mining on Antarctica for at least 50 years. Article 7 expressly prohibits "any activity relating to mineral resources other than scientific research."

2. **Amending the Protocol:** Although article 12 contains amendment and modification procedures that may be invoked at any time, amendments to ban require unanimity of the consultative parties. In the year 2041, the Protocol will be open for review by the parties, which will have an opportunity to amend the agreement. An amendment requires adoption by a majority of the parties, including three-fourths of the states that are consultative parties at the time of adoption of the Protocol. However, no amendment takes effect until ratification by three-fourths of the consultative parties, including all of the states that were consultative parties at the time of adoption of the Protocol. Under article 25, a party may opt out from article 7, effective two years after giving notice, if an amendment to the article has been successfully adopted but fails to be entered into force within three years of its adoption.

VII. DEFORESTATION

Deforestation involves the ***unsustainable use of forests and their genetic resources***. Of primary concern today is the destruction of tropical rainforests.

A. **Consequences:** Although states have not agreed on a definition of the problem, a ***fundamental cause is thought to be poverty***. Local impacts include floods and droughts, siltation of rivers, destruction of breeding areas, and the threat to the survival of over 140 million forest dwellers worldwide. Globally, deforestation is thought to be the primary cause of loss of biodiversity, including medicinal plants, and a major contributor to the greenhouse effect due to the release of carbon dioxide from forest burning and the loss of tropical forests as consumers of carbon dioxide.

B. **The 1984 International Tropical Timber Agreement:** This agreement, administered by the International Tropical Timber Organization (ITTO), is the only international agreement regulating tropical timber. It includes 33 producing states and 27 consuming states and accounts for 90 percent of the international trade in tropical timber. Although any trade restrictions on tropical timber would likely require action by the ITTO, the Timber Agreement is based on the principle of free trade, and it is unlikely to be changed for environmental reasons alone.

C. **The Rio Forest Principles:** The United States proposed a binding deforestation agreement during a preparatory meeting for UNCED, but it was met with considerable opposition from developing countries concerned about threats to sovereignty over their natural resources. The result was an agreement adopted by the Conference called the Non-Legally Binding Authoritative Statement of Principles for a Global Consensus on the Management, Conservation, and Sustainable Development of All Types of Forests—otherwise known as the Rio Forest Principles. In the Rio Forest Principles, the parties agree to promote international cooperation on forestry but do not commit to any specific actions or deadlines.

D. **Debt-for-nature swaps:** Debt-for-nature swaps, first introduced in 1987 by non-governmental organizations (NGOs), involve the purchase of foreign debts of debtor countries in exchange for the creation of domestic forest reserves or other environmental projects. Countries such as Bolivia, Ecuador, and Costa Rica have already participated in such swaps, and many other countries are currently considering similar plans.

1. **Public vs. private debt-for-nature swaps:** The first generation of debt-for-nature swaps were "private," meaning at least one of the parties involved was private. A "second generation" of swaps has recently emerged, called "public" swaps. These occur between sovereign states and, to date, have provided a greater amount of debt reduction than private swaps.
2. **New types of public debt-for-nature swaps:** Three types of public swaps have emerged, each with different enforcement mechanisms:

   a. **Government debt purchases:** Similar to private debt exchanges, this swap involves the government of one country agreeing to buy private debt of another in exchange for reforestation or conservation projects. Enforcement mechanisms are determined by the nature of the agreement between the parties. To date, these agreements have lacked traditional enforcement provisions and instead rely on the friendly relations between the parties.

   b. **Government grants to environmental groups:** The U.S. Agency for International Development has statutory authority to make grants to NGOs, which in turn may support reforestation efforts in countries that have "the capacity, commitment, and record of environmental concern to oversee the long-term viability of…the project." Although legal agreements are required prior to a grant, specific terms and enforcement provisions have not been mandated.

   c. **Debt forgiveness:** The largest debt-for-nature exchange is contained in the Enterprise for Americas Initiative (EAI) proposed by the United States. Within the EAI, the United States has structured a number of environmental framework agreements with countries such as Chile, Bolivia, and Jamaica that are designed to replace old debt with new and funnel funds directly to environmental projects. By statute, enforcement provisions of these agreements must be "reasonable." One example is a strong mechanism for dispute resolution: the host country can cut off all future funds to a country if a dispute cannot be resolved. Other exchanges proposed in Europe focus on environmental cleanup efforts rather than conservation.

VIII. DESERTIFICATION AND LAND DEGRADATION

Desertification is identified in Agenda 21 as one of the key global environmental problems that not only affects the quality of the environment but also is critically linked to the goal of achieving sustainable development in all countries. Desertification affects about one-sixth of the population and one-quarter of the total land area of the world. While some degraded lands can be reclaimed with a reasonable amount of effort and resources, severely or totally degraded land may be permanently lost.

A. **Definition:** Desertification is defined by the United Nations as land degradation in arid, semi-arid, and dry sub-humid areas (including irrigated cropland) resulting mainly from adverse human impact (improper land use). A number of factors are involved, including demographics, overgrazing, deforestation, sources of energy, water resources and irrigation, and erosion.

B. **The Lome IV Convention:** Signed in 1989 between the European Economic Community and the African, Caribbean, and Pacific States (ACP), this agreement specifically addresses the problem of desertification in Title I, which calls for specific actions on national, regional, and international levels to preserve resources and protect ecosystems against desertification and drought.

C. **Past U.N. efforts to combat desertification:** The U.N. Conference on Desertification (UNCOD), held at UNEP in Nairobi in 1977, was the first world conference to set out a plan of action for initiating and sustaining a cooperative effort to combat desertification. Focusing on technical and economic reforms, the plan attempted to reinforce and integrate national, regional, and global actions within and outside the United Nations. The status of the plan of action was reviewed in 1992, when it was found that little progress had been made.

D. **Current U.N. efforts:** Chapter 12 of Agenda 21 includes six program areas countries agree to focus on:

- Strengthening the knowledge base and developing information and monitoring systems for regions prone to desertification and drought;
- Combating land degradation through, *inter alia*, intensified soil conservation and reforestation activities;
- Creating integrated development programs for the eradication of poverty and promotion of alternative livelihood systems in areas prone to desertification;
- Developing comprehensive anti-desertification programs and integrating them into national development plans and national environmental planning;
- Developing drought preparedness and relief schemes and programs to cope with environmental refugees; and
- Promoting environmental education about desertification and drought.

E. Treaty envisioned: Paragraph 12.40 of Agenda 21 requires the U.N. General Assembly to establish a committee to oversee the creation of an international convention to combat land degradation and drought. The committee was established in 1992, and in 1994, it formulated the U.N. Convention to Combat Desertification in Those Countries Experiencing Serious Drought and/or Desertification, Particularly in Africa.

IX. MARINE ENVIRONMENT

The preservation of the marine environment is discussed at Chapter 10, §X.

X. INTERNATIONAL TRADE AND ENVIRONMENT

There is growing recognition that trade and the environment are inextricably linked, and trade implications of environmental policy and environmental implications of the world trade system are emerging as issues of international concern.

A. The General Agreement on Tariffs and Trade (GATT): Most of the rules governing international trade are codified in the General Agreement on Tariffs and Trade, which was first established in 1948 and is periodically negotiated by the parties. The rules are based primarily on the ideology of free trade, with a view that is skeptical of regulations that inhibit trade. Thus, many proponents of free trade see environmental regulations as a type of non-tariff barrier to be forbidden under GATT. The principal forum for resolution of trade disputes is the World Trade Organization (WTO), which refers to treaties such as GATT for its standards.

1. **Lack of environmental protection under GATT:** There is no mention in GATT of environmental protection as a justification for limiting trade; however, states may legitimately restrain trade under article XX if "necessary to protect human, animal, or plant life or health" and impose measures "relating to the conservation of natural resources."

2. **The Uruguay Round:** The Uruguay Round of GATT talks, begun in 1985 and concluded in 1994, was the first round to link international trade and the environment in the contexts of agricultural subsidies, harmonization of certain environmental standards, prohibition of export controls, and the liberalization of import restrictions. Although these issues were not resolved, the participants signed an agreement pledging to undertake a dialogue on the "interlinkages between environmental and trade policies."

   Despite opposition from environmental and consumer groups as well as some local governments, implementing legislation for the Uruguay Round of the General Agreement on Tariffs and Trade was approved by Congress at the end of 1994. Environmentalists expressed concern that GATT and the GATT implementing legislation, unlike the North American Free Trade Agreement (NAFTA), contain no environmental provisions and therefore leave U.S. conservation laws open to attack as unfair trade barriers. Also, under the prior GATT procedures, a nation could veto a GATT panel ruling with which it did not agree. Under the new procedures, trade disputes heard by the WTO cannot be vetoed. Failure to comply with a WTO ruling can lead to imposition of trade sanctions by other GATT parties.

   a. **Environmental impact statement rejected:** A suit filed by public interest groups to require the Office of the U.S. Trade Representative to prepare an environmental impact statement for the Uruguay Round of the GATT was dismissed by the District of Columbia federal district court. *Public Citizen v. Kantor*, 864 F. Supp. 208 (D.D.C. 1994). The court relied on *Public Citizen v. U.S. Trade Representative*, 5 F.3d 549 (1993), *cert. denied*, 114 S. Ct. 685 (1994), in which a federal appeals court had dismissed a similar challenge to NAFTA because there was no "final agency action" to trigger judicial review under the Administrative Procedure Act.

3. **GATT Group on Environment Measures and Trade:** First established in 1971, the Group on Environment Measures and Trade was dormant until first activated in 1991 following a GATT debate on environment and trade. The Group's initial agenda includes: (1) trade provisions in existing multilateral environmental agreements, (2) national environmental regulations likely to have an international effect, and (3) trade effects of packaging and labeling requirements aimed at protecting the environment.

B. **The World Trade Organization:** *See* Chapter 6, §IV.

C. **Conflicting views of traditional free trade theorists and environmentally oriented economists:** GATT negotiators have a difficult time coming to an agreement about issues concerning trade and environment because economists' theories in this area conflict. According to environmentally oriented economists, when the prices of goods that enter the international market do not reflect the environmental costs of production, the producers are receiving an effective subsidy equal to the resources used in the process. Thus, they claim that these goods distort the trade process, giving an unfair advantage to producers who degrade the environment, termed "ecological dumping." However, under the GATT, no such explicit environmental subsidy is recognized. Instead, these goods are viewed as having only an "implicit subsidy," one that is not forbidden.

D. **The Tuna/Dolphin Decision:** In February 1991, Mexico filed a formal complaint against the United States claiming that a U.S. embargo on Mexican yellowfin tuna was protectionist in nature and a violation of GATT. The United States had imposed the embargo pursuant to the Marine Mammal Protection Act as a trade sanction to compel Mexico (and other states) to bring its kill rate of dolphins in the harvesting of yellowfin tuna in the Eastern Tropical Pacific in line with U.S. standards. The United States argued that the measure was justified under article III of GATT, which requires only that imported products be accorded no less favorable treatment than products of national origin, or under the exemptions in article XX for protection of natural resources and animals. The panel concluded that the U.S. import ban violated GATT. Dispute Settlement Panel Report on United States Restrictions on Imports of Tuna, Aug. 16, 1991, *reprinted at* 30 I.L.M. 1594. According to the panel, article III allows for regulation of a product based only on the qualities of the product itself, not on the process by which it is made. The article XX exemptions can be used to protect living or natural resources only under the jurisdiction of the party invoking the exemptions. In May 1994, a second panel upheld the European Community's claim that GATT was also violated by the U.S. embargo on intermediary nations that import and then export yellowfin tuna harvested in violation of U.S. standards. The GATT panel concluded that the secondary embargo by the United States on imports of tuna from intermediary nations was inconsistent with its GATT obligations because the ban was too attenuated to the preservation of dolphins to be "necessary" to protect the life or health of dolphins or to be "related to" conserving dolphins.

E. **The Shrimp/Turtle Case:** In 1998, the WTO appellate body ruled that a U.S. law that protected endangered sea turtles violated the GATT. The law restricted imports of shrimp and shrimp products caught without using "turtle excluder devices" (TEDs). The WTO found that the implementation of this law amounted to arbitrary and unjustifiable discrimination. *See* Appellate Body Report, *United States—Import Prohibition of Certain Shrimp and Shrimp Products*, WT/DS58/AB/R (Oct. 12, 1998).

The United States made attempts to bring the law into compliance with GATT, and when the law was subsequently challenged by Malaysia, the WTO appellate body found the reformed U.S. law to be GATT-compliant. *See* Appellate Body Report, *United States—Import Prohibition of Certain Shrimp and Shrimp Products*, WT/DS58/AB/RW (Oct. 22, 2001).

F. The CAFE standards decision: In 1994, a GATT dispute settlement panel rejected an E.U. claim that U.S. fuel conservation and tax measures were discriminatory against European auto imports. The European Union had challenged the U.S. corporate average fuel economy standards, the "gas guzzler" tax, and the luxury tax on cars over $30,000. The decision upheld these taxes and the 19-year-old corporate average fuel economy (CAFE) standards, but the panel agreed with the European Union that the CAFE accounting rules that establish separate domestic and import fleets for determining overall fuel economy were discriminatory. The panel apparently rejected the E.U. claim that the United States had to take the least restrictive trade measures to serve environmental goals.

G. The Global Environment Facility (GEF): The Global Environment Facility was established by the World Bank, UNEP, and the U.N. Development Programme (UNDP) in 1991 as a pilot program under which grants or loans would be provided to developing countries to help them implement programs addressing problems of global environmental significance. These include protection of the ozone layer, limiting emissions of greenhouse gases, protection of biodiversity, and protection of international waters. A number of global environmental treaties that address these problems contain funding mechanisms provided by GEF, including the 1992 biodiversity treaty and the Montreal Protocol. Multilateral contributions to the GEF are currently made by participant states on a voluntary basis. Programs funded under the GEF are implemented through a "tripartite arrangement" by the World Bank, UNEP, and UNDP.

H. North American Free Trade Agreement (NAFTA): NAFTA is a unique trade agreement for its incorporation of environmental protections. The preamble states that trade must be consistent with environmental protection and conservation. The agreement calls for "harmonization of the parties' domestic standards with international environmental standards, while preserving in certain circumstances each country's ability to maintain domestic environmental standards that exceed prevailing international standards." Disputes over environmental standards may be resolved by an arbitral panel, with the burden under NAFTA on the party challenging the environmental measure. Although NAFTA by its terms is generally to be given priority over conflicting international agreements, exceptions are made for several major international environmental treaties. A separately negotiated environmental agreement focuses on cleanup of the Mexico/U.S. border area and establishment of a Commission on Environmental Cooperation to ensure enforcement of environmental standards by the parties.

In *Public Citizen v. U.S. Trade Representative*, 5 F.3d 549 (D.C. Cir. 1993), the D.C. Circuit Court of Appeals held that an environmental impact statement did not have to be prepared for NAFTA because it was not "final agency action" under the Administrative Procedures Act and NEPA itself does not create a private right of action.

I. Dominican Republic–Central American Free Trade Agreement (DR-CAFTA): Like NAFTA, DR-CAFTA contains provisions that set forth environmental priorities and guidelines for responding to violations of members' environmental laws. The Agreement establishes "incentives and other flexible and voluntary mechanisms" for addressing environmental concerns, focused primarily on establishing a framework for regional cooperation to mitigate the environmental effects of development and trade.

J. Equator Principles: Adopted in June 2003 and last revised in July 2006, the Equator Principles are voluntary guidelines for managing environmental and social issues in project finance lending.

They were created in response to the Collevecchio Declaration, which was signed by over 100 environmental advocacy groups at the 2003 Annual Meeting of the World Economic Forum, calling on financial institutions to make environmentally responsible lending decisions and policy. In July 2010, the Equator Principles formally adopted governance rules to set out the purpose and structure of the Principles and increase the transparency of the Association. As of February 2011, 69 international banking institutions had adopted the Principles, which are based on the International Finance Corporation's Performance Standards on Social and Environmental Sustainability. The Principles currently cover approximately 85-90 percent of global project lending.

K. **U.N. Resolution 2003/71:** Adopted on April 25, 2003, by the U.N. Commission on Human Rights, Resolution 2003/71 recognized the important connection between the environment and human rights in achieving goals of sustainable development.

XI. MILITARY ACTIVITIES AND THE ENVIRONMENT

The international community is increasingly willing to condemn military acts that harm the environment and may impose legal liability on an aggressor. Liability for environmental harm that results from military activities may arise from a number of international agreements.

A. **Protocol I to the 1949 Geneva Conventions Relating to the Protection of Victims of International Armed Conflicts:** Article 35 prohibits methods of warfare that "are intended, or may be expected, to cause widespread, long-term, and severe damage to the natural environment." Article 55 of Protocol I of the Geneva Conventions states that "care shall be taken in warfare to protect the natural environment against widespread, long-term, and severe damage. . . .Attacks against the natural environment by way of reprisals are prohibited." The status of the Protocol as customary international law is controversial.

B. **Environmental Modification Convention of 1977 (ENMOD):** This Convention was drafted during the Vietnam War in response to concern over the use of "deliberate manipulation of natural processes" that change the "dynamics, composition, or structure of the earth. . . ." ENMOD prohibits its member states from engaging in environmental modification techniques that have "widespread, long-lasting, or severe" effects as a means to harm another state.

C. **General customary laws of war:** The customary laws of war impose a requirement of proportionality and necessity on all methods of warfare. It has also been argued that the body of law restricting use of certain weapons gives rise to a more general prohibition of any method of warfare that causes unnecessary suffering. Finally, it is unclear whether the general norms of international environmental law are suspended in the context of armed conflict.

D. **Application of U.S. domestic law:** In 2005, the National Historic Preservation Act (NHPA), which requires the United States to avoid harming cultural properties on its own or other nations' registries, was invoked to protect the dugong, an animal that would have been endangered by the construction of a planned U.S. military base in Okinawa. The District Court for the Northern District of California ruled that the Japanese list protecting the dugong is equivalent to the U.S. National Register in purpose, effect, and consequence, and that the construction of a military base is a "federal undertaking," triggering the protection of the NHPA. This case marks the first time that an animal has been considered a cultural property for the purposes of the NHPA.

XII. EXTRATERRITORIAL APPLICATION OF U.S. ENVIRONMENTAL LAW

While some U.S. laws are intended for extraterritorial application, typically, environmental legislation is not considered one of these areas. U.S. courts have been reluctant to apply domestic environmental law to foreign countries because these laws were designed to address domestic environmental issues.

A. Refusal to apply U.S. domestic environmental law extraterritorially: In *Amlon Metals, Inc. v. FMC, Corp.*, 775 F. Supp. 668 (S.D.N.Y. 1991), the Resource Conservation and Recovery Act did not provide a cause of action for harm that occurred in the United Kingdom as a result of hazardous waste shipped from the United States. The court ruled that the cause of action should have been brought before a U.K. court applying U.K. law.

B. Exceptions to refusal to apply U.S. domestic environmental law extraterritorially: In *Environmental Defense Fund v. Massey*, 986 F.2d 528 (D.C. Cir. 1993), the court found that the NEPA required an environmental impact statement for actions affecting the environment in Antarctica. The court concluded that because the impact was occurring outside the jurisdiction of any nation, U.S. environmental law could be applied.

Furthermore, U.S. courts have also been willing to apply domestic environmental law in cases where the actions occur outside the jurisdiction of the United States, but the effects occur within the United States. In *Pakootas v. Teck Cominco Metals*, 452 F.3d 1066 (9th Cir. 2006), *cert. denied*, 128 S. Ct. 858 (2008), the court found that U.S. hazardous waste law (the "Superfund" Act) applies to discharges originating in Canada. The Ninth Circuit concluded that no extraterritorial application of the Act was involved because the discharges had reached U.S. territory.

Quiz Yourself on INTERNATIONAL ENVIRONMENTAL LAW

21. An accident occurs at a nuclear reactor in State *A*, with radioactive emissions crossing into other states' territories. Is State *A* liable for any damage caused by the emissions? ______

22. An exotic animal listed as an Appendix I species under CITES is shipped to a private person who maintains his own safari park with an accompanying permit under CITES. Is the permit permissible under CITES? ______

23. State *A* declares its intention to establish a research center in Antarctica to evaluate the potential for mining of oil and mineral resources. May State *A* establish such a center? ______

ANSWERS

21. Yes. The Stockholm Declaration, the Rio Declaration, the Draft Articles on State Responsibility, and the *Trail Smelter* case, among other international law sources, declare that a state is liable for transboundary environmental harm to another state. Although none of these sources is per se a binding source of international law, the accumulation of international authority recognizing this responsibility has created a norm of custom imposing liability for transboundary environmental harm. Somewhat less clear is the standard of liability—whether negligence, strict liability, or something more akin to nuisance and unreasonable interference standards. The Vienna Convention on Civil Liability for Nuclear Damage may be urged as establishing a standard of strict liability for nuclear-related accidents. Even more problematic is enforcement. There are many hurdles to enforcement in domestic state courts, and only a consenting state can be brought before the ICJ.

22. Yes. CITES is a permit system that prohibits only transport of a species in violation of the restrictions CITES imposes on the purposes of transfer. If an Appendix I species is not being transported for commercial use, transport and a permit for it are allowable so long as the transfer is not detrimental to the survival of the species and is done in keeping with transport requirements for the safety of the species and other procedural requirements.

23. Probably, but it would be subject to a number of restrictions. The 1959 Antarctic Treaty was designed to limit territorial claims but to assure freedom of scientific research on the continent. Many non-state parties questioned whether the treaty established binding customary law on non-parties. Although there were several specific treaties protecting specific resources of Antarctica, the 1992 Madrid Protocol was the first treaty to provide comprehensive environmental protection for the continent. Among other requirements, the center would have to be established and operated to "limit adverse impacts" on the environment and satisfy the procedures for doing an environmental impact assessment of the center before proceeding. The Protocol also bans actual mining. If State *A* is not a party to the Protocol, it may contend that the Protocol is not binding on it as customary international law. If that is the case, State *A* would still be bound by the more general (and less forceful) prohibitions on any state causing transboundary environmental harm.

Exam Tip on *INTERNATIONAL ENVIRONMENTAL LAW*

- The pervasive controversy over global warming is a good framework for preparing for an exam question on international environmental law. Possible issues include the following: Is the Kyoto Protocol binding as customary international law? If a treaty has a significant number of parties, but the major polluters are not parties, can the treaty be viewed as custom? What role will the grant of notice to neighboring states—or the failure to grant it in other cases—play in future transboundary pollution conflicts? Is a state that refuses to impose binding emission limitations on greenhouse gases liable for transboundary environmental harm to the global commons by its failure to regulate? Where could such a claim be brought in an international forum? By whom? What about in a state's domestic courts, for example in the United States? Who could bring such a claim, and on what theory? If the harm is global, who has injury-in-fact for standing in U.S. federal court? For further guidance, see *Massachusetts v. EPA*, 549 U.S. 297 (2007), and L. Malone & S. Pasternack, Defending the Environment: Civil Society Strategies to Enforce International Environmental Law (Island Press 2006).

CHAPTER 13

INTERNATIONAL CRIMINAL LAW

I. THE PRINCIPLES OF INDIVIDUAL RESPONSIBILITY AND CRIMINAL LIABILITY

International criminal law is the body of public international law that deals with the relationships between states and international criminal tribunals, between those criminal tribunals and individuals, and between states and individuals with respect to criminal trials and punishment.

A. Understanding international criminal law: Public international law has traditionally dealt only with the relations between states and between states and international organizations. Modern developments have led to more law governing the relationships between states and individuals or corporations. International criminal law primarily deals with the relationship between international organizations (criminal courts and tribunals) and individuals. International humanitarian law, including the customs and practice of criminal liability for its violators, is the area of public international law that has developed most in the past 20 years.

B. State responsibility: The purposes of international criminal law are bringing closure to victims, restoring people's belief in the operation of justice, expressing the condemnation of the international community, and deterring future crimes by holding individuals personally responsible for their actions. The International Court of Justice (ICJ) is available to hold states accountable for their breaches of international humanitarian law. In the case concerning the massacre at Srebrenica in the former Yugoslavia, the ICJ ruled that the state of Serbia had not committed genocide, but it had nonetheless violated the Genocide Convention by failing to prevent genocide and failing to punish the perpetrators or surrender them to the International Criminal Tribunal for the Former Yugoslavia (ICTY). *Application of the Convention on the Prevention and Punishment of the Crime of Genocide (Bosn. & Herz. v. Serb. & Mont.)* (Judgment of Feb. 26, 2007), *available at* http://www.icj-cij.org/docket/index.php?p1=3&p2=3&k=f4&case=91&code=bhy&p3=4 (last visited May 19, 2011). I.C.J. Report 1996, p. 595. Many commentators have argued against courts affixing state responsibility for crimes of genocide because ***judgments of collective guilt undermine efforts to prevent future genocides by holding individuals accountable for their actions***.

C. International humanitarian law: In order for a crime to be an "international crime" that carries individual liability and is subject to prosecution and punishment by the international community, it must be a violation of international humanitarian law. International humanitarian law is the body of treaty and customary law that governs the conduct of all individuals in conflict situations and protects the basic human rights of all people. International humanitarian law consists of the Geneva Conventions of 1949 that established *jus in bello* principles and all of the conventional and customary law prohibiting genocide and crimes against humanity.

D. The doctrine of command responsibility: At Nuremberg and other international criminal trials, a common defense proffered by those accused of crimes against humanity was that they were simply following the orders given to them by superiors. For international humanitarian law to have any practical application, ***someone in the chain of command must be personally accountable to the international community for his or her actions***. Criminal prosecutions have established the invalidity of the "following orders defense," but they have focused only on individuals in positions of power or command responsibility. International criminal prosecutions are usually reserved for individuals who "bear the most responsibility" for human rights disasters or individuals who were in a decision-making role and could have prevented the disaster. Further, international tribunals have recognized that criminal liability can attach to individuals for the actions committed by their subordinates.

1. ***Prosecutor v. Delalic*:** In *Prosecutor v. Delalic (Celebici Camp)*, Case No. IT-96-21-T, Judgment (Nov. 16, 1998), the ICTY Trial Chamber found that a Serbian general did not have sufficient command and control over the Celebici Camp or its personnel to trigger criminal liability for his role in the murder, torture, and inhumane treatment that occurred at the camp. The prosecutor appealed the acquittal, and the Appeals Chamber held that under article 7(3) of the ICTY statute, no criminal responsibility could attach for acts committed by other persons of completely equal rank or status. A military superior must have had "effective control" over the person committing a human rights violation in order to be held criminally liable for the violation. "Effective control" was defined as the "material ability to prevent and punish" the commission of offenses. The court held that a superior may be held responsible only if he or she had "reason to know" of offenses committed by subordinates.

2. ***Prosecutor v. Hadzihasanovic*:** In *Prosecutor v. Hadzihasanovic*, Decision on Jurisdiction in Relation to Command Responsibility, Case No. IT-01-47-AR72 (July 16, 2003), the ICTY Trial Chamber held that the doctrine of command responsibility was applicable in the context of an internal armed conflict under customary international law. The court also held that, in principle, a commander can be held liable for crimes committed prior to the moment that the commander assumed command. The defendants lodged an interlocutory appeal challenging both decisions by the Trial Chamber. The Appeals Chamber held that there was no evidence from any state practice that sustained the proposition that a commander can be held responsible for crimes committed by a subordinate prior to the commander's assumption of command over the subordinate.

E. **Broadening criminal liability:** Over the past 20 years, international criminal prosecutions have become more prevalent, and the international community has become more comfortable identifying new crimes.

1. **Aiding and abetting:** *Prosecutor v. Furundzija*, Case No. IT-95-17/1-T, Judgment (Dec. 10, 1998), established three very important precedents in international criminal law. First, the International Criminal Tribunal for Rwanda (ICTR) held that a prohibition against torture was a peremptory norm of international law. Second, the Tribunal found that rape committed during interrogation amounted to torture. Third, the Trial Chamber distinguished accomplice liability for torture from liability for aiding and abetting. To be guilty of torture as a co-perpetrator, the accused must have participated in an integral part of the torture. Furundzija was found ***guilty of torture as an aider or abettor, despite the fact that he wasn't physically present*** during the torture because he encouraged others to engage in torture with the knowledge that they would do so.

2. **Incitement:** In *Prosecutor v. Nahimana, Barayagwiza, and Ngeze*, Case No. ICTR-99-52-T, Judgment (Dec. 3, 2003), the director of Rwanda's Radio Television Libre Des Mille Collines (RTLM) during the 1994 genocide was convicted of the crime of ***direct and public incitement to commit genocide***. He was tried jointly before the ICTR with a co-director of the radio station and a newspaper publisher in what was known as "The Media Trial." The case set the important precedent that individuals can be held accountable for *all* of their actions that lead to humanitarian disasters.

3. **Recognition and definition of new crimes:** In *Prosecutor v. Sam Hinga Norman*, Decision on Preliminary Motion Based on Lack of Jurisdiction, Case No. SCSL-2003-14-AR72(E) (May 31, 2004), the Special Court for Sierra Leone considered whether the conscription of children into the armed forces was a recognized crime entailing individual criminal responsibility under customary international law. The court held that prohibitions on child recruitment existed *and* had crystallized as customary international law. When recognizing specific acts as international crimes (violations of international humanitarian law), ***courts typically look for treaty or convention law as evidence that an international norm exists***. In this case, the court used the 1990 African Charter on the Rights and Welfare of the Child to justify holding individuals criminally responsible. However, a norm does not need to be expressly stated in an international convention for its violation to be ruled a crime that carries individual liability.

II. THE INTERNATIONAL CRIMINAL TRIBUNALS

Throughout the 1990s, the creation of ad hoc criminal tribunals after wars or humanitarian disasters was widely viewed as a good way to bring closure to victims, restore people's belief in the operation of justice, express the condemnation of the international community, and deter future crimes by holding individuals personally responsible for their actions.

A. **Problems of legitimacy:** The tribunals face several major criticisms: local communities rather than the international community should try criminals and pass judgments; the international state system cannot allow a supranational judicial body to have personal jurisdiction over individuals; the international community is not well suited to pass judgment on individuals because it can never properly understand the conflicts that lead to massive human rights disasters; and the U.N. Charter does not permit the creation of criminal courts. The legitimacy of the tribunals has depended mostly on the cooperation of state governments in officially recognizing the tribunals, making arrests, and extraditing the accused to the tribunals. Legitimacy is also established with the consent and agreement of the governments of the states where the human rights violations occurred. Finally, the tribunals ensure their legitimacy by rendering "good" judgments and assigning sentences that are popularly viewed as fair.

1. **Creation and jurisdiction:** There are four major arguments that international criminal tribunals are illegitimate bodies in the international state system.

   a. **Usurpation of existing courts' jurisdiction:** Many critics of the tribunals have joined criminal defendants in arguing that *the tribunals supplant the jurisdiction of the existing courts of states recognized by the international community*. The co-equal sovereignty principle that every government must respect the jurisdiction of other governments is challenged by the assertion of the international tribunals that they can prosecute citizens of a state who are not being prosecuted by the courts of that state. The idea that an international judicial body can claim for itself the power to intervene to correct a failure of the justice systems of sovereign states is revolutionary.

   b. **Derogation of sovereign immunity:** The fact that the tribunals often indict government and military officials for crimes committed while serving in an official capacity puts ***stress on the principle of sovereign immunity and the state action doctrine***.

   c. **Risk of unequal treatment:** The use of ad hoc tribunals rather than a uniform international criminal court gives rise to ***variance in judicial process and unequal treatment*** of defendants. It also forces the international community to engage in a sort of judicial triage by creating tribunals for only some of the world's humanitarian disasters while leaving other genocidaires and war criminals to remain at large with impunity.

d. **Lack of authority:** Creation of the tribunals has challenged the contractual model of international relations. Many defendants have argued that ***the United Nations lacks the authority to create a criminal tribunal under its own Charter***. If the Charter does not give the United Nations the power to create criminal courts to try individuals, then the member states of the United Nations never agreed to their creation.

   Example: In *Prosecutor v. Tadic*, Case No. IT-94-1-I, Decision on Defense Motion for Interlocutory Appeal on Jurisdiction (Oct. 2, 1995), Dusko Tadic appealed his conviction by the ICTY claiming that the creation of the Tribunal by the U.N. Security Council was illegal under the U.N. Charter, and that the Tribunal had been given wrongful primacy over national courts. Tadic argued that the creation of a lawful war crimes tribunal required an international treaty or a vote by the U.N. General Assembly. The Appeals Chamber overturned the decision of the Trial Chamber and held that it had jurisdiction to hear the challenge to the invalidity of the Tribunal's establishment by the Security Council. The Chamber concluded that article 41 of Chapter VII of the U.N. Charter authorized the Security Council to create the ICTY as a "measure not involving the use of force" designed to give effect to its decisions concerning the maintenance and restoration of international peace and security.

2. **Recognition by state governments:** The international tribunals have cemented their legitimacy and overcome the problems and criticisms above primarily because they have been accepted by most states. Many states have officially recognized the legitimacy of the courts, and some have agreed to cooperate with them or even provide some funding. The tribunals cannot function unless state governments make arrests and extraditions and respect the judgments and sentences.

   a. **Extradition agreements:** States pledge to locate and arrest persons indicted by the tribunals who are located on their sovereign territory. States also pledge to extradite the indictees to the jurisdiction of the tribunal to stand trial.

   b. **Enforcement of sentences:** States conclude agreements with the tribunals agreeing to honor their judgments. Because of the ad hoc nature of the criminal tribunals, they do not have their own long-term detention facilities for the imprisonment of those convicted. The tribunals can release convicts into the custody of states to serve their sentences.

   Example: The ICTR has concluded agreements with the governments of Italy, France, Sweden, Swaziland, Mali, and Benin in which the states agreed to give effect to the judgments of the Tribunal. The government of the United Kingdom has agreed to jail some of those convicted by the Special Court for Sierra Leone.

3. **Punishment:** None of the international tribunals have the ability to sentence convicted criminals to death. Most states in the international community have recognized judicial death sentences as inhumane or degrading treatment in violation of various human rights treaties to which they are parties.

B. **The International Criminal Tribunal for the Former Yugoslavia (ICTY):** The ICTY is an ad hoc U.N. organ established ivn The Hague, Netherlands, to try those responsible for serious "violations of international humanitarian law" that occurred on the territory of the former Yugoslavia beginning in 1991. The ICTY, as well as the ICTR, was directed by the Security Council to complete all cases by the end of 2014.

1. **Creation:** The ICTY was established by U.N. Security Council Resolution 827 on May 25, 1993. It was the first ad hoc international criminal tribunal since Nuremberg, and it ushered in a new era of international criminal law. The ICTY was the first effort by the United Nations to try to punish individuals for human rights violations.

2. **Structure:** The ICTY has three organs: the Registry, the Prosecutor, and the Judges' Chambers. There are three trial chambers and one appeals chamber that is shared with the ICTR. Each trial chamber has three permanent judges and up to nine *ad litem* judges. The shared appeals chamber has seven judges, but each appeal is heard by a panel of five of those judges. The judges are elected by a vote of the General Assembly from a slate of candidates that is created by the Security Council. Judges serve four-year terms and are eligible for re-election.

3. **Rulings:** The Statute of the ICTY gives the Tribunal jurisdiction to hear prosecutions for four major crimes: grave breaches of the Geneva Conventions of 1949, violations of the laws or customs of war, genocide, and crimes against humanity. Under the umbrellas of each of these four major crimes are many specific offenses, and the judgments of the ICTY have become important precedents because they have defined these offenses.

   Example: *Prosecutor v. Kunarac, Kovac and Vukovic*, Case No. IT-96-23, Judgment on Appeal (June 12, 2002), was the first conviction by the ICTY for crimes against humanity based on incidences of rape and sexual enslavement. The Trial Chamber found that rape was used by members of the Bosnian Serb armed forces as an instrument of terror and that they were given free rein to act whenever and against whomever they wished. The decision sets an important precedent for expanding the definition of a "crime against humanity."

C. **The International Criminal Tribunal for Rwanda (ICTR):** The ICTR is a U.N. organization that was established in Arusha, Tanzania, to try those responsible for human rights violations during the genocide in Rwanda in 1994. The Tribunal had jurisdiction to hear criminal charges against *anyone* accused of committing crimes against humanity within Rwanda during the period of January 1, 1994, to December 31, 1994.

1. **Creation:** The ICTR was created on November 8, 1994, by Security Council Resolution 955.

2. **Structure:** The Tribunal has three organs: the Registry, the Office of the Prosecutor, and the Judges' Chambers. It has three trial chambers consisting of three judges each and one appeals chamber consisting of seven judges. The judges are nominated by the member states of the United Nations, vetted by the Security Council, and then elected to four-year terms by a vote of the General Assembly. No two judges may be nationals of the same state. The Tribunal also currently has nine sitting *ad litem* judges that were selected from a pool of 18 potential judges elected by the Security Council for possible participation in the two trial chambers. The pool of *ad litem* judges was created on August 14, 2002, by Security Council Resolution 1431. There is no jury for the criminal trials. The ICTR's appeals chamber is shared with the ICTY.

3. **Rulings:** Along with the ICTY, the ICTR revolutionized international criminal law and set all of the precedents for the criminal courts that followed. The Tribunal has *ratione materiae* jurisdiction over genocide, crimes against humanity, and violations of article 3 of the Geneva Conventions. The ICTR's most important work has been the definition of specific crimes and the identification of the elements that must be proved for a conviction. As of November 2010,

the Tribunal had rendered 45 judgments, with nine trials still in progress and four additional accused individuals awaiting trial.

a. ***Prosecutor v. Akayesu:*** This case was the first international genocide trial in history, and it established the definition of genocide with respect to the 1948 Convention on the Prevention and Punishment of Genocide. Akayesu was the *bourgmestre* (mayor) of Taba commune in Rwanda, and he wielded significant authority and influence over military, political, and civil activities in Taba. He was charged with genocide, crimes against humanity, and war crimes, including extermination, murder, rape, and torture. The Tribunal held that a conviction for "complicity in genocide" required proof that the defendant actually participated in the killing, but it also held that "direct, public incitement to commit genocide" is a crime that carries personal criminal liability. *Prosecutor v. Akayesu*, Case No. ICTR-96-4-T, Judgment (Sept. 2, 1998).

b. ***Prosecutor v. Karemera, Ngirumpatse, and Nzirorera:*** The Appeals Chamber of the ICTR ruled that all of the Tribunal's trial chambers had to take "judicial notice" of three facts: members of the Twa, Tutsi, and Hutu ethnicities were protected groups under the Genocide Convention; there were widespread systematic attacks throughout Rwanda against the civilian population based on Tutsi ethnic identification; and between April 1994 and July 1994, there was a genocide against the Tutsi. The instruction to take "judicial notice" required the trial chambers to establish the three facts at the outset of every trial as beyond any dispute and thus precluded the defendant from employing any testimony, evidence, or argument denying the genocide. This decision set an important precedent allowing future courts to issue similar orders so as to prevent international tribunals from becoming a forum where defendants can deny or obfuscate the larger truths of humanitarian disasters. *Prosecutor v. Karemera, Ngirumpatse, and Nzirorera*, Case No. ICTR-98-44-AR73(C), Decision on Prosecutor's Interlocutory Appeal of Decision on Judicial Notice (June 16, 2006).

c. ***Prosecutor v. Furundzija:*** This case established three very important precedents in international criminal law. First, the ICTR held that a prohibition against torture was a peremptory norm of international law. Second, the Tribunal found that rape committed during interrogation amounted to torture. *See also Prosecutor v. Gacumbitsi*, Judgment, Case No. ICTR-2001-64-T (June 17, 2004) (classifying rape as an international crime against humanity). Third, the Trial Chamber distinguished accomplice liability for torture from liability for aiding and abetting. To be guilty of torture as a co-perpetrator, the accused must have participated in an integral part of the torture. Furundzija was found guilty of torture as an aider and abettor, despite the fact that he wasn't physically present during the torture, because he encouraged others to engage in torture with the knowledge that they would do so. *Prosecutor v. Furundzija*, Case No. IT-95-17/1-T, Judgment (Dec. 10, 1998).

D. **The International Residual Mechanism:** As the ICTY and ICTR were directed by the U.N. Security Council to complete their cases by the end of 2014, an institution was needed to resolve lingering issues such as future trials for fugitives, retrials, enforcement of sentences made by either court, the ongoing protection of witnesses, and the maintenance of documents related to the tribunals. On December 22, 2010, the U.N. Security Council adopted U.N. Security Council Resolution 1966, which established the International Residual Mechanism for Criminal Tribunals to accomplish those goals. The Mechanism inherited the jurisdiction, rights, and obligations of both the ICTY and the ICTR and will continue the essential functions of both. After its initial period of four years, which ended in 2016, the Mechanism will be reviewed by the Security Council every two years and will only end by its determination. As this book goes to press, a top priority of the Mechanism is the arrest and prosecution of nine remaining fugitives from the genocide in Rwanda. The Statute of the Mechanism compels the cooperation of U.N. member states in the investigation and prosecution of these remaining fugitives.

E. Mixed or hybrid tribunals: Unlike the ICTY or ICTY, many tribunals developed in the past few decades to resolve international incidents have not been exclusively international or exclusively domestic. Instead, these mixed or hybrid tribunals incorporate elements of both international prosecution and domestic prosecution to varying degrees.

1. **Lockerbie:** One of the first hybrid tribunals arose out of a standoff between the Libyan government and the U.N. Security Council after the bombing of Pan Am Flight 103. The flight exploded over the village of Lockerbie, Scotland, en route to New York. After investigations revealed that two Libyan agents may have been involved, the United States. and the United Kingdom demanded their surrender. However, Libya refused to extradite the accused, leading to a U.N. embargo against the country. In order to defuse the tensions, in April 1999, both sides agreed to a criminal trial before a Scottish court, presiding in The Hague and applying Scottish law. After amending Scottish judicial procedures to allow the trial and an agreement allowing the Scottish High Court to sit in the Netherlands, both agents were tried beginning in May 2000. Following the trial, one Libyan was convicted of conspiracy and sentenced to life in prison, while the other was acquitted.

2. **East Timor:** After decades of violence which killed as many as 200,000 East Timorese, a United Nations–supervised referendum on independence from Indonesia was held in East Timor (Timor-Leste) in 1999. Following this referendum, however, still more East Timorese died and several hundred thousand were displaced before independence was finally achieved in 2002. In order to bring those responsible to justice, the U.N. Security Council created an interim government, which established "Special Panels for Serious Crimes." These Special Panels were charged with prosecuting those accused of war crimes, crimes against humanity, and genocide between the referendum and October 2000. The Panels consisted of one East Timorese judge working with two international judges within the District Court of Dili, the capital of East Timor. Of the nearly 300 persons against whom arrest warrants were issued by the Panels, only about 88 actually stood trial. Significant figures in the Indonesian government, as well as the former Governor of East Timor, all escaped trial by remaining outside the country.

   At the same time, the Indonesian government established its own *Ad Hoc* Human Rights Court for Timor-Leste in Jakarta. The court indicted around 20 individuals, most of whom were directly in charge of the military or police in East Timor.

3. **Cambodia:** From 1975 to 1979, nearly 2 million Cambodians lost their lives under the dictatorial regime of Pol Pot and the Khmer Rouge. Although the Khmer Rouge was eventually removed from power, until 1997, little was done to bring those responsible to justice. After requesting U.N. assistance in creating tribunals, the Cambodian government established the Extraordinary Chambers in the Courts of Cambodia for the Prosecution of Crimes Committed During the Period of Democratic Kampuchea (ECCC) in 2001. The ECCC is charged with prosecuting those "most responsible" for the genocide, crimes against humanity, grave breaches of the Geneva Convention, and other crimes under the Cambodian Penal Code. The U.N. assistance in creating the ECCC included a commitment by the Cambodian government to enforce its prosecutions and not to request amnesty for anyone investigated by the ECCC.

The ECCC has begun conducting trials of former Khmer Rouge leaders and officials. Kang Kek Iew (also romanized as Kaing Guek Eav), who managed the infamous Tuol Sleng prison outside the capital Phnom Penh, received a life sentence from the ECCC in 2010. Nuon Chea, the right-hand man of Pol Pot, and Khieu Samphan, an upper level administrator of the Khmer Rouge, have also received life sentences. However, death and dementia of the accused have prevented some from being put on trial. Additionally, allegations of corruption in Case 003, the case against Meas Muth, a naval official who currently lives comfortably in Battambang province of Cambodia, have hurt the ECCC's reputation. In that case, two arrest warrants have been made against Muth, but as this book goes to press, both Prime Minister Hun Sen and the three-judge panel investigating Case 003 are against an arrest.

The ECCC is also notable for creating the revolutionary Victims Support Service, which connects victims to the proceeding. In addition to helping victims find legal representation, the Victims Support Service also allows victims to join cases as complainants or civil parties seeking compensation.

4. **Iraqi Special Tribunal:** After Operation Iraqi Freedom deposed Iraqi President Saddam Hussein, the Iraqi Special Tribunal was established by the Iraqi Governing Council and the Coalition Provisional Authority in December 2003. The objective of the organization was to prosecute former President Hussein and other senior officials of the Ba'athist regime for war crimes, crimes against humanity, genocide, and other serious crimes committed since 1968. Although the Tribunal was initially independent of the Iraqi judicial system, the Tribunal is now known as the Iraqi High Tribunal and is part of the court system. To the chagrin of those who wished to see an independent, international tribunal similar to those in Rwanda and the former Yugoslavia, the Tribunal is run entirely by Iraqi judges, with occasional assistance from international experts. The most notable case tried before the Tribunal was the prosecution of Saddam Hussein for the execution of 148 Shiite civilians, in which the former president was sentenced to death.

5. **Lebanon:** Following the assassination of former Lebanese Prime Minister Rafic Hariri in February 2005, Lebanon and the United Nations agreed to establish a Special Tribunal. Unlike most Tribunals mentioned thus far, the Special Tribunal for Lebanon has a jurisdiction of only those responsible for a single event in a single country. Additionally, the Tribunal could expand its temporal jurisdiction to include other attacks in the preceding year if the attacks were "connected in accordance with the principles of criminal justice" and were of a similar nature and gravity. The Tribunal is also unique in that it is outside both the U.N. and the Lebanese judiciary. To maintain that independence, the Tribunal has primacy over the Lebanese national courts, and both Lebanese and international judges are employed by the Tribunal.

   The Special Tribunal for Lebanon defines terrorism as requiring the following elements: (a) the intent of the underlying crime; (b) the special intent to spread fear or coerce authority; (c) the commission of the criminal act; and (d) the transnational nature of the act. Although the Tribunal argues that this is the commonly accepted definition of terrorism, it has been met by criticism. The Tribunal began its first trial in January 2014 against four Hezbollah members.

6. **Kosovo:** Since neither the ICTY nor the Kosovar judicial system could handle the caseload of atrocities committed during the war in Kosovo in 1999, the U.N. Interim Administration Mission in Kosovo (UNMIK) established panels to ensure the impartiality of judges. Known

as Regulation 64 Panels, each panel would consist of two international judges and one Kosovar judge. More than 20 war crimes trials were handled by these panels.

7. **Bosnia:** The War Crimes Chamber of the State Courts of Bosnia and Herzegovina is a domestic court that handles the lower-level crimes against Croatian civilians. The cases are referred by the ICTY but are entirely operated under Bosnia and Herzegovinian law.

8. **Senegal/Chad:** After being deposed as President of Chad in 1990, Hissène Habré fled to Senegal. The former President was accused of more than 40,000 political killings, more than 20,000 cases of torture, and ethnic cleansing, which earned him the nickname "Africa's Pinochet" from Human Rights Watch. Although Senegal put Habré under house arrest in 2005, the country initially refused to prosecute him. In 2005, Habré was indicted in Belgium, followed by a trial *in absentia* in Chad in 2011. In 2012, however, Senegal bowed to international pressure and established the Extraordinary African Chambers in the Senegalese Courts with help from the African Union. The case was adjudicated by Senegalese judges and had authority to prosecute genocide, crimes against humanity, war crimes, and torture. In May 2016, Habré was convicted of rape, sexual slavery, and ordering of the killing of more than 40,000 persons.

9. **Bangladesh:** In 1971, Bangladesh declared its independence from Pakistan, sparking a war in which the Pakistani Army killed thousands of civilians. In 2009, Bangladesh established an International Crimes Tribunal as a domestic institution to prosecute members of the Pakistani Army and their collaborators for the genocide and war crimes of that war. After the first round of convictions, which included nine members of the Jamaat-e-Islami, the largest Islamist party of Bangladesh, demonstrations began in the capital of Dhaka. The Tribunal has been criticized for its lack of transparency and issues regarding independence and impartiality.

10. **Gacaca courts:** In Rwanda, the *Gacaca* ("justice from the grass") court was a domestic institution inspired by traditional community justice systems. Designed to supplement the ICTR in 2001, the Gacaca courts were more focused on healing and rebuilding after the Rwandan genocide. Because of this, these courts often resembled truth commissions rather than formal judicial systems. The Gacaca courts were officially closed in 2012.

11. **The Special Court for Sierra Leone—an in-depth look at one hybrid tribunal:** The Special Court is an independent judicial body established in Freetown to try those who bear the greatest responsibility for serious violations of international humanitarian law and Sierra Leonean law committed in the territory of Sierra Leone after November 30, 1996 (during the Sierra Leonean civil war). The independence of the court and its direct financing by the governments of other states make it a unique judicial entity.

    a. **Creation:** The Special Court for Sierra Leone was established with the Statute of the Special Court on January 16, 2002, by a special agreement between the United Nations and the government of the Republic of Sierra Leone. The court is completely independent and is not a part of the United Nations or the government of Sierra Leone. On June 12, 2000, the President of Sierra Leone wrote an official letter to the U.N. secretary-general requesting that the United Nations act to try to punish human rights violators who committed atrocities during the latter part of the country's 11-year civil war. On August 14, 2000, the U.N. Security Council passed Resolution 1315, authorizing the secretary-general to begin negotiations with Sierra Leone. The court officially began operations on July 1, 2002, and the first trials began in June 2004. The court has had a budget of around $30 million per year since its creation ($36 million in 2007 and $33 million for 2008) and it is funded by contributions from over 30 governments around the world.

b. **Structure:** The Special Court was modeled on the ICTR and the ICTY, and it is organized into four organs by the Special Court Statute: the Registry, the Prosecutor, the Defense Office, and the Judges' Chambers. The Registrar, Prosecutor, and Principal Defender are appointed by the U.N. secretary-general. There are three judicial decision-making bodies, two trial chambers, and an appeals chamber, staffed by 11 judges. Seven of the judges are appointed by the U.N. secretary-general and four are appointed by the government of Sierra Leone. Judges serve three-year terms and are eligible for reappointment. There is no jury at the trials, and the three judges of a trial chamber decide the guilt or innocence of the accused. A five-judge appeals chamber hears appeals based on jurisdictional issues, procedural issues, and new evidence.

i. **The Office of the Principal Defender—an innovation in international criminal law:** No other international tribunal has a permanent institution to ensure the rights of suspects and the accused. The Defense Office monitors trials and investigations and screens expert witnesses for the court to ensure impartial testimony. It can also provide courtroom counsel for defendants who are indigent or choose Defense Office representation.

c. ***Prosecutor v. Taylor*:** In the biggest case before the Special Court, Charles Taylor, the former president of Liberia, faced charges of crimes against humanity for his role in starting the civil war in Sierra Leone. In 2007, the case was moved to the International Criminal Court (ICC) in The Hague for trial, and Taylor boycotted the initial proceedings on June 4. The case is important because it was the first criminal trial of an individual for actions committed while he was a sitting head of state. *Prosecutor v. Taylor*, Case No. SCSL-03-01-I-059, Decision on Immunity from Jurisdiction (May 31, 2004). In 2012, Taylor was convicted on all 11 counts he faced and received a sentence of 50 years in prison.

III. THE INTERNATIONAL CRIMINAL COURT (ICC)

The ICC was established in The Hague, Netherlands, to hear prosecutions for genocide, crimes against humanity, war crimes, and crimes of aggression that occurred after July 1, 2002.

A. **A permanent criminal court:** The ICC is a U.N. organ and the first permanent criminal tribunal. As of 2010, it had 114 member states (membership requires signing and ratification of the Rome Statute). There are a number of states that have signed the Rome Statute but not yet ratified it.

1. **Creation and the Rome Statute:** The ICC was established when the Rome Statute of the International Criminal Court came into force on July 1, 2002. The Statute is the product of a General Assembly conference in Rome in June 1998, and it was adopted by the General Assembly on July 17, 1998.

2. **Structure and jurisdiction:** The court has four organs: the Presidency, the Registry, the Prosecutor, and the Judicial Divisions. There are three judicial bodies that hear the cases. The Pre-Trial Division has seven judges, the Trial Division has six judges, and the Appeals Division has five judges. Judges are elected by an assembly of the states parties to the Rome Statute to nine-year terms. The court can hear cases against persons who are citizens of states parties to the Rome Statute, against persons whose alleged crimes occurred on the territory of a state party, or against persons whose crimes occurred in connection with a situation referred to the court by the U.N. Security Council. The court ***does not have universal jurisdiction.*** With respect to *ratione materiae* jurisdiction, article 5 of the Rome Statute allows the court to

hear prosecutions for only four crimes: genocide, crimes against humanity, war crimes, and the crime of aggression. The court does not yet have jurisdiction over the crime of aggression, but a conference convened in June 2010 adopted a formal resolution defining the substance of the crime of aggression for the first time. The court cannot hear prosecutions for terrorism (because the states parties could not agree on a definition of the crime), drug-trafficking, or the use of weapons of mass destruction.

a. **The "complementarity" principle:** Article 17 of the Rome Statute limits the jurisdiction of the court with the complementarity principle. The ICC is supposed to be a "court of last resort" that hears cases only when there is a failure of the operation of justice in the domestic courts of states. The ICC cannot act unless a state is unwilling or unable to prosecute violators of international humanitarian law.

b. **Territorial Jurisdiction:** Article 12(2)(a) of the Rome Statute extends jurisdiction of the court, authorizing the ICC to hear cases where only part of a crime is committed within the borders of a state party to the Statute. For example, the ICC determined that the deportation of the Rohingya from Myanmar to Bangladesh, a state party, fell within the scope of article 12(2)(a). ICC-RoC46(3)-01/18, Decision on the "Prosecutor's Request for a Ruling on Jurisdiction under Article 19(3) of the Statute" (Sept. 6, 2018), https://www.icc-cpi.int/CourtRecords/CR2018_04203.pdf.

B. **Criticisms:** In 1998, seven states (including the United States) voted against the adoption of the Rome Statute, and in 2002, both Israel and the United States "unsigned" the treaty by expressing their intention never to become parties.

1. **Politically motivated prosecution:** Some states fear that their political leaders or military personnel will be subject to investigations and prosecutions by the ICC that are without merit and are driven by the desire to realize certain international political outcomes. The United States is particularly concerned about exposing its soldiers deployed abroad to prosecution by the ICC.
2. **National sovereignty:** Commentators have argued that the ICC infringes on the sovereignty of states in the international system by supplanting national judicial systems and interfering with state policymaking. The United States and Israel both fear that members of their governments could be exposed to ICC prosecution for their role in foreign policy decisions that are internationally unpopular.

C. **Early work:** The Office of the Prosecutor began investigating human rights violations that occurred in Uganda, the Democratic Republic of the Congo, the Central African Republic, and Sudan's Darfur region. The Ugandan case focused on the prosecution of the commanders of the Lord's Resistance Army (LRA), a militant group engaged in armed rebellion against the Ugandan government. However, at least two of the five commanders of the LRA have since been killed without being captured or prosecuted. The original case prosecuted against three Congolese rebel commanders was split into individual cases, and the court adjudicated a variety of alleged war crimes, including the conscription of child soldiers under the age of 15. One of these cases, *Prosecutor v. Thomas Lubanga Dyilo*, represents the problems faced by the early ICC. Although Lubanga was arrested in 2005, it took a pre-trial chamber in 2007 to decide there was sufficient evidence to proceed and the trial still did not begin until 2009. Following multiple interruptions, the court finally released its judgment in 2012, seven years after Lubanga's arrest. The judgment spanned hundreds of pages, encompassed three decisions, and was criticized for not including the testimony of any of the victims who had been child soldiers. *Prosecutor v. Thomas Lubanga Dyilo*, ICC-01/

04-01/06, Judgment Pursuant to Article 74 of the Statute (Mar. 14, 2012). The cases regarding Darfur included charges against the nation's sitting president, Omar al-Bashir, for crimes against humanity and other war crimes. Finally, charges for war crimes and crimes against humanity were filed against the former commander in chief, Jean-Pierre Bemba Gombo for the Movement for the Liberation of the Congo, a rebel group that participated in the put-down of a coup attempt in the Central African Republic from 2002-2003.

D. **Crimes the ICC can adjudicate:** Generally, the ICC only has jurisdiction over the "most serious crimes of concern to the international community as a whole." In article 5 of the Rome Statute, four crimes in particular are specified as meeting this criterion. The ICC only has jurisdiction over crimes committed after the Rome Statute entered into force in 2002. In order to exercise jurisdiction, the ICC requires a referral from a state party, a referral from the U.N. Security Council, or an investigation that has been initiated by the Prosecutor. *See* Rome Statute of the International Criminal Court, U.N. Doc. A/CONF.183/9 (1998).

1. **The crime of genocide:** Genocide is defined by the Rome Statute as committing any of the following crimes with the intent to destroy a national, ethnic, religious, or racial group: (a) killing members of that group; (b) causing substantial bodily or mental harm to members of that group; (c) deliberately imposing conditions on that group calculated to bring about its destruction in whole or part; (d) forced sterilization or other imposed measures to prevent births; or (e) taking children away from that group and giving them to another group.

2. **Crimes against humanity:** A crime against humanity, as defined by the Rome Statute, is any of the following crimes committed while part of a widespread or systemic attack against a civilian populace, with knowledge of the attack: (a) murder; (b) extermination; (c) enslavement; (d) deportation; (e) imprisonment in violation of international law; (f) torture; (g) rape, sexual slavery, enforced prostitution, forced pregnancy, enforced sterilization, or any other form of sexual violence; (h) persecution against an identifiable group; (i) enforced disappearances of persons; (j) apartheid; or (k) any other inhumane act of a similar character.

3. **War crimes:** The ICC will have jurisdiction for war crimes when committed as part of a plan, policy, or large-scale commission. War crimes are defined as severe breaches of the Geneva Convention or other serious violations of the international law of armed conflicts

4. **Aggression:** As defined in an Amendment adopted in 2010, aggression is the planning, preparation, initiation, or execution of an act of aggression which by its character, gravity, or scale represent a violation of the Charter of the United Nations. An act of aggression includes invasions, annexations, bombardments, blockades, the use of mercenaries, and other uses of armed forces against the sovereignty or territorial integrity of another state.

E. **Recent developments:** In 2016, the ICC took the following major actions: the opening of the trial against Ahmad Al Faqi Al Mahdi for the war crime of destroying historical and religious monuments in Timbuktu, Mali; the opening of the trial against Dominic Ongwen for his role as a commander of the LRA in Uganda; the opening of a Preliminary Examination of the situation in Burundi by the Prosecutor, and the conviction of Jean-Pierre Bemba Gombo of rape as a crime against humanity or war crime, the first time an individual was convicted of criminal rape at the ICC. *Prosecutor v. Gombo*, Case No. ICC-01/05-01/08, Judgment Pursuant to Article 74 of the Statute (Mar. 21, 2016), https://www.icc-cpi.int/CourtRecords/CR2016_02238.pdf. Other situations include the international armed conflict in Georgia in 2008, the conflicts in Central African Republic in 2002-2003 and the renewed violence in 2012, potential war crimes in Mali since 2012, alleged crimes against humanity in Côte d'Ivoire in 2010-2011, alleged crimes against humanity in Libya since 2011, post-election violence in Kenya in 2007-2008, alleged genocide and crimes against humanity in Darfur, Sudan since the Rome Statute entered into force in 2002, the LRA in Uganda since 2002, and the armed conflict in the Democratic Republic of the Congo since 2012. In 2017, the ICC found that South Africa had violated the Rome Statute by not arresting and surrendering Omar Al-Bashir during his visit in 2015. Two ICC warrants for his arrest were posted during that time – one for war crimes and crimes against humanity, and another for genocide.

IV. STATE PROSECUTION OF "INTERNATIONAL CRIMINALS"

After the close of Nuremberg, there were no international courts available to try war criminals, so state governments had to pass laws criminalizing the actions of foreign individuals committed on foreign territory and laws conferring extraterritorial jurisdiction on their courts. These laws put stress on both existing domestic criminal laws and established principles of state jurisdiction, and this type of criminal prosecution did not become popularly established.

A. Early development: The first prosecutions of individuals for crimes against humanity and war crimes by the domestic courts of a state occurred after World War II. Nazi-hunters found many Germans accused of crimes and brought them for trial in Europe and Israel.

Example: On May 11, 1960, Israeli Mossad agents abducted former Nazi SS officer Adolf Eichmann from a suburb of Buenos Aires and brought him for trial in Israel for war crimes, crimes against humanity, and crimes against the Jewish people. Eichmann was tried in the District Court of Jerusalem pursuant to Israel's 1950 Nazi and Nazi Collaborators Punishment Law and convicted of all charges. His defenses were that he was at all times simply following orders, that he was protected from prosecution by the act-of-state doctrine, and that Israel lacked jurisdiction to try him. Argentina protested the Israeli abduction in an appeal to the Security Council in June 1960, but bilateral diplomacy led to closure of the matter. Eichmann was hanged in the only civil execution in Israel's history. CrimC (Jer) 40/61; CrimA (S. Ct.) 336/61 *Att'y Gen. of Israel v. Adolf Eichmann* [1962] IsrSC.

Example: The former head of the Gestapo in Lyon, Klaus Barbie, was found in Bolivia in 1983 and extradited to France to stand trial for his actions during World War II. The French Cour de Cassation had to stretch domestic French criminal law to allow for his trial. The court held that the French statute of limitations did not apply because statutory limitations on claims for crimes against humanity were prohibited by customary international law. On July 4, 1987, Barbie received his sentence of life imprisonment from the Rhone Cour d'assises. *Federation Nationale des Deportes et Internes Resistants et Patriotes, et al. v. Barbie*, 78 I.L.R. 125 (October 6, 1983), and *Prosecutor v. Barbie*, Judgment of Oct. 6, 1983, Cass. crim., 1984 D.S. Jur. 113, J.C.P. 1983, II, G, No. 20, 107 (1983).

B. Statutory schemes and universal jurisdiction: Some states have conferred universal jurisdiction on their courts to hear criminal prosecutions for violations of international humanitarian law regardless of where the violations occurred, who allegedly committed them, or who the victims were. The universality principle is based on the idea that certain *jus cogens* norms of international humanitarian law carry *erga omnes* obligations. A violation of that law by an individual is a breach of the individual's obligation to the government and people of every state in the world, so every state has the right to prosecute. Spain, Germany, and Belgium have all experimented with universal jurisdiction laws.

1. ***Arrest Warrant of 11 April 2000*:** In this case, the ICJ held that the issuance and circulation of a Belgian arrest warrant for crimes against humanity violated the "full immunity from criminal jurisdiction and inviolability" of the Congolese minister of foreign affairs. The court ruled that because of the nature of the government position, no distinction could be made between the minister's private and official actions. The court found that customary international law provides no exception to the immunity of an incumbent minister of foreign affairs when he is abroad, even in cases of alleged war crimes or crimes against humanity. The holding contradicted Belgium's 1993 War Crimes Law, which granted universal jurisdiction to Belgian courts for the hearing of war crimes charges that arise from events anywhere in the world. The ICJ ruling was a setback to those seeking avenues for prosecution of the most grievous offenses committed by persons acting in their "official" capacity. Belgium's universal jurisdiction law was repealed on August 1, 2003. *Arrest Warrant of 11 April 2000 (Dem. Rep. Congo v. Belg.)*, 2002 I.C.J. 121 (Feb. 14).

C. **Civil liability and tort claims as alternatives to criminal law:** In many countries, and especially in the United States, national courts are available to foreign plaintiffs for civil actions against foreign defendants for extraterritorial violations of international humanitarian law. The development of civil liability for human rights violators is far ahead of the development of criminal liability. The United States is a leader in passing legislation that allows for civil suits by victims of human rights abuses. The Alien Tort Claims Act (ATCA), Alien Tort Statute (ATS), Torture Victim Protection Act (TVPA), Hostage Taking Act, and the Racketeer Influenced and Corrupt Organizations Act (RICO) can all be used to bring lawsuits for acts that occurred outside the United States.

Example: In *Republic of the Philippines v. Ferdinand Marcos*, 862 F.2d 1355 (9th Cir. 1988), the government of the Philippines sued former president Ferdinand Marcos and his wife for wire fraud and transportation of stolen goods in the foreign commerce of the United States under RICO, 18 U.S.C. §1961. The Ninth Circuit recognized that ***civil liability could exist for the acts of a former president committed while in office***, and it upheld an injunction prohibiting Marcos from disposing of his assets.

Example: In *Forti v. Suarez-Mason*, 694 F. Supp. 707 (N.D. Cal. 1998), the court recognized a cause of action for the tort of "causing disappearance" under the Alien Tort Statute after two Argentine plaintiffs presented evidence from legal scholars establishing an international consensus for defining the tort as "abduction by state officials or their agents; followed by official refusals to acknowledge the abduction or to disclose the detainee's fate." 694 F. Supp. at 710. The Argentine citizens were allowed to pursue their claims against Carlos Suarez-Mason, a former general in the military government of Jorge Videla, for compensation for the disappearance and presumed execution of family members during the "Dirty War" in Argentina waged by the junta against suspected dissidents.

V. BARRIERS TO PROSECUTION

The domestic law barriers to prosecution of international criminal law are extensive and often vaguely defined, allowing domestic courts to evade controversial, highly charged cases.

A. **Sovereign immunity and the state action doctrine:** A major barrier to the development of international criminal law is the principle of sovereign immunity. It is a recognized custom in international law that the courts of one state will not sit in judgment on the actions of another state committed on its own territory. It is also customary that members of the government of a state are immune from criminal prosecution by the courts of another state. It would be very difficult to hold government leaders accountable for violations of international humanitarian law if they could always hide behind their immunity, so courts have begun to chip away at the traditional rules of immunity.

Example: On December 9, 2002, the Republic of the Congo sued France in the ICJ seeking the annulment of all French investigation and prosecution of crimes against humanity and torture allegedly committed by the Congolese minister of the interior. Congo objected to France claiming jurisdiction to criminally try a member of its government for actions allegedly committed on Congolese territory. Congo also asserted that France violated the principle of sovereign immunity by issuing a warrant for the questioning of the president of the Congo. France consented to the jurisdiction of the ICJ. August 11, 2008, had been set as the deadline for the filing of the final rejoinder by France before oral argument. In November 2010, however, the agent for the Republic of the Congo informed the ICJ that his government sought to withdraw its application instituting proceedings and requested the ICJ to "make an order officially recording the discontinuance of the proceedings and directing the removal of the case from the list." France presented no objection to such removal. *Certain Criminal Proceedings in France (Congo v. Fr.), available at* http://www.icj-cij.org/docket/index.php?p1=3&p2=3&k=d2&case=129&code=cof&p3=3 (last visited May 19, 2011).

Example: In *Prosecutor v. Taylor*, Case No. SCSL-03-01-I-059, Decision on Immunity from Jurisdiction (May 31, 2004), Charles Taylor, the former president of Liberia, filed an application to quash the indictment and arrest warrant issued by the Special Court for Sierra Leone against him because he was a sitting head of state at the time of his alleged crimes. The court held that the principle that a sitting head of state is not immune from personal prosecution by international tribunals was sufficiently established in international law to dismiss the application.

Example: In *U.S. v. Noriega*, 117 F.3d 1206 (11th Cir. 1997), the court rejected Manuel Noriega's claim that the FSIA protected him from prosecution for drug-trafficking charges because he was the head of state of the Republic of Panama. The court held that the political branches of the U.S. government never recognized Noriega, the commander of the Panamanian Defense Forces, as the legitimate leader of Panama, so he was not entitled to immunity from the courts of the United States.

B. Extradition and problems with capture: Criminal prosecutions are obviously not very successful unless the accused is arrested and present before the court. Many international criminal defendants contest their prosecutions from the outset by challenging the circumstances of their arrest or extradition.

1. **Extradition:** In *Ntakirutimana v. Reno*, 184 F.3d 419 (5th Cir. 1999), the court denied a petition for the writ of habeas corpus filed by the president of the Seventh-Day Adventist Church for Rwanda. Petitioner Elizaphan Ntakirutimana was charged by the ICTR with genocide and other crimes and was requested for extradition by the U.S. government. Ntakirutimana argued that the U.S. Constitution required a treaty to authorize extradition to the ICTR, but the court concluded that 18 U.S.C. §3186 empowered the secretary of state to extradite fugitives from foreign countries.

2. **Illegal capture:** In *Prosecutor v. Nikolic*, Decision of the Interlocutory Appeal Concerning the Legality of Arrest, Case No. IT-94-02-AR73 (June 5, 2003), the ICTY held that the appropriate remedy for an illegal or improper arrest or capture was not dismissal of the criminal

charges that prompted the capture. Dragan Nikolic was violently abducted from his home in the Federal Republic of Yugoslavia by Serbian criminals before being transferred to the NATO-led Stabilization Force in Bosnia and Herzegovina. NATO then released Nikolic into ICTY custody for trial.

Exam Tips on INTERNATIONAL CRIMINAL LAW

- In an introductory course to public international law, the rapidly expanding area of international criminal law comes up in a number of different contexts. Keep in mind the following:
- Under the doctrine of command responsibility, a military or civilian authority is responsible for international crimes that he or she could have prevented or failed to punish.
- Human rights violations may rise to the level of international criminal offenses, such as crimes against humanity, war crimes, genocide, and crimes against peace. For war crimes that are grave breaches of the Geneva Conventions and the other criminal law violations, there is universal jurisdiction, which is significant in that every state can claim a right to prosecute such offenses in its own domestic courts.
- For violations of the Genocide Convention, Torture Convention, and for grave breaches of the Geneva Conventions, every state is obligated to prosecute and punish these violations so that inaction is a violation of international law in itself.

Multiple-Choice Questions

Instructions: Circle the correct response.

1. International customary law is the result of relations between
   A. nation-states and their citizens.
   B. nation-states and the citizens of other nations.
   C. nation-states and other nation-states.
   D. all of the above.
2. The most important source of international environmental law is
   A. customary law.
   B. treaties.
   C. general principles of law.
   D. none of the above.
3. "Agenda 21" is part of
   A. the Stockholm Conference of the Human Environment.
   B. the U.N. Convention of the Law of the Sea.
   C. U.N. Conference on the Environment and Development (1992).
   D. the World Summit on Sustainable Development.
4. The primary cause of the loss of biodiversity is
   A. introduced species.
   B. habitat destruction.
   C. overexploitation.
   D. agricultural pollution.
5. Which of the following is a "framework" agreement regarding biodiversity, containing no specific commitments?
   A. the Convention on Biological Diversity
   B. the UNESCO World Heritage Convention
   C. the 1979 Convention on the Conservation of Migratory Species
   D. the Cartagena Protocol on Biosafety
6. The concept of Common But Differentiated Responsibility is based upon
   A. the principle of equity between countries.
   B. the principle of sustainable development.
   C. both *A* and *B*.
   D. none of the above.

7. In addition to binding emissions reductions for developed nations, the Kyoto Protocol contained which of the following?

   A. a "joint implementation" provision

   B. a "clean development" mechanism

   C. an "international emissions trading" mechanism

   D. all of the above

8. Which of the following is a characteristic that helps identify a substance as toxic?

   A. its persistence over time

   B. its tendency to bioaccumulate

   C. its carcinogenic potential

   D. all of the above

9. The largest single source of hazardous pollutants is

   A. forestry.

   B. mining.

   C. industrial production.

   D. none of the above.

10. Which of the following is a method commonly used in disposing of hazardous wastes?

    A. incineration (burning)

    B. discharge into bodies of water

    C. neutralization or sequestration

    D. all of the above

11. Which of the following contains a strict ban on the import of hazardous wastes into its signatory nations?

    A. the 1987 London Guidelines

    B. the Rotterdam Convention

    C. the Basel Convention

    D. the Bamako Convention

12. Which of the following introduced the "prior informed consent" procedure for trade in hazardous chemicals and pesticides?

    A. the 1987 London Guidelines

    B. the Rotterdam Convention

    C. the Basel Convention

    D. the Bamako

13. Which of the following introduced the "managed trade" approach into the area of hazardous waste disposal?
    A. the 1987 London Guidelines
    B. the Rotterdam Convention
    C. the Basel Convention
    D. the Bamako Convention
14. Which of the following has the broadest (most inclusive) definition of "hazardous wastes"?
    A. the 1987 London Guidelines
    B. the Rotterdam Convention
    C. the Basel Convention
    D. the Bamako Convention
15. Which of the following have been shown to cause transboundary water pollution?
    A. industrial production
    B. agricultural production
    C. discharge of municipal (urban) waste
    D. all of the above
16. The success of the international response to stratospheric ozone depletion is attributable to
    A. scientific consensus as to the problem and its solutions.
    B. strong leadership on the part of the United States.
    C. the use of incentives for industries to participate.
    D. all of the above.
17. The Vienna Ozone Convention was most significant for its
    A. specific and strongly worded performance requirements.
    B. high levels of funding for research.
    C. agreement to address an environmental challenge before its effects were felt or even proved scientifically.
    D. all of the above.
18. The Montreal Protocol
    A. rejected the so-called precautionary principle.
    B. incorporated an "essential uses" exception into its requirements.
    C. neglected to provide for technological assistance to developing nations.
    D. all of the above.

19. The Montreal Protocol

    A. has elimination of ozone-depleting substances as its ultimate objective.

    B. governs CFCs but exempts other ozone-depleting substances.

    C. provides no financial assistance for compliance.

    D. none of the above.

20. The Montreal Protocol is generally considered a success because

    A. nearly every country in the world has signed it.

    B. it has resulted in very large reductions in the emission of ozone-depleting substances.

    C. both *A* and *B*.

    D. The Montreal Protocol is not generally considered to be a success.

21. The Antarctic Treaty

    A. is the first international agreement governing the use of Antarctica.

    B. has as its goal to assure continued scientific research.

    C. suspends all states' right to claim "sectors" of the continent.

    D. all of the above.

22. Parties to the Antarctic Treaty include

    A. only states that make territorial claims to Antarctica.

    B. only states that have conducted substantial scientific research there.

    C. states that make territorial claims and states that have conducted substantial scientific research in Antarctica.

    D. any state that wishes to be a party to the treaty.

23. The first treaty to provide comprehensive environmental protection for Antarctica is

    A. the Convention for the Conservation of Antarctic Seals.

    B. the Convention on the Conservation of Antarctic Marine Living Resources.

    C. the Agreed Measure for the Protection of Antarctic Flora and Fauna.

    D. the 1991 Madrid Protocol.

24. The 50-year ban on mining in the 1991 Madrid Protocol

    A. is likely to be amended.

    B. cannot be amended.

    C. has been frequently amended.

    D. is unlikely to be amended because of the votes necessary for amendment.

25. The first treaty to address the problem of desertification was

    A. the Lome IV Convention.

    B. the Madrid Protocol.

    C. the Rio Principles.

    D. the U.N. Convention to Combat Desertification.

26. The first global treaty containing extensive provisions to protect the marine environment was

    A. the 1958 Convention on the High Seas.

    B. the 1982 U.N. Convention on the Law of the Sea.

    C. the 1958 Convention on the Territorial Sea and Contiguous Zone.

    D. the Madrid Protocol.

27. A merchant ship in the territorial sea of a state is subject to the pollution laws of

    A. the flag state of the ship.

    B. the coastal state.

    C. any applicable international treaty standard.

    D. all of the above.

28. The right of innocent passage is available to a ship passing through

    A. a state's territorial sea.

    B. a state's territorial sea and contiguous zone.

    C. a state's territorial sea, contiguous zone, and exclusive economic zone.

    D. the high seas.

29. Under the rule of the *Trail Smelter* case, liability for the 2010 BP oil spill in the United States' Gulf of Mexico potentially may be imposed:

    A. only on BP.

    B. on the United States.

    C. on the United States if it has failed to take reasonable measures to prevent such accidents.

    D. none of the above.

30. One way in which a non-governmental organization could bring public attention to damage from climate change is to

    A. bring a lawsuit before the International Court of Justice against polluting companies.

    B. file a petition with UNESCO to list a site threatened by climate change as a UNESCO World Heritage site.

    C. both of the above.

    D. none of the above.

31. In the U.S. Supreme Court decision of *Massachusetts v. EPA,* the Court held

    A. that Massachusetts had sufficient individualized injury for standing even though global warming has a worldwide impact.

    B. that greenhouse gases are air pollutants.

    C. that the U.S. Environmental Protection Agency had to regulate greenhouse gases under the Clean Air Act if greenhouse gases come from mobile and stationary sources and are harmful to the public health and welfare.

    D. all of the above.

Answers to Multiple-Choice Questions

1. D
2. B
3. C
4. B
5. A
6. C
7. D
8. D
9. C
10. D
11. D
12. A
13. C
14. D
15. D
16. D
17. D
18. B
19. A
20. C
21. D
22. C
23. D
24. D
25. D
26. B
27. D
28. A
29. C
30. B
31. D

Table of Cases

Table of Conventions on the Law of the Sea

Table of U.N. Charter References

Table of Advisory Opinions, Reports, and Declarations

Table of Statutes and Restatement Provisions

Table of International Agreements

Subject Matter Index

NOTE: For International Agreements, please refer to the separate Table of International Agreements.

U